Integrating Digital Public Infrastructure in Emerging Economies

Sherif Mohamed A. Ismail
https://orcid.org/0009-0000-0852-873X
American University in Cairo, Egypt

Lyudmyla Symochko
University of Coimbra, Portugal

Mohammad Israr
https://orcid.org/0000-0002-6770-9570
Maryam Abacha American University, Nigeria

Ajay B. Gadicha
College of Engineering and Management Amravati, India

IGI Global
Scientific Publishing
Publishing Tomorrow's Research Today

Vice President of Editorial	Melissa Wagner
Director of Acquisitions	Mikaela Felty
Director of Book Development	Jocelynn Hessler
Production Manager	Mike Brehm
Cover Design	Jose Rosado

Published in the United States of America by
IGI Global Scientific Publishing
701 East Chocolate Avenue
Hershey, PA, 17033, USA
Tel: 717-533-8845 | Fax: 717-533-7115
Website: https://www.igi-global.com E-mail: cust@igi-global.com

Library of Congress Cataloging-in-Publication Data

LCCN: 2025039423 (CIP Data Pending)
ISBN13: 979-8-3373-6380-6
Isbn13Softcover: 979-8-3373-6381-3
EISBN13: 979-8-3373-6382-0

British Cataloguing in Publication Data
A Cataloguing in Publication record for this book is available from the British Library.

Table of Contents

Detailed Table of Contents

Rapidly economies, fundamentally altering the structures of industries, labour markets, productivity patterns, and value creation mechanisms. As nations and economic impact is both profound and multifaceted. AI serves as a general-purpose technology, similar to electricity or the internet, with broad applications that permeate virtually every sector and manufacturing education, logistics, agriculture, creative industries. Ubiquitous integration of AI is driving new forms of automation, accelerating innovation cycles, reducing operational costs, and reshaping competitive landscapes. Consequently, AI is emerging not only as a productivity enhancer but also as a catalyst for entirely paradigms. Most significant the enhancement of productivity. AI labor, enabling faster decision-making, improved forecasting, and optimal resource allocation. In sectors like manufacturing, AI-powered robotics and predictive maintenance are reducing downtime and improving efficiency. In are revolutionizing traditional workflows.

The electronic industry is changing the process of providing services of governments, as well as the way people interact with the government. Countries across the world are establishing Digital Public Infrastructure (DPI) - shared systems to support such priority services as identity cheques, online payments, along with data sharing. In this chapter, Empowering Citizens through Code explains how software and digital innovation can be used to help create open, transparent, inclusive systems that can benefit everyone. It further indicates that good public policies are also required to complete this task; technology will not assist in this task. Good policies ensure the safety of the data of people, a tool does not belong to a few individuals and that innovation could be useful. The chapter describes the reasons why laws, open standards, and intergovernmental cooperation can make digital platforms more secure, efficient and scalable.

Digital Public Infrastructure (DPI)—the interoperable stack of foundational digital rails for identity, payments, data exchange, consent, and trusted services—has emerged as a powerful lever for inclusive development. Yet deployment in emerging economies is uneven, and the digital divide persists along axes of income, gender, geography, language, age, and disability. This chapter proposes a strategic, end-to-end framework for designing, deploying, and governing inclusive DPI. Drawing on lessons from diverse contexts, it synthesizes policy, technical, institutional, and societal levers into a practical roadmap emphasizing inclusion-by-design, safety, accountability, and sustainability. The chapter provides conceptual foundations, a typology of divides, case mini-studies, actionable design principles, governance models, financing options, risk management, monitoring and evaluation (M&E) metrics, and an implementation playbook.

The intersection of Artificial Intelligence (AI) and blockchain technology is reshaping not only industries but also labor markets, offering new pathways for job creation and transforming the nature of work itself. As digital transformation accelerates across sectors, the integration of these two disruptive technologies—AI with its capability to mimic human cognition, and blockchain with its secure, decentralized data handling—has introduced both opportunities and challenges for employment. While there has been considerable concern about automation displacing jobs, a

processing, and data exchange. The convergence of DPI with Web3 technologies and decentralized infrastructure creates unprecedented opportunities for inclusive economic development. This chapter examines how blockchain, distributed ledger technologies, and decentralized protocols enhance traditional DPI frameworks, analyzing implementations across emerging markets with emphasis on India's pioneering India Stack model. Through examination of 220 million active blockchain addresses globally and DPI implementations reaching 1.3 billion citizens, this research demonstrates that Web3-enabled DPI can overcome institutional voids, reduce transaction costs by up to 70%, and facilitate financial inclusion for 730 million unbanked adults. The chapter analyzes technical architectures, governance models, security frameworks, and socioeconomic impacts while addressing challenges including digital divides, regulatory gaps, and sustainability concerns. Key findings reveal that DPI integrated with Web3 infrastructure contributed 0.9% to GDP in 2022, projected to reach 4.2% by 2030, with the global blockchain market valued at $31.18 billion in 2025 and forecasted to reach $393.42 billion by 2032.

Strong, easily available, and digital financial services which are creative are becoming increasingly important for the growth of world economy, the financial industry is undergoing a revolution in the emerging economies due to the convergence of digital public infrastructure (DPI), blockchain technology, and artificial intelligence (AI), which offers an unprecedented chance to promote financial inclusion, increase efficiency, along with establishing confidence in digital finance. And due to these game-changing technologies, the emerging FinTech industry has accelerated and established itself as both a force behind and a recipient of the extensive digitisation initiatives around the globe. In this proposed chapter "Leveraging Blockchain and AI to Advance Digital Public Infrastructure: Boosting FinTech Development in emerging economies" we aim to thoroughly investigate the ways in which blockchain, AI, and DPI work together to influence the course of FinTech expansion in the emerging markets. We will be presenting a holistic approach, which offers a comprehensive analysis, exposing the complexities of this technological shift and its influence on the emerging economies.

Preface

In an era increasingly defined by connectivity, data, and digital interdependence, Digital Public Infrastructure (DPI) has emerged as a cornerstone of inclusive, sustainable, and equitable development. DPI encompasses the shared digital systems that enable societies to operate efficiently—identity systems, payment networks, data-sharing frameworks, and the regulatory and ethical structures that underpin them. As emerging economies seek to bridge development gaps, these infrastructures hold transformative potential: they not only digitize services but democratize access to opportunity, innovation, and governance.

This book, *Integrating Digital Public Infrastructure in Emerging Economies*, explores how digital ecosystems—rooted in openness, interoperability, and trust—are reshaping the economic, social, and institutional landscapes of the Global South. The chapters collectively interrogate the multidimensional impacts of technologies such as artificial intelligence (AI), blockchain, and decentralized networks on productivity, inclusion, and sustainability. Through interdisciplinary lenses, the contributing authors examine case studies, theoretical frameworks, and policy pathways that illuminate the strategic role of DPI in national and regional transformation.

The volume seeks not merely to describe technological change but to contextualize it within human and institutional frameworks. In doing so, it emphasizes that successful digital transformation in emerging economies depends as much on governance, ethics, and public trust as on technological innovation. The editors have curated a diverse range of perspectives—from engineering and economics to policy and social science—to ensure a comprehensive understanding of how nations can design digital systems that serve people first and foremost.

Chapter 1, *AI and the Economy: Innovation Policy and the Economy*, by SudhaAnanthi G, lays the foundation by discussing how artificial intelligence functions as a general-purpose technology transforming production, labor, and policy innovation.

The chapter identifies AI's role as both an enabler of productivity and a catalyst for new economic paradigms.

Chapter 2, *Empowering Citizens through Code: Policy Pathways for Scalable Digital Public Infrastructure*, co-authored by Ajay Gadicha, Sherif Ismail, and colleagues, examines how digital governance can be made more transparent and participatory. It highlights the crucial interplay between technological advancement and sound public policy in safeguarding data and promoting equitable innovation.

Chapter 3, *Bridging the Digital Divide: A Strategic Framework for Deploying Inclusive DPI in Emerging Economies*, by Barkha Dange, presents a comprehensive framework for inclusive DPI design. It integrates technical, institutional, and social dimensions into an actionable roadmap for ensuring equitable access and long-term sustainability.

Chapter 4, *Artificial Intelligence and Blockchain as a Driver of Job Creation*, authored by Anuradha Phadnis and collaborators, investigates the dual potential of AI and blockchain in shaping future labor markets. It argues that, beyond automation, these technologies can stimulate new employment sectors and redefine digital labor ecosystems.

Chapter 5, *Artificial Intelligence and Blockchain and the Growth of the FinTech Industry*, by Neetal Vyas and co-authors, explores how AI and blockchain accelerate financial innovation, foster credit inclusion, and transform risk management within emerging FinTech ecosystems.

Chapter 6, *Cashless Confidence: Exploring the Influence of Digital Payments on Gen Z Consumption Patterns*, led by Yuvraj Shergill and the CHRIST University team, focuses on behavioral finance and generational shifts in digital payment adoption. It offers insight into how digital-native consumers shape the evolution of financial technologies.

Chapter 7, *DPI in the Age of Web3 and Decentralized Infrastructure*, by Deepak Gupta and collaborators, investigates how blockchain and decentralized technologies integrate with DPI frameworks. It assesses the potential of Web3 to create transparent, secure, and citizen-empowered ecosystems.

Chapter 8, *Leveraging Blockchain and AI to Advance Digital Public Infrastructure: Boosting FinTech Development in Emerging Economies*, by Samarth Saksena, bridges theory and practice, illustrating how converging technologies can accelerate FinTech innovation while enhancing institutional trust in emerging markets.

Chapter 9, *Sustainable Digital Evolution: Addressing Challenges and Embracing Opportunities*, by Girisaran K. S. and Pooja Khanna, emphasizes environmental, ethical, and social considerations in digital progress. It underscores the importance of sustainability as a guiding principle in digital transformation.

Finally, Chapter 10, *Strategic Roadmap for DPI in 2030: Vision and Implementation*, by Ajay Gadicha, Sherif Ismail, and colleagues, envisions a global framework for future-ready DPI. The roadmap outlines strategies for integrating next-generation technologies, harmonizing policy environments, and ensuring universal digital inclusion by the year 2030.

As editors, we believe that the evolution of Digital Public Infrastructure is not merely a technological journey—it is a societal one. The chapters in this volume demonstrate that inclusive digital systems must be designed with intention: grounded in ethics, governed with transparency, and guided by sustainability. DPI should be understood as a public good, fostering equitable access to opportunity and participation in the digital economy.

The lessons drawn from this collection reveal a shared truth across diverse geographies and disciplines: digital transformation cannot succeed without trust, interoperability, and human-centric design. Emerging economies, in particular, stand at a defining moment where technology can serve as a bridge between innovation and inclusion, or—if poorly governed—a driver of inequality. Our collective challenge is to ensure it becomes the former.

We hope that *Integrating Digital Public Infrastructure in Emerging Economies* serves as a timely contribution to both academic and policy discourses. By combining empirical insight, conceptual analysis, and strategic foresight, this book aims to guide practitioners, policymakers, and researchers toward building digital systems that empower, connect, and sustain.

Chapter 1
AI and the Economy Innovation Policy and the Economy

G. SudhaAnanthi
https://orcid.org/0009-0001-5062-5311
Winners Academy, India

ABSTRACT

Rapidly economies, fundamentally altering the structures of industries, labour markets, productivity patterns, and value creation mechanisms. As nations and economic impact is both profound and multifaceted. AI serves as a general-purpose technology, similar to electricity or the internet, with broad applications that permeate virtually every sector and manufacturing education, logistics, agriculture, creative industries. Ubiquitous integration of AI is driving new forms of automation, accelerating innovation cycles, reducing operational costs, and reshaping competitive landscapes. Consequently, AI is emerging not only as a productivity enhancer but also as a catalyst for entirely paradigms. Most significant the enhancement of productivity. AI labor, enabling faster decision-making, improved forecasting, and optimal resource allocation. In sectors like manufacturing, AI-powered robotics and predictive maintenance are reducing downtime and improving efficiency. In are revolutionizing traditional workflows.

UNDERSTANDING THE ECONOMIC IMPACT OF AI

Rapidly economies, fundamentally altering the structures of industries, labour markets, productivity patterns, and value creation mechanisms. As nations and economic impact is both profound and multifaceted. AI serves as a general-purpose

DOI: 10.4018/979-8-3373-6380-6.ch001

technology, similar to electricity or the internet, with broad applications that permeate virtually every sector and manufacturing education, logistics, agriculture, creative industries. Ubiquitous integration of AI is driving new forms of automation, accelerating innovation cycles, reducing operational costs, and reshaping competitive landscapes. Consequently, AI is emerging not only as a productivity enhancer but also as a catalyst for entirely paradigms. Most significant the enhancement of productivity. AI labor, enabling faster decision-making, improved forecasting, and optimal resource allocation. In sectors like manufacturing, AI-powered robotics and predictive maintenance are reducing downtime and improving efficiency. In are revolutionizing traditional workflows. Applications crop monitoring, supply chain optimization are enhancing food production and reducing waste. These applications collectively contribute to economic efficiency and growth. However, the economic impact of AI is not uniformly positive or evenly distributed. The rise of AI-driven automation has profound implications for labor markets. While AI creates new jobs in data science, AI ethics, particularly those involving repetitive, rule-based tasks. Sectors such as transportation, retail, and customer service are witnessing disruptions as AI-powered systems replace human labor. This technological displacement raises concerns about structural unemployment, wage stagnation, and the widening of socio-economic inequalities, especially in regions or communities that are less equipped to adapt to rapid technological change.

At the same time, AI contributes to the creation of new markets and economic opportunities. The emergence of the AI ecosystem—including startups, AI-as-a-Service platforms, data providers, and hardware manufacturers—has spurred a vibrant innovation economy. Countries and corporations investing in AI research and development are gaining competitive advantages, attracting foreign investments, and positioning themselves as global leaders in the digital economy. Additionally, the application of AI in public sector governance, such as urban planning, traffic management, healthcare delivery, and environmental monitoring, is enabling more efficient public services and fostering socio-economic development. The adoption of AI is also stimulating global competition and geopolitical shifts in economic power. Nations several EU countries—are increasingly shaping global standards, intellectual property regimes, and regulatory frameworks. This digital race for AI supremacy is intensifying investment in education, research, and infrastructure, further accelerating AI's economic influence. Simultaneously, there is a growing recognition of driven growth, preventing a digital divide that could deepen global inequalities. Furthermore, AI's role in augmenting human capabilities cannot be overlooked. By complementing human intelligence with machine precision and speed, AI enables professionals in medicine, law, education, and creative fields to achieve greater outcomes. In medicine, for instance, AI-assisted diagnostics and drug discovery are speeding up treatment protocols and expanding access to healthcare. In creative sectors, generative AI tools are unlocking new avenues for artistic expression and content generation, giving rise to hybrid forms of economic value. These collaborative human-AI synergies are fostering a more dynamic and diverse economic environment.

The Role of AI in Driving Innovation and Growth: Innovation driver

Innovation landscape, acting as a transformative force that propels economic growth, enhances productivity, and accelerates the development of new ideas, services, and technologies. (Abisoye A. et al. 2022) As a powerful general-purpose technology, AI is not merely an enhancement of existing tools—it is a foundational enabler of cross-sectoral innovation. By leveraging its. AI is opening previously unimaginable frontiers in science, business, and society. It is driving innovation not only by automating processes but also by generating novel solutions, unlocking new business models, and reconfiguring entire value chains. The synergy between AI and innovation is creating a dynamic feedback loop where AI-powered tools stimulate new discoveries, which in turn feed further technological advancement and economic expansion. One of the most prominent ways AI drives innovations is through its massive unprecedented speed. This capacity enables researchers, developers, and businesses to gain deeper insights, identify hidden that would be infeasible using traditional methods. In the pharmaceutical industry, for instance, screening, reducing development timelines. Revolutionizing engineering and manufacturing. (Abisoye A. et al. 2022) In agriculture, AI technologies support innovation through precision farming techniques, enabling optimal crop management, soil analysis, and pest control. These advancements contribute not only to industrial growth but also to addressing global healthcare access. Create smart, adaptive products. For example, AI-powered recommendation engines drive personalization in e-commerce and entertainment, while chatbots and virtual assistants improve customer service and engagement. In the automotive sector, AI is at the heart of autonomous vehicle development, pushing the boundaries of transportation innovation. In education, adaptive learning platforms use AI to tailor content delivery to individual learners, enhancing educational. These innovations not only improve user satisfaction and engagement but also contribute to competitive differentiation and market expansion.

Moreover, AI fosters innovation in business models and organizational processes. (Agrawal A. et al. 2019) Traditional industries are being reimagined through platform-based models, intelligent automation, and data-driven decision-making. Startups and digital-native firms are leveraging AI to disrupt legacy systems, offering innovative services such as AI-driven financial advising, telemedicine, and supply chain optimization. This democratization of AI tools—fueled by open-source platforms, cloud computing, and AI-as-a-Service—lowers the barriers to innovation, allowing even small firms and individuals to experiment, create, and compete in global markets. The result is a more dynamic and inclusive innovation ecosystem where ideas can scale rapidly and reach broader audiences. AI also serves as a catalyst for scientific discovery and technological advancement. In fields such as genomics, climate modeling, and quantum computing, AI is enabling researchers to analyze complex phenomena, simulate scenarios, and test hypotheses with greater efficiency. This accelerates the pace of scientific progress and leads to breakthroughs that have far-reaching economic and societal implications. AI-powered simulations are aiding space exploration, while predictive models are improving disaster preparedness and response. These applications underscore AI's potential not only to solve existing problems but also to redefine the frontiers of human knowledge and capability. In addition, AI is reshaping the innovation process itself. Traditional innovation cycles—often linear and time-consuming—are being replaced by agile, iterative, and data-informed approaches. (Agrawal A. et al. 2019) AI tools facilitate rapid prototyping, real-time feedback, and continuous improvement, enabling organizations to innovate faster and more effectively. For instance, in the design and manufacturing sectors, generative design algorithms use AI to explore countless design permutations based on specified constraints, producing optimized solutions that human designers might not conceive. This shift towards AI-enhanced creativity is blurring the lines between human and machine-led innovation, leading to a collaborative paradigm where AI augments human ingenuity.

AI Applications in Various Industries: Economic Benefits: AI applications.

Artificial Intelligence (AI) is playing a transformative role across multiple industries, revolutionizing traditional operations, creating new avenues for value generation, and yielding substantial economic benefits. (Ai H. et al. 2024) As become increasingly sophisticated and accessible, their integration into various sectors is reshaping business models, improving efficiency, global competitiveness. Economic impact these applications is not confined to isolated pockets but extends across entire value chains, influencing everything from production and logistics to customer engagement and strategic planning. As a general-purpose technology, AI is delivering economic dividends through cost reduction, productivity enhancement, revenue generation, innovation acceleration, and service improvement in virtually every industry. Predictive maintenance, process optimization streamlines operations. Intelligent machines can autonomously detect equipment failures, analyze performance in real-time, and suggest interventions, significantly remarkable precision, improving output consistency and reducing waste. (Ai H. et al. 2024) Additionally, AI supports demand forecasting and supply chain management, enabling manufacturers to respond more effectively to market fluctuations. These advancements contribute directly to higher productivity, cost efficiency, and global competitiveness, especially in economies where manufacturing remains a key growth driver. In the healthcare industry, AI is transforming medical diagnostics, treatment personalization, drug development, and administrative workflows. Optimize resource allocation, and expand access to care—producing substantial economic and social value.

The financial services sector has emerged. (Akram R. et al. 2024) Natural language processing tools automate compliance monitoring by scanning communications and documents for regulatory breaches. Additionally, AI enhances customer service through chatbots and virtual agents capable of managing complex queries. The economic benefits include improved security, reduced operational expenses, increased accessibility, and the generation of new financial products and services. Purchasing behavior, optimizing revenue generation. AI also enhances inventory forecasting and supply chain logistics, ensuring stock availability and reducing storage costs. Virtual try-on tools and AI-based customer service agents create more interactive and efficient shopping experiences. These applications improve customer retention, boost revenue, and enable retailers to stay competitive in a fast-evolving digital marketplace. The transportation and logistics sector benefits from AI through route optimization, demand prediction, fleet management, and autonomous vehicles. Suggest optimal delivery routes, reducing fuel consumption and delivery times. In public transport, AI helps manage schedules and predict passenger demand, enhancing service efficiency. Autonomous drones and vehicles are being tested and deployed for last-mile delivery and mobility services, promising to reshape urban logistics and reduce human labor dependency. (Akram R. et al. 2024) These innovations improve operational efficiency, lower environmental impact, and offer cost savings across transportation networks.

AI-Powered Innovation: New Products and Services: AI-powered innovation.

Offerings that were once unimaginable. (Avalekar U. A. et al. 2025) From virtual assistants and generative content platforms to autonomous vehicles and precision healthcare tools, AI-powered innovations are creating value, solving complex problems, and meeting evolving consumer demands. These breakthroughs are not just enhancing competitiveness but are also opening up new markets, business models, and economic opportunities globally. Queries, schedule tasks, manage smart home devices, and provide personalized information. These AI-driven platforms have evolved into essential interfaces for digital interaction, deeply integrated into smartphones, smart speakers, and even vehicles. Their expanding functionalities continue to influence how consumers engage with technology, making everyday life more convenient and productive. The services built around these assistants are now integral to ecosystems of apps, connected devices, and cloud-based services, generating significant economic value through user engagement, data monetization, and subscription models. In the realm of creative industries, AI has led to the emergence of generative tools capable of producing music, art, text, and even video content. Platforms like DALL·E, Midjourney, and RunwayML allow users to generate stunning visuals from text prompts, democratizing creativity and reducing reliance on traditional design workflows. (Avalekar U. A. et al. 2025) Similarly, AI music composition tools can create melodies, harmonies, and soundscapes based on user-defined inputs or emotional tone. In publishing and media, AI is used to generate news articles, social media content, and advertising copy at scale, accelerating production and enhancing personalization. These generative capabilities are revolutionizing how content is conceived, created, and distributed, offering cost-effective, scalable solutions for creators, marketers, and publishers alike.

In transportation mobility, AI is driving innovation navigation systems suggest optimal routes by analyzing traffic data, weather conditions, and road closures. (Boonman H. et al. 2023) In logistics, predictive algorithms forecast demand, optimize delivery schedules, and enhance fleet efficiency. These technologies reduce operational costs, minimize fuel consumption, and improve delivery reliability—benefits that are translating into new service models such as mobility-as-a-service (MaaS) and autonomous freight transportation. Retail and e-commerce are undergoing rapid transformation due to AI-powered innovation. Personalized shopping experiences are now driven. AI chatbots offer instant customer support, product suggestions, and transaction assistance. (Boonman H. et al. 2023) Visual search tools allow users to upload images and find similar products, improving product discovery. AI is also being used in virtual fitting rooms, where customers can try on clothes using augmented reality and body scanning technology. In-store AI systems track customer movement and behavior, enabling retailers to optimize store layouts and marketing strategies. These innovations increase customer satisfaction, boost sales, and streamline operations, offering retailers a competitive edge in an increasingly digital marketplace. Improving engagement and outcomes. AI tutors provide personalized feedback, identify knowledge gaps, and offer targeted interventions, mimicking one-on-one instruction. Automated grading systems evaluate assignments and tests quickly and consistently, saving educators time and effort. Language learning apps like Duolingo use AI to adjust difficulty and provide instant corrections, enhancing the learning experience. By lifelong learning and workforce development.

The Impact of AI on Productivity and Efficiency: Productivity impact.

Work processes. (Chib S. et al. 2025) It is not just a tool for automation—it is an enabler of smarter, data-driven decision-making, proactive problem-solving, and strategic innovation. By augmenting human capabilities and optimizing systems, AI is leading to a significant increase in output and resource utilization, resulting in major gains in productivity and efficiency at both micro and macroeconomic levels. Inventory tracking, and scheduling—can be executed more quickly and with fewer errors by AI systems. In back-office operations, Robotic Process Automation (RPA) powered by AI is streamlining workflows across finance, human resources, and procurement departments. (Chib S. et al. 2025) For example, AI bots can reconcile financial records, manage payroll, and handle compliance reporting far more efficiently than human workers, allowing employees to improves overall organizational agility and productivity. AI's impact on decision-making processes is another key driver of efficiency. Traditional decision-making often relies on historical data, intuition, or limited datasets. AI, particularly through machine learning and predictive analytics, can process massive, real-time datasets to generate actionable insights that guide more accurate, timely, and data-informed decisions. In sectors like logistics, AI-driven in finance, AI-powered risk assessment tools enable better credit scoring and investment strategies. This enhanced decision-making accelerates response times, improves strategic alignment, and reduces the risks and costs associated with trial-and-error approaches.

In the manufacturing industry, AI technologies are at the core of smart factory initiatives, transforming production lines into adaptive and self-optimizing environments. AI-enabled predictive maintenance tools monitor machinery in real-time, detecting signs of wear or malfunction before they cause breakdowns inspectors. (Chowdhary S. et al. 2025) These applications significantly reduce waste, rework, and energy consumption while enhancing throughput and consistency, contributing directly to improved operational efficiency. The integration of AI in supply chain and logistics operations has revolutionized how goods are moved, stored, and delivered. AI-powered algorithms optimize routing and scheduling, leads to reduced fuel consumption, lower transportation costs, and faster delivery times. In warehouses, AI-driven robotics and automation systems manage sorting, picking, and packing processes with high precision and speed. Additionally, AI tools forecast demand trends and supply disruptions, allowing businesses to respond proactively and maintain service levels. These enhancements in supply chain agility and reliability contribute to a more productive and resilient logistics ecosystem. (Chowdhary S. et al. 2025) In customer service and support, AI-powered chatbots, virtual assistants, and sentiment analysis tools are significantly improving efficiency and customer experience. Chatbots can identify emerging concerns or negative trends, allowing companies to address problems proactively. These tools reduce wait times, lower customer service costs, and allow human agents to focus on complex or high-priority cases, thereby increasing the productivity of service teams.

Innovation Policy Frameworks for AI Adoption: Policy frameworks.

National economies, public services, and industries require thoughtful and comprehensive innovation policy frameworks. (Coates J. M. et al. 2025) As AI reshapes the global innovation landscape, countries and institutions are recognizing the urgency of formulating adaptive, forward-looking policies that not only foster technological advancement manage. An effective innovation policy framework for AI balances the need to drive rapid AI deployment with safeguards that ensure inclusivity, accountability, sustainability, and long-term societal benefit. Such frameworks are essential to building innovation ecosystems. At core of an AI innovation policy framework lies the promotion of research and development (R&D). Governments must invest in foundational and applied AI research across sectors, supporting universities, public research institutions, and private sector initiatives. Funding programs, grants, and incentives are crucial mechanisms for encouraging AI experimentation and pushing. Many countries have created dedicated AI research institutes or centers of excellence, such as Canada's CIFAR, the UK's Alan Turing Institute, and India's AI Mission. (Coates J. M. et al. 2025) These institutions serve as innovation hubs that foster interdisciplinary collaboration, advance state-of-the-art AI technologies, and develop indigenous capabilities that reduce dependency on foreign innovations. In tandem, public-private partnerships (PPPs) have emerged as essential tools within innovation policy frameworks. AI development often requires substantial investments, cross-sector expertise, and access to diverse datasets. Through PPPs, governments can facilitate collaboration between startups, tech giants, academia, and civil society. These partnerships accelerate innovation by aligning public interests with private capabilities, ensuring that AI applications address real-world needs such as healthcare access, smart mobility, and climate resilience. Moreover, PPPs enable knowledge transfer, incubate entrepreneurship, and create testbeds for real-world AI deployment—driving economic development and capacity building.

Another critical element of AI-focused innovation policy is human capital development. The success of AI adoption hinges on transition into emerging AI-related roles. (Cockburn I. M. et al. 2018) Policies must also address gender and social inclusion in AI education, promoting diversity in the tech workforce and avoiding the entrenchment of existing inequalities. Countries such as Singapore and Finland have launched national AI training programs aimed at equipping both professionals and the general population with essential AI skills. Data which necessitates the development of data ecosystems that are open, interoperable, secure, and privacy-preserving. Innovation policies must encourage the creation of data-sharing frameworks that enable collaboration while respecting ethical and legal boundaries. Initiatives spaces, India's Data Empowerment and Protection Architecture (DEPA), and the US National AI Research Resource exemplify efforts to build shared data infrastructure for innovation. Furthermore, innovation frameworks must promote computing power—that support scalable AI experimentation and deployment, particularly in underserved regions. A robust policy framework must also embed ethical, legal, financial services, innovation policies must incorporate guidelines for transparency, fairness, accountability, and explainability. Regulatory sandboxes, for instance, allow for the safe testing of AI applications under regulatory oversight, facilitating iterative learning and adaptive policymaking. (Cockburn I. M. et al. 2018) Ethical AI principles, such as those proposed by UNESCO, the OECD, and national AI strategies, must be translated into enforceable standards and integrated into product development lifecycles. In addition, policies should mandate algorithmic audits, impact assessments, and the inclusion of where appropriate maintain prevent harm.

Government Initiatives and Funding for AI Research: Government initiatives.

Taking proactive steps development through targeted initiatives and strategic funding. These efforts reflect a growing understanding critical factor in economic growth, national competitiveness, and social development. Government initiatives international collaboration, governments are laying the groundwork for sustainable, inclusive, and responsible AI advancement. A central component of government support for AI is the formulation of national AI strategies. (Ernst E. et al. 2019) These comprehensive policy documents outline long-term visions, goals, and investment plans to guide AI development within countries. They typically include priorities such as enhancing R&D capacity, fostering innovation ecosystems, building ethical and regulatory frameworks, and addressing skills gaps. For example, the European Union's Coordinated Plan on AI sets forth a shared roadmap among member states to boost AI capabilities and competitiveness, while India's National Strategy for AI (NSAI) emphasizes inclusive agriculture. Similarly, the United States' National AI Initiative Act promotes AI leadership through investments in research, education, infrastructure, and ethical guidelines. These strategies reflect the central role governments play in orchestrating AI development at the national level. (Ernst E. et al. 2019) Direct funding for AI research is a primary mechanism through which governments stimulate innovation. Public investment supports both foundational and applied AI research, enabling breakthroughs in program, funding research chairs and labs in Toronto, Montreal, and Edmonton. In addition to research grants, governments are investing in the creation of AI centers of excellence and innovation hubs. These institutions serve as focal points for interdisciplinary collaboration, cutting-edge research, and the commercialization of AI technologies. For instance, Germany's AI Competence Centers promote cooperation between academia and industry, while France's INRIA focuses on digital science and AI innovation.

Figure 1. Entrepreneurship Sustains Barriers in the Entrepreneurial Process

Singapore has established AI Singapore (AISG), which supports translational research, AI product development, and industry deployment. These hubs facilitate knowledge transfer, entrepreneurship, and experimentation by creating environments where scientists, startups, corporations, and policymakers interact. (Filiou D. et al. 2023) Public sector AI challenge funds and innovation prizes are also being used to encourage targeted research in high-impact areas. These initiatives often support AI applications that Advanced Research Projects Agency (DARPA) runs AI competitions and challenge programs to spur innovations in autonomous systems, adversarial AI, and defense applications. These initiatives stimulate creative problem-solving and attract multidisciplinary teams to tackle complex problems using AI. Beyond direct funding, governments are playing. Research Resource Task Force is working on creating a shared research infrastructure that democratizes access to data, tools, and computing power for AI researchers. Such infrastructure initiatives aim to level the playing field and reduce the barriers to entry for researchers and institutions with limited resources. Another significant government role is in promoting interdisciplinary and inclusive AI research. Governments are encouraging cross-sectoral and cross-disciplinary approaches that combine computer science with social sciences, humanities, law, and medicine. (Filiou D. et al. 2023) This enables Funding programs now often include requirements for addressing fairness, bias, transparency, and privacy in AI applications. For example, Canada's CIFAR AI Chairs program includes mandates for responsible AI development, while the U.S. National AI Research Institutes are focused on AI for societal benefit, including education, public health, and environmental sustainability.

Collaboration between Industry, Academia, and Government: Collaboration.

Often referred to as the triple helix model—has emerged as a cornerstone of successful innovation ecosystems. (Furman & Seamans, 2019) These synergistic partnerships pool resources, knowledge, and expertise from each sector to accelerate AI research, development, and deployment. By aligning commercial interests, academic rigor, and public priorities, such collaboration ensures that AI innovations are not only cutting-edge and market-ready but also ethically responsible, socially beneficial, and strategically aligned with national and global development goals. In the context of AI, where complexity, interdisciplinarity, and rapid change are the norm, the tri-sector collaboration is more essential than ever. Industry, with its focus on product development, scale, and commercialization, brings the technical infrastructure, funding, and practical insights necessary to drive AI applications. research into usable technologies, services, and platforms that reach end users. Tech giants like Google, Microsoft, IBM, and Amazon invest billions in AI R&D and frequently partner with universities to support research labs, provide data access, and test applications. Startups, too, contribute by offering agile environments for experimentation and market responsiveness, often acting as early adopters and innovators in niche AI domains such as healthcare diagnostics, smart agriculture, or financial automation. (Furman & Seamans, 2019) Academia, on the other hand, offers a foundation of deep scientific inquiry, long-term research perspectives, and a critical lens for examining AI's implications. Universities and research institutions are responsible for producing fundamental breakthroughs natural language processing algorithms. Furthermore, they are central to talent development, training the next generation of AI scientists, engineers, and ethicists. Academic freedom allows scholars to explore unconventional and high-risk ideas that might not receive funding in a purely commercial setting. Through peer-reviewed publications, conferences, and collaborative projects, academia contributes to the diffusion of knowledge and the continuous evolution of AI as a field.

Government, as a regulator, funder, and strategic planner, plays a catalytic role in fostering and sustaining the collaboration between industry and academia. (Hunjra A. I. et al. 2024) Public policies set the direction for national AI agendas, allocate funding for research and innovation, and establish ethical and legal frameworks to ensure responsible AI development. Governments also act as conveners, bringing together disparate stakeholders to align efforts, eliminate duplication, and solve public-interest problems. Through public procurement, challenge grants, tax incentives, and national strategies, they can steer AI innovation toward societal needs, such as public health, education, climate action, and equitable access to technology. A prime example of such collaboration can be seen in joint research programs and public-private research consortia. (Hunjra A. I. et al. 2024) These initiatives unite universities, private companies, and government agencies to work on shared research goals. For instance, the Partnership on AI includes members from academia (e.g., MIT, Oxford), industry (e.g., Google, Facebook, IBM), and civil society, focusing on ethical AI and best practices. The AI4EU platform in Europe connects academic research with industrial use cases and public policy, enabling cross-border collaboration. In the U.S., the National AI Research Institutes initiative brings together university-led research hubs with support private sector partners to explore applications ranging from food systems to climate modeling and human-AI interaction.

Economic Benefits of AI Adoption: Economic benefits.

Adoption rapidly reshaping global economies, offering a wide array of economic benefits that span across industries, sectors, and regions. (Kim & Choi, 2019) AI's transformative capabilities—ranging from automation and optimization to intelligent data analysis and prediction—are enabling organizations and governments to increase productivity, reduce costs, enhance service quality, and generate new value. As a general-purpose technology, AI is poised to become a key driver of economic growth in the 21st century, akin to past technological revolutions like electricity, the steam engine, or the internet. With its ability to unlock efficiencies, foster innovation, and catalyze new markets, the economic impact of AI adoption is profound and multi-dimensional. (Kim & Choi, 2019) Beyond cost savings, AI adoption drives revenue growth dynamically adjust pricing, inventory, and promotions. In the entertainment industry, AI powers recommendation engines and content creation, expanding engagement and monetization opportunities. Moreover, AI facilitates the rise of data-driven business models where data is monetized as a strategic asset, such as in insurance, telecommunications, and digital advertising. These AI-enabled innovations open up new revenue streams and markets, fostering business expansion and job creation. AI adoption also contributes to macroeconomic competitiveness by enhancing national productivity, innovation capacity, and global market positioning. Countries that lead Union—are reaping significant economic dividends in the form of increased GDP, foreign investment, and technological sovereignty. A PwC study estimates that AI could contribute up to $15.7 trillion to the global economy by 2030, with $6.6 trillion coming from increased productivity and $9.1 trillion from consumption-side effects. Nations with proactive AI strategies and ecosystems attract top talent, investment, and corporate headquarters, strengthening their economic influence in the digital age.

Furthermore, AI adoption enhances decision-making and strategic planning through advanced data analytics, pattern recognition, and forecasting. (Levidow L. et al. 2012) Businesses and governments can now analyze anticipate market trends, respond swiftly to changes. Retailers use AI to forecast demand, tailor inventory, and plan product launches. Urban planners use AI-powered simulations to optimize infrastructure development, transportation, and resource allocation. During crises such as managing logistics. These applications improve efficiency, reduce uncertainty, and support evidence-based policymaking, leading to better economic outcomes. Another critical benefit is AI's role in stimulating innovation ecosystems. AI serves as an enabling technology that accelerates research and development across domains including pharmaceuticals, energy, agriculture, and materials science. In drug discovery, AI shortens the R&D cycle by identifying promising compounds and predicting efficacy. In agriculture, AI supports precision farming, crop monitoring, and yield optimization, enhancing food security and rural economies. (Levidow L. et al. 2012) These innovations not only drive sectoral productivity but also generate high-value intellectual property, strengthen domestic industries, and support export growth. AI also acts as a magnet for entrepreneurship, with a proliferation of AI startups emerging across sectors, backed by venture capital and supported by public-private innovation programs. The economic benefits of AI adoption are also reflected in job creation and labor market evolution. Transitions smoothly and benefits from new employment opportunities. By fostering human-AI collaboration rather than substitution, economies can unlock a more dynamic, inclusive labor market.

Challenges and Risks Associated with AI Adoption: Challenges and risks.

While Artificial Intelligence (AI) promises vast economic and social benefits, its widespread adoption presents a complex landscape of challenges and risks that must be thoughtfully addressed. (Li B. et al. 2022) These challenges economic, geopolitical dimensions. As AI becomes increasingly embedded in critical systems—healthcare, finance, education, security, and governance—the consequences of its failures, biases, or misuse grow more serious. Navigating these challenges is essential. Misdiagnoses, disproportionately affecting underrepresented populations. Moreover, data silos, proprietary restrictions, and lack of interoperability limit access to high-quality, diverse datasets essential for building robust and generalizable AI models. The issue, as users and regulators struggle to understand how or why specific outcomes were produced. Mitigating algorithmic bias requires concerted efforts in fairness-aware model development, diverse data representation, algorithmic audits, and explainable AI research. Ethical dilemmas represent another significant challenge. Questions about the moral boundaries of AI are increasingly central, particularly in areas involving surveillance, predictive policing, autonomous weapons, and personal data use. For example, facial recognition technologies—deployed for security or marketing—raise concerns about consent, surveillance, and civil liberties. (Li B. et al. 2022) The deployment of autonomous decision-making systems in life-critical also poses ethical questions: Who is responsible when things go wrong? What ethical framework should guide machine decisions in ambiguous or life-threatening scenarios? Without clear ethical standards and governance mechanisms, AI risks being applied in ways that conflict with human rights and democratic values.

Security vulnerabilities and cyber threats pose another critical risk associated with AI adoption. AI systems can inversion techniques. In adversarial attacks, subtle perturbations in input data—imperceptible to humans—can cause AI systems to make incorrect predictions, such as misclassifying road signs or bypassing facial recognition systems. (Limbore N. V. et al. 2025) Hackers may exploit AI-driven automation in critical infrastructure—like energy grids, financial markets, or autonomous vehicles—potentially leading to widespread disruption or damage. Additionally, AI can be weaponized for cybercrime, misinformation campaigns, deepfakes, and automated hacking, amplifying the scale and impact of malicious activity. Ensuring therefore paramount for safe deployment. The loss of introduces further complexity. there is a risk of delegating too much authority to machines without sufficient human involvement or understanding. blind reliance on AI may lead to decisions that lack empathy, context-awareness, or moral judgment. Furthermore, when AI decisions cause harm or violate rights, determining liability and accountability becomes challenging. (Limbore N. V. et al. 2025) The lack of clear accountability frameworks can hinder redress mechanisms and erode public trust. Another major concern creates new opportunities and job categories, it also displaces traditional roles, especially those involving repetitive or routine tasks. Highly skilled workers and large tech firms,

The Impact of AI on Employment and Labor Markets: Employment impact.

Artificial Intelligence (AI) is fundamentally reshaping the landscape of employment and labor markets worldwide. (Lokhande M. et al. 2025) As AI technologies continue to advance and become more deeply embedded in economic systems, their effects on jobs, work structures, skills demand, and workforce dynamics are becoming increasingly significant and complex. While AI offers immense institutions to manage workforce transitions. Understanding and addressing these multifaceted impacts is essential for fostering inclusive and sustainable labor markets in the AI era. Studies by organizations like McKinsey and the OECD estimate that up to 14–30% of current jobs could be automated by the mid-2030s, with varying impact across industries and regions. However, the narrative of widespread job loss must be balanced with recognition of AI-driven job creation and transformation. AI does not merely replace human labor—it also complements it and creates new roles and occupations. As AI automates certain tasks, it frees AI ethicists, algorithm auditors, and human-AI interaction designers. The labor market impact of AI is thus characterized not only by displacement but also by reconfiguration of job roles and required skills. Many existing occupations are evolving as AI tools become standard components of the workflow. For instance, marketing professionals now use AI for predictive analytics and campaign optimization, while lawyers employ AI for legal research and contract analysis. This transformation demands driven insights. (Lokhande M. et al. 2025) As a result, the ability to adapt and learn continuously has become a central requirement in the AI-influenced labor market. Skill mismatches and digital divides, however, pose significant challenges in the context of AI adoption. Not all workers have equal access to the education, training, and digital infrastructure needed to acquire AI-relevant skills. Low-income workers, those in rural areas, and workers in developing countries may be particularly vulnerable to being left behind.

Older workers and those with limited formal education also face greater risk of displacement due to slower adaptation to technological changes. These disparities can job decline. Without targeted interventions, such polarization could undermine social cohesion and economic stability. (Lundvall B. Å. et al. 2022) In response to these shifts, Programs offering training in coding, data literacy, cybersecurity, digital marketing, and AI fundamentals are expanding, often with support from public-private partnerships. (Lundvall B. Å. et al. 2022) For example, initiatives like Singapore's SkillsFuture, Germany's AI Campus, and India's FutureSkills Prime aim to equip workers with future-ready skills. However, the effectiveness of these programs depends on their accessibility, relevance, and ability to reach vulnerable populations. Continuous investment in human capital development is essential to ensure that workers are not just displaced but repositioned in more productive and rewarding roles. Occupations. In agriculture, AI is enhancing productivity through precision farming and crop monitoring, potentially reducing the need for manual labor but increasing demand for agricultural technologists. In finance, AI is automating routine tasks like compliance checks and risk assessments while creating new roles in AI governance and financial modeling. In education, AI-powered tools support personalized learning, creative industries, AI-generated content is reshaping roles in design, music, and writing, prompting debates about authorship and originality. These sectoral dynamics highlight the need for nuanced labor market policies that consider industry-specific impacts and workforce characteristics.

The Future of AI in the Economy: Future directions.

Transformative forces shaping the global economy in the 21st century. As technological capabilities continue to advance, AI will increasingly underpin economic systems, drive industrial innovation, enhance productivity, and alter the structure of labor markets. Progress but also how societies, governments, and businesses choose to harness its power responsibly, equitably, and sustainably. (Luo S. et al. 2023) Looking ahead, life—from manufacturing and services to governance and global trade—presents trajectory of future development. One of the most significant future directions is the mainstreaming of AI, once confined to research labs and elite technology firms, is becoming increasingly accessible due to advances in computing power, open-source software, and cloud-based infrastructure. This democratization of AI will enable its widespread adoption across small and medium-sized enterprises (SMEs), public institutions, and developing countries. In manufacturing, AI-driven smart factories will enable real-time optimization of supply chains, predictive maintenance, and adaptive production systems. In agriculture, AI will support precision farming through automated drones, weather prediction, and soil monitoring. In finance, AI will power intelligen. This horizontal expansion of AI technologies economic, especially as traditional industries integrate digital intelligence into their core operations. (Luo S. et al. 2023) The future economy will also witness models driven by AI innovation. Just as the internet gave rise to e-commerce, social media, and the gig economy, AI will catalyze novel economic activities. These may include personalized AI healthcare platforms, autonomous transportation ecosystems, virtual assistants for professional tasks, synthetic media production, and advanced human-computer interaction services. New business models will emerge around data monetization, AI-as-a-service (AIaaS), and decentralized autonomous organizations (DAOs). This proliferation of AI-driven entrepreneurship will reshape competitive landscapes, disrupt incumbents, and offer dynamic new avenues for job creation, investment, and global trade.

A critical future trend will be the transition from narrow AI to more generalized and context-aware systems. Current AI systems are typically. However, advances in multimodal learning, reinforcement learning, and neural-symbolic systems are pushing AI towards more adaptive and generalized capabilities. (Mehra J. et al. 2025) These next-generation AI models will be able to reason, learn from fewer examples, and transfer knowledge across domains—unlocking new possibilities for automation and augmentation across complex, dynamic environments. In economic terms, this means AI will increasingly move beyond back-office automation into roles that require decision-making, problem-solving, and policy analysis. As AI becomes more embedded in economic infrastructures, its role in boosting productivity and economic efficiency will intensify. (Mehra J. et al. 2025) AI-powered analytics, digital twins, robotic process automation, and intelligent resource allocation will enable firms to optimize operations, reduce costs, and innovate faster. This could lead to sustained productivity growth, reversing the stagnation observed in many advanced economies over the past decade. At the macroeconomic level, boost GDP growth public service delivery, fostering innovation. According to various economic forecasts, including those by PwC and McKinsey, AI could contribute between $13 trillion and a central engine future economic expansion. While AI will create high-skill, high-wage jobs in data science, AI development, and digital design, it may simultaneously displace routine jobs in sectors like transportation, manufacturing, and clerical work. If left unmanaged, this bifurcation could lead to a divided economy where the benefits of AI accrue to a narrow segment of society, exacerbating income inequality, social unrest, and political instability. Future economic policies must therefore prioritize inclusive AI deployment, support for displaced workers, universal access to digital education, and social safety nets.

Emerging Trends in AI and Economic Development: Emerging trends.

National development strategies and economic planning. Governments around the world are recognizing the strategic importance of AI as a catalyst for innovation, productivity, and industrial modernization. (Nisha Angeline M. et al. 2025) As a result, countries are embedding AI initiatives into their economic blueprints, investing in AI research and infrastructure, and promoting AI education and entrepreneurship. For instance, China's AI Development Plan, India's National AI Strategy ("AI for All"), and the all reflect a growing focus on AI as a core pillar of economic policy. This integration signifies a shift from reactive adoption to proactive leadership, with AI becoming a central component in national efforts to compete in the global digital economy. Open-source platforms, cloud computing, and low-code or no-code development tools. These innovations are lowering the barriers to entry for individuals, startups, and small enterprises, enabling broader participation in the AI economy. Platforms like TensorFlow, PyTorch, and OpenAI's APIs provide access to powerful machine learning capabilities, while cloud-based AI services from companies like AWS, Google, and Microsoft allow users to deploy AI solutions without the need for deep technical expertise or expensive infrastructure. This democratization is empowering a new wave of digital entrepreneurs, fostering local innovation, and enabling bottom-up economic growth, particularly in emerging markets. (Nisha Angeline M. et al. 2025) A major trend reshaping AI and powered platforms and ecosystems that facilitate new forms of value creation and exchange. Platform-based business models—such as those used by Uber, Amazon, and Alibaba—rely heavily on AI for personalized recommendations, dynamic pricing, supply chain optimization, and fraud detection. These platforms are not only transforming traditional industries like retail, logistics, and mobility but also giving rise to new forms of informal digital work and micro-entrepreneurship. AI-enhanced platforms are also being developed for agriculture (e.g., precision farming tools), education (e.g., adaptive learning platforms), and healthcare (e.g., remote diagnostics), extending their impact into sectors critical to human development.

The intersection smart cities are leveraging AI and IoT to manage traffic, energy use, and waste systems more efficiently; AI and blockchain are being used in supply chain transparency and digital identity systems; and AI with 5G is enabling real-time industrial automation and remote surgeries. (Park M. S. et al. 2022) These technological synergies are opening up new pathways for economic development that are faster, smarter, and more interconnected than ever before. The growing importance of ethical and inclusive AI is also emerging as a crucial trend in economic development. As AI becomes more embedded in economic systems, concerns around fairness, transparency, accountability, and privacy are coming to the forefront. There is increasing recognition that the benefits of AI must be distributed equitably and that its development must avoid reinforcing existing social and economic inequalities. Inclusive AI design practices are now emphasizing diverse data representation, gender equity, cultural sensitivity, and accessibility for persons with disabilities. International bodies like the OECD, UNESCO, and the Global Partnership on AI are promoting global norms and ethical frameworks to guide AI deployment in development contexts. The future of economic development will depend not just on the power of AI, but on its ability to uplift all communities. Another emerging trend is the rise of AI-led innovation hubs and clusters as engines of regional economic development. (Park M. S. et al. 2022) Around the world, cities and regions are establishing AI-focused innovation districts that bring together academia, industry, and government to foster research, commercialization, and talent development.

Examples include Silicon Valley in the U.S., Shenzhen in China, Toronto's MaRS Discovery District in Canada, and Bengaluru's AI centers in India. These hubs often act as magnets for venture capital, tech startups, and multinational investment, generating high-skilled employment and regional economic diversification. As these clusters grow, they also contribute to global knowledge networks and cross-border innovation collaboration.

Harnessing AI for Sustainable Economic Growth: Sustainable growth.

A key driver of AI's contribution to sustainable growth is its ability to optimize resource efficiency across sectors, reducing waste and minimizing environmental impact. In manufacturing, AI-powered systems such as predictive maintenance, digital twins, and real-time analytics can dramatically cut down energy consumption, reduce material usage, and improve production yields. Similarly, in agriculture, AI enables precision farming techniques that boosting crop yields while minimizing ecological harm. In logistics and transportation, AI supports dynamic routing and fleet management systems that cut emissions and improve fuel efficiency. (Popkova E. G. et al. 2020) These improvements economic growth from environmental degradation—a core principle of sustainability. In the energy sector, consumption patterns. AI algorithms are also used in battery optimization, predictive maintenance of wind turbines, and the design of energy-efficient buildings. As countries seek to meet climate targets and reduce their carbon footprints, AI's capacity to enable smart, decentralized, and low-carbon energy systems will be critical in supporting green growth strategies. AI also contributes economy models, where waste is minimized, and resources are continuously reused. AI tools help companies identify opportunities to extend product life cycles, improve recycling processes, and develop new materials that are more sustainable. For example, machine learning algorithms can detect inefficiencies in supply chains and suggest ways to reduce overproduction and inventory waste. (Popkova E. G. et al. 2020) Companies are using AI to track and analyze product use, enabling business models based on product-as-a-service, refurbishment, or upcycling. By enabling smarter design, distribution, and consumption practices, AI can help shift economies away more circular and regenerative system.

Sustainable growth also depends on inclusive development—ensuring that help bridge gaps in access and quality, especially in rural or marginalized communities. In healthcare, AI enables mobile diagnostics, remote monitoring, and early detection of diseases, improving access to services for populations in remote or under-resourced areas. (Soni N. et al. 2020) These inclusive applications of AI have the potential to empower individuals, reduce inequality, and promote broad-based human development as a pillar of sustainable growth. Another vital contribution of AI lies in strengthening public service delivery and governance, which are foundational to sustainable economic development. AI can improve government efficiency by administrative data-driven policymaking, enabling real-time monitoring of public programs. For example, AI-based systems can detect fraud in tax and welfare programs, allocate resources more effectively, and analyze social data to anticipate and address emerging challenges. In urban development, AI technologies support smart city initiatives that improve traffic management, waste collection, water distribution, and emergency response. By enhancing institutional effectiveness and accountability, AI helps build the governance infrastructure necessary for long-term economic sustainability. (Soni N. et al. 2020) As environmental degradation and climate change pose existential threats to economies worldwide, resilience. Climate modeling powered by AI enables more accurate prediction of weather patterns, sea-level rise, and natural disasters. AI tools help governments and humanitarian organizations prepare for and respond to floods, wildfires, droughts, and hurricanes, reducing their human and economic costs. Moreover, AI is being deployed to monitor deforestation, track pollution, and manage biodiversity, contributing to the stewardship of natural capital. These applications demonstrate AI's critical role in aligning economic activities with environmental protection, ensuring that growth today does not compromise the prospects of future generations.

Policy Considerations for AI-Driven Economic Growth: Policy considerations.

As Artificial Intelligence (AI) becomes a pivotal force in shaping the global economy, governments and policymakers face the critical challenge of developing comprehensive and forward-thinking policy frameworks that guide its responsible adoption while unlocking its vast economic potential. (Tam P. H. et al. 2024) AI has the power to stimulate innovation, enhance productivity, create new markets, and improve public service delivery. However, without robust policy considerations, its deployment can also exacerbate inequality, displace workers, concentrate economic power, and raise ethical concerns. Therefore, AI-driven economic growth must be anchored in policies that are inclusive, adaptive, and grounded in long-term societal interests. Effective AI policy must balance innovation with regulation, growth with equity, and global competitiveness with domestic development. One of the primary policy considerations is establishing a promote investment, research, and integration across sectors. These strategies must be tailored to each country's unique strengths, capacities, and development needs. (Tam P. H. et al. 2024) For instance, advanced economies may focus on frontier AI research and global competitiveness, while developing countries might prioritize inclusive applications in agriculture, healthcare, and education. A national AI strategy should outline clear objectives, sectoral priorities, institutional responsibilities, timelines, and metrics for success. It should also be periodically updated to reflect technological advances and evolving economic realities. Investment in AI research and infrastructure is another critical pillar of AI-driven economic policy. Public funding plays a catalytic role in supporting fundamental and applied AI research, particularly in areas where market incentives are weak but societal needs are high—such as climate change mitigation, public health, and inclusive education. Governments must also invest in digital infrastructure, including cloud computing, high-performance computing (HPC) facilities, data centers, and broadband connectivity, especially in underserved regions. These infrastructure investments enable ecosystem.

Central to AI policy is the development is the lifeblood of AI. Policymakers must establish clear rules around data access, ownership, privacy, sharing, and security. This includes fostering open data initiatives, health, while also ensuring safeguards for sensitive personal data. (Upadhyaya A. N. et al. 2025) Transparent and fair data governance is essential for enabling innovation, building trust, and protecting citizens' rights. Additionally, policies should promote the creation of representative, high-quality datasets that reflect the diversity of the population to mitigate algorithmic bias and support equitable AI development. Another key policy consideration involves reforming supporting lifelong learning through micro-credentials, online courses, and public-private partnerships. Special attention should be given to ensuring that women, marginalized groups, and workers in vulnerable sectors have access to these opportunities. AI-driven economic growth also demands regulatory. International cooperation on AI regulation is essential to harmonize standards, prevent regulatory arbitrage, and promote responsible innovation globally. Policymakers must also address the risks of market concentration and monopolization in the AI economy. A small number of technology giants currently dominate the development and deployment of large-scale AI systems, data platforms, and cloud infrastructure. (Upadhyaya A. N. et al. 2025) This concentration of power can stifle competition, restrict innovation, and create economic dependencies. Antitrust and competition policies should be adapted to address these new dynamics, including regulating data access, promoting interoperability, and supporting open-source alternatives. Encouraging startups space is also vital for ensuring a dynamic and diverse innovation ecosystem.

Regulatory Frameworks for AI Adoption: Regulatory frameworks.

One of the central goals of AI regulation is ensuring transparency and explainability in algorithmic systems. (Van Roy V. et al. 2020) Stakes domains, be explainable, interpretable, and auditable. Explainability requirements can include the ability to trace decision-making processes, provide meaningful information to affected parties, and ensure that humans can override or contest AI-generated outcomes. Closely related is the issue of algorithmic fairness and non-discrimination. Even amplify existing social inequalities. To address this, regulatory frameworks must include provisions for fairness audits, bias detection tools, and impact assessments prior to deployment. These mechanisms should evaluate how AI systems affect different demographic groups and ensure compliance with anti-discrimination laws. Regulations may also mandate the use of diverse training datasets, encourage inclusive design processes, and require organizations to implement safeguards to prevent disparate impact on vulnerable populations. A foundational element of any AI regulatory framework is data governance. AI systems depend heavily on large volumes of data, and the way this data is collected, stored, shared, and processed has profound implications for individual privacy and autonomy. Regulations must define clear standards for data protection, informed consent, data minimization, and data anonymization. (Van Roy V. et al. 2020) Moreover, frameworks should establish mechanisms for data access and sharing that promote innovation while respecting privacy and proprietary rights. For example, regulated access to anonymized public data can spur innovation in health or urban planning without compromising individual privacy. Interoperable and standardized data governance policies also enhance cross-border collaboration and compliance.

Another core consideration is the classification of AI systems based on risk. Many policymakers advocate for a tiered or risk-based regulatory approach, where higher-risk applications—such as facial recognition for surveillance, autonomous weapons, or predictive policing—are subject to stricter controls or outright bans, while low-risk uses—like AI-driven spell checkers or content recommendations—face lighter regulation. Obligations accordingly. This approach ensures that regulatory burdens are proportional and do not stifle low-risk innovation. (Wang S. et al. 2024) Human oversight and accountability are also key pillars of effective AI regulation. Regulatory frameworks must ensure that human operators remain in control and bear ultimate responsibility for AI-driven decisions, especially in contexts where rights and freedoms are at stake. (Yang Y. et al. 2024) This involves defining legal liability for harm caused by AI systems, setting standards for designs, and creating mechanisms for redress. Regulations should also require that users are informed when they are interacting with AI systems, and that they can opt out or seek human intervention where appropriate. Sector-specific regulation is another important consideration. (Wang S. et al. 2024) While some regulatory principles apply universally, others must be tailored to specific sectors. For example, AI in healthcare must comply with medical device regulations and patient safety standards, while AI in finance must meet requirements for transparency, fraud prevention, and consumer protection. In autonomous vehicles, safety testing, operational boundaries, and accident liability require detailed regulatory attention. (Yang Y. et al. 2024) Policymakers must work with sectoral regulators, industry experts, and civil society to co-develop context-sensitive rules that balance innovation with safety and public interest.

CONCLUSION

Education and skills development are critical levers for inclusive AI adoption. The shift toward an AI-enabled economy is altering the nature of work, increasing demand for digital literacy, coding, data analysis, and problem-solving skills. To ensure that all individuals can benefit from these changes, educational institutions must integrate AI-related content into curricula at all levels—from primary schools to universities. Vocational and technical training programs should be expanded and modernized to equip workers with practical AI competencies. Equally important is the promotion of lifelong learning and upskilling opportunities, especially for those whose jobs are at risk of automation. Governments should provide scholarships, grants, and incentives to support training initiatives, with targeted outreach to women, people with disabilities, indigenous communities, and other historically excluded groups. Representation and diversity in the AI workforce and leadership is essential for equitable outcomes. Currently, AI development is dominated by a relatively narrow demographic profile—often skewed toward wealthy, urban, and predominantly male populations. This lack of diversity can lead to the creation of technologies that do not reflect the experiences, needs, or values of wider society. To counter this, inclusive AI growth must involve active policies to AI research, design, and policymaking. This includes creating inclusive hiring practices, mentorship programs, and leadership pipelines in tech companies and academic institutions. Ensuring, accountability, also supports inclusion. When individuals are affected by AI-driven decisions—such as being denied a loan, misdiagnosed by a medical algorithm, or excluded from job opportunities—they must. Regulatory policies should require organizations to disclose the use of AI, provide clear explanations for automated outcomes, and establish accessible mechanisms for recourse and appeal. Transparent AI systems empower users and protect their rights, especially those from communities historically excluded from systems of power and decision-making. Inclusive AI governance means involving a wide range of voices in shaping the policies, standards, and norms that guide AI deployment. Historically marginalized groups must be given a seat at the table in policy consultations, regulatory design, and ethics boards. This democratization of AI governance helps ensure that the technology serves diverse interests and reduces the risk of harm to vulnerable communities. Governments should facilitate participatory policymaking processes, including public consultations, citizen assemblies, and stakeholder forums, where civil society organizations, grassroots groups, and everyday citizens can influence AI development and deployment. In the labor market, supporting workers displaced or affected by AI is crucial for inclusive economic growth. Automation driven by AI is expected to transform employment patterns, potentially displacing workers in manufacturing, logistics, retail, and administrative roles. Inclusive policies must offer comprehensive social safety nets, job transition assistance, and income support for those impacted by technological disruption.

REFERENCES

Abisoye, A., & Akerele, J. I. (2022). A practical framework for advancing cybersecurity, artificial intelligence and technological ecosystems to support regional economic development and innovation. *Int J Multidiscip Res Growth Eval*, *3*(1), 700–713. DOI: 10.54660/.IJMRGE.2022.3.1.700-713

Agrawal, A., Gans, J., & Goldfarb, A. (2019). Economic policy for artificial intelligence. *Innovation Policy and the Economy*, *19*(1), 139–159. DOI: 10.1086/699935

Ai, H., Islam, N., Mangla, S. K., Song, M., & Tan, X. (2024). Circular economy, open innovation, and green innovation: Empirical evidence from prefecture-level cities in China. *IEEE Transactions on Engineering Management*, *71*, 5706–5719. DOI: 10.1109/TEM.2024.3357350

Akram, R., Li, Q., Srivastava, M., Zheng, Y., & Irfan, M. (2024). Nexus between green technology innovation and climate policy uncertainty: Unleashing the role of artificial intelligence in an emerging economy. *Technological Forecasting and Social Change*, *209*, 123820. DOI: 10.1016/j.techfore.2024.123820

Avalekar, U. A., Mehta, V., Mishra, B. R., Prasanna, L., Rajlakshmi, P. V., Manjunath, T. C., & Selvakumar, P. (2025). The Current Advances in AI-Driven Education. In Babulak, E. (Ed.), *Educational AI Humanoid Computing Devices for Cyber Nomads* (pp. 173–196). IGI Global Scientific Publishing. DOI: 10.4018/979-8-3693-8985-0.ch008

Boonman, H., Verstraten, P., & van der Weijde, A. H. (2023). Macroeconomic and environmental impacts of circular economy innovation policy. *Sustainable Production and Consumption*, *35*, 216–228. DOI: 10.1016/j.spc.2022.10.025

Chib, S., Mehta, A. K., Selvakumar, P., Saravanan, A., Mishra, B. R., & Manjunath, T. C. (2025). Mental Health Challenges and Solutions in High-Pressure Work Environments. In Harriott, S. (Ed.), *Innovative Approaches to Managing Conflict and Change in Diverse Work Environments* (pp. 247–272). IGI Global Scientific Publishing. DOI: 10.4018/979-8-3693-9556-1.ch011

Chowdhary, S., Selvakumar, P., Sangeetha, B., Sarvaani, V. V., Anute, N., & Sharma, M. (2025). The Role of Social Capital in Entrepreneurial Development. In Martínez-Falcó, J., Sánchez-García, E., & Marco-Lajara, B. (Eds.), *Support Networks for Entrepreneurs: Social Capital and Strategic Collaborations* (pp. 311–338). IGI Global Scientific Publishing. DOI: 10.4018/979-8-3693-9836-4.ch013

Coates, J. M., Santhanalakshmi, K., Dinesh, N., Gandhimathi, S., & Chandel, P. S. Mohit, & Selvakumar, P. (2025). Assessment and Evaluation in Transnational Staff Development. In G. Morris & J. Ye (Eds.), *Training and Development in Transnational Higher Education* (pp. 387-406). IGI Global Scientific Publishing.

Cockburn, I. M., Henderson, R., & Stern, S. (2018). The impact of artificial intelligence on innovation: An exploratory analysis. In *The economics of artificial intelligence: An agenda* (pp. 115–146). University of Chicago Press.

Ernst, E., Merola, R., & Samaan, D. (2019). Economics of artificial intelligence: Implications for the future of work. *IZA Journal of Labor Policy*, *9*(1), 1–35. DOI: 10.2478/izajolp-2019-0004

Filiou, D., Kesidou, E., & Wu, L. (2023). Are smart cities green? The role of environmental and digital policies for Eco-innovation in China. *World Development*, *165*, 106212. DOI: 10.1016/j.worlddev.2023.106212

Furman, J., & Seamans, R. (2019). AI and the Economy. *Innovation Policy and the Economy*, *19*(1), 161–191. DOI: 10.1086/699936

Hunjra, A. I., Zhao, S., Goodell, J. W., & Liu, X. (2024). Digital economy policy and corporate low-carbon innovation: Evidence from a quasi-natural experiment in China. *Finance Research Letters*, *60*, 104910. DOI: 10.1016/j.frl.2023.104910

Kim, S. S., & Choi, Y. S. (2019). The innovative platform programme in South Korea: economic policies in innovation-driven growth. *Foresight and STI governance, 13*(3), 13.

Levidow, L., Birch, K., & Papaioannou, T. (2012). EU agri-innovation policy: Two contending visions of the bio-economy. *Critical Policy Studies*, *6*(1), 40–65. DOI: 10.1080/19460171.2012.659881

Li, B., Jiang, F., Xia, H., & Pan, J. (2022). Under the background of AI application, research on the impact of science and technology innovation and industrial structure upgrading on the sustainable and high-quality development of regional economies. *Sustainability (Basel)*, *14*(18), 11331. DOI: 10.3390/su141811331

Limbore, N. V., Anute, N., Ahluwalia, G. K., Chordiya, P. B., Kalshetti, P., & Selvakumar, P. (2025). Ethical Leadership and Corporate Responsibility. In Harriott, S. (Ed.), *Innovative Approaches to Managing Conflict and Change in Diverse Work Environments* (pp. 193–218). IGI Global Scientific Publishing. DOI: 10.4018/979-8-3693-9556-1.ch009

Lokhande, M., John Deva Prasanna, D. S., Selvakumar, P., Ragupathi, T., Vaissnave, V., & Manjunath, T. C. (2025). Novel ML Algorithms for Healthcare. In A. Ajibesin, N. G., & S. Thangavel (Eds.), *Synergizing Data Envelopment Analysis and Machine Learning for Performance Optimization in Healthcare* (pp. 113-134). IGI Global Scientific Publishing. DOI: 10.4018/979-8-3373-0081-8.ch005

Lundvall, B. Å., & Rikap, C. (2022). China's catching-up in artificial intelligence seen as a co-evolution of corporate and national innovation systems. *Research Policy, 51*(1), 104395. DOI: 10.1016/j.respol.2021.104395

Luo, S., Yimamu, N., Li, Y., Wu, H., Irfan, M., & Hao, Y. (2023). Digitalization and sustainable development: How could digital economy development improve green innovation in China? *Business Strategy and the Environment, 32*(4), 1847–1871. DOI: 10.1002/bse.3223

Mehra, J., Madaan, S., & Balu, N. Mohit, Selvakumar, P., & Manjunath, T. C. (2025). The Ubiquitous Internet and Smart Computation Available 24/7 for Anyone and Anywhere. In E. Babulak (Ed.), *Educational AI Humanoid Computing Devices for Cyber Nomads* (pp. 247-270). IGI Global Scientific Publishing.

Nisha Angeline, M., Selvakumar, P., Gupta, M. K., Nazar, N., Elumalai, D., & Bhattacharya, S. (2025). Emerging Materials for Energy Storage and Environmental Applications. In K. Muduli, B. Moharana, S. Ales, & D. Biswal (Eds.), *Using Computational Intelligence for Sustainable Manufacturing of Advanced Materials* (pp. 53-72). IGI Global Scientific Publishing. DOI: 10.4018/979-8-3693-7974-5.ch003

Park, M. S., & Chang, S. D. (2022). Review of Artificial Intelligence Platform Policies and Strategies in South Korea, United States, China and the European Union Using National Innovation Capacity. *International Journal of Knowledge Content Development & Technology, 12*(3).

Popkova, E. G., Alekseev, A. N., Lobova, S. V., & Sergi, B. S. (2020). The theory of innovation and innovative development. AI scenarios in Russia. *Technology in Society, 63*, 101390. DOI: 10.1016/j.techsoc.2020.101390

Soni, N., Sharma, E. K., Singh, N., & Kapoor, A. (2020). Artificial intelligence in business: From research and innovation to market deployment. *Procedia Computer Science, 167*, 2200–2210. DOI: 10.1016/j.procs.2020.03.272

Tam, P. H., Hong, T. P., Thanh, C. N., & Tran, P. (2024). AI Innovation and Economics Growth: A Global Evidence. *WSB Journal of Business and Finance, 58*(1), 198–216. DOI: 10.2478/wsbjbf-2024-0017

Upadhyaya, A. N., Debnath, P., Rani, P., Selvakumar, P., Manjunath, T. C., & Bhattacharya, S. (2025). AI-Based Disaster Prediction and Early Warning Systems. In Mobo, F. (Ed.), *AI and Emerging Technologies for Emergency Response and Smart Cities* (pp. 55–74). IGI Global Scientific Publishing. DOI: 10.4018/979-8-3693-9770-1.ch003

Van Roy, V., Vertesy, D., & Damioli, G. (2020). AI and robotics innovation. In *Handbook of labor, human resources and population economics* (pp. 1–35). Springer International Publishing. DOI: 10.1007/978-3-319-57365-6_12-2

Wang, S., Huang, X., Xia, M., & Shi, X. (2024). Does artificial intelligence promote firms' innovation efficiency: Evidence from the robot application. *Journal of the Knowledge Economy*, *15*(4), 16373–16394. DOI: 10.1007/s13132-023-01707-w

Yang, Y., Zhang, C., Liu, B., Huang, Y., & Tai, Y. (2024). Mystery of special government subsidies: How does digital transformation promote enterprise innovation and development? *Economic Analysis and Policy*, *83*, 1–16. DOI: 10.1016/j.eap.2024.06.003

Chapter 2
Empowering Citizens Through Code:
Policy Pathways for Scalable Digital Public Infrastructure

Ajay B. Gadicha
https://orcid.org/0000-0002-5496-3334
P. R. Pote Patil College of Engineering and Management, Amravati, India

Sherif Ismail
https://orcid.org/0009-0000-0852-873X
American University in Cairo, Egypt

Riya Dolas
https://orcid.org/0009-0002-0704-1588
P. R. Pote Patil College of Engineering and Management, Amravati, India

Vijay B. Gadicha
https://orcid.org/0009-0006-4939-9026
P. R. Pote Patil College of Engineering and Management, Amravati, India

Mohini M. Mohod
P. R. Pote Patil College of Engineering and Management, Amravati, India

ABSTRACT

The electronic industry is changing the process of providing services of governments, as well as the way people interact with the government. Countries across the world are establishing Digital Public Infrastructure (DPI) - shared systems to support such priority services as identity cheques, online payments, along with data sharing. In this chapter, Empowering Citizens through Code explains how software and digital

DOI: 10.4018/979-8-3373-6380-6.ch002

innovation can be used to help create open, transparent, inclusive systems that can benefit everyone. It further indicates that good public policies are also required to complete this task; technology will not assist in this task. Good policies ensure the safety of the data of people, a tool does not belong to a few individuals and that innovation could be useful. The chapter describes the reasons why laws, open standards, and intergovernmental cooperation can make digital platforms more secure, efficient and scalable.

INTRODUCTION

The new era of digital has been transforming how government is being operated, how service delivery is being done in the system as well as how the citizens are relating to the systems. The digital platforms ceased being communication platforms or business platforms, but they are created and predetermined structure of infrastructure that determines economic growth, development and governance (Digital Cooperation Organization, 2025; World Bank Group, 2025). Digital Public Infrastructure (DPI) is a trend that is being embraced by governments worldwide in an effort of simplifying service delivery to the citizens hence, making the process more efficient, transparent and inclusive (Carnegie Endowment for International Peace, 2025; International Telecommunication Union, 2025). DPI is a coalition of integrated electronic services and offers certain of the key services include identity cheques, electronic transactions, safe transfer of data and access to state programmes (Organisation for Economic Co-operation and Development, 2024). Similar, to roads and electricity, DPI constitutes the backbone of the digital society, which is present in the real world, and individuals as well as organisations can comfortably speak in the public and the private world (Digital Cooperation Organization, 2025).

The point of the concept of Empowering Citizens through Code identifies the problem of technology in the specific case of empowering the citizens which includes the usage of open-source software, compatible systems, and digital platform as one of the systems which gives the citizens either direct payoffs of the direct benefits of citizen participation and access to the services provided by governments (World Bank Group, 2025). Meaning In this sense, code goes beyond programming, yet it is design and structure of systems that will encourage more transparent and responsive and cantered governance (Gadicha et al., 2024). The citizens are able to have access to significant services, keep personal documents, do business and even engage in the governing process directly through well developed digital systems in a fast and safe manner (International Telecommunication Union, 2025).

However, technology is not the solution in empowerment. The policy designs have to be robust such that the digital systems are secure, non-bias and scalable

(Gadicha et al., 2024). The policies which follow development and growth of digital infrastructures impinge on the areas of data privacy, cybersecurity, open digital inclusiveness, open standards and cooperation with the government (Organisation for Economic Co-operation and Development, 2024; Carnegie Endowment for International Peace, 2025). The digital platforms that have the inclusive policies can introduce equity, accountability, and economic inclusion such that the citizens of the various socio-economic classes can be able to enjoy the fruits of the digital transformation (Digital Cooperation Organization, 2025).

The examples of Aadhaar, UPI and DigiLocker can prove this in India. CoWIN (health services) and many others prove that it is possible to offer the service to more than a billion citizens in the conditions of economic efficiency of the implementation of the digital platform with the policy support (World Bank Group, 2025; Carnegie Endowment for International Peace, 2025). In other cases whereby, integrated DPI framework can improve governance, service delivery and a country that a citizen can trust it is in Estonia and Singapore in the world (International Telecommunication Union, 2025). The chapter talks about the issue of empowering the citizens through the help of scalable digital public infrastructure by governments supported by solid policy frameworks (Digital Cooperation Organization, 2025). It outlines the concepts, design, advantages, issues and international case study of DPI and how a new technology and a policy can work together to establish a transparent and inclusive digital society that is citizen-centric (Organisation for Economic Co-operation and Development, 2024; World Bank Group, 2025). Both innovation and regulation are perceived as the tool, which can be utilized by the nations to make sure that the act of digital transformation has already become the instrument of fair development, empowerment, and social progress (Carnegie Endowment for International Peace, 2025).

EMPOWERING CITIZENS THROUGH CODE

The term Empowering Citizens through Code is the focus on the direct experience of citizens, their access to, and independence of governance and public services with the help of digital technology and open-source and interoperable software in particular (World Bank Group, 2025). In that regard, the term code is understood as something beyond programming, as it is also the image of the design and structure of digital systems that render governance efficient, transparent and inclusive (Gadicha et al., 2024). Developing the services offered to the population by the governments using the solid digital infrastructure, the governments provide the citizens with chances to be active in the state, receive the benefits without any problems, and engage in economic and social life without any risks (Digital Cooperation Organization, 2025; International Telecommunication Union, 2025).Part of Code in Empowering the Citizens —

Incidence and Availability - Code-based digital systems have the potential to eliminate access barriers, particularly in marginalized communities and rural populations as well as people with disabilities (Digital Cooperation Organization, 2025). As an illustration, services are availed to more people using platforms that are multilingual, user-friendly, and mobile friendly (World Bank Group, 2025). The Aadhaar system of India, which implements biometric authentication, enables the country to grant millions of unofficially documented citizens access to banking, welfare, and social services (Carnegie Endowment for International Peace, 2025).

Students should have transparency and accountability - Computerized procedures limit the amount of human being involvement, which limits corruption and mistakes (Organisation for Economic Co-operation and Development, 2024). This is possible by an open-source code that makes sure that the design and functioning of the systems are transparent so that the citizens, auditors and the developers can check and enhance services (Gadicha et al., 2024). This openness enhances confidence in government organizations (Digital Cooperation Organization, 2025).

Economic Participation - The code-based digital infrastructure can make financial services, entrepreneurship, and employment accessible to everyone democratically (International Telecommunication Union, 2025). India has an example of the UPI (Unified Payments Interface) that enables individuals and small businesses to pay in real time online, which has led to financial inclusion and innovation in the fintech market (World Bank Group, 2025).

Enhanced Service Delivery - Citizens have an opportunity to use various services on one interface through interoperable platforms (Organisation for Economic Co-operation and Development, 2024). As an example, DigiLocker combines the document storage with the government services, decreasing papers and time delays and enhancing the efficiency of the services (Carnegie Endowment for International Peace, 2025).

Policy Pathways in Support of Empowerment.

Although technology facilitates empowerment, policy frameworks are necessary in order to make systems secure, equitable, and scalable. Key policy pathways include:

- Data Privacy and Security: Policies should safeguard the personal data of citizens and make sure that the information is used in a moral way.
- Digital Inclusion Policies: Governments are supposed to offer affordable connectivity, digital literacy initiatives, and accessibility interventions of vulnerable segments of society.

- Open Standards and Interoperability: Open-source solutions and interoperable systems policies will help to avoid monopolies, encourage innovation and enable scaling.
- Public-Private Collaboration: The collaboration with the private businesses, start-ups, and civil society can help to improve service delivery, technological innovation, and engagement with the citizens.

Global Examples India: Aadhaar, UPI, DigiLocker - making it possible to verify identity and establish financial transactions and document management of more than a billion citizens.

Estonia: e-Residency and X-Road — offers the service of secure data exchange and digital governance.

Challenges However, regardless of the potential, there are a number of challenges:

Digital Divide: The absence of any of the devices, internet or even digital literacy can alienate citizens.

Cybersecurity Risks: The systems should be secured against hacking, fraud, and abuse.

Policy Gaps: The weak regulation may result in either personal data misuse or vendor lock-in.

Scalability and Sustainability: Infrastructure should be able to respond to the needs of more users without losing its performance.

Figure 1. Empowering Citizens through Code

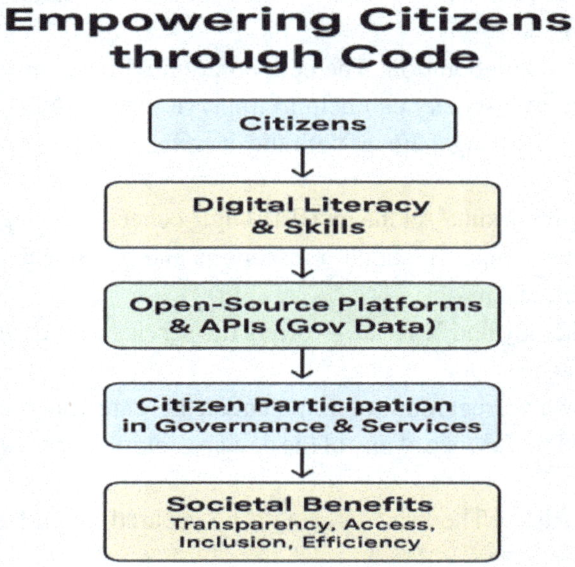

PRINCIPLES FOR SCALABLE DIGITAL PUBLIC INFRASTRUCTURE (DPI)

Construction of a scalable DPI is not just a technological issue but should be planned, administered and in line with the said requirements by the citizenry. A good DPI framework is a framework that can balance between technical efficiency, accessibility, security and compliance. It is a planned and implemented scaled digital public infrastructure according to the following principles.

Interoperability—Interoperability ensures that different electronic systems, platforms, and apps can interact and exchange data regardless of the technology or vendor (Organisation for Economic Co-operation and Development, 2024). It facilitates various aspects of DPI to cooperate to create one digital ecosystem (International Telecommunication Union, 2025). An example here is the India Stack, which brings together such systems as Aadhaar, UPI, and DigiLocker—utilizing common protocols and open APIs—which enables the easy exchange of data and interoperable services among different industries (World Bank Group, 2025; Carnegie Endowment for International Peace, 2025).

Modularity—Modularity is the nature of design of digital systems as modules that are independent and self-contained yet prescriptive, which may be developed, upgraded, or substituted without disrupting the support structure as a whole (Gadicha et al., 2024). The design is flexible, innovative, and cost-effective (Digital Cooperation Organization, 2025). In the case of GovTech of Singapore, the platform organizes its services (such as health, transport, and education) into building blocks that could be updated or replaced individually (International Telecommunication Union, 2025). Along the same line, governments throughout the world are transitioning to the application of open-source modules when executing their activities—including authentication, data storage, and analytics—that can be reused in multiple undertakings (World Bank Group, 2025).

Privacy and Security—One of the fundamental requirements of DPI is the safety of individual and sensitive information of the citizens (Organisation for Economic Co-operation and Development, 2024). The intensive privacy and security design must ensure legal data collection, secure storage, and controlled access to personal data by the customers (Gadicha et al., 2024). The General Data Protection Regulation (GDPR) of the EU is a global standard because of the enforced strict data protection and consent levels (Digital Cooperation Organization, 2025). Along this line, the proposed Data Protection Act in India establishes wide-ranging policies on responsible data use, transparency, and accountability (Carnegie Endowment for International Peace, 2025).

Accessibility and Inclusion—The idea of accessibility implies that digital services are available and can be utilized by anyone, such as marginalized communities, older adults, people with disabilities, and those with low levels of digital literacy (Digital Cooperation Organization, 2025). Inclusive design facilitates social justice and digital empowerment (World Bank Group, 2025). The other one is M-Pesa, a mobile-based financial service in Kenya that assisted people who do not access conventional banks to participate in the digital economy (Carnegie Endowment for International Peace, 2025). In the same vein, one can ensure that visually impaired individuals can access public services effectively by making sure that government portals support screen readers (International Telecommunication Union, 2025).Sustainability Sustainability in DPI is realized to make sure the digital solutions would be long-lasting in terms of strength, resourcefulness and adapting to novelties in technologies and policy changes. The long term planning reduces wastage and it enables it to become flexible. The example of the digital identity system designed in Estonia is designed to be regularly updated with new security provisions and functionality of the system being added. Cloud infrastructure and containerization technology also enhance energy efficiency and increase scalability and diminish environmental impact.

Open APIs and Open Standards: Framework Interoperability and Open DPI innovation Open Application Programming Interfaces (APIs) in combination with Open Standards enable framework interoperability. Open APIs facilitate the interaction of a number of services and may be linked to a common back end without any difficulties to optimize the effectiveness of its operation and the experience of citizens. As the example, the UPI platform of the India Stack is open API and it enables fintech startups to build secure payment solutions that are interoperable. Similarly, X-Road API of Estonia there provides a secure framework whereby government and non-government service providers are able to access and share datasets without breaking the privacy of data.

Figure 2. Digital Public Infrastructure

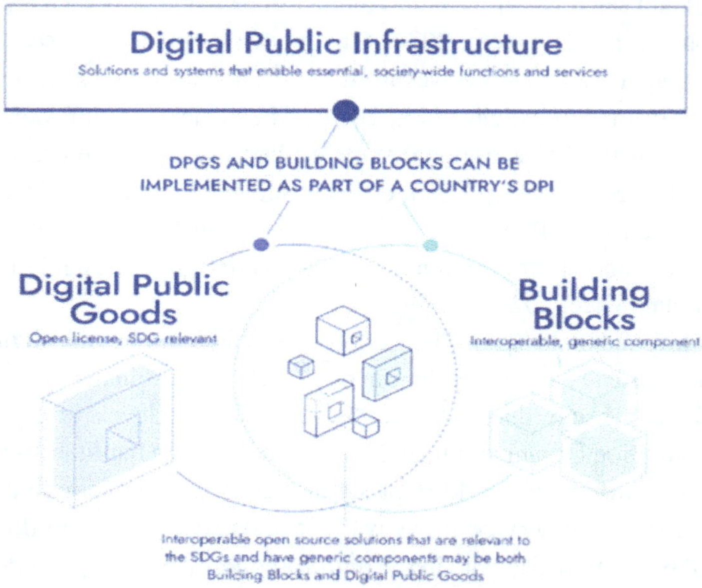

POLICY FRAMEWORKS FOR DIGITAL INFRASTRUCTURE

Digital Public Infrastructure (DPI) cannot be considered merely a collection of technical devices, but rather more of a socio-technical ecosystem, in which policy frameworks are important elements, influencing the nature of inclusive, secure, and scalable digital systems (Digital Cooperation Organization, 2025; World Bank Group, 2025). DPI depends on effective policies because they provide simplicity, structure of governance, and incentives for design, deployment, and management of digital services (Organisation for Economic Co-operation and Development, 2024). Having no good policy underpinning, even very progressive technological systems can fail to provide equal results and win the trust of citizens (Carnegie Endowment for International Peace, 2025).

Inclusiveness is one of the areas of focus of policy structures. Policies must ensure that the digital services are available to the entire society—such as marginalized groups, rural areas, the elderly, and people with disabilities (Digital Cooperation Organization, 2025). Accessibility standards and digital literacy programs are some of the regulatory measures that would make sure that DPI can be used and be of good use to all citizens (International Telecommunication Union, 2025). As an example, governments can provide frameworks that will declare that digital services will be supported to include various languages, low-bandwidth, and mobile-first designs to enhance accessibility (World Bank Group, 2025).

Key Policy Levers

Government Initiatives—Governments can be foundational in facilitating DPI by funding, regulating, and providing strategic support with the goal of facilitating (World Bank Group, 2025). Efforts facilitating open-source civic technology enable civic institutions to develop reusable and open architecture (Gadicha et al., 2024). Through investment in the underlying digital infrastructure—e.g., secure identity systems, digital payment gateways, or open data repositories—governments can usher in faster innovation, as well as enable less duplication of efforts (Digital Cooperation Organization, 2025). These measures would make it possible to maintain the infrastructure that is socially open and meet social demands as opposed to proprietary solutions (International Telecommunication Union, 2025).

Regulatory Incentives—Incentives that instill privacy, interoperability, and standards on data-sharing are the key factor in establishing trust and usability of DPI (Organisation for Economic Co-operation and Development, 2024). Privacy requirements will keep the personal information of citizens out of the hands of any third party and ensure that the information does not get abused (Gadicha et al., 2024). Standardized APIs enable various digital services to interact smoothly to promote integration of various fields like health, education, and finances (World Bank Group, 2025). Open data policies empower startups, researchers, and non-governmental organizations to develop on top of government services, which provide a vibrant ecosystem of citizen-facing services (Carnegie Endowment for International Peace, 2025).

Public-Private Collaboration—Governments do not have the capacity to construct all the elements of DPI efficiently (Digital Cooperation Organization, 2025). The policies that promote partnering with private companies, startups, and non-governmental organizations (NGOs) can use the experience and responsiveness of the private sector but ensure responsibility to the people (International Telecommunication Union, 2025). Such partnerships are usually in the form of co-development, innovation grants, or joint infrastructure programmes (World Bank Group, 2025). Through engaging several stakeholders, the digital platforms are in a position to scale more quickly, cost-effectively, and can meet the needs of citizens in the real world (Carnegie Endowment for International Peace, 2025).

International Standards—Conformance with international standards enables digital platforms to be cross-border interoperable and in harmonious agreement with international best practices (Organisation for Economic Co-operation and Development, 2024). Adherence to standards like the ISO standard of information security, the W3C standard of web accessibility, or the GDPR standard of data protection will improve not only trust between users but support cross-border cooperation and the adoption of technologies (Digital Cooperation Organization, 2025). The standardization promotes DPI scalability (International Telecommunication Union, 2025).

Singapore Smart Nation Initiative example The Smart Nation Initiative of Singapore offers a practical example of a sound policy framework of DPI. Introduced as a way of applying technology to enhance urban life and the services provided to citizens, the project incorporates the concept of collaboration with the business and an emphasis on the citizens.

- Citizen-Centric Design: Policies make sure that the adoption of technology (e.g. an instance of digital identity) has usability, security, and accessibility considerations across all residents.
- Private Sector Involvement: The startup and technological firms are actively promoted to share innovations and this is an excellent promotion of a competitive and innovative climate.
- Regulatory Oversight: Unambiguous principles of data privacy, ease of interoperability, and digital governance will contribute to the fact that people will not be afraid of their information and will be able to integrate seamlessly across platforms.
- Scalability and Innovation:
- Singapore is designed with modular and open systems which mean it can easily add new services to enable a sustainable and advancing digital ecosystem.

On the whole, all policy frameworks in DPI form a guiding framework balancing innovation, security, inclusiveness, and scalability. States such as Singapore show

how strategic planning of policies with the help of effective governance and cooperation may drive powerful, citizen-cantered digital environments.

Figure 3. Policy Frameworks for Digital Infrastructure.

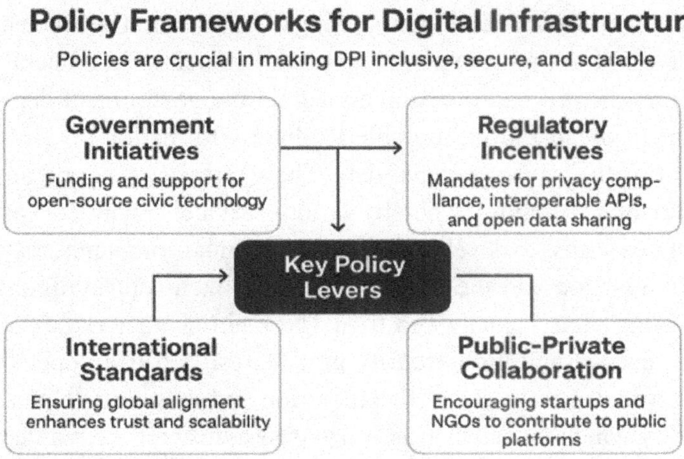

DIGITAL PUBLIC INFRASTRUCTURE (DPI) CONCEPT: THE BUILDING BLOCKS OF DIGITAL PUBLIC INFRASTRUCTURE.

Digital Public Infrastructure (DPI) is changing how citizens, businesses, and governments relate with each other by establishing a platform of efficient inclusive and open digital ecosystems Foundation of DPI are Digital Identity Systems because they allow a person to generate identity in a unique, verifiable, and universal manner. Aadhaar platform in India, the e-ID system in Estonia and the SingPass in Singapore have transformed the manner in which citizens receive services. Such digital identity systems can prevent frauds, enable a secure authentication process and can access the required services like healthcare, banking, welfare programs, and education easily. More so because they offer stepping ground to financial inclusion, that allows even people who do not have conventional methods of identification to participate in the formal economy and enjoy digital services delivery.

Another pillar of DPI is called The Digital Payment Systems. One example of such recently adopted payment infrastructures include the Unified Payments Interface (UPI), M-Pesa in Kenya, and Swish in Sweden that allow individuals and businesses and government departments to write and read payment transactions in real time and fast. It is through such systems that transparency and economic efficiency is facilitated by the economy because the reliance on cash is minimised. Moreover, e-payment systems are significant in payment of the social welfare fund such as subsidies and direct transfer of money to the citizens in a timely and specific manner, Data Exchange and Integration Platforms will enlarge the comprehensive functioning and efficiency of DPI and sharing of information between institutions in an unassailable and smooth manner. Examples of models of interoperability include India Stack and the X-Road of Estonia wherein the government departments and non-government organizations are able to share information on a real-time basis without violating the privacy policies data. These interfaces support authentication, validation and interoperability whereby various services can interact as a unit. They will give them an access to developers and to individual companies that will be open to promote innovation and the development of citizen-centric digital application without violating their security and trust.The main characteristics of DPI are its transparency, access, and high-security procedures. DPI is an open-source-based project and promotes cross-sector collaboration and versatility. Open APIs enable interoperability which means that the various systems can easily interact with one another and provide a smooth user experience. Another key principle is inclusive access the ability to make all citizens, no matter which geography they belong to, whether they have a physical disability or not, and whether they are digitally literate or not, access digital services. This inclusiveness must be designed to be user-friendly as well as multilingual and at low costs in terms of connectivity. Also critical is the focus on privacy and security, which is provided by encryption, consent-based sharing of data usage, and open governance systems that ensure that citizens do not lose faith in digital ecosystems.

DPI has a significant socio-economic and governance implication in addition to its technological elements. It improves the delivery of services to the people through automation, minimisation of administrative delays and minimisation of human error and thus faster results are obtained which are more reliable. Digital transparency is an accountability measure of governance as it generates digital trails and audit logs that discourage corruption and misappropriation of public resources. DPI was especially useful in the management of vaccine distribution, financial aid, and public health communication during the crises, including the COVID-19 pandemic, especially in a large scale. DPI is an economic driver of innovation and entrepreneurship by developing the ability of startups and private businesses to create upon open digital frameworks. This does not only spur competition and creativity but provides jobs and boosts the national economic growth.

Challenges and Considerations

Although Digital Public Infrastructure (DPI) is a tool that can provide enormous improvements to inclusiveness, efficiency and transparency, it still has some challenges that should be taken into consideration. The digital divide is one such challenge that is rather problematic because unequal access to digital devices, internet connectivity, and lack of digital literacy poses challenges to disadvantaged groups. Rural communities, older citizens, and communities with fewer economic means tend to not be able to participate in digital ecosystems with full participation which contributes to social and economic marginalization. It is thus important to ensure universal access and offer digital education as the key to ensuring the real inclusivity.

Cybersecurity is another issue of great concern. DPI systems have a high tendency to store and process large volumes of sensitive personal and financial information, which makes them an ideal target of attack by hackers and cybercriminals. Without strong encryption, well-developed authentication procedures and constant security control, centralized databases and interconnected networks can be exposed to the threats of data breaches, fraud, and identity theft. The only way of keeping the social trust is being able to protect this information against the changing digital threats.

There are also policy and regulatory loopholes which are dangerous. The absence of the clearly spelled out data protection and consent administration and accountability frameworks may result in abuse of personal data or excessive exploitation of private vendors. Poor governance frameworks may lead to vendor lock-in in which governments will be locked to particular technology providers and that restricts flexibility and innovation. To strike a balance between innovation, privacy and ethical concerns, it is necessary to come up with clear and enforceable policies on data.

Finally, there is a technical and operational challenge of scalability. With the rise in population and demand of digital services, DPI should be able to fulfill the needs of large volumes of transactions, real time data exchanges and user authentication without interfering with the speed, reliability or security of the services. Scalability means that infrastructure has to be upgraded continuously, interoperability has to be tested and performance has to be optimized.

Global Examples

- India: Aadhaar, UPI, DigiLocker — supporting financial inclusion and service delivery for over a billion citizens.
- Estonia: X-Road platform — enabling secure, nationwide data exchange.
- Singapore: SingPass and Smart Nation initiatives — integrating digital ID, payments, and government services seamlessly.

Figure 4. Digital Public Infrastructure (DPI) Concept: The Components of Digital Public Infrastructure

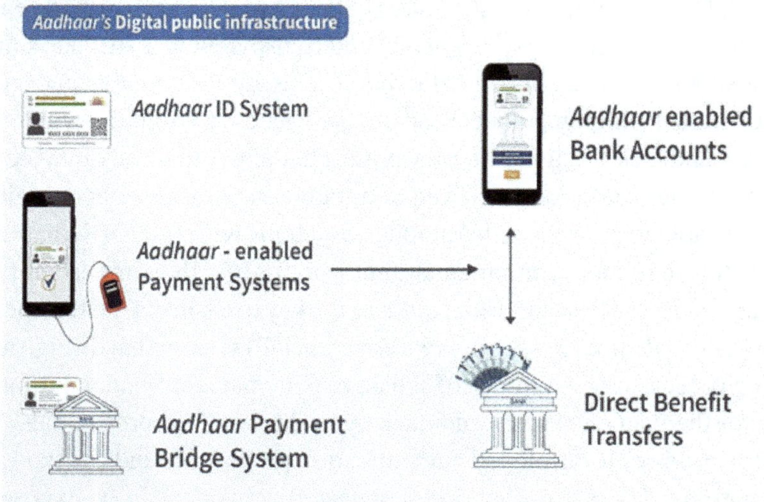

CHALLENGES AND RISKS OF (DPI)

1. Technical Challenges

Data and Information- DPI Systems that deal with cybersecurity threats generate and store enormous personal and financial information. This makes it easy to target them in cyberspace attacks, hacks, and identity stealing. To keep the citizens trustful, it is important to ensure the security of the data and systems. Lack of strong cybersecurity may result in massive intrusions, loss of money, and lack of trust in governmental bodies.

Scalability and Performance-Digital systems should be able to support millions or even billions of users at the same time without interruption. Infrastructure may be poorly designed which may result in slowness of services, crashing systems or non-availability especially in times of high-demand such as natural disaster times or even pandemics.

Technology Obsolescence-Quick Changes in technology implies that infrastructure may easily become obsolete. Unless updated on a regular basis, old systems may not keep pace with increasing demands or be able to incorporate new innovations.

2. Social Challenges

Unequal access to technology Digital Divide-Unequal access to technology continues to be a major obstacle. DPI may not work in favor of citizens in the rural regions, those with low income or those who lack digital literacy. This poses a danger of exclusion, which increases the disparity between the individuals who have access to services digitally and those who do not.

Privacy Concerns and Public Trust-Citizens can be worried about the misuse of personal information, surveillance or theft. Without the transparency of the data collection, storage, and sharing processes, the lack of trust can destroy the trust people have in digital systems.

Resistance to Adoption-Some citizens will be particularly opposed to the usage of digital platforms especially elderly citizens or those who are not technologically savvy and would wish to stick to the traditional methods of service delivery. This will limit the extent and performance of DPI.

3. Policy and Governance Problems.

Regulatory Gaps-A good number of nations are in the process of building laws on data privacy, cybersecurity and digital ethics. In the absence of robust regulations the DPI systems can be abused, unaccountable or lose to safeguard the rights of citizens.

Accountability and Oversight-Automation and digital processes may complicate the process of responsibility allocation in the event of mistakes or fraud. This requires proper governance framework and accountability in order to remain reliable and trusted by the citizens.

Vendor Lock-In and Proprietary Systems-Dependence on the proprietary technology providers may diminish the flexibility and raise the cost. There has to be policies on open-source platforms and interoperability that are created to make them long term sustainable.

Ethical Issues- DPI Application of AI, predictive analytics or automated decision-making may lead to bias, discrimination, and unintended social outcomes unless strictly controlled and monitored.

4.Policy and Governance Attributes.

Digital Public Infrastructure (DPI) requires effective policy and governance to be built on a scale. They offer the strategic outline to the extent that digital services are interoperative, inclusive, safe, and flexible. The three paths below identify some of the most important ways of governing DPI in a citizen-focused and sustainable way.

Key Approaches

Multi-Stakeholder Governance- DPI initiatives have a merit in that there is a large number of stakeholders in the initiative like the government agencies, civil society organization, academia, and the players in the private sector. This type of collaborative governance is used to ensure that a broad spectrum of different points of views is considered in formulation of the policies, they are innovative as well as are balanced in both regard to the interests of the people and effectiveness. The models with multi-stakeholders can include the advisory boards, public-private associations, and citizen councils in the decision-making and supervision. Standardization- Standardization is critical in interoperability of systems and platforms. The different digital services can communicate with one another through open-source frameworks, standardized APIs (Application Programming Interfaces) and common protocols. Standardization eliminates redundancy, cuts costs of implementation and makes sure that a new solution can interface with the existing infrastructure without causing significant discontinuity.

Regulator Sandbox- A regulatory sandbox is a testing environment in which new solutions in digital form can be tested under controlled conditions. It enables innovators to test the water and check compliance as well as risks without engaging in a full-scale regulatory commitment at once. This will foster experimentation without exposing the citizens to possible detriments thereby balancing between innovation and responsibility.

Scaling Local Solutions- Effective DPI may be initiated with localized pilot projects, which will be addressing the needs of a particular community. Winning local projects can then be expanded at the national level with the infrastructure being modular, adjustable and receptive to real world needs. Local first testing enables governments to develop technology and processes and policies that are improved before undertaking a nationwide deployment.

Example: India Stack

- Modularity: Every element like the digital ID, e-KYC, and payment services can be utilized on its own without the need to be interconnected with other modules.
- Interoperability: Open APIs enable third party developers as well as the platforms of the private sector to interface with the services of the state.
- Scalable Policy Design: The structure allowed pilot projects to take local decisions to help control national implementation plans, so the needs of citizens and governance requirements could be achieved.

FUTURE DIRECTIONS AND OPPORTUNITIES IN DIGITAL PUBLIC INFRASTRUCTURE

1.The integration of Emerging Technologies (AI) and (ML):

Automated decision-making, needs prediction and optimal service delivery.

2.Distributed Ledger Technologies and Blockchain.

Smart Cities and Internet of Things (IoT), Edge Technologies and Cloud Computing.

3.Policy/Regulatory Opportunities.

Make sure that data ownership and ethical use of citizen data, Enhance the digital inclusion of underserved populations and enhance digital literacy, Develop interoperability requirements on how systems can integrate well, Institute sustainability guidelines (e.g. green computing policies and energy efficient infrastructure),Global Trends and Lessons, Estonia: X-Road facilitates the secure data exchange and intercountry cross-border digital services, Singapore: Smart Nation is the fusion of digital identity, payments, and city services, Kenya: M-Pesa shows how mobile-first payment systems can promote financial inclusion in the developing world.

These examples can serve to guide governments in predicting their challenges, innovating sustainably, and service scaling.

4.Citizen Empowerment Opportunities.

Participatory Governance: Citizens are able to give feedback, track services, and take part in policy-making online, Financial and Social Inclusion: Enhances the availability of banking, insurance as well as welfare services to marginalized populations, Education and Skill Development: Digital platforms have the potential to become more employable and better digital literate, Technological policy assimilation can promote equity, trust, and social mobility.

5.Objections to Future Implementation

AI and IoT data collection privacy issues.

6.Cybersecurity threats of increasingly networked systems.

Lacuna in policies that control up and coming technologies, As digital systems get more complicated, providing a fair access is necessary

METHODOLOGY

1.Research Approach

- The theoretical, practical, and policy aspects of DPI have been investigated by use of a qualitative and descriptive research approach. This approach allows for:
- Learning the theoretical underpinnings of technology-based citizen empowerment.
- Assessing policy trajectories and government systems enabling scalable DPI.
- Looking at practical cases to determine the best practices, problems, and lessons learned.

2.Data Collection

The research relies on the secondary data such as:

- Academic Journals and Research Papers: Academic research publications in e-governance, digital infrastructure and public policy.
- Government Reports and Policy Documents: Government reports on such efforts as India Stack, DigiLocker, CoWIN, and other international DPI frameworks in Estonia and Singapore.
- International examples of DPI implementation and citizen-centric policies Global Case Studies and Best practices: International examples of DPI implementation and citizen-centric policies.
- News Articles, White Papers, and Industry Reports: Current data on technological advances, policy modifications and usage patterns of DPI.

There was no major data collection (e.g., no surveys or interviews, etc.), the methodology is based on the available literature and other authoritative sources to extract insights.

3.Analytical Framework

This analysis in this chapter is based on a multi-dimensional framework, which addresses:

1.Technological Dimension

- The analysis of the design, scalability and interoperability of digital public systems.
- Assessing the new technologies (AI, blockchain and IoT) in DPI.

2.Policy and Governance Dimension.

- Scanning legislation, policies and control systems that empower or inhibit digital infrastructure.
- Evaluation of structures regarding data privacy, cybersecurity, open standards, and inclusion policies.

3.Social Impact Dimension

- The evaluation of the impact of DPI on citizen empowerment, digital inclusion, efficiency of service delivery and transparency.
- Determining the obstacles including the digital divide, accessibility issues, and unwillingness to adoption.

4.Comparable Case Study Analysis.

In order to present the practical knowledge, comparative approach has been used based on the examples of: India: Cowin, Aadhaar, UPI, Digi Locker, Estonia: X-Road, e-Residency.

Singapore: Smart Nation and SingPass, Kenya: M-Pesa cell phone payment platform.

The following cases were chosen under the criteria of scale, innovation, impact on citizens and policy support. A comparative analysis shows successful factors, issues, and strategies that can be scaled to digital infrastructure.

LIMITATIONS

The work is based mainly on secondary sources, which restrict admission to adoption statistics in real-time and direct experience of the citizens.

Emerging tendencies in the swift technological advancement might be not reflected in the existing literature.

The differences in cultures, economies, and politics can make the policy and implementation of policies different in different countries.

Figure 5. Methodology

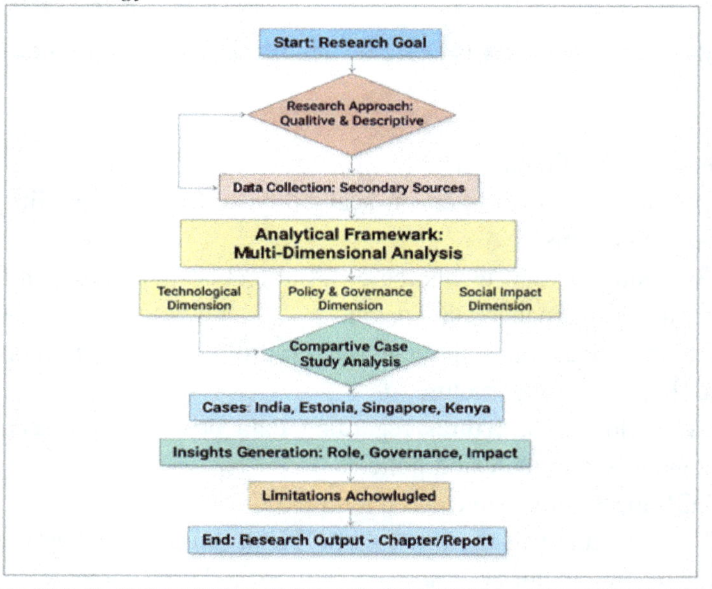

Publication of Generative AI Assistance

The authors admit that neither any generative AI tools were applied in the writing or editing of this chapter, nor in research. All responsibilities of AI systems were not assigned any tasks according to the GAIDeT taxonomy (2025) at any level of development. It is the original work of the authors, who also have full responsibility regarding the accuracy and integrity of the manuscript. Generative AIs are not mentioned as participants or creators and are not responsible for the end results.

CONCLUSION

Digital Public Infrastructure (DPI) is a revolutionary way of governing, delivering services and empowering the citizens. Through the use of technology, code and policy frameworks, governments can develop systems which are inclusive, transparent, secure and scalable. This chapter has explored the fact that DPI when properly led by good policies and ethical technological applications can be a public good, enhancing access to key services, financial and social inclusion, and citizen involvement in governance.

The analysis represents the importance of the so-called code open-source, interoperable, and scalable digital systems, which facilitates the empowerment of citizens. Code is not merely a technical resource, it is the basis of platforms that help verify identity, do secure payments, manage documents, and provide a smooth service delivery. These systems, combined with facilitating policy routes, guarantee privacy, accountability, inclusivity, and sustainability and mitigate cybersecurity threats, digital inequalities, and the absence of governance.

The case studies in the world, covering India, Estonia, Singapore, and Kenya, provide examples of how proper DPI structures may empower citizens, enhance innovation, and efficiency in administration. There is a good example of Aadhaar, UPI, DigiLocker and CoWIN systems in India, which demonstrate that with support of clear policies, scalable infrastructure can be used to serve a billion citizens. On the same note, the e-governance ecosystem in Estonia and the Smart Nation initiatives in Singapore are clear indicators of the significance of interoperability, secure data exchange, and the need to design with the citizens in mind.

In the future, the incorporation of new technologies like AI, blockchain, IoT, and cloud computing will provide an opportunity to take DPI to a new level. These technologies can enhance predictive service provision, automatize governance procedures, enhance security, and create participatory governance. Nevertheless, they need to have strong policy frameworks, ethical rules, and inclusion efforts in order to make sure that technology is used as a form of empowerment and not exclusion.

Primarily, the chapter points out that the process of the code empowerment of the citizens is not only technological, but also socio-political and policy, process. Under the condition of a reasonable design of the technology and a cautious approach to the policies, the DPI may reduce the distance between citizens and the state, create trust and develop fairly. The future of governance is the establishment of digital ecosystems that are scalable, secure, inclusive, and human-focused to make sure that all citizens have full access to the digital society.

REFERENCES

Carnegie Endowment for International Peace. (2025, February). Digital public infrastructure: A practical approach for Africa.

Digital Cooperation Organization. (2025, June). Digital public infrastructure: A key building block for social inclusion and economic development.

Gadicha, A. B., Gadicha, V. B., Obaid, A. J., & Abbood, Z. A. (2024). An in-depth examination of cyberbullying detection utilizing machine learning techniques. AIP Conference Proceedings, 3207(1), Article 060002. [Note: Replace with actual DOI if available; “This link is disabled” suggests access issue]DOI: 10.1063/5.0234200

Gadicha, A. B., Gadicha, V. B., Zuhair, M., Ingole, V. A., & Saraf, S. S. (2024). ZTA-DEVSECOPS: Strategies towards network zero trust architecture and DevSecOps in cybersecurity and IIoT environments. In Smart and agile cybersecurity for IoT and IIoT environments (pp. 306–324).

International Telecommunication Union. (2025). Building digital public infrastructure for cities and communities.

Organisation for Economic Co-operation and Development. (2024, December). Digital public infrastructure for digital governments.

World Bank Group. (2025, March). Digital public infrastructure and development: A World Bank Group approach.

Chapter 3
Bridging the Digital Divide:
A Strategic Framework for Deploying Inclusive Digital Public Infrastructure in Emerging Economies

Barkha Sachin Dange
https://orcid.org/0009-0009-3804-2090
Ramdeobaba University, Nagpur, India

ABSTRACT

Digital Public Infrastructure (DPI)—the interoperable stack of foundational digital rails for identity, payments, data exchange, consent, and trusted services—has emerged as a powerful lever for inclusive development. Yet deployment in emerging economies is uneven, and the digital divide persists along axes of income, gender, geography, language, age, and disability. This chapter proposes a strategic, end-to-end framework for designing, deploying, and governing inclusive DPI. Drawing on lessons from diverse contexts, it synthesizes policy, technical, institutional, and societal levers into a practical roadmap emphasizing inclusion-by-design, safety, accountability, and sustainability. The chapter provides conceptual foundations, a typology of divides, case mini-studies, actionable design principles, governance models, financing options, risk management, monitoring and evaluation (M&E) metrics, and an implementation playbook.

DOI: 10.4018/979-8-3373-6380-6.ch003

SUMMARY

Digital transformation is one of the defining forces of the 21st century, reshaping how societies organize, how economies grow, and how governments interact with citizens. For emerging economies, the stakes are particularly high. These countries face the dual challenge of catching up with global technological advances while also addressing deep structural inequalities in access to electricity, connectivity, education, and financial services. Against this backdrop, Digital Public Infrastructure (DPI) has emerged as a transformative lever. DPI refers to a modular and interoperable stack of digital identity systems, real-time payments, data exchange frameworks, consent managers, and secure registries that together create the rails for both public service delivery and private sector innovation. When designed inclusively, DPI can accelerate development by lowering transaction costs, enabling direct benefit transfers, fostering financial inclusion, and expanding access to healthcare, education, agriculture, and justice systems. It can empower women, rural populations, and marginalized groups who have historically been excluded from formal systems of state and market.

CONTEXTUAL BACKGROUND

Digitalization is not merely about technology adoption; it represents a profound reconfiguration of how states, markets, and societies function. In emerging economies, where gaps in physical infrastructure, financial inclusion, and public service delivery persist, digital systems offer an unprecedented opportunity to leapfrog traditional constraints (Qiang et al., 2009). The spread of mobile phones, cloud computing, and affordable connectivity has created the possibility of building digital-first service models that can reach citizens at scale, often bypassing legacy bottlenecks such as bureaucratic red tape or underdeveloped physical infrastructure (GSMA, 2022). For governments, this means lowering transaction costs in welfare distribution, tax collection, and regulatory oversight (Muralidharan et al., 2016). For individuals and enterprises, it means faster access to credit, healthcare, markets, and educational opportunities (Aker & Mbiti, 2019).

The COVID-19 pandemic underscored the indispensability of digital systems. Remote work, online education, digital payments, and telemedicine became lifelines during lockdowns. However, the crisis also magnified exclusionary patterns: students without devices were cut off from learning, rural households struggled with patchy connectivity, and small merchants without digital payment options lost customers (Alliance for Affordable Internet, 2021). These experiences highlighted that digital divides are not peripheral—they are central determinants of resilience and development in the 21st century (ITU, 2020). At the same time, global institutions such as the World Bank's ID4D (ID4D Initiative, World Bank, 2022), UNDP's digital strategy (UNDP, 2022), and the OECD's digital government frameworks (OECD, 2021) are converging on the idea that DPI is foundational to achieving the Sustainable Development Goals (SDGs). Digital ID directly supports SDG 16.9 (legal identity for all), while digital payments and interoperable data platforms contribute to poverty reduction, gender equality, decent work, and innovation (Gelb & Diofasi Metz, 2018; Suri & Jack, 2016).

In this sense, the contextual backdrop is clear: emerging economies stand at a crossroads. Digital rails can either deepen fragmentation and inequality or become the connective tissue of more inclusive, accountable, and resilient societies (Heeks, 2017).

THE CENTRAL QUESTION

The central question animating this chapter is deceptively simple yet profoundly complex: How can emerging economies deploy digital public infrastructure in ways that reduce, rather than reproduce, inequalities? The framing matters. Too often, debates on digital transformation focus narrowly on technology adoption or economic growth, neglecting deeper concerns of equity, justice, and trust. For example, a biometric identity system may achieve near-universal coverage, but if grievance redressal mechanisms are weak, even minor authentication failures can exclude vulnerable groups from essential services. Similarly, a digital payments platform may thrive in urban centres but remain irrelevant for rural women without smartphones or digital literacy.

Answering this question requires a holistic approach that integrates legal frameworks, technical design, inclusive practices, institutional capacity, and robust governance. It cannot be reduced to a matter of hardware distribution or app deployment. Instead, inclusive DPI demands attention to power dynamics—who controls the infrastructure, who benefits, who bears risks, and who is left out. It requires grounding in rights-based principles such as privacy, dignity, and non-discrimination, while also remaining pragmatic about fiscal, institutional, and technological constraints faced by low- and middle-income countries.

What Counts as DPI?

As illustrated in Figure 1, the layers of Digital Public Infrastructure include identity, payments, data exchange, registries, messaging, and analytics (Open Government Partnership, 2021).

Defining Digital Public Infrastructure (DPI) is both straightforward and contested. At its core, DPI refers to the foundational, interoperable systems that enable the provision of digital services across public and private sectors (CGAP, 2021; Open Government Partnership, 2021).These typically include:

- Digital Identity & Credentials (e.g., Aadhaar in India, NID in Bangladesh), which provide secure recognition of individuals and organizations.
- Payments Systems (e.g., UPI, PIX, M-Pesa), enabling real-time, low-cost, and widely accessible financial transactions.
- Data Exchange & Consent Frameworks (e.g., Estonia's X-Road, India's Data Empowerment and Protection Architecture), which allow safe, auditable data sharing under user control.
- Core Registries & Messaging Systems (e.g., civil registries, land records, SMS-based notifications), which anchor public services.

However, what counts as DPI is broader than a mere technical stack. For some scholars, DPI encompasses legal and institutional scaffolding—data protection laws, competition policies, and governance structures—that ensure inclusivity and accountability (Singh & Mohan, 2021). For others, it also includes enablers like open APIs, developer ecosystems, and community intermediaries that operationalize these rails in practice (CGAP, 2021). In short, DPI is not just infrastructure; it is an ecosystem (Open Government Partnership, 2021).

A crucial feature is modularity: each layer (identity, payments, data exchange) should function independently yet integrate seamlessly. This avoids lock-in and enables innovation (Estonian Government, 2020). Equally vital is openness: DPI should be built on open standards to prevent monopolistic capture and encourage diverse participation (Heeks, 2017). Finally, DPI must be governance-neutral yet rights-anchored, allowing countries to adapt models to local contexts while upholding fundamental protections (Financial Action Task Force, 2020; Gelb & Diofasi Metz, 2018).

In this chapter, DPI is thus conceptualized as a socio-technical system: not only hardware and software, but also laws, norms, institutions, and human capacities that together determine whether infrastructure empowers or excludes (Heeks, 2017).

DPI can either narrow or widen these divides depending on choices made at the design, deployment, and governance layers. Technology by itself is not enough.

Inclusive DPI requires a whole-of-ecosystem approach that integrates policy reform, supply-side investments (in networks, devices, and platforms), demand-side enablement (literacy, skills, content), community participation (last-mile intermediaries, local innovation), and continuous guardrails for rights (data protection, algorithmic accountability, grievance redress) (GSMA, 2021; Alliance for Affordable Internet, 2021; UNDP, 2022).

The message is clear: DPI is not a magic bullet, but when designed inclusively, governed transparently, and implemented with accountability, it becomes a powerful equalizer that bridges divides and accelerates progress toward the SDGs (World Bank, 2021). Conversely, without inclusion-by-design, DPI risks becoming another tool that amplifies exclusion (ITU, 2020).

The digital divide is not a single gap but a stack of interlocking gaps: access (devices, electricity, connectivity), affordability (of data, devices, and services), digital skills, safety and trust, relevant local content, and meaningful usage that leads to developmental outcomes. DPI can either narrow or widen these gaps depending on choices made at the design and governance layers. Inclusive DPI requires an ecosystem approach—one that integrates policy reform, supply-side investments, demand-side enablement, community participation, and continuous guardrails for rights.

Crucially, the urgency for inclusive DPI has never been greater. The COVID-19 pandemic exposed the costs of digital exclusion, as millions of students, workers, and small businesses were left behind. The rise of artificial intelligence and data-driven governance amplifies both opportunities and risks, demanding infrastructures that are transparent, accountable, and inclusive. Moreover, the Sustainable Development Goals (SDGs)—from poverty reduction and gender equality to health, education, and climate resilience—cannot be achieved without digital rails that serve all citizens fairly.

At the same time, failure to act carries steep consequences. Countries that neglect inclusive DPI risk creating new "data divides," entrenching monopolistic platforms, and undermining public trust. Without safeguards, digital infrastructure can enable surveillance, exclusion, and cyber vulnerability. Thus, inclusive DPI is not just a technical agenda—it is a moral, economic, and geopolitical imperative.

This chapter proposes the Inclusive DPI Strategy Framework (IDSF) with seven pillars:

1. Foundations & Policy Enablement: spectrum policy and connectivity, rights-based data protection, competition and interoperability mandates, procurement reform.
2. Core DPI Rails: digital identity, verifiable credentials, payments, consent and data exchange, registries, messaging.

3. Inclusion-by-Design: universal accessibility, multilingual interfaces, assisted service models, safety-by-default, grievance redressal, offline-first operation.
4. Ecosystem Enablement: developer platforms, open APIs, SDKs, sandboxes, standards, interoperability testing, civic-tech co-creation.
5. Affordability & Access: device financing, targeted subsidies, community networks, shared access points, zero-rated public services following net-neutrality-compatible designs.
6. Capacity & Adoption: digital literacy, institutional capacity, change management, last-mile intermediaries, social protection linkages.
7. Governance, Assurance & M&E: accountability boards, algorithmic audits, SRIAs (Socio-Technical Risk Impact Assessments), incident reporting, outcome metrics, independent evaluation.

The chapter translates the framework into a phased roadmap (0–5 years), a RACI template, a risk register, and a KPI suite that policymakers and implementers can adapt.

Glossary

1. INTRODUCTION

1.1 Contextual Background

Digitalization has fundamentally transformed how states deliver services, how markets transact, and how citizens interact with both government and private actors. In advanced economies, digital platforms are often seen as convenience-enhancers, but in emerging economies, they are increasingly viewed as development accelerators—tools that can expand financial inclusion, enhance social protection, reduce administrative costs, and provide citizens with access to essential services at scale (World Bank, 2021).

The COVID-19 pandemic dramatically accelerated the urgency of digital transformation. Lockdowns and mobility restrictions exposed the fragility of traditional service delivery and forced governments to experiment with digital rails for cash transfers, vaccine registrations, remote education, and telehealth (UNDP, 2022). Yet the pandemic also revealed how deeply uneven digital capabilities were: households without smartphones or reliable internet were effectively excluded from these emergency lifelines (Alliance for Affordable Internet, 2021). In rural South Asia, for instance, many families could not access online schooling, creating what UNESCO has called a "generational learning crisis."

At the same time, global institutions such as the World Bank's ID4D Initiative (ID4D Initiative, World Bank, 2022), UNDP's Digital Strategy (UNDP, 2022), and the OECD Digital Government Index (OECD, 2021) have increasingly positioned Digital Public Infrastructure (DPI) as a cornerstone for achieving the Sustainable Development Goals (SDGs). Digital IDs directly support SDG 16.9 (legal identity for all), while real-time payments systems contribute to SDG 8.10 (financial inclusion) and SDG 1.3 (social protection coverage) (Gelb & Diofasi Metz, 2018). The logic is clear: DPI, when designed inclusively, multiplies state capacity and lowers transaction costs across entire economies (Muralidharan et al., 2016).

However, technological optimism must be tempered with caution. Evidence shows that DPI, if poorly designed or implemented, can entrench inequality, enable surveillance, or create monopolistic ecosystems that disadvantage smaller players (Singh & Mohan, 2021). The dual nature of DPI—as both a public good and a potential instrument of exclusion—frames the challenge for emerging economies (Heeks, 2017).

1.2 The Central Question

This chapter asks a central policy and design question: How can emerging economies deploy DPI in ways that actively reduce, rather than reproduce, inequalities?

Addressing this question requires moving beyond purely technological debates to adopt a socio-technical systems lens. DPI is not just about digital rails—it is about the surrounding ecosystem:

- Legal and regulatory scaffolding (data protection, competition, procurement).
- Technical architecture (interoperability, open standards, modularity).
- Inclusive design (multilingual, accessible, offline-first).
- Capacity building (human intermediaries, digital literacy, institutional skills).
- Governance and accountability (independence, transparency, trust).

The framework presented in this chapter—the Inclusive DPI Strategy Framework (IDSF)—integrates all of these dimensions into a holistic model. Unlike vendor-driven or siloed approaches, it is technology-neutral, vendor-neutral, and grounded in open standards and rights-based principles (Heeks, 2017; Financial Action Task Force, 2020). Its adaptability across diverse political economies makes it a practical tool for policymakers in Africa, South Asia, Latin America, and beyond (African Union, 2020; UN ESCAP, 2021).

1.3 What Counts as DPI?

While the definition of DPI is evolving, most frameworks converge on a layered architecture comprising:

1. Digital Identity & Credentials – Foundational ID systems that enable authentication, verification, and issuance of verifiable credentials (e.g., Aadhaar in India, e-Residency in Estonia).
2. Payments – Low-cost, real-time, interoperable payments systems that facilitate peer-to-peer (P2P), government-to-person (G2P), and business-to-business (B2B) transfers (e.g., PIX in Brazil, M-Pesa in Kenya).
3. Data Exchange & Consent Layers – Systems that allow secure, auditable, and user-consented data flows across government and private actors (e.g., India's Data Empowerment and Protection Architecture).
4. Common Registries – Population, land, business, and vehicle registries that underpin service delivery.
5. Messaging & Notification Systems – Government-to-citizen communication channels via SMS, email, or app-based notifications.
6. Analytics & Insights – Aggregate-level data systems to inform policymaking and service improvements.

Key to DPI design is modularity: each layer should be independently governable and upgradeable, preventing single points of failure or monopolistic lock-in. For example, payments systems should not depend exclusively on one ID provider, and data exchange protocols should allow private innovation without undermining user rights.

1.4 The Stakes for Inclusion

Inclusion is not merely a normative imperative (grounded in human rights), but also an instrumental necessity for DPI success. Systems that exclude large portions of the population suffer from:

- Lower adoption rates, reducing network effects.
- Weaker fiscal efficiency, since benefits (e.g., cash transfers) fail to reach intended recipients.
- Reduced trust, undermining long-term sustainability.

Conversely, inclusive DPI expands adoption and drives value creation. Examples include:

- Cash transfer programs that reach women and rural households directly via mobile wallets.
- Immunization reminders sent through SMS in multiple languages, improving health outcomes.
- Telemedicine triage platforms that connect rural patients with urban doctors.
- Farmer advisory systems integrated with digital IDs and mobile payments, improving crop yields and reducing input costs.
- Job matching portals linked to digital credentials that certify skills and training.

Ultimately, DPI that is inclusive by design not only upholds equity but also enhances state capacity and accelerates development outcomes.

2. CONCEPTUALIZING THE DIGITAL DIVIDE

2.1 Theoretical Underpinnings

The "digital divide" is not a single binary gap (connected vs. unconnected). Instead, it is a multi-dimensional, path-dependent phenomenon. Classic ICT4D scholarship identifies it as comprising both first-order divides (access to infrastructure and devices) and second-order divides (skills, usage, and outcomes) (Heeks, 2017). More recent work adds a third-order divide: the ability to translate digital access into meaningful social and economic gains (Alliance for Affordable Internet, 2021; GSMA, 2022).

We conceptualize the divide as five interlocking dimensions:

1. Access Divide – Whether people have reliable electricity, devices, and connectivity (fixed and mobile), and whether the quality of service (bandwidth, latency, uptime) is sufficient for meaningful use.
2. Affordability Divide – Whether total cost of ownership (devices, data, maintenance) is affordable relative to household income.
3. Skills & Literacy Divide – Whether individuals have the basic digital and information literacy to navigate platforms safely, in their own languages, and with assistive technologies if needed.
4. Usage & Value Divide – Whether individuals use digital tools in ways that generate real value (e.g., education, health, jobs) or remain confined to entertainment/social media.
5. Trust & Safety Divide – Whether users feel safe from fraud, harassment, surveillance, algorithmic bias, and misuse of their data.

2.2 Reinforcing Feedback Loops

These divides are mutually reinforcing. For instance:

- Low trust discourages people from adopting digital services → reducing usage levels.
- Low usage discourages service providers from localizing content → reducing relevance.
- High costs make devices unaffordable → exacerbating the access divide.
- Low digital literacy amplifies safety risks → further reducing trust.

Without deliberate intervention, these loops create self-perpetuating exclusion cycles. For example, in rural Sub-Saharan Africa, limited broadband coverage leads to low usage, which reduces incentives for providers to invest, reinforcing the divide.

2.3 Empirical Illustrations

- Sub-Saharan Africa: Mobile coverage exceeds 80%, yet affordability remains a barrier. Data costs can exceed 10% of monthly income, far above the UN Broadband Commission's affordability target of 2%.
- South Asia: Gender divides are particularly acute. Women are 30% less likely to use mobile internet compared to men, reflecting both affordability and cultural constraints.
- Latin America: Urban-rural broadband gaps exceed 40%, with many rural schools and clinics lacking reliable connectivity.
- Global North: Even advanced economies face divides—for example, elderly populations in Europe often struggle with e-government portals due to low digital literacy.

These empirical patterns underscore that the digital divide is not static but evolves with technology. Today's challenge is not only connecting the unconnected but ensuring equitable, safe, and valuable participation in digital societies.

3. LITERATURE AND PRACTICE: LESSONS TO DATE

The deployment of DPI across diverse contexts has generated a rich body of literature and practical lessons. These lessons span technical, institutional, and societal dimensions and collectively underscore that technology is only one component of

DPI success. Institutional design, user trust, and ecosystem enablement are equally vital. The following six themes emerge as particularly instructive.

3.1 Open Standards and Modularity

Scholars and practitioners consistently emphasize the importance of open standards in preventing vendor lock-in, avoiding monopolistic control, and ensuring long-term sustainability (Heeks, 2017). For example, India's Unified Payments Interface (UPI) was deliberately designed with open APIs and standardized protocols that allow banks, fintech startups, and payment service providers to innovate on a common platform (Chatterjee & Saha, 2021). This open architecture resulted in explosive growth—processing over 10 billion transactions monthly in 2023—while maintaining interoperability across hundreds of providers (Ministry of Electronics and Information Technology, Government of India, 2022). Similarly, Estonia's X-Road operates as an open, modular data exchange layer, enabling secure interoperability across government and private services (Estonian Government, 2020). Modularity ensures that individual layers (identity, payments, consent) can be upgraded or replaced without destabilizing the entire stack, allowing flexibility in adapting to new technologies such as blockchain or privacy-preserving computation (Estonian Government, 2020). The literature stresses that without openness and modularity, DPI risks creating "walled gardens" that replicate inequalities and reduce innovation potential (Singh & Mohan, 2021).

3.2 Universal Design and Accessibility

Evidence from both high- and low-income countries demonstrates that accessibility is not a marginal concern but a design principle with broad benefits (Heeks, 2017). In Sub-Saharan Africa, voice-based interfaces and IVR systems designed for low-literate rural populations have since become widely used by urban consumers who value convenience (GSMA, 2021). Similarly, screen-reader compatibility and text-to-speech features initially developed for persons with disabilities now benefit wider user bases in education and elderly care (ITU, 2020). The principle of universal design—ensuring that digital infrastructure is accessible to the widest range of users regardless of literacy, language, or disability—creates positive spillovers (Alliance for Affordable Internet, 2021). For instance, Brazil's PIX incorporated QR-code based payments, which are easier for older and low-literate populations to use, while also aligning with merchant adoption needs (Central Bank of Brazil, 2022). Literature also points out that when accessibility is treated as an afterthought, costly retrofitting is required, and exclusionary patterns become entrenched (GSMA,

2022). Thus, universal design is not merely an ethical imperative but a practical strategy for adoption at scale (UNDP, 2022).

3.3 Human Infrastructure

While DPI often evokes images of servers, protocols, and cryptographic layers, human infrastructure—the networks of agents, mediators, and facilitators—is equally crucial (GSMA, 2021). The success of M-Pesa in Kenya rested not only on mobile technology but also on the extensive network of agents who provided cash-in and cash-out services, often located in rural and remote areas (Mas & Radcliffe, 2011; Jack & Suri, 2014). In Bangladesh, Union Digital Centers provide local citizens with assisted access to government services, ensuring that digital exclusion does not translate into service exclusion (Digital Bangladesh Vision, 2021). Literature highlights that human intermediaries are vital in contexts of low literacy, gender barriers, or weak connectivity (Duncombe & Boateng, 2009). They build trust, provide guidance, and act as the bridge between abstract digital platforms and tangible user needs (Cummings & O'Neil, 2015). In many emerging economies, investment in training these intermediaries yields higher returns than investments in pure technological upgrades (Bill & Melinda Gates Foundation, 2021).

3.4 Consumer Protection and Trust

Trust emerges repeatedly in the literature as the critical determinant of sustained usage. Digital systems that are technically robust but lack grievance mechanisms, fraud protections, or redressal channels often fail to gain traction. For example, early implementations of Aadhaar-based welfare delivery in India faced backlash due to authentication failures and lack of grievance escalation pathways. Subsequent improvements—such as offline verification options, virtual IDs, and better helpdesk systems—were essential in restoring trust. Kenya's mobile money ecosystem also faced agent fraud challenges, prompting the introduction of consumer protection guidelines and stronger central bank oversight. Trust-building mechanisms include clear privacy policies, transparent consent management, independent oversight boards, and rapid grievance redressal mechanisms. Without them, users hesitate to engage deeply with DPI systems, limiting adoption and undermining the intended inclusion benefits.

3.5 Governance Independence

Another recurring theme is the importance of institutional independence in DPI governance. Systems run directly by political administrations risk perceptions of partisanship, instability, and surveillance misuse. Brazil's Central Bank governance of PIX illustrates how an independent, statutory institution can credibly operate a nationwide payments system while maintaining public trust. Estonia's digital governance is similarly anchored in independent, rules-based institutions that transcend electoral cycles. In contrast, countries where DPI is closely tied to ruling parties often face public skepticism, lower adoption, and international concerns over surveillance. Literature from ICT4D and political economy stresses that independent governance structures—separated from day-to-day politics but accountable to law and civil society—are essential for both credibility and longevity of DPI.

3.6 Iterative Rollout

Finally, a strong body of literature advocates for iterative and phased rollouts. DPI systems are too complex to be successfully deployed in "big bang" implementations (Heeks, 2017). India's Aadhaar began as a pilot project in a few states before scaling nationally, allowing for testing and correction of authentication failures (Bhatia & Bhabha, 2017; Gelb & Diofasi Metz, 2018). Similarly, Estonia's X-Road underwent sandbox testing with multiple agencies before full adoption (Estonian Government, 2020). Iterative rollouts allow policymakers to learn from user feedback, adapt to unforeseen challenges, and gradually build the institutional and technical capacity required for scale (Cummings & O'Neil, 2015). Moreover, sandboxes and pilot projects lower political and financial risks, enabling innovation while minimizing systemic failures (OECD, 2021). Literature shows that where governments attempted top-down nationwide DPI launches without phased testing, outcomes often included costly failures, user backlash, and loss of credibility (Gelb & Diofasi Metz, 2018).

4. CASE MINI-STUDIES

4.1 India – Aadhaar + UPI + ONDC

India is often cited as the world's most ambitious DPI ecosystem. Aadhaar, a biometric digital ID launched in 2009, now covers over 1.3 billion residents. It enabled direct benefit transfers (DBT), where government subsidies for food, fuel, and social protection are deposited directly into beneficiary bank accounts, reducing leakage and corruption. Aadhaar also streamlined KYC processes for opening bank accounts and mobile connections. The Unified Payments Interface (UPI), launched in 2016, took inclusion to the next level. By 2024, UPI was processing more than 10 billion monthly transactions, far outpacing comparable systems worldwide. Its open API model allowed fintech, rural cooperative banks, and global players like

Google Pay to innovate atop the same rail. Importantly, UPI supported zero-cost transactions for users, breaking the reliance on cash in both urban and rural markets. More recently, the Open Network for Digital Commerce (ONDC) seeks to replicate UPI's success for digital marketplaces. It allows kirana stores, small merchants, and artisans to join e-commerce ecosystems without being locked into platforms like Amazon or Flipkart. While challenges include ensuring data privacy (Aadhaar controversies) and safeguarding competition, India demonstrates how layered DPI design—identity, payments, commerce—can generate powerful network effects.

4.2 Estonia – X-Road & e-Residency

Estonia's digital state is built on X-Road, an interoperable data exchange backbone launched in 2001. The system allows secure, real-time sharing of data across over 1,000 public and private institutions. Citizens can complete tax returns in minutes, access electronic health records, and sign legally binding contracts digitally using their ID cards. One of Estonia's major innovations is e-Residency, enabling global entrepreneurs to register EU-based companies and conduct business remotely. By 2023, over 100,000 e-residents from 170+ countries had established businesses in Estonia, generating significant revenue. Estonia has also faced challenges. The 2007 cyberattacks from Russia forced the country to pioneer cyber defence strategies, including data embassies (backups stored abroad) and strong cryptographic protections. The Estonian case underscores how trust, security, and resilient governance are as important as technical rails in DPI deployment.

4.3 Kenya – M-Pesa & eCitizen

Launched in 2007, M-Pesa transformed Kenya into the global epicentre of mobile money. By 2022, more than 90% of adults used M-Pesa to transfer money, pay bills, and access microloans. This leapfrogged traditional banking, extending financial access to rural and low-income populations. Integration with the government's eCitizen portal further expanded utility. Citizens could pay for licenses, taxes, and public services via mobile money, reducing bureaucratic delays. Research indicates that M-Pesa lifted 2% of Kenyan households out of poverty, with women benefiting disproportionately due to easier access to credit and savings. However, risks included fraud in agent networks and concerns over Safaricom's market dominance. Regulatory balancing acts—encouraging innovation while ensuring consumer protection—remain ongoing. Kenya's model shows how private-led DPI (M-Pesa) can integrate with state platforms to drive broad inclusion.

4.4 Brazil – PIX and Open Finance

Brazil's Central Bank launched PIX in 2020, an instant payment system offering 24/7, real-time, zero-cost transfers for individuals. Within three years, PIX adoption exceeded 70% of the adult population, with transaction volumes surpassing $300 billion per month. By mandating open participation, PIX dismantled barriers for smaller banks and fintech, ensuring fair competition. The rollout of Open Finance further expanded consumer empowerment by allowing individuals to share their financial data across institutions. This enhanced portability of services—such as loans or investments—without lock-in. A key factor was strong state-led governance: the Central Bank designed, launched, and oversees PIX, lending it institutional credibility. Challenges include cybersecurity threats and digital literacy gaps in rural areas. Still, Brazil demonstrates how government-driven DPI with inclusive design can succeed at national scale.

4.5 Bangladesh – Digital Bangladesh Vision

Bangladesh's Digital Bangladesh Vision 2021 integrated ID, payments, and service delivery into a cohesive national strategy. The rollout of smart national ID cards enabled authentication across banking, elections, and social protection. The rise of bKash, a private-sector mobile financial service, brought millions into the financial system. By 2022, bKash had over 60 million users, many from rural households. To complement this, the government established over 8,000 Union Digital Centres (UDCs), acting as rural service hubs where citizens could access digital services with assisted support. The Bangladesh case illustrates how public-private synergy—government vision + private fintech innovation—can drive inclusive DPI. Remaining gaps include broadband penetration (particularly in rural areas) and gender disparities in mobile access.

4.6 Mexico – Red Compartida (Shared Network)

Mexico's Red Compartida represents a unique DPI approach: wholesale mobile broadband infrastructure. Operated in the 700 MHz spectrum band, the network provides capacity to retail telecom providers—including smaller operators and MVNOs—lowering entry barriers. By decoupling infrastructure from retail services, Red Compartida expanded 4G coverage to underserved areas. It also reduced data costs by increasing competition. By 2021, coverage extended to 70% of the population, including rural communities traditionally excluded from broadband markets. Challenges include slow uptake from private operators and sustainability of financing. Still, Mexico highlights how spectrum policy and shared infrastructure can be powerful DPI enablers.

4.7 African Union – Regional DPI Initiatives

The African Union's Digital Transformation Strategy for Africa (2020–2030) aims to harmonize DPI across member states. The Smart Africa Alliance promotes cross-border collaboration on broadband and e-services. The Pan-African Payment and Settlement System (PAPSS) supports regional trade by enabling instant cross-border payments in local currencies. These initiatives address fragmentation, but face challenges: diverse regulatory regimes, limited institutional capacity, and financing constraints. Nevertheless, continental-scale DPI offers immense potential for migrant workers, traders, and SMEs, lowering transaction costs and improving service portability.

4.8 Indonesia – e-KTP & GoPay Integration

Indonesia launched e-KTP, a biometric national ID program, covering more than 190 million citizens. This ID underpins access to government programs, health insurance, and banking. On the payments side, Indonesia witnessed rapid uptake of GoPay (linked to the Gojek ecosystem) and OVO. By 2023, digital wallet usage exceeded 80 million active users, many of them unbanked or underbanked. The government encouraged interoperability through the QRIS standard, allowing any QR code payment app to function nationwide. The integration of e-KTP and QRIS demonstrates how government standards + private innovation can create inclusive DPI. However, governance issues—such as corruption scandals in the e-KTP rollout—underline the need for transparency and accountability.

4.9 Nigeria – NIN & Mobile Money Expansion

Nigeria rolled out the National Identification Number (NIN) as a foundational ID. By 2022, more than 80 million Nigerians were registered, though challenges remain in reaching rural and nomadic populations. On the payments front, Nigeria licensed mobile money operators such as Paga and bank-led systems. However, adoption has lagged behind Kenya's M-Pesa, due to regulatory bottlenecks and lack of trust. The Central Bank of Nigeria's eNaira (a retail CBDC) represents another DPI experiment, though uptake has been limited. Nigeria illustrates the difficulties of harmonizing ID, payments, and telecom regulation in a large, diverse federal system. Lessons point to the need for strong institutional coordination and grassroots outreach.

4.10 Philippines – PhilSys & GCash

The Philippines launched PhilSys, its national ID system, with the goal of covering 92 million citizens by 2025. The ID is designed for use across government subsidies, healthcare, and financial services. In parallel, GCash emerged as the country's most widely used e-wallet, with more than 60 million users by 2023. Integration with government transfers during the COVID-19 pandemic highlighted the role of mobile money in crisis response. Challenges include archipelagic geography (making last-mile service delivery difficult) and privacy concerns. Still, the Philippines demonstrates how mobile-first DPI ecosystems can bridge divides in geographically complex nations.

4.11 European Union – eIDAS & GDPR

The European Union has taken a regulatory-first approach to DPI. The eIDAS regulation harmonizes digital identity across member states, enabling cross-border recognition of IDs and electronic signatures. The GDPR serves as a global gold standard for data protection, influencing DPI governance worldwide. By mandating data minimization, consent, and portability, it shapes how both governments and private platforms design digital systems. The forthcoming EU Digital Identity Wallet aims to provide every citizen with a secure, interoperable identity credential by 2030. The EU model shows the importance of legal frameworks as DPI enablers, complementing technical rails.

4.12 China – Digital Yuan & Health Codes

China has pioneered state-led DPI with global implications. The Digital Yuan (e-CNY), piloted in dozens of cities, represents one of the world's most advanced CBDC experiments. It enables programmable payments and direct state-to-citizen transfers. During the COVID-19 pandemic, health code apps integrated ID, mobility, and health data, governing access to public spaces. While effective in containment, they sparked debates about surveillance and privacy. China's experience demonstrates both the power and risks of DPI: when deployed without strong privacy protections, systems risk becoming tools of digital authoritarianism.

4.13 Comparative Lessons and Insights

A cross-case analysis reveals several shared success factors:

Success Factors:

- Open standards & interoperability (India's UPI, Indonesia's QRIS, EU's eIDAS).
- Strong state-led governance (Brazil's PIX, Estonia's X-Road).
- Public-private synergy (Bangladesh's bKash + UDCs, Kenya's M-Pesa + eCitizen).
- Inclusion-by-design (Mexico's Red Compartida, Philippines' GCash).

Pitfalls & Challenges:

- Privacy concerns (Aadhaar in India, health codes in China).
- Monopoly risks (Safaricom in Kenya, GoPay in Indonesia).
- Institutional fragmentation (Nigeria's ID + payments struggles).
- Cybersecurity threats (Estonia, EU-wide harmonization).

The comparative takeaway is clear: DPI succeeds when it balances innovation with safeguards, competition with inclusion, and central leadership with ecosystem participation.

5. THE INCLUSIVE DPI STRATEGY FRAMEWORK (IDSF)

The seven pillars of the proposed framework are summarized in Figure 3.

The Inclusive DPI Strategy Framework (IDSF) is designed to help emerging economies build Digital Public Infrastructure (DPI) in a way that is not only technologically sound but also inclusive, sustainable, and future-proof. It synthesizes lessons from theoretical foundations, practical implementation experiences, and global case studies of successful DPI initiatives.

At its core, the IDSF emphasizes that DPI is not just about technology; it is about creating a social and institutional ecosystem where citizens, governments, and private actors can interact safely, equitably, and productively.

Seven Core Pillars of IDSF

Each pillar represents a key domain necessary for inclusive and effective DPI in emerging economies:

1. Accessibility and Affordability

- o DPI must ensure universal access, regardless of geography, income, gender, or disability.
- o Affordable connectivity, multilingual interfaces, and offline capabilities are crucial.
- o Example: India's UPI system works on both smartphones and basic feature phones.

2. Interoperability and Standards
   - o Systems should be interoperable across sectors (finance, health, education, transport).
   - o Open standards and APIs prevent vendor lock-in and foster innovation by startups.
   - o Example: Estonia's X-Road framework enables secure data exchange across agencies.
3. Security and Privacy
   - o Strong cybersecurity measures and data protection frameworks are foundational.
   - o Trust is built by ensuring users' data is not exploited, misused, or left vulnerable.
   - o Example: EU's GDPR serves as a global reference point for data privacy.
4. Institutional and Governance Capacity
   - o Effective DPI requires clear institutional responsibilities, regulatory frameworks, and capacity building.
   - o Collaboration between government, private sector, and civil society is essential.
   - o Example: Rwanda's IremboGov platform was developed through strong public–private partnerships.
5. Innovation and Local Ecosystem Development
   - o DPI should stimulate local entrepreneurship and innovation ecosystems.
   - o Sandboxes, accelerators, and developer-friendly APIs can empower startups.
   - o Example: UPI in India has enabled an explosion of fintech innovation.
6. Financial and Operational Sustainability
   - o DPI must be designed for long-term viability.
   - o Public–private funding models, transaction-based revenue streams, and international development support can ensure sustainability.
   - o Example: Mobile money platforms like M-Pesa scaled sustainably through partnerships.
7. Inclusivity and Citizen Empowerment
   - o Digital systems should empower citizens, not exclude them.

- o Special attention to gender digital divide, rural communities, and marginalized groups is key.
- o Example: Bangladesh's digital birth registration program has improved service delivery to rural mothers and children.

5.1 Cross-Cutting Principles

Rights

Anchoring DPI within human rights ensures that citizens retain agency and protection. For example, the EU's GDPR emphasizes *data minimization* and *purpose limitation*, preventing excessive data harvesting. Embedding such safeguards prevents DPI from morphing into surveillance tools. In emerging economies, constitutional guarantees and independent data protection authorities are critical.

Resilience

DPI must be robust against cyberattacks, systemic outages, and climate shocks. Resilience requires redundant infrastructure, offline-first services, and cybersecurity protocols. Estonia pioneered "data embassies," storing critical datasets in foreign jurisdictions to withstand local disruptions—a practice others can adopt.

Responsibility

Responsibility entails transparent governance, accountability mechanisms, and ethical stewardship. For example, Brazil's Central Bank publishes real-time PIX adoption data, enhancing transparency. Responsibility also means ensuring grievance redressal: citizens must have recourse if services malfunction or rights are violated.

5.2 Pillar A — Foundations & Policy Enablement

A robust DPI ecosystem rests on a strong policy and legal foundation.

- Legislative Frameworks: Independent data protection laws with enforceable rights (as in Kenya's 2019 Data Protection Act).
- Spectrum & Connectivity Policy: Prioritize affordable broadband, license community networks, and support innovative spectrum models (e.g., Mexico's Red Compartida).
- Procurement Reform: Mandate open-source preference or open standards compliance to avoid vendor lock-in.

- Competition Policy: Prevent monopolies by enforcing interoperability (e.g., interoperability mandates for mobile money in Ghana).

Action Point: Governments should publish a *DPI Readiness Baseline Report*—assessing regulatory, connectivity, and institutional conditions—before rollout.

5.3 Pillar B — Core DPI Rails

DPI is typically composed of modular, interoperable rails:

1. Identity & Credentials
    - Should accommodate marginalized groups (refugees, undocumented citizens).
    - Models include community attestations (as in ID4Africa pilots) or biometrics (as in India).
    - Privacy safeguards (virtual IDs, tokenization) must be mandatory.
2. Payments
    - Low-cost, real-time systems (PIX, UPI).
    - Features: *offline capability* (USSD, NFC), fraud detection, consumer protection.
    - Central bank oversight builds trust.
3. Data Exchange & Consent
    - Consent managers enable granular, revocable permissions (India's Data Empowerment and Protection Architecture – DEPA).
    - Secure APIs for government-to-government and government-to-business transactions.
4. Common Registries & Messaging
    - Land, business, and vehicle registries serve as foundational assets.
    - Messaging platforms (e.g., Estonia's e-notifications) provide trusted citizen communication.

Action Point: Countries should adopt a layered modular architecture with clear separation of control to prevent monopolization.

5.4 Pillar C — Inclusion-by-Design

Inclusion is not an afterthought—it must be designed into every layer.

- Universal Accessibility: Interfaces that support text-to-speech, sign language, and minority languages (e.g., Bangladesh's multilingual UDC portals).

- Safety-by-Default: Child protection mechanisms in education DPI (Philippines' digital classrooms).
- Offline-First Services: QR/NFC tokens, SMS/USSD payments, and voice IVR ensure resilience in low-connectivity areas.
- Grievance Redressal: Mandatory grievance dashboards with escalation pathways.

Case Insight: Mexico's Red Compartida expanded coverage but combined it with shared public access points, ensuring affordability in rural communities.

5.5 Pillar D — Ecosystem Enablement

No DPI succeeds in isolation; it requires a vibrant innovation ecosystem.

- Open APIs & SDKs: India's UPI growth was driven by open APIs accessible to fintech startups.
- Developer Sandboxes: Regulatory testbeds for piloting new services (UK's FCA sandbox as a model).
- Civic-Tech Co-creation: Hackathons and community-led service design (Kenya's open data initiative).
- Interoperability Testing: Neutral labs to ensure cross-compatibility.

Action Point: Governments should establish a DPI Innovation Lab—jointly run with universities and civil society—to prototype services and test inclusivity.

5.6 Pillar E — Affordability & Access

Bridging affordability divides requires multi-pronged approaches:

- Device Financing: Micro-loan models for smartphones (Kenya's M-KOPA).
- Community Networks: Locally owned ISPs serving villages (Zenzeleni in South Africa).
- Subsidized Data Packs: Zero-rated government services but aligned with net neutrality.
- Refurbished Device Markets: Circular economy approaches reduce device costs.

Action Point: Deploy Universal Service Funds (USF) toward devices, not just connectivity—since both are critical for access.

5.7 Pillar F — Capacity & Adoption

Capacity building ensures citizens and institutions can use DPI meaningfully.

1. Citizen Capacity
   - o Digital literacy tailored by demographic (youth, elderly, women).
   - o Awareness campaigns to build trust (Brazil's national campaigns for PIX).
2. Institutional Capacity
   - o Civil service training in cybersecurity, product management, and data stewardship.
   - o Creation of CIO academies within governments.
3. Community Capacity
   - o Last-mile intermediaries (Bangladesh's UDC agents, India's Common Service Centers).
   - o Peer-to-peer training networks in rural areas.

Action Point: Link DPI adoption programs to social protection schemes (e.g., conditional cash transfers requiring digital IDs).

5.8 Pillar G — Governance, Assurance & M&E

Effective governance is the backbone of DPI success.

- Independent DPI Authorities: With statutory independence and open board structures.
- Algorithmic Audits: Regular third-party audits of AI/ML systems in DPI (to detect bias).
- Socio-Technical Risk Impact Assessments (SRIAs): Mandatory before large-scale rollouts.
- Outcome Metrics: Example KPIs include % women with active digital IDs, median grievance resolution time, and reduction in transaction costs.

Case Insight: Brazil's Central Bank publishes transparent performance data for PIX—an accountability measure emerging economies can replicate.

5.9 Integrating the Framework into Practice

The IDSF is not a static blueprint but a living framework. Countries must adapt based on political economy, capacity, and cultural context. For fragile states, focusing on foundational ID and payments may be the starting point; for middle-income economies, emphasis may shift to ecosystem enablement and advanced data exchange.

The framework's strength lies in balancing technical rails with human infrastructure, central governance with ecosystem participation, and innovation with rights-based safeguards.

6. IMPLEMENTATION ROADMAP (0–5 YEARS)

DPI deployment in emerging economies must follow a phased, iterative, and adaptive approach, ensuring learning-by-doing while safeguarding inclusion. The roadmap spans five phases:

Phase 0: Pre-Rollout Diagnostics (0–6 months)

- Stakeholder Mapping: Identify all actors—ministries, regulators, private providers, CSOs, community groups.
- Baseline Assessment: Connectivity penetration, device ownership, gender gaps, institutional capacity.
- Legal Gap Analysis: Data protection, competition, and telecom frameworks reviewed.
- Digital Divide Dashboard: Publicly available data disaggregated by gender, age, disability, income, and geography.

Output: *DPI Readiness Report* with risks and policy recommendations.

Phase 1: Core Foundation Setup (6–18 months)

- Establish a National DPI Authority (NDPIA) with statutory independence.
- Pilot foundational ID and payments systems.
- Launch open API developer sandbox.
- Begin public awareness campaigns on rights, safety, and grievance redressal.

Output: *Pilot ID system, payment platform, and NDPIA governance structure.*

Phase 2: Assisted Rollout & Registries (Year 2)

- Expand ID and payments to rural service centres and last-mile agents.
- Launch priority registries (land, business, vehicle).
- Deploy grievance portals and multilingual helplines.

- Train 5,000–10,000 last-mile intermediaries.

Output: *50% population with digital ID; first registries live.*

Phase 3: Ecosystem Integration (Year 3)

- Interlink government ministries via data exchange layer.
- Scale APIs to fintech's, SMEs, civic-tech organizations.
- Incentivize private innovation via hackathons, seed funding.
- Expand assisted services to 80% of rural districts.

Output: *Ecosystem of 500+ third-party apps/services on DPI rails.*

Phase 4: Safeguards & Advanced Features (Year 4)

- Implement Privacy-Enhancing Technologies (PETs) (ZKPs, tokenization).
- Roll out advanced consent managers.
- Conduct independent algorithmic audits.
- Introduce digital credential wallets for health, education, and employment.

Output: *Rights-based, privacy-protected DPI stack with sectoral applications.*

Phase 5: Consolidation & Sustainability (Year 5)

- Transition NDPIA into a permanent statutory body.
- Ensure financial sustainability (via PPPs, levies, blended finance).
- Conduct external evaluation against SDG-linked KPIs.
- Expand regional interoperability (cross-border IDs, payments).

Output: *Mature, inclusive DPI ecosystem aligned with SDGs.*

7. GOVERNANCE MODELS AND INSTITUTIONAL DESIGN

Governance determines whether DPI deepens democracy or fosters digital authoritarianism. Successful DPI requires separation of powers, transparency, and citizen participation.

7.1 Institutional Structures

- NDPIA (National Digital Public Infrastructure Authority): Independent statutory body overseeing architecture, compliance, and inclusion.
- Sectoral Councils: Health, education, agriculture, fintech councils feeding into NDPIA.
- Citizen Advisory Forum: Civil society, academia, SMEs, disability advocates included.

7.2 Independence and Accountability

- Statutory independence (like Brazil's Central Bank).
- Mandatory public consultations for policy changes.
- Annual *Digital Rights Report* published by NDPIA.

7.3 Governance Models

1. Centralized State-Led (Brazil PIX, China e-CNY) → Fast, but risk of overreach.
2. Federated/Decentralized (EU eIDAS, Estonia X-Road) → Strong checks, but requires capacity.
3. Public-Private Hybrid (Kenya's M-Pesa, Bangladesh bKash) → Innovation-friendly, but risks monopoly capture.

Recommendation: Emerging economies should adopt a hybrid model: state-led governance + open ecosystem + strong independent oversight.

7.4 Tools for Trust

- Algorithmic Transparency Dashboards: Public audits of DPI algorithms.
- Grievance Escalation Chains: Local → Regional → National.
- Whistleblower Protections: Legal shields for exposing abuse.
- Cross-Border Data Embassies: Secure backups (Estonia model).

8. FINANCING THE DPI STACK

Financing determines both scalability and sustainability of DPI. Emerging economies need innovative, blended models.

8.1 Public Finance

- National budgets must fund *foundational rails* (ID, payments).
- Earmark Universal Service Funds (USF) for device access, not just connectivity.

8.2 Private Participation

- PPPs with performance-linked incentives (e.g., outcome-based financing).
- Allow fintechs/startups to innovate via DPI APIs.
- Telecom operators can co-invest in shared infrastructure.

8.3 Blended Finance

- Combine donor grants, development loans, and domestic capital.
- Instruments: concessional loans, guarantee funds, impact bonds.
- Example: African Union's DPI strategy calls for blended funds to finance cross-border rails.

8.4 Innovative Mechanisms

- Transaction Levy: Small charge on high-value payments (not basic ones) funds DPI maintenance.
- Digital Infrastructure Bonds: Long-term sovereign bonds dedicated to DPI expansion.
- Open-Source Costing: Reduces licensing costs and fosters innovation.

9. CRITICAL PERSPECTIVES & DEBATES

While Digital Public Infrastructure (DPI) promises inclusion and empowerment, it also raises fundamental ethical, economic, and social debates. These debates determine whether DPI becomes a tool for democratic participation and inclusion, or for exclusion and control.

9.1 Ethical Perspectives

Privacy vs. Utility

- Proponents' View: DPI systems like Aadhaar or eIDAS enable service delivery at scale, reducing leakages and corruption.
- Critics' View: Centralized databases risk mass surveillance, data breaches, and mission creep.
- Middle Path: Adoption of *privacy-enhancing technologies* (e.g., zero-knowledge proofs, tokenization, differential privacy).

Surveillance and Civil Liberties

- In China, health codes and the Social Credit System illustrate how DPI can be harnessed for surveillance and behavior control.
- In democratic contexts like Estonia, the same digital rails are paired with independent oversight and citizen transparency rights.
- The question is not just what DPI does, but who controls it.

Algorithmic Fairness

- Biometric systems may misidentify women, darker-skinned populations, or elderly users, leading to wrongful exclusion.
- Example: Aadhaar authentication failures among manual laborers due to fingerprint wear.
- Solutions include multi-modal biometrics, fallback mechanisms, and human-in-the-loop grievance processes.

9.2 Economic Perspectives

Monopoly Risks vs. Open Competition

- Pro-Monopoly Argument: A dominant platform (like M-Pesa in Kenya) can accelerate adoption by creating a de facto standard.
- Counter-Argument: Over-concentration creates lock-in, suppresses innovation, and inflates costs.
- Middle Path: Regulatory mandates for *interoperability* (as Brazil did with PIX and Open Finance).

Public vs. Private Models

- Public-Led (Brazil PIX): Ensures low costs and universal access, but may limit private innovation if overregulated.
- Private-Led (M-Pesa): Rapid scaling, but high dependency on one operator.
- Hybrid (India's UPI): Government provides rails, private firms innovate on top.

Affordability Trade-offs

- Zero-cost transactions may boost adoption, but raise questions of sustainability.
- A balanced model includes tiered cost structures—free for basic services, small levy on high-value commercial transactions.

9.3 Societal Perspectives

Gender Digital Divide

- GSMA data: women in South Asia are 30% less likely to use mobile internet than men.
- Causes: affordability, restrictive norms, safety concerns.
- Remedies: subsidized devices for women, female-led digital literacy programs, safety-by-design features (SOS alerts, privacy modes).

Disability Inclusion

- Global disability population: ~1 billion people.
- Many DPI systems lack accessibility (e.g., screen-reader compatibility, voice interfaces).
- Example: Bangladesh's UDC introduced text-to-speech for rural elderly users.
- Principle: Universal Design must be mandatory in DPI standards.

Linguistic and Cultural Barriers

- Multilingual societies (India, Nigeria, Philippines) risk exclusion if DPI supports only dominant languages.
- Example: India's DigiLocker now supports regional languages, increasing uptake.

- Cultural norms (e.g., guardianship rules in Middle Eastern contexts) affect adoption, requiring contextual tailoring.

Youth vs. Elderly Divide

- Youth are early adopters; elderly face barriers due to lack of skills or trust.
- Example: Estonia runs "digital elder" programs, training seniors in basic e-services.
- Adoption strategies must target age-specific needs.

9.4 Political Perspectives

Democratic Safeguards vs. Digital Authoritarianism

- DPI can empower citizens with transparency (e.g., Estonia's e-governance).
- But it can also centralize control, as in China's Digital Yuan deployment.
- The difference lies in governance safeguards, independent audits, and civic participation.

Cross-Border Data Sovereignty

- Developing countries fear dependency on global tech giants (AWS, Microsoft, Huawei).
- Regional approaches (African Union's PAPSS, EU's Gaia-X cloud) emphasize digital sovereignty.
- Debate: Should emerging economies pursue national data centers, or integrate into regional cloud federations?

9.5 Environmental Perspectives

Sustainability of DPI Infrastructure

- Data centers consume vast energy and water resources.
- Example: India's data center sector projected to require 2.5 GW power by 2025.
- Remedies: green energy mandates, carbon-neutral cloud, circular economy for devices.

E-Waste Challenges

- Device-driven DPI expansion risks creating e-waste mountains.
- Example: Africa already receives large quantities of discarded electronics.
- Solutions: enforce Right to Repair, develop local refurbishing markets, integrate e-waste management into DPI financing.

9.6 Integrative Insight

DPI is neither inherently emancipatory nor inherently authoritarian. Its impact depends on design choices, governance models, and safeguards.

- A rights-first, open, inclusive DPI can accelerate SDGs, improve governance, and expand opportunity.
- A closed, opaque, monopolistic DPI can deepen divides, undermine rights, and entrench elite capture.

Thus, the critical debates are not academic abstractions—they directly shape adoption, trust, and developmental impact.

10. RISK MANAGEMENT AND SAFEGUARDS

Risks fall into technical, social, market, and operational categories.

- Technical: system outages, cybersecurity breaches.
- Social: exclusion of vulnerable groups, surveillance.
- Market: monopolies, unfair pricing.
- Operational: shortage of skilled talent.

Mitigation measures include redundancy, oversight boards, algorithmic audits, anti-monopoly legislation, and capacity-building programs.

11. MONITORING, EVALUATION, AND LEARNING (MEL)

A strong MEL system includes logic models, KPIs, and participatory evaluations. For example, indicators include % of women with active digital IDs, average grievance resolution time, and transaction costs per capita. Dashboards should be open to the public. Independent third-party evaluations provide credibility.

12. TECHNICAL ARCHITECTURE PATTERNS

- Modularity: independent scaling of ID, payments, and data layers.
- Interoperability: adherence to ISO 20022, FIDO2, OIDC.
- Privacy-Enhancing Technologies: zero-knowledge proofs, secure enclaves.
- Offline-first: SMS/USSD, QR codes, sound-based transactions.
- Observability: system logs, runbooks, chaos testing.

13. CAPACITY BUILDING AND CHANGE MANAGEMENT

Capacity development must occur at three levels:

1. Human capacity: trained product managers, SREs, accessibility experts.
2. Institutional capacity: CIO academies, digital policy training for civil servants.
3. Community capacity: grassroots intermediaries bridging the gap between citizens and systems.

14. INCLUSION PLAYBOOK

Accessibility Checklist: WCAG compliance, voice interfaces, sign-language support. Gender-Safe Design: anti-harassment mechanisms, guardian-aware flows. Low-Connectivity Patterns: adaptive payloads, progressive enhancement. Assisted Services: trained local agents, grievance escalation trees.

15. SECTORAL BLUEPRINTS

- Health: e-prescriptions, telemedicine, immunization tracking.
- Agriculture: farmer IDs, e-marketplace access, land registry integration.
- Education: digital credential wallets, school connectivity.
- MSMEs: e-invoicing, credit scoring from consented data.
- Social Protection: targeted transfers, grievance portals, offline tokens.

Each blueprint demonstrates how DPI integrates with sectoral outcomes.

16. LOCALIZATION AND CULTURAL CONTEXT

Localization requires multilingual design, co-creation with communities, and support for minority scripts. Festivals, cultural calendars, and local norms must shape service rollout.

17. ETHICAL, LEGAL, AND HUMAN RIGHTS CONSIDERATIONS

Key principles include dignity, non-discrimination, and privacy. Algorithmic accountability is vital, ensuring explainability in decisions affecting rights. Child-safety by design is mandatory in education and social protection services.

18. FUTURE TRENDS & POLICY RECOMMENDATIONS

Digital Public Infrastructure (DPI) is still evolving. While foundational layers like identity, payments, and data exchange are stabilizing, new technological and governance frontiers are rapidly emerging. The next decade will determine whether DPI narrows or widens the digital divide in emerging economies.

18.1 Future Trends in DPI

Trend 1: AI-Enabled DPI

- Use Cases: Automated fraud detection in payments, smart grievance redressal chatbots, personalized citizen services.
- Risks: Algorithmic bias, opacity in decision-making, exclusion of marginalized groups.
- Safeguard: Algorithmic impact assessments + explainable AI (XAI) embedded into DPI governance.

Trend 2: Blockchain and Decentralized Trust

- Blockchain and distributed ledgers can enhance auditability of identity credentials, land registries, and supply chains.
- Example: Georgia's land registry blockchain pilot improved trust in property transfers.
- Caution: High energy use, governance complexity, and risks of "crypto-hype."

Trend 3: Cross-Border DPI Interoperability

- Regional economic blocs are piloting DPI that transcends national borders.
- African Union (PAPSS): Facilitates cross-border payments.
- EU (eIDAS 2.0): Enables mutual recognition of digital IDs.
- Potential: Enables migrant workers to use home-country IDs abroad for remittances, banking, and welfare.

Trend 4: Digital Currencies and Payment Futures

- Central Bank Digital Currencies (CBDCs) are being tested in over 100 countries.
- Examples: China's e-CNY, Nigeria's eNaira, India's Digital Rupee.
- Promise: Inclusion of unbanked populations.
- Risks: State surveillance of transactions, displacement of private fintech innovation.

Trend 5: Green and Sustainable DPI

- Governments are embedding climate goals into digital policy.
- Example: EU's Green Digital Agenda requires cloud providers to achieve carbon neutrality by 2030.
- Future DPI may mandate renewable-powered data centers and e-waste recycling targets.

Trend 6: Human-Centered Design at Scale

- Future DPI must adapt to cultural diversity, disability inclusion, and offline-first operation.
- Multimodal interfaces (voice, gesture, local language text) will dominate in low-literacy contexts.
- Assisted service models will expand to bridge human and digital infrastructures.

Trend 7: Cybersecurity as a Public Good

- Cyber threats (ransomware, supply-chain attacks) will increasingly target DPI.
- Some countries may treat cyber defense of DPI like public health, with global coordination and rapid response mechanisms.

18.2 Policy Recommendations

Drawing from global lessons, the following 10 recommendations form a strategic playbook for inclusive DPI in emerging economies:

1. Adopt Rights-Based DPI by Design
   - Enshrine privacy, non-discrimination, and accessibility in DPI legislation.
   - Make *data fiduciary obligations* mandatory for both public and private actors.
2. Ensure Independent DPI Governance
   - Establish National DPI Authorities (NDPIA) with statutory independence.
   - Mandate open consultations, public audits, and annual reports.
3. Mandate Open Standards and Interoperability
   - Prevent monopolies by requiring open APIs, standards-based registries, and vendor-neutral procurement.
   - Benchmark: India's UPI, Brazil's PIX.
4. Prioritize Inclusion-by-Design
   - Accessibility (WCAG), multilingual support, offline tokens, and grievance redressal must be default requirements, not add-ons.
5. Bridge the Affordability Divide
   - Use Universal Service Funds (USFs) for device subsidies, community Wi-Fi, and targeted vouchers.
   - Promote refurbished device ecosystems to reduce cost + e-waste.
6. Build Human Infrastructure
   - Train last-mile intermediaries, female digital champions, and grassroots organizations.
   - Establish Civil Service Digital Academies to train government staff in DPI management.
7. Embed Safeguards Against Misuse
   - Introduce Socio-Technical Risk Impact Assessments (SRIAs) before rolling out large-scale DPI.
   - Mandate algorithmic audits, breach notification protocols, and whistleblower protections.
8. Diversify Financing Models
   - Blend public budgets, development aid, and private innovation.
   - Experiment with digital infrastructure bonds and transaction levies on high-value transfers to fund DPI sustainability.
9. Promote Regional and Cross-Border DPI

- Harmonize ID, payments, and data exchange at regional levels (AU, ASEAN, SAARC).
- Support migrant workers with portable IDs and interoperable wallets.

10. Monitor, Evaluate, and Adapt
    - Create open public dashboards on inclusion metrics (gender, disability, geography).
    - Conduct independent evaluations every 3 years with civil society participation.

18.3 Integrative Outlook

The future of DPI is not technological—it is political and ethical.

- Countries that adopt inclusive, rights-based, interoperable DPI will unlock productivity, expand social protection, and reduce inequality.
- Countries that adopt opaque, monopolistic, surveillance-driven DPI risk deepening divides, eroding rights, and losing public trust.

Thus, the challenge for emerging economies is clear: build DPI as a public good, not as a tool of control.

REFERENCES

African Union. (2020). *Digital transformation strategy for Africa*. African Union Commission.

Aker, J., & Mbiti, I. (2019). Mobile phones and economic development in Africa. *The Journal of Economic Perspectives*, *33*(3), 207–232. DOI: 10.1257/jep.24.3.207

Alliance for Affordable Internet. (2021). *The affordability report*. Web Foundation.

Bhatia, A., & Bhabha, J. (2017). India's Aadhaar scheme and the promise of inclusive social protection. *World Development*, *98*, 222–240. DOI: 10.1016/j.worlddev.2017.04.013

Bill & Melinda Gates Foundation. (2021). *Level one project guide: Principles for financial inclusion*. Bill & Melinda Gates Foundation.

Central Bank of Brazil. (2022). PIX: The instant payments system in Brazil. https://www.bcb.gov.br

CGAP. (2021). *Building digital public goods for inclusive finance*. CGAP.

Chatterjee, P., & Saha, S. (2021). UPI and digital payments transformation in India. *Economic and Political Weekly*, *56*(12), 35–41.

Cummings, C., & O'Neil, T. (2015). *Do digital technologies improve service delivery? Evidence from developing countries*. Overseas Development Institute.

Digital Bangladesh Vision. (2021). Government of Bangladesh ICT Division. a2i. https://a2i.gov.bd

Duncombe, R., & Boateng, R. (2009). Mobile phones and financial services in developing countries: A review of concepts, methods, issues, evidence and future research directions. *Third World Quarterly*, *30*(7), 1237–1258. DOI: 10.1080/01436590903134882

Estonian Government. (2020). X-Road data exchange platform. e-Estonia. https://e-estonia.com

Financial Action Task Force. (2020). *Guidance on digital identity*. FATF.

Gelb, A., & Diofasi Metz, A. (2018). *Identification revolution: Can digital ID be harnessed for development?* Center for Global Development.

GSMA. (2021). *Driving digital inclusion in emerging economies*. GSMA Intelligence.

GSMA. (2022). *The state of mobile internet connectivity*. GSMA Intelligence.

Heeks, R. (2017). *Information and communication technology for development (ICT4D)* (2nd ed.). Routledge. DOI: 10.4324/9781315652603

ID4D Initiative, World Bank. (2022). Global ID coverage report. World Bank.

ITU. (2020). *Measuring digital development: Facts and figures*. International Telecommunication Union.

Jack, W., & Suri, T. (2014). Risk sharing and transactions costs: Evidence from Kenya's mobile money revolution. *The American Economic Review, 104*(1), 183–223. DOI: 10.1257/aer.104.1.183

Mas, I., & Radcliffe, D. (2011). *Mobile payments go viral: M-Pesa in Kenya*. Bill & Melinda Gates Foundation.

Ministry of Electronics and Information Technology, Government of India. (2022). *Digital India programme annual report*. Government of India.

Muralidharan, K., Niehaus, P., & Sukhtankar, S. (2016). Building state capacity: Evidence from biometric smartcards in India. *The American Economic Review, 106*(10), 2895–2929. DOI: 10.1257/aer.20141346

OECD. (2021). *Digital government index 2020: Shaping the digital transformation of the public sector*. OECD Publishing., DOI: 10.1787/9789264314610-

Open Government Partnership. (2021). Digital public infrastructure for inclusive governance. https://www.opengovpartnership.org

Pan-African Payment and Settlement System. (2022). *Implementation report*. Afreximbank.

Qiang, C. Z., Rossotto, C. M., & Kimura, K. (2009). Economic impacts of broadband. In *Information and communications for development 2009: Extending reach and increasing impact* (pp. 35–50). World Bank.

Singh, P. J., & Mohan, S. (2021). Platform governance in India: Lessons from digital commerce. *Economic and Political Weekly, 56*(18), 44–51.

Suri, T., & Jack, W. (2016). The long-run poverty and gender impacts of mobile money. *Science, 354*(6317), 1288–1292. DOI: 10.1126/science.aah5309 PMID: 27940873

UN ESCAP. (2021). *Asia-Pacific digital transformation report*. United Nations Economic and Social Commission for Asia and the Pacific.

UNDP. (2022). *Human development report 2022: Uncertain times, unsettled lives*. United Nations Development Programme.

World Bank. (2021). *World development report 2021: Data for better lives*. World Bank., DOI: 10.1596/978-1-4648-1600-0

World Bank & ITU. (2021). *The digital regulation handbook. World Bank*. International Telecommunication Union.

DPI (Digital Public Infrastructure): Foundational, interoperable digital systems—identity, payments, data exchange—that enable public and private services.

Verifiable Credentials (VCs): Cryptographically secure attestations of attributes held by individuals or organizations.

Federated Identity: Identity model where multiple identity providers interoperate through standards.

Data Fiduciary: Entity with duties of care, loyalty, and purpose limitation in handling personal data.

Consent Manager: Independent layer that manages user permissions for data sharing with auditability.

Last-Mile Intermediary: Trained local agent/organization providing assisted digital services.

Digital KYC (Know Your Customer): A digital verification process that authenticates individuals' identity using government-recognized documents or biometric credentials, reducing onboarding costs for financial and social services.

Interoperability Framework: A set of standards and protocols that allow diverse digital platforms and services to exchange data seamlessly, ensuring that users are not locked into single vendors.

Public Key Infrastructure (PKI): Cryptographic system that secures digital communication and transactions by providing authentication, integrity, and non-repudiation.

Zero-Rating: Policy where access to certain online services or applications is made free of data charges, often debated for its impact on net neutrality and equity.

Digital Literacy: The set of cognitive, technical, and safety skills required to effectively navigate digital tools, evaluate information, and engage meaningfully online.

Universal Service Obligation (USO): A regulatory requirement for telecom providers to ensure affordable access to basic connectivity in underserved and rural areas.

Privacy-Enhancing Technologies (PETs): Tools like differential privacy, homomorphic encryption, and secure multiparty computation that protect individual data while allowing aggregate analysis.

Algorithmic Audit: An independent review of automated decision-making systems to detect bias, ensure fairness, and verify accountability.

Resilience-by-Design: A principle of building digital systems with redundancy, offline capability, and disaster recovery to ensure continuity in crises.

Digital Sovereignty: The capacity of a nation to control and govern its own digital infrastructure, data flows, and technology standards without overdependence on foreign platforms or vendors.

Inclusive Design: A design philosophy that proactively addresses barriers related to language, literacy, disability, gender, and cultural diversity, ensuring digital systems are usable by all segments of society.

RegTech (Regulatory Technology): Technology-driven solutions that help governments and regulators monitor compliance, automate reporting, and enforce safeguards in digital ecosystems.

Tokenization: The process of replacing sensitive data (e.g., account numbers or IDs) with unique tokens, enhancing security while enabling efficient data exchange.

Digital Twins: Virtual replicas of infrastructure, ecosystems, or even populations, used for simulation, monitoring, and policy planning in digital governance.

Chapter 4
Artificial Intelligence and Blockchain as a Driver of Job Creation

Anuradha Phadnis
https://orcid.org/0000-0002-3387-9520
Indira Global School of Business, Pune, India

Syed Hassan Imam Gardezi
https://orcid.org/0009-0006-6171-1238
Union Investments LLC, UAE

Jyothi Pawar
Sri Balaji University, Pune, India

Sweta Banerjee
https://orcid.org/0000-0001-9987-9067
Sri Balaji University, Pune, India

P. Selvakumar
https://orcid.org/0000-0002-3650-4548
Department of Science and Humanities, Nehru Institute of Technology, Coimbatore, India

S. Madhu
https://orcid.org/0009-0000-8816-5798
Jyothy Institute of Commerce and Management, India

ABSTRACT

The intersection of Artificial Intelligence (AI) and blockchain technology is reshaping not only industries but also labor markets, offering new pathways for job creation and transforming the nature of work itself. As digital transformation accelerates across sectors, the integration of these two disruptive technologies—AI with its capability to mimic human cognition, and blockchain with its secure, decentralized data handling—has introduced both opportunities and challenges for employment. While there has been considerable concern about automation displacing jobs, a deeper exploration reveals that AI and blockchain are also engines of job creation, fostering entirely new roles, industries, and business models. Understanding how this dual force operates requires unpacking both the technologies' fundamental

DOI: 10.4018/979-8-3373-6380-6.ch004

principles and the ecosystems they enable. AI, at its core, involves the development of algorithms and models that allow machines to perform tasks that would typically require human intelligence.

UNDERSTANDING THE ROLE OF AI AND BLOCKCHAIN IN JOB CREATION

The intersection of Artificial Intelligence (AI) and blockchain technology is reshaping not only industries but also labor markets, offering new pathways for job creation and transforming the nature of work itself. As digital transformation accelerates across sectors, the integration of these two disruptive technologies—AI with its capability to mimic human cognition, and blockchain with its secure, decentralized data handling—has introduced both opportunities and challenges for employment. While there has been considerable concern about automation displacing jobs, a deeper exploration reveals that AI and blockchain are also engines of job creation, fostering entirely new roles, industries, and business models. Understanding how this dual force operates requires unpacking both the technologies' fundamental principles and the ecosystems they enable. AI, at its core, involves the development of algorithms and models that allow machines to perform tasks that would typically require human intelligence. These include decision-making, pattern recognition, language processing, and even creativity. On the other hand, blockchain is a distributed ledger technology that ensures transparent, immutable, and secure record-keeping without the need for centralized authorities. When combined, these technologies reinforce each other: AI enhances the efficiency and intelligence of blockchain systems, while blockchain adds trust, transparency, and auditability to AI outputs. Together, they are spawning hybrid systems that underpin emerging sectors such as decentralized finance (DeFi), autonomous supply chains, digital identity verification, and smart legal contracts—all of which demand human expertise to build, maintain, and evolve.

One of the foundational ways AI and blockchain create jobs is through the development and maintenance of infrastructure. Skilled professionals such as data scientists, machine learning engineers, AI researchers, blockchain developers, cryptographers, and smart contract auditors are in high demand. These roles require advanced knowledge of programming, mathematics, and cybersecurity, reflecting a shift in labor demand toward highly skilled, technical work. The growth in decentralized application (dApp) development, NFT platforms, AI-driven healthcare tools, and digital asset exchanges illustrates how these technologies are fueling a demand for talent that did not exist a decade ago. Startups and enterprises alike are hiring not only technical staff but also project managers, compliance officers, legal experts, and product designers who can navigate the regulatory, ethical, and user-experience challenges associated with these emerging systems. Beyond core technical roles, AI and blockchain are also catalyzing job growth in peripheral and supporting industries. As businesses integrate AI-blockchain solutions, they require professionals who can train and manage AI systems, curate data, assess blockchain governance models, conduct impact assessments, and handle customer engagement. For instance, the rise of AI in customer support has led to a surge in demand for chatbot trainers, UX designers, and conversational AI specialists. Similarly, blockchain-based platforms dealing with identity, logistics, or finance require people to manage ecosystem partnerships, onboard users, conduct tokenomics analyses, and educate stakeholders. In sectors such as agriculture, education, energy, and real estate, tailored AI-blockchain implementations are creating niche job categories—like agricultural data modelers, energy tokenization analysts, or AI-driven edtech consultants—blending domain expertise with technological fluency.

The Impact of AI and Blockchain on Employment Opportunities

The integration of Artificial Intelligence (AI) and blockchain technologies is redefining the employment landscape, generating far-reaching impacts on how jobs are created, transformed, or even made obsolete. (Banala S. et al. 2025) These two transformative forces are not only catalyzing industrial revolutions but also reshaping the very fabric of global labor markets. On one hand, AI enables automation, intelligent decision-making, and unprecedented efficiency across sectors, while blockchain ensures decentralized, secure, and transparent data systems. Together, their synergy is bringing about a paradigm shift in employment opportunities, simultaneously disrupting traditional job structures and spawning a vast array of novel roles, professions, and income streams. The impact is multidimensional—ranging from the emergence of new high-skilled jobs and entrepreneurial ventures to the reconfiguration of job categories, shifts in required skillsets, and the democratization of work in decentralized environments. AI is already being deployed across diverse industries—finance, healthcare, education, logistics, retail, entertainment, agriculture, manufacturing, and beyond—to automate processes, extract insights from data, personalize user experiences, and predict outcomes. This automation, while improving efficiency, can displace certain types of jobs, especially those involving repetitive, rule-based tasks such as data entry, basic customer service, and routine manufacturing. At the same time, the deployment of AI systems creates demand for new roles such as data scientists, machine learning engineers, AI ethicists, and algorithm auditors. These positions often require advanced technical competencies, opening up high-paying opportunities for workers equipped with relevant digital skills. Similarly, as blockchain systems gain adoption in areas like supply chain management, identity verification, finance, and contract automation, there is an increasing need for blockchain developers, cryptographers, smart contract engineers, and cybersecurity specialists. As a result, while some low-skill or routine jobs may decline, a new tier of employment opportunities is flourishing, particularly in technology development and system maintenance.

Importantly, AI and blockchain are not limited to back-end technical roles. Their implementation also necessitates an ecosystem of professionals to ensure ethical, regulatory, operational, and human-centric integration. For example, AI systems must be audited for fairness, bias, and accountability, requiring roles like AI ethics consultants, governance analysts, and legal advisors. (Banala S. et al. 2025) Blockchain, particularly in areas involving decentralized finance (DeFi) or non-fungible tokens (NFTs), demands expertise in regulatory compliance, tokenomics, digital asset management, and community building. Furthermore, these technologies often require cross-disciplinary collaboration, thereby giving rise to hybrid roles—such as fintech strategists, AI-powered healthcare consultants, edtech innovators, and decentralized governance architects—that blend domain-specific knowledge with technological fluency. The proliferation of such hybrid roles is expanding employment opportunities beyond traditional disciplinary boundaries, making space for professionals from humanities, law, education, design, and business to contribute to technology-driven innovation. Moreover, AI and blockchain are fostering entirely new business models that are fueling entrepreneurial growth and job creation. Startups are leveraging AI for everything from predictive analytics and autonomous vehicles to personalized marketing and automated legal services. At the same time, blockchain is enabling peer-to-peer marketplaces, tokenized economies, decentralized applications (dApps), and smart contracts that automate business logic and payments. These innovations are removing intermediaries and reducing entry barriers, allowing individuals to monetize their skills, launch businesses, and participate in global markets. For instance, a digital artist can now use blockchain to authenticate and sell NFTs directly to buyers, while a developer can earn cryptocurrency by contributing code to decentralized open-source projects. This democratization of entrepreneurship is particularly impactful in emerging economies, where traditional employment infrastructures are underdeveloped. By enabling trustless transactions and verifiable digital identities, blockchain and AI open up employment opportunities to a global workforce, reducing dependence on centralized institutions.

AI Applications in Emerging Industries: New Job Opportunities

The proliferation of Artificial Intelligence (AI) technologies is revolutionizing emerging industries and giving rise to an unprecedented wave of job opportunities. As AI evolves from a theoretical concept to a transformative force, its applications are driving innovation across sectors that are still developing or rapidly evolving—such as renewable energy, digital health, space technology, precision agriculture, smart manufacturing, edtech, fintech, and creative media. (Upadhyaya A. N. et al. 2025) These industries are integrating AI-driven systems to boost productivity, personalize services, optimize resource allocation, and automate complex processes, thereby fundamentally reshaping the nature and structure of employment. What distinguishes AI's influence in emerging sectors is not merely the replacement of routine tasks but the enabling of entirely new business models, professions, and collaborative ecosystems that would have been unimaginable a decade ago. One of the most dynamic examples of AI's application in an emerging industry is digital health and biotechnology. AI-powered tools are now being employed for disease detection, medical imaging interpretation, personalized medicine, drug discovery, and virtual care. Machine learning models trained on vast datasets can identify patterns in patient health data, predict disease progression, and assist clinicians in making data-driven decisions. (Upadhyaya A. N. et al. 2025) This paradigm shift has resulted in the rise of roles such as biomedical data scientists, AI health algorithm developers, clinical informatics specialists, and digital diagnostics engineers. These professionals are tasked with developing, testing, and deploying AI models while ensuring compliance with regulatory standards and ethical guidelines. Simultaneously, demand has grown for health technology educators, digital wellness coaches, and telehealth coordinators who help bridge the gap between high-tech systems and human-centered care. As AI continues to revolutionize healthcare delivery, the employment landscape is expanding to include multidisciplinary experts with skills in medicine, AI, software engineering, and ethics.

Similarly, renewable energy and climate technology are emerging fields where AI is unlocking new possibilities. (Nisha Angeline M. et al. 2025) Smart energy grids powered by AI can forecast energy demand, manage distribution, and optimize renewable inputs like solar and wind energy. In energy trading markets, AI algorithms enable real-time analytics and predictive pricing models. These innovations are creating roles for renewable energy data analysts, grid optimization engineers, AI-based energy efficiency consultants, and sustainable infrastructure designers. (Nisha Angeline M. et al. 2025) Additionally, climate scientists are now working with AI to model climate patterns, assess risk, and design interventions. In urban planning and environmental monitoring, AI applications generate demand for geospatial analysts, environmental AI engineers, and sustainability technologists. By integrating AI into climate-focused industries, organizations are not only enhancing operational efficiency but also creating green jobs that align with global sustainability goals. In the realm of precision agriculture, AI is transforming traditional farming into a data-intensive, high-efficiency enterprise. Technologies such as drone-based monitoring, automated irrigation systems, AI-powered yield prediction, and crop disease diagnostics are enhancing productivity while minimizing environmental impact. These developments have led to the creation of specialized roles like agritech AI developers, precision farming analysts, drone operation managers, and agricultural robotics engineers. Moreover, agricultural cooperatives, NGOs, and startups are hiring AI literacy trainers to educate farmers on how to use mobile-based AI tools. As the global demand for food increases and the agricultural sector faces pressures from climate change and resource scarcity, AI's integration ensures the generation of both direct and ancillary employment opportunities across rural and urban economies.

AI-Powered Entrepreneurship: Creating New Business Models

The advent of Artificial Intelligence (AI) has redefined the entrepreneurial landscape, unlocking unprecedented opportunities for innovation, disruption, and value creation. As a transformative general-purpose technology, AI is not merely an enabler of efficiency or automation—it is a powerful catalyst for developing entirely new business models, reshaping traditional industries, and fostering entrepreneurial ecosystems that are agile, data-driven, and scalable. (Coates J. M. et al. 2025) From solopreneurs building intelligent tools to startups revolutionizing global markets, AI-powered entrepreneurship represents a paradigm shift where data, algorithms, and human creativity converge to generate adaptive, personalized, and highly responsive products and services. As entrepreneurs leverage AI's capabilities to solve complex problems, the structure, strategies, and scope of businesses are undergoing radical evolution. One of the foundational changes AI brings to entrepreneurship is the ability to create data-centric and intelligence-driven business models. Unlike traditional enterprises that rely on human judgment and linear planning, AI-driven startups use algorithms to collect, process, and interpret massive datasets in real time. (Coates J. M. et al. 2025) This ability to generate actionable insights from diverse data streams enables entrepreneurs to identify market gaps, predict consumer behavior, and iterate products rapidly based on feedback. For instance, AI-driven market research platforms help entrepreneurs understand emerging trends, segment audiences, and test product-market fit with far greater precision and speed. As a result, the entrepreneurial process becomes more scientific, reducing risk and increasing the likelihood of success in competitive markets.

AI also enables hyper-personalization at scale, a capability that has given rise to new consumer-focused business models in sectors such as retail, health, education, and entertainment. AI systems analyze individual user data to tailor recommendations, services, and content dynamically. Startups like Stitch Fix, Duolingo, and Spotify use machine learning algorithms to personalize experiences for millions of users—transforming how products are consumed and monetized. (Chowdhary S. et al. 2025) Entrepreneurs can now launch platforms that cater to niche audiences with individualized services, a model known as the "segment of one." This has led to the rise of AI-powered personalized wellness apps, customized learning platforms, intelligent news aggregators, and tailored financial planning tools, each representing a sustainable business model rooted in continuous user engagement and algorithmic adaptation. In the B2B space, AI is enabling automation-as-a-service and AI-as-a-service (AIaaS) models, where entrepreneurs build tools that automate repetitive tasks, enhance decision-making, or streamline operations for other businesses. These platforms, which often rely on APIs and cloud-based AI engines, provide intelligent capabilities such as customer segmentation, invoice processing, supply chain forecasting, and anomaly detection. (Chowdhary S. et al. 2025) AI-based SaaS startups—like Gong, which analyzes sales conversations, or UiPath, which builds robotic process automation bots—offer modular, scalable services to enterprises seeking digital transformation. These ventures capitalize on subscription or usage-based revenue models, lowering entry barriers for clients while ensuring steady income streams for entrepreneurs. In this framework, AI becomes a commodity that can be embedded into any business workflow, turning intelligence into a monetizable resource.

Upskilling and Reskilling for AI-Driven Jobs

As Artificial Intelligence (AI) continues to transform the global labor market, the need for upskilling and reskilling has become not only a strategic priority but also a societal imperative. (Limbore N. V. et al. 2025) AI-driven disruption is reshaping how work is performed, who performs it, and what skills are most valuable in the digital economy. While AI automates repetitive and routine tasks across various sectors—ranging from manufacturing and logistics to finance and customer service—it simultaneously generates demand for new competencies that combine technical literacy, critical thinking, creativity, and adaptability. In this rapidly evolving context, upskilling and reskilling efforts are central to ensuring that individuals, organizations, and entire nations can navigate the transition toward an AI-powered future with resilience, inclusivity, and economic viability. (Limbore N. V. et al. 2025) Upskilling refers to the process of building upon existing skills to adapt to more advanced or AI-integrated roles, while reskilling involves learning entirely new competencies to transition into different job functions or industries. Both are essential responses to the dynamic demands of the AI-driven economy. As businesses increasingly embed AI technologies into their core operations—such as predictive analytics, intelligent automation, natural language processing, machine learning, and computer vision—there is a growing need for employees who can work alongside AI systems, interpret data insights, and contribute to the design, deployment, and oversight of AI tools. The World Economic Forum, among other global bodies, has emphasized that over a billion people will require upskilling or reskilling by the end of this decade to stay relevant in their careers and to meet the labor needs of the Fourth Industrial Revolution.

One of the most significant drivers of upskilling in the AI era is the widespread adoption of digital technologies across traditional sectors. (Mehra J. et al. 2025) Manufacturing firms are implementing smart robotics and AI-powered quality control; logistics companies are using route optimization algorithms; banks and insurers are deploying AI for risk modeling, fraud detection, and customer engagement; healthcare providers are integrating AI for diagnostics and virtual care. (Mehra J. et al. 2025) In these contexts, existing workers—be they factory technicians, financial analysts, nurses, or logistics coordinators—must acquire new competencies that enable them to work effectively in AI-augmented environments. For instance, a manufacturing worker may need training in robot maintenance or digital twins; a financial advisor may require proficiency in AI-based investment platforms; a healthcare professional may benefit from learning how to interpret AI-generated diagnostic recommendations. These are examples of targeted upskilling that enhances performance, improves job security, and fosters career advancement. Simultaneously, reskilling is vital for workers whose roles are at high risk of displacement due to AI automation. Jobs that consist primarily of routine, repetitive, and predictable tasks—such as data entry, telemarketing, basic accounting, or manual assembly line work—are particularly vulnerable. For individuals in these positions, transitioning into new job roles through reskilling programs offers a pathway to sustainable employment. Governments, employers, and educational institutions are increasingly offering reskilling programs that focus on in-demand roles such as data analysts, cybersecurity specialists, cloud computing professionals, AI model trainers, digital marketers, and UX designers. These programs often combine technical training with soft skills development, project-based learning, and real-world application to ensure learners can effectively adapt to new job contexts.

Blockchain Applications in Various Industries: Job Creation

The emergence of blockchain technology has significantly impacted multiple industries, reshaping business processes and catalyzing new waves of job creation across both traditional and digitally native sectors. (Avalekar U. A. et al. 2025) Originally conceptualized as the backbone of cryptocurrencies like Bitcoin, blockchain has since evolved into a foundational technology with far-reaching implications beyond digital assets. At its core, blockchain is a decentralized, immutable, and transparent digital ledger that facilitates trustless transactions and verifiable record-keeping across distributed networks. As industries increasingly integrate blockchain into their operations, a broad spectrum of employment opportunities is emerging—spanning technical, managerial, regulatory, creative, and educational roles. This shift is transforming the nature of work in finance, healthcare, supply chain, real estate, energy, entertainment, government, and more, resulting in not only new job titles but also entirely new career trajectories and entrepreneurial ventures. In the financial sector, blockchain has laid the groundwork for decentralized finance (DeFi), digital asset exchanges, and tokenized investment platforms. (Avalekar U. A. et al. 2025) These innovations are enabling peer-to-peer lending, automated market making, decentralized insurance, and real-time settlements—reducing dependence on intermediaries and increasing efficiency and transparency. As a result, job roles such as DeFi protocol developers, smart contract engineers, blockchain analysts, tokenomics consultants, and crypto compliance officers have become highly sought-after. Additionally, financial institutions that are adopting blockchain for internal processes, such as cross-border payments, identity verification, and anti-money laundering (AML) tracking, are hiring blockchain integration specialists, cybersecurity experts, and blockchain auditors. These roles require a blend of traditional finance knowledge and blockchain fluency, opening the door for both upskilled professionals and new entrants to the workforce.

Figure 1. Benefits of combining AI and Blockchain

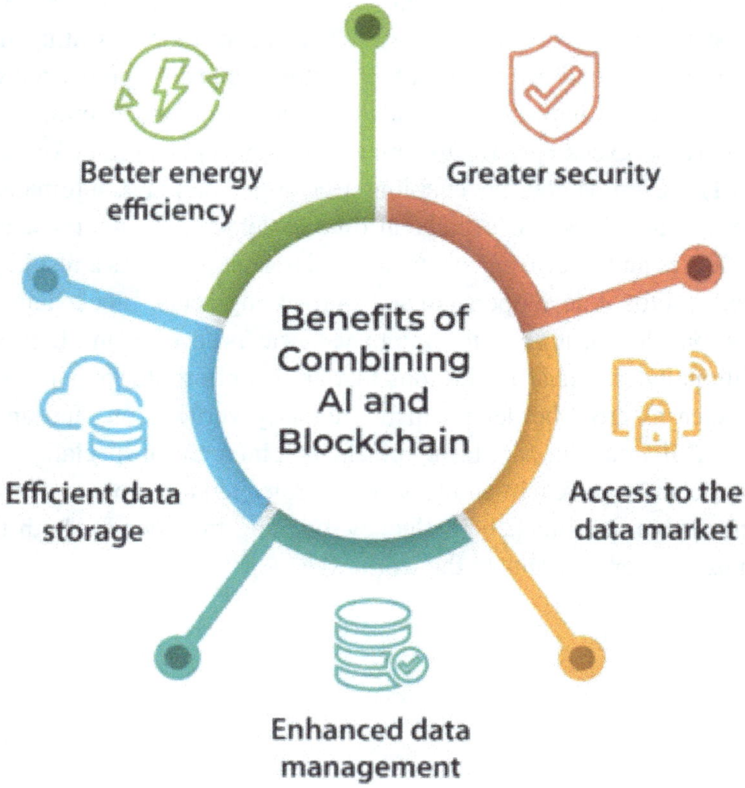

The supply chain and logistics industry is also being transformed by blockchain's capabilities in traceability, transparency, and automation. Companies are using blockchain to track goods from origin to destination, verify product authenticity, prevent counterfeiting, and ensure ethical sourcing. (Sarwer M. H. et al. 2022) For example, food supply chains can use blockchain to verify organic certification and expiration data, while the fashion industry can track materials for sustainability reporting. This has created demand for supply chain blockchain architects, logistics analysts with blockchain expertise, digital ledger project managers, traceability system developers, and implementation consultants. Governments and regulatory bodies are also exploring blockchain for customs and trade documentation, creating job opportunities for blockchain policy advisors and international trade technologists. As blockchain solutions become more prevalent in global commerce, job creation expands across both technology providers and end-user industries. In healthcare, blockchain is revolutionizing data management, patient privacy, and pharmaceutical supply chains. By allowing secure and interoperable medical records, blockchain ensures patient data is tamper-proof, accessible only with consent, and transferable across healthcare providers. Pharmaceutical companies are leveraging blockchain to authenticate drugs and combat counterfeit medicines. These applications are creating roles for healthcare blockchain developers, digital health consultants, medical data integrity officers, compliance specialists, and blockchain-enabled patient platform designers. (Sarwer M. H. et al. 2022) Hospitals, insurers, and telehealth providers require professionals who understand both healthcare regulations and blockchain infrastructure, facilitating a convergence of medical and technological expertise that generates cross-disciplinary employment opportunities.

Blockchain-Based Entrepreneurship: New Opportunities: Blockchain entrepreneurship.

The rise of blockchain technology has ushered in a new era of entrepreneurship characterized by decentralization, transparency, and digital ownership. Entrepreneurs are leveraging blockchain to create novel business models, disrupt traditional industries, and tap into global markets without the need for centralized intermediaries. (Pandey A. et al. 2025) As blockchain evolves beyond its foundational role in cryptocurrencies like Bitcoin and Ethereum, it now serves as the infrastructure for a wide range of applications—from decentralized finance (DeFi) and digital identity to tokenized assets and Web3 ecosystems. This transformation is enabling a new breed of blockchain-based entrepreneurship, where startups, individual creators, and communities alike are empowered to launch decentralized platforms, issue native tokens, and build permissionless systems that challenge the status quo. One of the most impactful developments in blockchain entrepreneurship is the emergence of Decentralized Finance (DeFi). DeFi refers to financial services—such as lending, borrowing, trading, and insurance—offered through decentralized platforms that operate autonomously via smart contracts. Entrepreneurs have launched DeFi protocols that eliminate intermediaries like banks, enabling peer-to-peer transactions on blockchain networks. (Pandey A. et al. 2025) These ventures not only democratize access to financial services but also offer new income-generating mechanisms such as yield farming, liquidity mining, and staking. Founders of DeFi startups need not rely on traditional venture capital; instead, they can bootstrap their projects through Initial Coin Offerings (ICOs), Initial DEX Offerings (IDOs), or token sales, attracting a global user base and funding community.

Another transformative avenue is the tokenization of assets, which allows entrepreneurs to digitize ownership of real-world and digital assets on blockchain. (Agarwal J. D. et al. 2021) From real estate and fine art to intellectual property and commodities, tokenization enables fractional ownership, enhances liquidity, and broadens access to investment opportunities. Startups are creating token marketplaces, custody solutions, and smart contract protocols that facilitate compliant asset tokenization. Entrepreneurs can tokenize equity, revenue streams, or project governance rights, offering investors a transparent and secure method of engagement. (Agarwal J. D. et al. 2021) This is particularly beneficial for small businesses and creators who may otherwise face barriers to capital markets. Non-Fungible Tokens (NFTs) have unlocked massive opportunities for entrepreneurship in the creative economy. By enabling digital scarcity and provable ownership, NFTs allow artists, musicians, writers, and game developers to monetize their content directly and maintain control over royalties. Platforms such as OpenSea, Rarible, and Foundation have enabled a wave of NFT creators and collectors, while new ventures have emerged to build NFT infrastructure, marketplaces, tools, and services. Blockchain entrepreneurs are also exploring utility NFTs, which offer real-world benefits such as event access, merchandise, and exclusive community memberships. The play-to-earn (P2E) and create-to-earn (C2E) models further incentivize user participation, spawning entrepreneurial ecosystems around NFT gaming and metaverse experiences.

Blockchain-Related Jobs: Development, Implementation, and Management: Blockchain jobs.

The rapid advancement and adoption of blockchain technology have given rise to a wide array of job opportunities across various sectors, fundamentally reshaping the employment landscape. (Owotemu A. E. et al. 2025) Blockchain-related jobs encompass a spectrum of roles involving development, implementation, and management, requiring diverse skill sets that blend technical proficiency, business acumen, and strategic oversight. As more industries—from finance and healthcare to logistics and government—integrate blockchain solutions to enhance transparency, security, and efficiency, the demand for professionals with blockchain expertise is surging. These roles not only offer high salaries and international exposure but also provide opportunities to work on innovative, decentralized, and future-forward projects that challenge conventional systems. At the core of blockchain careers lies the role of the Blockchain Developer, one of the most sought-after and foundational positions in the field. These professionals are responsible for designing, coding, and maintaining blockchain protocols, building smart contracts, and developing decentralized applications (dApps) that run on blockchain networks. There are two primary types of blockchain developers: core blockchain developers, who focus on protocol-level development and architecture, and blockchain software developers, who create apps and interfaces that interact with existing blockchain platforms. (Owotemu A. E. et al. 2025) Proficiency in programming languages such as Solidity (for Ethereum), Rust, Go, JavaScript, and Python is essential. Developers must also understand cryptography, consensus algorithms, peer-to-peer networking, and the specific workings of platforms like Ethereum, Solana, or Hyperledger.

Closely related are Smart Contract Engineers, who specialize in writing, testing, and deploying smart contracts—self-executing code that facilitates transactions or enforces rules on the blockchain. (Hussain A. A. et al. 2021) These engineers must ensure that smart contracts are secure, gas-efficient, and bug-free, as exploits or errors in smart contract logic can lead to catastrophic financial losses. Auditing smart contracts for vulnerabilities is another critical task, often carried out by dedicated Blockchain Security Analysts or Auditors, who conduct formal verifications and penetration testing to safeguard the integrity of blockchain systems. Another vital job category in the blockchain domain is Blockchain Solution Architect. These professionals bridge the gap between business needs and technical implementation by designing end-to-end blockchain solutions for enterprises. They assess organizational requirements, choose appropriate blockchain platforms, define system architecture, and ensure interoperability with existing infrastructure. (Hussain A. A. et al. 2021) Blockchain architects must also navigate trade-offs between decentralization, scalability, privacy, and performance. They often collaborate with developers, UX designers, legal teams, and product managers to deliver cohesive solutions tailored to specific industry use cases. Blockchain Project Managers play a central role in overseeing the successful execution of blockchain initiatives. They coordinate cross-functional teams, manage timelines, track deliverables, and communicate progress to stakeholders. Project managers must understand blockchain concepts deeply enough to make informed decisions and troubleshoot roadblocks, while also ensuring compliance with industry standards and regulations. Agile methodologies, such as Scrum and Kanban, are frequently employed in blockchain projects due to their iterative and collaborative nature.

Emerging Job Roles in AI and Blockchain: Emerging job roles.

The convergence of Artificial Intelligence (AI) and Blockchain technologies has not only transformed traditional industries but also spawned a new generation of job roles that were virtually nonexistent a decade ago. (Wang Z. et al. 2022) These emerging job roles are reshaping the global employment landscape, requiring interdisciplinary skill sets that blend data science, software engineering, distributed computing, cybersecurity, ethics, economics, and regulatory compliance. As organizations across sectors recognize the disruptive potential of AI and blockchain, the demand for specialized talent capable of navigating this technological frontier has grown exponentially. These roles are dynamic, often remote-friendly, and open to global participation, creating opportunities for innovation, entrepreneurship, and inclusive economic growth. At the forefront of this revolution is the AI Blockchain Engineer, a hybrid professional skilled in designing systems that integrate AI algorithms with blockchain protocols. This role involves developing smart contracts that can autonomously execute decisions based on AI-driven data analysis, as well as ensuring data provenance, privacy, and auditability through decentralized architectures. (Wang Z. et al. 2022) These engineers must understand machine learning frameworks such as TensorFlow, PyTorch, or scikit-learn, alongside blockchain platforms like Ethereum, Hyperledger Fabric, or Polkadot. They also need proficiency in programming languages like Python, Solidity, and Rust. AI Blockchain Engineers are crucial in industries such as supply chain, healthcare, and finance, where AI-driven insights must be securely and transparently recorded on blockchain networks.

A closely related emerging role is the Decentralized AI Developer, who focuses on creating AI models that operate on decentralized infrastructure, such as federated learning systems or edge computing devices. (Patnaik B. C. M. et al. 2025) These developers work to eliminate centralized data silos by building AI systems that learn from distributed datasets without compromising privacy. Blockchain technology is often used to manage identity, incentivize data sharing, and track model performance. This role is essential in privacy-sensitive fields like personalized medicine, autonomous vehicles, and smart cities, where data ownership and security are paramount. (Patnaik B. C. M. et al. 2025) As decentralized data becomes a cornerstone of future digital economies, the Data Tokenization Expert has emerged as a key figure in designing systems that convert data into digital assets. These professionals are responsible for creating data token models that allow users to monetize their personal or enterprise data while retaining control. Data Tokenization Experts work at the intersection of AI, blockchain, and digital rights management, ensuring that data is accurately valued, securely transferred, and used ethically. Their work enables the rise of data marketplaces and supports AI model training with verified, user-consented datasets. Another vital emerging role is the AI Ethics Officer for Decentralized Systems, who ensures that AI algorithms integrated with blockchain comply with ethical standards, legal norms, and social expectations. These professionals evaluate AI fairness, transparency, and accountability while also assessing the ethical implications of immutable data storage and decentralized governance. With concerns around surveillance, bias, and algorithmic discrimination rising, this role is critical to fostering responsible innovation in AI-blockchain applications. It is especially relevant for public sector deployments, humanitarian initiatives, and social-impact technologies.

New Industries and Business Models: New industries.

The integration of Artificial Intelligence (AI) and Blockchain technologies has catalyzed the emergence of entirely new industries and business models, reshaping the global economic landscape and redefining how value is created, exchanged, and managed. These technologies, each transformative in their own right, are synergistic when combined—AI brings intelligence and automation, while blockchain ensures trust, transparency, and decentralized governance. (Kwok A. O. et al. 2024) This confluence has given rise to innovative industries and ecosystems that were once unimaginable, driving economic diversification, enhancing productivity, and empowering a new generation of digital entrepreneurs and creators. One of the most prominent industries born out of this fusion is Decentralized Finance (DeFi). DeFi represents a paradigm shift in financial services, eliminating traditional intermediaries like banks and enabling peer-to-peer financial transactions via smart contracts on blockchain platforms. (Kwok A. O. et al. 2024) AI enhances DeFi by optimizing lending protocols, automating risk assessments, detecting fraudulent activities, and managing algorithmic trading strategies. AI-driven credit scoring models analyze user behavior and on-chain history, allowing individuals without traditional financial records to access loans and insurance products. Meanwhile, blockchain ensures that all transactions are transparent, auditable, and resistant to tampering. Together, they create an open, inclusive financial system that challenges the centralization of legacy banking institutions.

Another groundbreaking industry is the Tokenized Data Economy, where data is treated as a valuable digital asset. (Johnson M. et al. 2021) Powered by blockchain, individuals and organizations can tokenize their data—whether personal, behavioral, or sensor-generated—and trade it in decentralized marketplaces. AI plays a vital role by analyzing this data for predictive modeling, personalized services, and automated decision-making. This model empowers data owners to retain control over their information, monetize it, and contribute to AI training processes without compromising privacy. (Johnson M. et al. 2021) Industries such as healthcare, advertising, mobility, and smart cities are embracing this model to unlock the economic potential of big data while respecting user consent and data sovereignty. The convergence has also given rise to the AI-as-a-Service (AIaaS) on Blockchain industry. This model democratizes access to AI capabilities by allowing users to access AI tools, models, and computation on demand through blockchain-based platforms. Blockchain ensures transparent usage tracking, secure micropayments, and fair revenue sharing with model creators. This has enabled small businesses, developers, and researchers to leverage powerful AI services without needing extensive infrastructure. Additionally, federated learning systems built on blockchain enable collaborative AI development without centralized control, preserving privacy and encouraging wider participation from diverse stakeholders. In the realm of Digital Identity and Reputation Systems, new models are emerging that leverage AI for behavior analysis and blockchain for verifiable credentials. These systems allow individuals and organizations to build decentralized digital identities composed of attributes, history, and endorsements validated on-chain. AI algorithms can continuously update reputational scores based on transactional behavior, contributions, and feedback across various platforms. Such models are essential in gig economies, freelancing platforms, DAOs (Decentralized Autonomous Organizations), and online marketplaces where trust and accountability are paramount. They also provide underserved populations with access to formal digital identities, unlocking new economic opportunities.

The Gig Economy and Freelance Opportunities: Gig economy.

The gig economy, defined by short-term, flexible, and task-based employment, has undergone a dramatic transformation with the integration of Artificial Intelligence (AI) and Blockchain technologies. (Bhumichai D. et al. 2024) Traditionally characterized by freelancers, independent contractors, and part-time workers providing services across sectors such as transportation, hospitality, and digital services, the gig economy is now evolving into a more intelligent, decentralized, and inclusive ecosystem. This transformation is being fueled by the technological capabilities of AI to match, manage, and optimize labor, and blockchain's ability to foster transparency, security, and trust without the need for centralized intermediaries. Together, these technologies are reshaping the nature of work, expanding the range of freelance opportunities, and creating a new paradigm in employment that is more dynamic, globally connected, and economically empowering. AI is at the forefront of driving efficiency and innovation in the gig economy. (Bhumichai D. et al. 2024) Intelligent algorithms power job-matching platforms that analyze worker profiles, performance history, client reviews, and preferences to recommend the most relevant projects or gigs. Natural language processing (NLP) enables automatic parsing of resumes, job descriptions, and communication between clients and freelancers. AI-powered tools also assist in pricing optimization by analyzing market trends and individual skill levels, enabling freelancers to competitively price their services. Moreover, AI facilitates remote work by automating tasks such as transcription, translation, graphic design, and content creation, allowing freelancers to scale their productivity without requiring large teams or infrastructure. These advancements significantly enhance the user experience, reduce inefficiencies in hiring, and lower entry barriers for workers from diverse backgrounds.

Furthermore, AI has spawned entirely new freelance domains. Data labeling for machine learning models, AI model training supervision, synthetic data generation, chatbot development, virtual assistant services, and content moderation are just a few of the novel jobs emerging as AI becomes more prevalent. (Ahmed I. et al. 2022) Freelancers are increasingly engaging in these high-value roles that contribute directly to the AI development pipeline. Freelancers also leverage generative AI tools for creativity in writing, music production, video editing, and game development, enabling them to offer high-quality digital products without extensive technical expertise. This democratization of advanced capabilities empowers freelancers to become micro-entrepreneurs, offering premium services and generating multiple revenue streams. (Ahmed I. et al. 2022) On the other hand, blockchain technology addresses some of the longstanding challenges faced by gig workers—particularly issues related to trust, payment delays, contract enforcement, and verification. Through smart contracts, blockchain ensures that freelancers are paid automatically and promptly upon task completion, with conditions coded into immutable agreements that execute without human intervention. This eliminates dependency on centralized platforms that may withhold payments, charge high fees, or impose opaque rules. Additionally, blockchain-based platforms allow for peer-to-peer engagements where clients and freelancers interact directly, reducing administrative overhead and enhancing transparency. One of the most impactful applications of blockchain in the gig economy is the creation of decentralized freelance marketplaces such as Braintrust, LaborX, and Ethlance. These platforms operate without central authorities and allow users to maintain ownership of their work history, ratings, and credentials. By eliminating intermediaries, freelancers receive a greater share of their earnings while clients access talent at lower costs. Blockchain also enables the creation of verifiable digital identities and reputational systems, which are critical for building trust in a trustless digital environment. Workers can port their records across platforms, retaining control over their professional history and reputational capital regardless of platform changes or policies.

Skills Required for AI and Blockchain Jobs: Required skills.

As artificial intelligence (AI) and blockchain technologies increasingly transform industries and economies, the demand for a skilled workforce that can develop, implement, and manage these systems is rapidly growing. (Kalai M. et al. 2024) These jobs require a multidisciplinary blend of technical, analytical, and soft skills, spanning computer science, mathematics, cybersecurity, data science, cryptography, business, and design. While AI and blockchain each have distinct technological foundations, there is significant overlap in the skillsets needed to thrive in this evolving job market. Individuals aiming to build successful careers in these domains must possess both foundational knowledge and the ability to adapt to rapid technological change. Moreover, as these technologies evolve, so too must the workforce—requiring a continuous commitment to upskilling and lifelong learning. At the heart of AI jobs lie strong programming capabilities. (Kalai M. et al. 2024) Proficiency in languages such as Python, R, and Java is essential for implementing algorithms, data pipelines, and machine learning models. Python, in particular, is the de facto language for AI development due to its extensive libraries such as TensorFlow, PyTorch, Scikit-learn, and Keras, which support a wide range of AI tasks from neural networks to natural language processing. Understanding data structures, object-oriented programming, and software engineering principles are crucial for building scalable AI solutions.

Mathematics and statistics form the theoretical backbone of AI. Knowledge of linear algebra, probability, calculus, optimization, and statistical modeling is vital for understanding how machine learning algorithms work. (Chandrasekaran N. et al. 2019) These skills allow professionals to design and interpret models rather than merely apply existing tools. For deep learning, concepts such as backpropagation, gradient descent, activation functions, and convolutional networks require a strong grounding in advanced mathematical principles. Data handling is another key area. AI professionals must be adept at data collection, cleaning, preprocessing, transformation, and augmentation. Skills in SQL, NoSQL databases, and big data tools like Hadoop and Spark are important for managing and querying large datasets. Additionally, familiarity with cloud platforms such as AWS, Google Cloud, and Azure is increasingly critical as AI workloads are often deployed in cloud environments. Machine learning (ML) and deep learning (DL) expertise are at the core of most AI roles. Candidates must be comfortable with supervised and unsupervised learning techniques, including regression, classification, clustering, recommendation systems, and anomaly detection. For DL, knowledge of architectures like CNNs, RNNs, GANs, transformers, and attention mechanisms is essential for tasks in computer vision, speech recognition, and language modeling. (Chandrasekaran N. et al. 2019) Experience in model evaluation, cross-validation, hyperparameter tuning, and deployment practices ensures that models perform effectively in real-world scenarios. In the blockchain domain, skills in decentralized architecture and distributed computing are foundational. Developers must understand how peer-to-peer networks function, how consensus algorithms (like Proof of Work, Proof of Stake, and Byzantine Fault Tolerance) ensure agreement across nodes, and how distributed ledgers maintain integrity without central control.

Training and Development Programs for AI and Blockchain Professionals: Training programs.

As the demand for skilled professionals in artificial intelligence (AI) and blockchain continues to surge, comprehensive training and development programs have become indispensable in preparing the global workforce to meet the rapidly evolving technological landscape. These programs are designed not only to build foundational knowledge but also to provide hands-on experience, practical exposure, and interdisciplinary expertise needed to succeed in these complex domains. (Khan A. A. et al. 2023) AI and blockchain are no longer niche technologies; they are becoming integral to industries such as finance, healthcare, logistics, education, energy, and public services. Therefore, training and development programs must be holistic, modular, flexible, and accessible—empowering individuals at all career stages, from students and early-career professionals to mid-level executives and entrepreneurs, to acquire and refine the competencies necessary to thrive in the digital economy. Universities around the world are integrating AI and blockchain modules into their degree programs in computer science, engineering, business, law, and data science. Some institutions offer specialized undergraduate and postgraduate degrees in AI, machine learning, data analytics, or distributed ledger technologies. (Khan A. A. et al. 2023) For example, institutions such as MIT, Stanford, Carnegie Mellon, and the University of Oxford have developed world-class curricula that combine theoretical rigor with real-world applications. Blockchain-focused programs often include cryptography, smart contract design, distributed computing, and tokenomics. In contrast, AI programs emphasize machine learning, neural networks, natural language processing, and robotics.

In addition to full-time programs, many universities offer online and part-time professional certificates tailored for working professionals. (Chhibber S. et al. 2025) These academic offerings are often supplemented with capstone projects, internships, and collaborations with industry partners, providing participants with direct exposure to current challenges and opportunities in the field. Collaborative university-industry research centers are also becoming popular, serving as innovation hubs where students and researchers work closely with companies to co-develop AI and blockchain solutions. (Chhibber S. et al. 2025) The rise of massive open online courses (MOOCs) has revolutionized access to AI and blockchain education. Platforms like Coursera, edX, Udacity, FutureLearn, and Khan Academy offer specialized training programs, often developed in collaboration with top universities and technology companies. For AI, popular courses include Andrew Ng's "Machine Learning" on Coursera, MIT's "Introduction to Deep Learning," and Stanford's "CS229: Machine Learning." These courses cover core concepts such as supervised and unsupervised learning, neural networks, model evaluation, reinforcement learning, and AI ethics. For blockchain, MOOCs such as the University at Buffalo's "Blockchain Basics," Princeton's "Bitcoin and Cryptocurrency Technologies," and ConsenSys Academy's "Blockchain Developer Program" are widely recognized. These courses teach essential blockchain principles, including consensus mechanisms, smart contracts, Ethereum, Hyperledger Fabric, and decentralized application (dApp) development.

Lifelong Learning and Continuous Professional Development: Lifelong learning.

In the rapidly evolving landscape of technology, lifelong learning and continuous professional development have emerged as critical imperatives for professionals seeking to remain relevant, agile, and future-ready. (Xuan T. R. et al. 2023) The emergence of artificial intelligence (AI) and blockchain technologies has dramatically transformed industries, business models, and the nature of work itself. As automation, decentralization, and digital innovation accelerate, traditional career trajectories are being redefined, rendering static skill sets obsolete and creating unprecedented demand for ongoing education. Lifelong learning—the continuous, self-motivated pursuit of knowledge and skills across one's lifespan—has become essential not only for career advancement but for professional survival. In the age of AI and blockchain, it is no longer sufficient to master a domain once and apply that knowledge indefinitely; instead, the workforce must cultivate adaptive learning habits, cross-disciplinary competence, and digital fluency through structured and informal learning pathways. The rapid pace of technological innovation, particularly in AI and blockchain, is fundamentally reshaping the skill requirements across virtually all sectors. Job roles are becoming more complex, requiring hybrid expertise that blends technical acumen with soft skills such as creativity, ethical reasoning, communication, and problem-solving. AI is automating repetitive and rule-based tasks, while blockchain is decentralizing systems of trust, governance, and transaction. These forces are disrupting established workflows in finance, healthcare, supply chains, education, legal services, media, and governance. Consequently, professionals in these fields must continuously update their knowledge to work alongside intelligent systems, harness distributed networks, and adapt to new compliance, security, and innovation frameworks.

Lifelong learning enables individuals to proactively respond to these disruptions by re-skilling and up-skilling in real time. It also fosters resilience, employability, and long-term career growth in volatile job markets. Rather than being seen as a reactive measure to job displacement, lifelong learning must be embedded as a proactive and strategic approach to workforce development in the digital age. (Xuan T. R. et al. 2023) Higher education institutions are increasingly redesigning their programs to support lifelong learning. Modular degrees, stackable credentials, and flexible online platforms now allow learners to access education at various life stages without committing to full-time, multi-year programs. Universities offer micro-degrees, postgraduate certificates, and continuing education units in AI, machine learning, blockchain development, data analytics, and related fields. These programs are often updated regularly to reflect the latest technological and industry trends. Moreover, academic institutions are building partnerships with corporations and tech firms to align curriculum with workforce demands. Co-branded learning pathways, such as the MIT xPro in AI and the Oxford Blockchain Strategy Programme, exemplify how traditional educational institutions are adapting to the needs of lifelong learners. They offer flexible schedules, hybrid formats, and industry-relevant projects that cater to mid-career professionals seeking to pivot or grow within their industries. Digital learning platforms have become the cornerstone of lifelong learning ecosystems, democratizing access to high-quality education worldwide. Platforms such as Coursera, edX, Udacity, DataCamp, and LinkedIn Learning offer thousands of courses in AI and blockchain, from beginner to advanced levels. These courses, often created by leading universities or tech companies, cover a wide array of subjects, including deep learning, neural networks, reinforcement learning, natural language processing, computer vision, cryptography, decentralized applications (dApps), smart contracts, and token economics.

The Future of Work: AI and Blockchain-Driven Job Creation: Future of work.

The future of work is undergoing a radical transformation, catalyzed by the dual forces of artificial intelligence (AI) and blockchain technology. (Reilly Marulanda M. S. et al. 2021) These two technological paradigms are not merely disrupting existing job structures—they are fundamentally reimagining how labor is organized, how value is created, and how economic participation is distributed. AI, with its ability to automate cognitive and physical tasks, analyze large datasets, and enable intelligent decision-making, is already augmenting and replacing many traditional roles. Simultaneously, blockchain, with its decentralized and tamper-proof architecture, is introducing new frameworks for trust, transparency, and peer-to-peer interactions across industries. As these technologies mature and converge, they are giving rise to entirely new categories of work, reshaping old ones, and creating innovative opportunities that transcend geographical, institutional, and structural barriers. At the heart of AI and blockchain's impact on the future of work is their capacity to redefine job functions. AI is facilitating automation in areas like manufacturing, logistics, finance, customer service, and even professional services such as law and healthcare. However, this automation does not merely eliminate jobs—it also leads to the emergence of new ones in AI development, algorithm supervision, data annotation, model evaluation, ethics oversight, and human-AI collaboration design. These roles demand not only technical skills but also nuanced understanding of human behavior, domain knowledge, and critical thinking. Blockchain, on the other hand, is transforming roles related to compliance, auditing, transactions, and record-keeping. It is decentralizing trust mechanisms, reducing the need for intermediaries, and enabling direct value exchange. This shift opens up new employment avenues in smart contract development, blockchain architecture, tokenomics, cryptographic security, decentralized finance (DeFi), and governance systems. Moreover, by enabling transparent, peer-verified work histories and credentials, blockchain is also supporting the rise of borderless labor markets and reputation-based employment systems.

The convergence of AI and blockchain is giving birth to hybrid job roles that did not exist a decade ago. Examples include AI ethicists, blockchain legal consultants, machine learning operations (MLOps) engineers, decentralized application (dApp) developers, smart contract auditors, and digital identity architects. (Reilly Marulanda M. S. et al. 2021) These roles combine elements of data science, software engineering, cybersecurity, legal compliance, and business strategy. As demand for these skills increases, educational institutions and training platforms are rapidly evolving to support new career trajectories. In addition to technical roles, there is growing demand for professionals who can bridge technology and business—such as product managers for AI solutions, blockchain business analysts, and innovation strategists. These professionals must understand how to translate complex algorithms and distributed systems into usable products and scalable services, while also addressing regulatory, ethical, and user-experience concerns. Blockchain technology is also paving the way for new models of decentralized work and organizational structures. The rise of decentralized autonomous organizations (DAOs) allows individuals to contribute to projects and earn income without being formally employed by a traditional corporation. Through smart contracts, contributors can be paid instantly and transparently for their work based on pre-agreed terms, reducing dependency on centralized payroll and HR systems. AI supports these decentralized models by enabling automated task distribution, performance tracking, and decision-making within DAOs. As a result, individuals are empowered to engage in multiple projects simultaneously, build diverse income streams, and curate their professional identities in more flexible and autonomous ways. This shift has profound implications for how work is defined, how careers are shaped, and how power is distributed within the economy.

Emerging Trends in AI and Blockchain Job Market: Emerging trends.

The global job market is undergoing a paradigm shift, driven in large part by the accelerating integration of Artificial Intelligence (AI) and blockchain technologies across various sectors. These innovations are not only revolutionizing existing industries but also laying the foundation for entirely new job categories, employment models, and skill demands. As AI becomes increasingly embedded in decision-making, automation, and predictive analytics, and as blockchain reshapes trust, transparency, and decentralization in data and transactions, their combined impact is catalyzing a transformation of labor markets worldwide. (Lokhande M. et al. 2025) The emerging trends in the AI and blockchain job market reflect the convergence of these technologies with economic, social, and organizational transformations, signaling a future where agility, interdisciplinary expertise, and lifelong learning will be key determinants of employability. One of the most defining trends in the AI and blockchain job market is the emergence of hybrid roles that blend technical acumen with domain-specific knowledge. No longer confined to the realm of data scientists or software developers, AI and blockchain roles increasingly require knowledge in finance, healthcare, law, education, supply chain, and other verticals. For instance, the rise of roles like "AI Compliance Officer," "Blockchain Policy Analyst," and "AI-enabled Legal Advisor" highlights the growing need for professionals who can interpret technical solutions within regulatory and sector-specific frameworks. These interdisciplinary roles demand a fusion of computer science fundamentals with ethics, law, sociology, and business strategy, fostering the need for adaptive educational and training programs.

Decentralized Autonomous Organizations (DAOs) are reshaping traditional organizational models by enabling collaborative work without centralized authority. (Lokhande M. et al. 2025) Enabled by smart contracts on blockchain networks, DAOs allow contributors from around the world to participate in decision-making, project execution, and governance based on token-based incentives and voting mechanisms. This trend has created demand for roles such as DAO Facilitator, Governance Strategist, and Token Economist. Simultaneously, blockchain-powered freelancing platforms are supporting decentralized hiring, payment, and reputation systems, offering greater autonomy and access to global gig workers. As blockchain continues to decentralize labor relations, we are witnessing the emergence of new forms of employment contracts, decentralized payroll systems, and on-chain credentials that redefine what it means to be "employed." Startups leveraging AI and blockchain are rapidly growing across fintech, healthtech, edtech, legaltech, and supply chain management, among other domains. These startups are driving innovation at a much faster pace than traditional enterprises and are contributing significantly to job creation. Roles such as machine learning engineers, natural language processing (NLP) specialists, blockchain developers, cybersecurity experts, and product managers are in high demand within these fast-moving environments. Additionally, startup culture often promotes fluid job roles where employees engage in multiple functions—technology development, market research, and customer engagement—further supporting the hybridization of professional skills. This trend signals an entrepreneurial ecosystem where jobs are not only abundant but are also dynamic and innovation-centric.

CONCLUSION

As the global economy experiences one of the most profound technological transformations in history, the twin forces of Artificial Intelligence (AI) and blockchain are reshaping labor markets in ways that hold immense promise for sustainable job creation. While much discourse has focused on the potential job displacement brought about by automation and decentralization, a more nuanced and optimistic perspective reveals how these technologies—when implemented thoughtfully—can serve as powerful engines for inclusive, equitable, and long-term employment generation. The integration of AI and blockchain into public and private sector systems offers opportunities to create new industries, enable entrepreneurship, revitalize existing sectors, and foster a global digital workforce. To ensure these opportunities are sustainable, strategic interventions must be made in policy, education, and innovation ecosystems to align technological advancement with societal needs and long-term development goals. AI and blockchain require robust digital infrastructures, including high-speed connectivity, cloud computing, edge devices, and distributed ledger networks. The design, development, deployment, and maintenance of these infrastructures demand a wide range of skilled labor—software developers, network engineers, cybersecurity specialists, and data center operators. As governments and corporations invest in smart cities, digital public services, and financial inclusion platforms powered by these technologies, they generate demand for a scalable digital workforce. In developing countries, where digital infrastructure is still nascent, the rollout of AI and blockchain systems can create employment at multiple levels—from technicians installing IoT networks to entrepreneurs building localized applications. This infrastructure-centric job creation fosters sustainability by embedding long-term technological capabilities in local economies.Blockchain's most transformative application lies in decentralized finance (DeFi), which allows peer-to-peer transactions, micro-lending, digital savings, and asset tokenization without the need for traditional banking intermediaries. When integrated with AI-driven credit scoring, fraud detection, and customer support tools, blockchain-based financial systems become more efficient, secure, and user-friendly. These technologies enable millions of unbanked and underbanked individuals to participate in the formal economy, unlocking avenues for entrepreneurial ventures and employment. Job creation occurs both directly (e.g., blockchain developers, AI finance analysts) and indirectly (e.g., rural artisans accessing global markets via NFTs or micro-traders using AI-driven investment tools). By democratizing access to capital and market participation, AI and blockchain promote financial inclusion that drives equitable economic growth and sustains livelihoods over time. AI and blockchain are transforming agriculture, an industry employing over a quarter of the global population. AI-powered solutions—such as precision agriculture, predictive analytics for crop yields, and automated irrigation systems—optimize productivity and reduce resource waste. Blockchain, on the other hand, enables transparent supply chains, land ownership verification, and fair-trade certification. These technologies support farmers by reducing dependency on intermediaries, increasing trust among buyers, and improving access to subsidies and markets. Startups and cooperatives developing these solutions generate employment in agri-tech development, drone maintenance, data annotation, and rural ICT training.

REFERENCES

Agarwal, J. D., Agarwal, M., Agarwal, A., & Agarwal, Y. (2021). Economics of cryptocurrencies: Artificial intelligence, blockchain, and digital currency. In *Information for efficient decision making: big data, blockchain and relevance* (pp. 331-430).

Ahmed, I., Zhang, Y., Jeon, G., Lin, W., Khosravi, M. R., & Qi, L. (2022). A blockchain-and artificial intelligence-enabled smart IoT framework for sustainable city. *International Journal of Intelligent Systems*, *37*(9), 6493–6507. DOI: 10.1002/int.22852

Avalekar, U. A., Mehta, V., Mishra, B. R., Prasanna, L., Rajlakshmi, P. V., Manjunath, T. C., & Selvakumar, P. (2025). The Current Advances in AI-Driven Education. In Babulak, E. (Ed.), *Educational AI Humanoid Computing Devices for Cyber Nomads* (pp. 173–196). IGI Global Scientific Publishing. DOI: 10.4018/979-8-3693-8985-0.ch008

Banala, S., Panyaram, S., & Selvakumar, P. (2025). Artificial Intelligence in Software Testing. In Chelliah, P., Venkatesh, R., Natraj, N., & Jeyaraj, R. (Eds.), *Artificial Intelligence for Cloud-Native Software Engineering* (pp. 237–262). IGI Global Scientific Publishing. DOI: 10.4018/979-8-3693-9356-7.ch009

Bhumichai, D., Smiliotopoulos, C., Benton, R., Kambourakis, G., & Damopoulos, D. (2024). The convergence of artificial intelligence and blockchain: The state of play and the road ahead. *Information (Basel)*, *15*(5), 268. DOI: 10.3390/info15050268

Chandrasekaran, N., Somanah, R., Rughoo, D., Dreepaul, R. K., Cunden, T. S. M., & Demkah, M. (2019, January). Digital transformation from leveraging blockchain technology, artificial intelligence, machine learning and deep learning. In *Information Systems Design and Intelligent Applications: Proceedings of Fifth International Conference INDIA 2018* Volume 2 (pp. 271-283). Singapore: Springer Singapore. DOI: 10.1007/978-981-13-3338-5_25

Chhibber, S., Rajkumar, S. R., & Dassanayake, S. (2025). Will Artificial Intelligence Reshape the Global Workforce by 2030? A Cross-Sectoral Analysis of Job Displacement and Transformation. *Blockchain, Artificial Intelligence, and Future Research*, *1*(1), 35–51. DOI: 10.70211/bafr.v1i1.178

Chowdhary, S., Selvakumar, P., Sangeetha, B., Sarvaani, V. V., Anute, N., & Sharma, M. (2025). The Role of Social Capital in Entrepreneurial Development. In Martínez-Falcó, J., Sánchez-García, E., & Marco-Lajara, B. (Eds.), *Support Networks for Entrepreneurs: Social Capital and Strategic Collaborations* (pp. 311–338). IGI Global Scientific Publishing. DOI: 10.4018/979-8-3693-9836-4.ch013

Coates, J. M., Santhanalakshmi, K., Dinesh, N., Gandhimathi, S., & Chandel, P. S. Mohit, & Selvakumar, P. (2025). Assessment and Evaluation in Transnational Staff Development. In G. Morris & J. Ye (Eds.), *Training and Development in Transnational Higher Education* (pp. 387-406). IGI Global Scientific Publishing.

Hussain, A. A., & Al-Turjman, F. (2021). Artificial intelligence and blockchain: A review. *Transactions on Emerging Telecommunications Technologies*, *32*(9), e4268. DOI: 10.1002/ett.4268

Johnson, M., Jain, R., Brennan-Tonetta, P., Swartz, E., Silver, D., Paolini, J., Mamonov, S., & Hill, C. (2021). Impact of big data and artificial intelligence on industry: Developing a workforce roadmap for a data driven economy. *Global Journal of Flexible Systems Managment*, *22*(3), 197–217. DOI: 10.1007/s40171-021-00272-y

Kalai, M., Becha, H., & Helali, K. (2024). Effect of artificial intelligence on economic growth in European countries: A symmetric and asymmetric cointegration based on linear and non-linear ARDL approach. *Journal of Economic Structures*, *13*(1), 22. DOI: 10.1186/s40008-024-00345-y

Khan, A. A., Laghari, A. A., Li, P., Dootio, M. A., & Karim, S. (2023). The collaborative role of blockchain, artificial intelligence, and industrial internet of things in digitalization of small and medium-size enterprises. *Scientific Reports*, *13*(1), 1656. DOI: 10.1038/s41598-023-28707-9 PMID: 36717702

Kwok, A. O., & Treiblmaier, H. (2024). Blockchain technology as a driver of economic development in small economies: A dynamic capabilities framework. *Journal of Decision Systems*, *33*(3), 413–438. DOI: 10.1080/12460125.2023.2214304

Limbore, N. V., Anute, N., Ahluwalia, G. K., Chordiya, P. B., Kalshetti, P., & Selvakumar, P. (2025). Ethical Leadership and Corporate Responsibility. In Harriott, S. (Ed.), *Innovative Approaches to Managing Conflict and Change in Diverse Work Environments* (pp. 193–218). IGI Global Scientific Publishing. DOI: 10.4018/979-8-3693-9556-1.ch009

Lokhande, M., John Deva Prasanna, D. S., Selvakumar, P., Ragupathi, T., Vaissnave, V., & Manjunath, T. C. (2025). Novel ML Algorithms for Healthcare. In A. Ajibesin, N. G., & S. Thangavel (Eds.), *Synergizing Data Envelopment Analysis and Machine Learning for Performance Optimization in Healthcare* (pp. 113-134). IGI Global Scientific Publishing. DOI: 10.4018/979-8-3373-0081-8.ch005

Mehra, J., Madaan, S., & Balu, N. Mohit, Selvakumar, P., & Manjunath, T. C. (2025). The Ubiquitous Internet and Smart Computation Available 24/7 for Anyone and Anywhere. In E. Babulak (Ed.), *Educational AI Humanoid Computing Devices for Cyber Nomads* (pp. 247-270). IGI Global Scientific Publishing.

Nisha Angeline, M., Selvakumar, P., Gupta, M. K., Nazar, N., Elumalai, D., & Bhattacharya, S. (2025). Emerging Materials for Energy Storage and Environmental Applications. In K. Muduli, B. Moharana, S. Ales, & D. Biswal (Eds.), *Using Computational Intelligence for Sustainable Manufacturing of Advanced Materials* (pp. 53-72). IGI Global Scientific Publishing. DOI: 10.4018/979-8-3693-7974-5.ch003

Owotemu, A. E., & Ibaru, A. (2025). Technological Transformation in Infrastructure & Real Estate: Artificial Intelligence (AI), Blockchain (DLT), Project Management & Policy Implications across Leading Markets in Africa (Egypt, South-Africa & Nigeria). *American Journal of Industrial and Business Management*, *15*(1), 155–174. DOI: 10.4236/ajibm.2025.151009

Pandey, A., & Joseph, J. (2025). Integral Role of Blockchain and Artificial Intelligence in Sustainable Economic Development. In *Driving Socio-Economic Growth With AI and Blockchain* (pp. 271–290). IGI Global Scientific Publishing. DOI: 10.4018/979-8-3693-8664-4.ch012

Patnaik, B. C. M., Satpathy, I., Jain, V., & Patnaik, A. (2025). Artificial Intelligence and Blockchain as the Driver of Banking Growth. In *Driving Socio-Economic Growth With AI and Blockchain* (pp. 45–64). IGI Global Scientific Publishing. DOI: 10.4018/979-8-3693-8664-4.ch003

Reilly Marulanda, M. S., & López Sarabia, P. (2021). Artificial Intelligence & Blockchain: The Path to Generate Value for Companies After the COVID-19 Pandemic. In *The Future of Companies in the Face of a New Reality: Impact and Development in Latin America* (pp. 185–201). Springer Singapore. DOI: 10.1007/978-981-16-2613-5_10

Sarwer, M. H., Saha, T. R., & Hossain, D. (2022). Driving business innovation with artificial intelligence, machine learning and blockchain technology. *Journal of Business and Management Studies*, *4*(3), 221–230. DOI: 10.32996/jbms.2022.4.3.21

Upadhyaya, A. N., Debnath, P., Rani, P., Selvakumar, P., Manjunath, T. C., & Bhattacharya, S. (2025). AI-Based Disaster Prediction and Early Warning Systems. In Mobo, F. (Ed.), *AI and Emerging Technologies for Emergency Response and Smart Cities* (pp. 55–74). IGI Global Scientific Publishing. DOI: 10.4018/979-8-3693-9770-1.ch003

Wang, Z., Li, M., Lu, J., & Cheng, X. (2022). Business Innovation based on artificial intelligence and Blockchain technology. *Information Processing & Management*, *59*(1), 102759. DOI: 10.1016/j.ipm.2021.102759

Xuan, T. R., & Ness, S. (2023). Integration of Blockchain and AI: Exploring application in the digital business. *Journal of Engineering Research and Reports*, *25*(8), 20–39. DOI: 10.9734/jerr/2023/v25i8955

Chapter 5
Artificial Intelligence and Blockchain and the Growth of Fintech Industry

Neetal Vyas
https://orcid.org/0009-0004-4926-8443
School of Business, Indira University, Pune, India

Avinash Hanmant Ghadage
https://orcid.org/0009-0000-9877-8520
Global Business School and Research Centre, D.Y. Patil Vidyapeeth's, India

Pradip Sanatkumar Padhye
https://orcid.org/0000-0002-1444-840X
Symbiosis School of Banking and Finance, Symbiosis International University, Pune, India

P. Selvakumar
https://orcid.org/0000-0002-3650-4548
Department of Science and Humanities, Nehru Institute of Technology, Coimbatore, India

T. C. Manjunath
https://orcid.org/0000-0003-2545-9160
Rajarajeswari College of Engineering, India

S. Madhu
https://orcid.org/0009-0000-8816-5798
Jyothy Institute of Commerce and Management, India

ABSTRACT

Financial Technology, commonly known past decade, the FinTech landscape evolved rapidly, with startups and established institutions leveraging innovative solutions to address longstanding inefficiencies in banking, payments, insurance, investments, lending, and wealth management. Among the most groundbreaking technologies reshaping the FinTech industry are Artificial Intelligence (AI) and Blockchain, which have emerged as pivotal drivers of innovation and change. Assess creditworthiness more accurately and inclusively. This not only improves the precision of credit evalua-

DOI: 10.4018/979-8-3373-6380-6.ch005

tions but also opens access to credit for underbanked and marginalized communities. AI is also extensively used in fraud detection and cybersecurity. Machine learning significantly enhancing user experience while reducing operational costs. Another significant application of AI lies in algorithmic trading and robo-advisory services. High-frequency trading platforms use AI These innovations democratize investment opportunities and offer affordable asset management options to retail investors.

INTRODUCTION ABOUT THE ROLE OF AI AND BLOCKCHAIN

Financial Technology, commonly known past decade, the FinTech landscape evolved rapidly, with startups and established institutions leveraging innovative solutions to address longstanding inefficiencies in banking, payments, insurance, investments, lending, and wealth management. Among the most groundbreaking technologies reshaping the FinTech industry are Artificial Intelligence (AI) and Blockchain, which have emerged as pivotal drivers of innovation and change. Assess creditworthiness more accurately and inclusively. This not only improves the precision of credit evaluations but also opens access to credit for underbanked and marginalized communities. AI is also extensively used in fraud detection and cybersecurity. Machine learning significantly enhancing user experience while reducing operational costs. Another significant application of AI lies in algorithmic trading and robo-advisory services. High-frequency trading platforms use AI These innovations democratize investment opportunities and offer affordable asset management options to retail investors. In tandem with AI, intermediaries. One of its most prominent applications is in cryptocurrencies such as Bitcoin and Ethereum, which function as decentralized digital currencies independent of traditional banking systems. These digital assets have challenged conventional financial models and opened new avenues for cross-border transactions, micropayments, and decentralized finance (DeFi). Blockchain's immutability and transparency are particularly valuable in areas such as transaction verification, auditing, and regulatory compliance yndicated loans. Moreover, blockchain is reshaping identity managemen. Digital identity solutions powered by blockchain offer a secure and verifiable way of managing user identities, reducing duplication of efforts across institutions and minimizing fraud. These solutions empower users reducing onboarding time for financial service providers. Despite their potential, the adoption also brings challenges. Concerns regarding algorithmic bias, data privacy, and accountability in AI systems necessitate transparent model governance, regular audits, and regulatory oversight. In the blockchain realm, issues legal uncertainty surrounding and decentralized platforms must be addressed to ensure sustainable and responsible growth. Regulators around the world are increasingly focusing on establishing frameworks that encourage innovation while safeguarding financial stability. Sandboxing initiatives, AI governance principles, and blockchain compliance protocols are being tested and refined to strike the right balance. At the same time, industry players are collaborating to set interoperability standards, promote data-sharing ecosystems, and enhance cybersecurity frameworks. In conclusion, FinTech is fundamentally reshaping the global financial landscape, with AI and blockchain serving as cornerstone technologies driving this transformation. AI enhances decision-making, operational efficiency, and customer engagement, while blockchain.

THE IMPACT OF AI AND BLOCKCHAIN ON FINTECH GROWTH

Blockchain technology have become fundamental drivers of growth in the global Financial Technology (FinTech) sector. (Adigun O. A. et al. 2024) Together, these two transformative technologies are not only revolutionizing traditional financial services but also shaping entirely new business models, markets, and economic paradigms. Their convergence is catalyzing unprecedented innovation, operational efficiency, scalability, trust, and inclusivity in financial systems, contributing significantly to the exponential growth and global expansion of the FinTech industry. Artificial Intelligence, in particular, has enabled FinTech firms to enhance automation, personalization, and created new revenue streams for FinTech companies by offering value-added services and hyper-personalized financial products. One of the most impactful contributions of AI to FinTech growth lies in democratizing access to financial services. By leveraging machine learning algorithms that assess. The ability to offer tailored products through mobile platforms has significantly expanded the customer base of FinTech companies and driven financial inclusion, one of the core pillars of sustainable FinTech growth. AI also fosters growth through its role in real-time decision-making and risk analytics. Financial markets are highly volatile, and the ability to respond quickly to changes is essential for maintaining competitiveness. AI systems equipped with natural language processing (NLP) and sentiment analysis can monitor global news, social media, and financial reports to detect events that may impact market movements. FinTech firms use this information to adjust investment strategies, detect early signs of systemic risk, and provide timely advice to clients. This agility enhances the reliability and appeal of FinTech services, fostering customer trust and loyalty, which are essential for growth.

Remittance services, where traditional systems are often slow, expensive, and opaque. By simplifying and securing these transactions, Blockchain empowers FinTech firms to offer faster, cheaper, and more reliable financial solutions—thereby attracting a global customer base and driving business growth. One of the primary growth levers provided by blockchain is the development. (Adigun O. A. et al. 2024)

This model lowers barriers to entry, enhances transparency, and creates a more participatory financial ecosystem. As DeFi platforms proliferate, they are expanding the scope of FinTech by introducing new financial instruments and services. (An Y. J. et al. 2021) Moreover, blockchain is a catalyst for growth in digital asset markets, including cryptocurrencies, tokenized securities, and non-fungible tokens (NFTs). These innovations are reshaping capital formation, ownership models, and investment opportunities. FinTech startups are developing platforms for secure trading, custody, and management of digital assets, opening new revenue streams and attracting both retail and institutional investors. (An Y. J. et al. 2021) The global interest in digital currencies, including central bank. FinTech engagement with national monetary systems. Another powerful driver of FinTech growth enabled by blockchain is efficiency in regulatory compliance and auditing. Through automated, transparent, and time-stamped records, blockchain simplifies regulatory reporting, ensures real-time auditing capabilities, and reduces the cost of compliance. This has encouraged more players, including traditional financial institutions, to collaborate with or adopt FinTech solutions, further expanding the market and increasing trust in digital financial services.

AI Applications in FinTech: Automation and Analytics

Optimized. (Ahmad S. et al. 2022) Its applications span the entire spectrum of FinTech, from customer engagement and credit scoring to fraud detection and investment management—anchored in two core pillars: automation and analytics. Automatically extract data from unstructured documents (e.g., invoices, loan applications, KYC forms), validate the information, and populate internal systems without manual intervention. (Ahmad S. et al. 2022) In 24/7 assistance across multiple channels. Whether helping users check account balances, initiate payments, or resolve issues, AI chatbots enhance user experience while significantly reducing response times and support costs. Some advanced virtual assistants also offer personalized financial advice by analyzing user spending patterns, savings behavior, and financial goals. In the realm of regulatory compliance, AI automates the tracking and implementation of changing financial regulations. Regulatory Technology (RegTech) solutions use AI to monitor transactions for compliance violations, flag potential issues, and generate reports for regulators. For example, AI tools can detect discrepancies in anti-money laundering (AML) processes, conduct real-time screening against sanction lists, and identify suspicious transaction patterns. Automating these complex compliance tasks not only ensures regulatory adherence but also reduces the cost and burden of manual compliance efforts. Beyond automation, AI's analytical capabilities provide FinTech firms with powerful tools for extracting insights from vast and complex data sets. Financial services generate enormous amounts of structured and unstructured data daily—from transaction logs and credit histories to social media activity and market news. AI enables the real-time analysis of this data to uncover trends, predict outcomes, and support informed. Enabling the detection of anomalies in real time. Machine learning models flag suspicious activities—such as unauthorized access, abnormal spending behavior, or identity theft—based on deviations from normal behavior. This proactive approach significantly improves fraud prevention, reduces financial losses, and enhances consumer trust.

AI is also revolutionizing credit risk assessment holistic credit profiles. This is especially valuable in developing economies where many individuals and small businesses lack formal financial records. (Anjum M. F. et al. 2023) By providing more accurate risk predictions, AI analytics enable FinTech firms to offer responsible lending products to a broader segment of the population. In investment and wealth management, AI is used to power reducing volatility in investment strategies. Personalized financial insights are another key application of AI analytics. FinTech applications can analyze an individual's financial behavior to offer real-time recommendations—such as budgeting tips, savings plans, or customized product suggestions. (Anjum M. F. et al. 2023) By leveraging behavioral analytics, FinTech platforms enhance customer engagement and retention, while simultaneously promoting financial literacy and better money management. In insurance technology (InsurTech), AI analytics are used for dynamic pricing, risk modeling, and claims processing. Insurers use AI to assess policyholder risk based on behavior (e.g., driving habits in auto insurance), personalize premium pricing, and automate claim adjudication processes. For example, AI can analyze photos of vehicle damage, verify documentation, and make settlement recommendations within minutes, dramatically improving customer experience and operational efficiency. This is particularly valuable in forecasting market trends, identifying customer churn, estimating credit default probabilities, and anticipating cash flow fluctuations. FinTech platforms can use these predictions to offer proactive solutions to clients, such as overdraft protection, investment rebalancing, or early warning alerts.

Machine Learning for Risk Management and Fraud Detection

Such as flagging transactions over a certain amount or those originating from unusual locations. While such systems are useful, they often fail to catch sophisticated fraud tactics and generate high false-positive rates, leading to customer frustration and inefficiencies. Machine learning addresses these limitations by learning from historical fraud patterns, adapting to new tactics, and identifying subtle deviations in behavior that may indicate fraudulent activity. (Avalekar U. A. et al. 2025) For instance, ML algorithms are trained to analyze real-time transactional data across multiple dimensions—such as transaction size, frequency, location, device ID, and user behavior—to build baseline user profiles. Any deviation from this profile, such as a sudden high-value transaction from a new device or a location mismatch, can trigger an alert. Importantly, ML models improve with time and data, constantly refining their fraud detection capabilities while minimizing false alarms. (Avalekar U. A. et al. 2025) Some financial institutions employ emerging fraud schemes, such as synthetic identity fraud or insider threats. In addition to transaction-level monitoring, ML is used for behavioral biometrics, analyzing how users interact with devices—like typing speed, screen swipes, or mouse movements—to authenticate identities and detect account takeovers. These techniques are unobtrusive and user-friendly, yet remarkably effective in preventing sophisticated fraud attempts. Combined with traditional authentication methods, behavioral ML models form a multilayered security architecture that enhances both safety and user experience. Another emerging area is the use of reinforcement learning in fraud mitigation. These algorithms operate in environments where outcomes are uncertain and evolve over time. They learn optimal actions by receiving feedback from their environment—such as identifying fraud, issuing alerts, or blocking transactions—and adjusting their strategies to maximize long-term rewards. This dynamic learning capability is essential in dealing with adversaries who constantly evolve their methods to circumvent detection systems.

The deployment of ML for fraud detection also extends to associated with layering or structuring, and generate actionable insights for compliance officers. (Banala S. et al. 2025) Some systems use graph-based models to map the flow of funds across networks and uncover hidden relationships between seemingly unrelated entities. This network-based approach is particularly effective in revealing complex fraud schemes involving shell companies or offshore accounts. (Banala S. et al. 2025) Despite its transformative benefits, is often siloed, inconsistent, or limited due to privacy constraints. There is also the risk of model bias, where training data may reflect existing prejudices or systemic inequalities—leading to unfair or discriminatory outcomes. Ensuring ethical ML practices through fair data sampling, continuous model auditing, and algorithmic transparency is essential to mitigate these risks. Moreover, adversarial actors are increasingly using AI themselves to test and exploit vulnerabilities in detection systems. (Chib S. et al. 2025) This has sparked the development of adversarial machine learning, where models are trained to withstand manipulation and deception attempts. As both attackers and defenders become more technologically advanced, the field of ML-based fraud detection is evolving into a dynamic, high-stakes contest requiring constant innovation and vigilance. Looking ahead, the future of machine learning in FinTech risk management and fraud detection is poised for further sophistication. (Chib S. et al. 2025) The integration of maintaining performance. Additionally, the convergence of ML with other technologies like blockchain will offer immutable data trails and enhanced auditability, further supporting risk mitigation efforts.

AI-Powered Chatbots for Customer Service

Artificial Intelligence (AI)-powered chatbots have revolutionized customer service across the FinTech industry, enabling organizations to deliver faster, smarter, and more personalized support at scale. (Chowdhary S. et al. 2025) These digital assistants leverage advanced technologies such as Natural Language Processing (NLP), machine learning, and sentiment analysis to simulate human-like accurate, real-time responses. As the FinTech sector becomes increasingly digital, with users expecting seamless, on-demand service, AI chatbots have emerged as a critical solution to meet these demands while improving efficiency, reducing operational costs, and enhancing overall user experience. The key advantage of AI chatbots lies in their 24/7 availability and instant response capability, which addresses one of the major pain points in traditional customer service: long wait times and limited-service hours. FinTech users often require immediate support, especially when dealing with time-sensitive financial issues such as failed transactions, payment delays, suspicious activity, or account access problems. (Chowdhary S. et al. 2025) AI chatbots can handle thousands of such inquiries simultaneously without fatigue, ensuring uninterrupted service delivery and reducing customer churn due to frustration or dissatisfaction. AI-powered chatbots are not limited to answering frequently asked questions; they are capable of contextual understanding and dynamic conversation management. Through continuous learning and the use of NLP, these bots interpret user queries, detect intent, and respond with relevant information even when the questions are phrased in natural, informal, or ambiguous language. Over time, chatbots learn from interactions and become better at handling complex conversations, including multilingual queries and slang, making them more adaptable to diverse customer bases across regions and demographics.

In the FinTech context, AI chatbots support a wide range of customer service functions, including balance inquiries, transaction tracking, loan application updates, card activation, fund transfers, investment assistance, insurance queries, and more. For instance, when a user wants to check the status of a loan application, the chatbot can instantly retrieve and present the latest information. (Coates J. M. et al. 2025) If a user forgets their password or needs to update personal details, the chatbot can initiate the necessary verification steps and guide them through the process securely and efficiently. Security and privacy are paramount in financial services, and AI-powered chatbots are designed to adhere to stringent authentication and encryption standards. Multi-factor authentication (MFA), biometric verification, and secure socket layer (SSL) protocols are integrated into chatbot frameworks to ensure that sensitive information is protected. (Coates J. M. et al. 2025) Additionally, chatbots are often programmed to recognize when a request involves high-risk actions—such as large fund transfers or account changes—and escalate the conversation to a human agent or require further verification to proceed, thus maintaining compliance with security and regulatory requirements. Beyond transactional support, AI chatbots that delivers real value to the user. AI chatbots also contribute significantly to customer onboarding and education. FinTech platforms, especially those offering innovative or complex financial products, often face challenges in guiding new users through sign-up processes, product features, and regulatory disclosures. Chatbots can simplify onboarding by answering questions, verifying documents, and walking users through compliance steps such as Know Your Customer (KYC) requirements. They can also offer tutorials, product comparisons, and real-time assistance, helping users make informed decisions and reducing drop-off rates.

Blockchain Technology: Secure and Transparent Transactions

Points of failure and enhances the resilience and integrity of the system. Transactions on a blockchain are grouped into blocks and linked sequentially using cryptographic hashes, forming an unalterable chain of records. (Dewasiri N. J. et al. 2023) Each block contains a set of validated transactions, a timestamp, and a reference to the previous block's hash, making the entire chain tamper-evident. Environment for digital interactions. Security in blockchain is achieved through multiple layers of cryptographic mechanisms. Public key cryptography ensures that only the rightful owner of a digital asset can initiate a transaction, while the distributed consensus mechanisms prevent unauthorized alterations to the ledger. Modify it without altering all subsequent blocks and gaining majority control over the network, an endeavor considered virtually impossible in large-scale public blockchains. This immutability feature serves as a powerful deterrent to malicious actors and makes blockchain an ideal solution for scenarios requiring auditability and long-term data integrity. (Dewasiri N. J. et al. 2023) In public administration, the immutable record-keeping offered by blockchain is transforming the way sensitive information is stored, accessed, and verified. For instance, in financial services, blockchain is being used to securely process cross-border payments, issue digital identities, and automate complex contracts through smart contracts operational. Transparency providing unprecedented transparency while still maintaining user anonymity through pseudonymous addresses. This openness fosters trust among participants, as all actions are verifiable and traceable on a public ledger.

Even in permissioned or private blockchains, which restrict access to authorized participants, transparency is enhanced through shared access to a common source of truth among stakeholders. (Gitobu C. et al. 2024) This facilitates better governance, accountability, and compliance with regulatory requirements. This level of transparency not only combats counterfeiting and fraud but also strengthens consumer confidence in product quality and ethical sourcing practices. The combination of security and transparency offered by blockchain has far-reaching implications for the evolution of trust-based systems. Traditionally, intermediaries between parties engaged in transactions. However, blockchain introduces a new trust model—often referred to as "trustless trust"—where the integrity of transactions is ensured by the technology itself, reducing the need for intermediaries. This disintermediation can lead to significant cost savings, faster transaction times, and greater accessibility. Furthermore, the programmable nature of blockchain allows for the creation of decentralized applications (dApps) and smart contracts that execute predefined conditions without human intervention. These self-executing contracts are particularly useful in automating agreements, ensuring compliance, and minimizing disputes. For example, in insurance, a smart contract can automatically trigger a payout when specific such as flight delays or weather-related crop damage, enhancing efficiency and customer satisfaction. Integration, ongoing advancements and increasing institutional interest signal a strong trajectory toward mainstream adoption. As organizations continue to explore and implement blockchain solutions, the promise of secure, transparent, and efficient transactions is poised to become a foundational element of the digital economy. (Gitobu C. et al. 2024) The evolution of blockchain is not merely a technological trend but a fundamental transformation in the way value and trust are exchanged in an increasingly connected world.

Blockchain Applications in Payments and Settlements

Blockchain technology is revolutionizing the global payments and settlements landscape by introducing faster, more secure, and cost-effective methods for transferring value. (Go E. J. et al. 2020) Traditional payment and settlement systems are often encumbered by complex intermediary networks, high transaction fees, lengthy processing times, and operational inefficiencies, especially in cross-border transactions. These conventional systems typically rely on centralized financial institutions, such as correspondent banks, clearinghouses, and central banks, which introduce latency and vulnerability removing the need for intermediaries, blockchain significantly accelerates settlement times—from days to mere seconds—and reduces associated costs, while simultaneously enhancing transparency, auditability, and trust among transacting parties. One of the key innovations in blockchain-enabled payments is the concept of real-time gross settlement (RTGS) on decentralized networks. In traditional banking, RTGS systems, though secure, often function during limited operating hours and are not interoperable across jurisdictions. Blockchain-based RTGS systems can function continuously, 24/7, and across borders, thereby enhancing liquidity management and enabling continuous settlement of obligations. (Go E. J. et al. 2020) A notable application of blockchain in payments is in the realm of cross-border remittances, a domain plagued by high fees, slow processing, and limited transparency. Traditional remittance corridors—especially those involving developing nations—are often characterized by long settlement times and an average cost of over 6% of the transaction amount, according to the World Bank. Blockchain-based remittance platforms, such as RippleNet and Stellar, utilizes its consensus ledger and native digital asset (XRP) to bridge different fiat currencies, allowing banks and payment providers to settle cross-border payments in real time without the need for nostro/vostro accounts.

Figure 1. Artificial Intelligence and Machine Learning in Fintech and It's Application

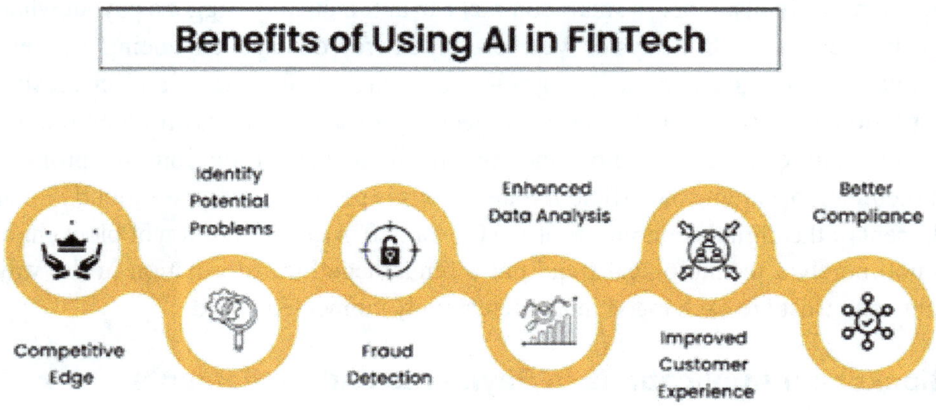

Stellar, on the other hand, focuses on financial inclusion by connecting financial institutions, payment systems, and individuals in underbanked regions through its open-source blockchain network. (Hosen M. et al. 2022) These systems enhance the transparency and traceability of remittance flows, and for recipients to track payments. Beyond remittances, blockchain is also gaining traction in interbank payments and wholesale settlements. Several central banks and financial institutions are exploring or piloting blockchain-based systems for interbank transfers and settlement of high-value settlements on distributed ledgers. In the private sector, platforms like JPMorgan's Onyx and its native JPM Coin exemplify the practical implementation of blockchain in facilitating instantaneous interbank payments and liquidity management. These platforms offer real-time settlement capabilities for institutional clients, reducing the reliance on traditional batch-processing systems and enhancing operational efficiency. Similarly, Fnality International, a consortium backed by major global banks, is developing the Utility Settlement Coin (USC) to enable tokenized payments backed by central bank money, further demonstrating the utility of blockchain in wholesale financial markets. In the retail payments sector, blockchain enables decentralized payment solutions that empower consumers and merchants alike. (Hosen M. et al. 2022) Accepted for goods and services, providing alternatives to traditional payment gateways. Blockchain wallets and QR code-based payment systems allow users to make direct payments without intermediaries, often with lower fees and higher privacy. Decentralized finance (DeFi) platforms also support payment functionalities by allowing users to send, receive, and exchange tokens seamlessly across decentralized applications (dApps). Furthermore, the rise of stablecoins, which bridge between traditional finance and the decentralized ecosystem, facilitating seamless integration and real-world applicability of blockchain payment systems.

Smart Contracts: Automating Financial Agreements: Smart contracts.

Programmable blockchains like Ethereum, which provide a decentralized platform for deploying and interacting with such contracts using languages like Solidity and Vyper. oracles—external systems that feed trustworthy information into the blockchain—smart contracts can execute claims without manual processing, improving customer experience and reducing settlement times. Another notable application of smart contracts is in the derivatives and securities markets, where they facilitate automated settlement, margining, and compliance checks. (Kazachenok O. P. et al. 2023) Traditional derivatives contracts, such as options and futures, involve complex, multi-party agreements that require continuous monitoring and reconciliation. Smart contracts simplify these processes by encoding the terms of the contract directly on the blockchain and ensuring that each step—exercise, expiry, or settlement—is executed precisely as intended. Decentralized finance (DeFi) platforms have capitalized on this capability to offer synthetic assets, decentralized exchanges, and automated market-making (AMM) services, all governed by smart contracts. (Kazachenok O. P. et al. 2023) These platforms eliminate the need for centralized custodians, brokers, and clearinghouses, thereby democratizin, and jurisdiction-specific regulations directly into financial agreements, ensuring that they remain compliant by design rather than requiring post hoc checks manage escrow accounts, automate title transfers, and release payments upon confirmation of milestones, streamlining the process and eliminating potential fraud. In trade finance, smart contracts can automate letters of credit, shipment tracking, and invoice financing, reducing paperwork and enhancing cross-border trust.

Despite their numerous advantages, smart contracts also face several technical, legal, and operational where attackers siphoned millions of dollars due to a coding loophole, underscore the importance of rigorous code auditing, formal verification, and testing before deployment. (Keshari A. et al. 2024) Additionally, smart contracts currently lack flexibility in handling complex real-world contingencies, such as force majeure events, ambiguous terms, or renegotiation. Unlike traditional contracts, which are interpreted by legal professionals within the context of law, smart contracts execute logic without nuance, which can lead to unintended outcomes if not carefully programmed. The interpretability of traditional legal agreements, facilitated by natural language interfaces and legal codification standards. Legal recognition and enforceability also present significant challenges for smart contracts, especially across jurisdictions with varying regulatory frameworks. Questions regarding the legal status of smart contracts—such as whether they constitute valid and enforceable agreements under contract law, who is liable in the event of errors or breaches, and how disputes are resolved—remain subjects of ongoing debate. While some jurisdictions, including several U.S. states and countries like Estonia and Malta, have introduced legislation recognizing the validity of smart contracts, many others have yet to provide clear guidance. (Keshari A. et al. 2024) Addressing these regulatory gaps is essential for encouraging institutional adoption and ensuring legal certainty. Furthermore, the reliance on oracles—external data sources that feed information into smart contracts—introduces potential points of failure and trust dependencies. If an oracle is compromised or provides inaccurate data, it can lead to erroneous contract execution. To mitigate this, decentralized oracle networks like Chainlink have emerged, offering cryptographically secured, reputation-based models to ensure data integrity.

Combining AI and Blockchain for Enhanced Security

Without reliance on central authorities. When combined, these two technologies can create a secure, intelligent, and autonomous ecosystem capable of detecting, preventing, and responding to security threats with unprecedented accuracy and speed. (Kliestik T. et al. 2024) This powerful convergence not only enhances security in traditional IT systems but also lays the foundation for a resilient digital infrastructure in emerging domains. Internet of Things (IoT). By addressing their individual limitations and leveraging each other's strengths, AI and blockchain form a robust, adaptive, and trustless security architecture suited for the complex and dynamic threat landscape of the modern digital world. Protocols that are both proactive and tamper-resistant. Traditional cybersecurity models often rely on predefined rules and centralized oversight, which can be slow to adapt to novel attack vectors and susceptible to single points of failure. AI enhances this by deploying machine learning algorithms to monitor system behavior, detect anomalies, and anticipate potential breaches. When these AI-driven insights are recorded and verified enables distributed AI systems to operate securely across multiple nodes. (Kliestik T. et al. 2024) This is especially beneficial in large-scale networks where the attack surface. Identity management and authentication, AI and blockchain can be combined to create highly secure, adaptive, and user-centric access control mechanisms. Traditional identity systems are vulnerable to data theft, phishing, and password breaches, partly due to their reliance on centralized databases and static authentication methods. Blockchain introduces credentials stored on a decentralized ledger. AI complements this by enabling behavioral biometrics, facial recognition, and adaptive risk-based authentication methods that analyze a user's interaction patterns in real-time. Together, they enable multi-factor authentication schemes that are dynamic, decentralized, and resistant to spoofing or impersonation. Across platforms, while AI continuously assesses the legitimacy of user behavior, blocking access in case of suspicious activity. This convergence supports both high assurance and user convenience, balancing security with usability.

The combination of AI and blockchain also strengthens data privacy and protection, especially in domains where sensitive personal or enterprise data is at risk. (Kumar A. et al. 2022) Blockchain enables secure data sharing through cryptographic techniques such as hashing, zero-knowledge proofs, and homomorphic encryption, which allow verification of data without revealing its content. AI, in turn, can manage the classification of data sensitivity levels, monitor data flows, and detect unauthorized access or misuse. One practical implementation of this combination is in healthcare, where patient data enforces accountability and transparency in data usage. (Kumar A. et al. 2022) Another vital area where AI and blockchain converge for enhanced security is in cyber threat detection and response systems. AI-powered systems can detect malware, ransomware, phishing attempts, and network intrusions by continuously analyzing traffic patterns, system behavior, and user activity. These intelligent detection systems become significantly more reliable and transparent when their outputs are stored on a blockchain, enabling traceable and verifiable alert logs. Moreover, AI can be used to assess the credibility of blockchain transactions and participants in real-time, flagging anomalies such as sudden transaction spikes, fraudulent token behaviors, or double-spending attempts. Blockchain smart contracts can then autonomously trigger defensive actions based on AI-generated alerts, such as freezing wallets, initiating alerts to system administrators, or executing contingency plans. This creates a closed-loop system where AI detects and evaluates threats, response without human intervention, minimizing response time and error rates in critical scenarios.

AI-Powered Blockchain: Improved Efficiency and Scalability

The convergence of overhead. (Lăzăroiu G. et al. 2023) AI, with its adaptive learning capabilities and optimization potential, can dramatically improve the performance of blockchain systems by optimizing consensus protocols, resource allocation, network configuration, data sharding, transaction validation, and overall system architecture. By integrating AI into the blockchain ecosystem, it becomes possible to achieve higher efficiency, faster transaction speeds, better network utilization, and increased scalability—without compromising the core principles of decentralization and security. This symbiotic relationship not only enhances the technical performance of blockchain platforms but also facilitates their deployment across high-demand industries such as finance, logistics, healthcare, and IoT. One of the most promising areas where AI improves blockchain efficiency is in consensus mechanism optimization. (Lăzăroiu G. et al. 2023) Traditional PoW protocols, while secure, are notoriously energy-intensive and computationally inefficient, often requiring vast amounts of electricity and time to validate a single block. AI can address this by analyzing blockchain performance metrics and dynamically adjusting consensus parameters based on network conditions. For instance, AI algorithms can predict optimal block sizes, mining difficulty levels, or stake weights to reduce latency and maximize throughput. Moreover, emerging can be further enhanced through AI-driven modeling and prediction tools that select validators or miners more intelligently based on historical performance, trustworthiness, or node reliability. These adaptive consensus strategies reduce the likelihood of network congestion, minimize energy wastage, and accelerate block validation—improving the overall responsiveness and sustainability of blockchain networks.

AI also plays a critical role in transaction prioritization and dynamic resource allocation, which are essential for maintaining scalability in high-traffic blockchain environments. With increasing numbers of users and decentralized applications (dApps) operating simultaneously, blockchain networks often suffer from bottlenecks that result in delayed confirmations, high gas fees, and failed transactions. (Limbore N. V. et al. 2025) AI algorithms can be trained to forecast transaction loads, predict network congestion, and allocate computational resources more efficiently across the blockchain. For example, AI models can dynamically reorder transaction queues based on priority, fee structures, or behavioral analysis to ensure equitable processing and optimal throughput. In Ethereum-based networks, AI-powered gas prediction tools can suggest optimal gas prices in real time, allowing users to balance cost and speed effectively. Additionally, AI can manage node clustering, network topology, and bandwidth distribution to enhance peer-to-peer communication and reduce latency. These optimizations lead to more reliable and predictable blockchain performance, which is vital for large-scale commercial and financial applications.

(Limbore N. V. et al. 2025) Another impactful application of AI in blockchain scalability is in data management and storage efficiency. As blockchain networks grow in size, they accumulate large volumes of data, leading to increased storage requirements, slower synchronization times, and reduced node participation. Stored on-chain. Furthermore, the use of AI-enabled sharding techniques—where a blockchain is partitioned into smaller, more manageable segments (shards)—can improve parallel transaction processing and significantly increase the network's capacity. AI can dynamically manage shard allocation, balance loads among shards, and predict cross-shard communication needs to maintain system coherence and performance.

Blockchain-Based AI: Secure Data Sharing and Management.

This convergence integrity and authenticity of data but also fosters collaborative intelligence, democratizes access to data, and enables responsible data monetization—ushering in a new era modification. (Mehra J. et al. 2025) Furthermore, blockchain's decentralized architecture prevents any single entity from unilaterally altering or deleting records, making it ideal for multi-stakeholder environments where trust is limited and transparency is vital. Access control and data privacy are further enhanced through the use of blockchain-based identity and permission systems. By leveraging decentralized identity (DID) frameworks, users and devices can maintain applications based on granular permissions. For example, individuals can authorize researchers to use anonymized healthcare records for AI training decentralized AI data marketplaces, blockchain-based smart contracts can enforce these access permissions automatically, ensuring that only authenticated users can retrieve or analyze specific datasets under agreed-upon terms. (Mehra J. et al. 2025) These contracts can also track and log every data transaction, providing complete transparency and auditability for all participants. Moreover, self-sovereign identity (SSI) models allow information. Interoperability sharing across organizational boundaries is another critical advantage enabled by blockchain-based AI. Traditional data-sharing frameworks often struggle with fragmented systems, incompatible formats, and institutional reluctance to share proprietary data. Blockchain mitigates these barriers by offering a neutral, shared ledger that acts as a single source of truth for all parties involved. Through tokenization metadata standardization, datasets can be indexed and referenced on-chain while remaining stored off-chain in secure, distributed data lakes or federated learning environments. AI models can then query or train on these datasets without requiring physical data transfers, thereby preserving privacy and minimizing storage duplication. This architecture supports cross-institutional collaboration in sectors such as or in scientific research, where labs across the globe collaborate on shared datasets to train models in genomics, climate modeling, or epidemiology. Blockchain ensures that the data used in such collaborations remains consistent, traceable, and resistant to tampering, thereby enabling scalable and secure AI development across ecosystems.

Moreover, blockchain enables data monetization and incentive mechanisms that reward data providers for sharing valuable insights with AI developers or other stakeholders. Using tokenized data economies, contributors can receive compensation in the form of digital tokens when their data is accessed or utilized by others. (Mhlanga D. 2023) These mechanisms are governed by smart contracts that automatically execute payment upon data usage, creating a transparent and automated value exchange. For instance, in the agriculture sector, farmers can tokenize and sell sensor data about soil moisture or crop health to agricultural AI platforms that analyze this data to optimize yield predictions or irrigation schedules. Similarly, consumers can license anonymized behavioral data from IoT devices to advertisers or researchers in exchange for digital rewards. These blockchain-based models incentivize high-quality data sharing, reduce reliance on centralized intermediaries, and make data-driven AI innovation more inclusive and economically sustainable. Importantly, smart contracts also enforce compliance with agreed-upon data usage terms, preventing misuse and promoting trust in the data economy. In the context of AI model management, blockchain facilitates verifiable AI training and auditing. (Mhlanga D. 2023) As AI models become increasingly influential in high-stakes domains, the need for transparency in their training processes, data sources, and performance metrics becomes paramount. Blockchain can record and certify each stage of the AI lifecycle—from dataset selection and preprocessing to model architecture and validation outcomes. This immutable audit trail supports model explainability, accountability, and reproducibility, which are essential for regulatory compliance and ethical AI deployment. In sectors such as finance or insurance, where AI-driven decisions can significantly impact individuals' lives, blockchain-based AI governance ensures that models are not trained on biased or manipulated datasets. It also allows regulators or external auditors to independently verify that models perform as intended and do not exhibit discriminatory behaviors. Furthermore, blockchain can facilitate federated learning networks, where multiple participants collaboratively train AI acts as a coordination layer that validates model updates, ensures data integrity, and rewards contributors—all while preserving data locality and privacy.

FinTech Growth: Opportunities and Challenges

The global financial technology (FinTech) sector has undergone unprecedented growth in recent years, transforming the landscape of financial services and redefining how individuals, businesses, and governments interact with money. (Nisha Angeline M. et al. 2025) This rapid expansion is driven by the convergence of advanced digital and mobile platforms—with innovative business models that challenge traditional banking paradigms. FinTech offers an array of opportunities that fuel financial inclusion, enhance operational efficiency, reduce transaction costs, and personalize financial products for diverse user groups. These opportunities are particularly significant in emerging markets, where traditional banking infrastructure is often inadequate or inaccessible. (Nisha Angeline M. et al. 2025) The proliferation of mobile devices, increased internet penetration, and rising consumer expectations for seamless digital experiences have catalyzed the growth of digital wallets, peer-to-peer (P2P) lending platforms, robo-advisors, decentralized finance (DeFi), and neobanks. FinTech startups and technology-driven financial institutions are leveraging agile methodologies and customer-centric innovations to fill gaps left by conventional financial services, thereby democratizing access to credit, savings, insurance, and investment products. However, alongside this growth lie several persistent challenges, including regulatory uncertainty, cybersecurity threats, data privacy concerns, financial exclusion risks, and issues of ethical use of technology. Navigating defines the sustainable trajectory of FinTech in the coming decades. Beyond inclusion, FinTech significantly enhances efficiency and agility in financial operations. Traditional financial institutions are often encumbered by legacy systems, hierarchical decision-making, and regulatory rigidity. In contrast, FinTech startups employ cloud-native technologies, agile development, and API-driven ecosystems to deliver services that are faster, cheaper, and more adaptable. Automated loan underwriting, digital onboarding, biometric authentication, and chatbot-driven customer support streamline operational processes while improving user experiences. In capital markets, algorithmic trading, predictive analytics, and blockchain-based settlement systems reduce latency, eliminate intermediaries, and improve transparency.

FinTech also creates opportunities for personalized and data-driven financial services. Leveraging big data and AI, FinTech companies can deliver tailored products that match individual preferences, financial goals, and risk appetites. Robo-advisors use machine learning algorithms to create and manage investment portfolios based on user inputs such as age, income, and financial objectives. (Noman R. et al. 2023) InsurTech firms offer dynamic pricing models based on driving behavior or health indicators collected through wearable devices. Personal finance management (PFM) apps provide users with budgeting tools, savings advice, and spending insights in real time, often gamifying financial literacy and promoting better money habits. The rise of open banking, driven by regulatory initiatives such as PSD2 in the EU and UPI in India, accountable financial system. Despite its promise, the FinTech sector faces significant challenges that could hinder its growth if not addressed strategically. Regulatory uncertainty and fragmentation are among the most pressing issues. FinTech innovations often outpace existing legal frameworks, creating ambiguities around licensing, consumer protection, taxation, and cross-border operations. The lack of harmonized regulations across jurisdictions complicates the scalability of FinTech platforms and increases compliance costs. (Noman R. et al. 2023) In some regions, but broader regulatory coherence and adaptive oversight mechanisms are needed to balance innovation with systemic stability. Additionally, FinTech firms are increasingly targets of and phishing schemes. As these platforms handle sensitive financial and personal data, ensuring robust cybersecurity frameworks, encryption protocols, and incident response mechanisms operational continuity. Technology also pose challenges in the FinTech landscape. The extensive use of AI, big data, and behavioral analytics raises concerns about consent, surveillance, algorithmic bias, and discrimination. For example, opaque credit scoring models may unintentionally reinforce socioeconomic disparities or exclude certain demographic groups due to biased training data. The commodification of personal data for targeted advertising or behavioral manipulation—especially in lending or insurance—can also erode user trust and regulatory compliance. Addressing these concerns requires a combination of ethical design principles, independent audits, and robust data governance frameworks that prioritize user agency, informed consent, and data minimization.

AI and Blockchain: Driving Innovation in FinTech

The fusion of artificial intelligence (AI) and blockchain technology is profoundly transforming the FinTech ecosystem, emerging as a powerful innovation engine that redefines the foundational architecture of modern financial services. Both technologies, while revolutionary on their own, create a synergistic effect when combined—enabling unprecedented capabilities in automation, security, scalability, personalization, and operational transparency. Their convergence is fueling disruptive business models and reshaping traditional financial paradigms across domains. (Rjoub H. et al. 2023) Together, these technologies are not only addressing the inefficiencies of legacy financial systems but also unlocking new possibilities for inclusive, intelligent, and resilient financial architectures. One of most compelling innovation vectors enabled by FinTech is autonomous finance algorithms automate complex tasks without human intervention. (Rjoub H. et al. 2023) AI algorithms are trained on historical data to make real-time investment decisions, monitor creditworthiness, detect fraud, and optimize portfolios. When these intelligent functions are embedded within blockchain-based smart contracts, they gain an additional layer of security and self-execution, reducing the need for third-party oversight. For example, assess market conditions and manage liquidity pools, while blockchain ensures the transparency and enforceability of loan terms through code. This fusion enables peer-to-peer financial services that are faster, cheaper, and less prone to bias or manipulation. Robo-advisors enhanced by AI can offer highly personalized investment strategies, while blockchain immutability guarantees auditability and compliance. As these platforms mature, they may evolve into self-governing autonomous financial entities—Decentralized Autonomous Organizations (DAOs)—capable of running entire investment or insurance operations through coded logic and data-driven decision-making, significantly lowering operational costs and enhancing trust.

Fraud detection and risk management represent another critical frontier where AI and blockchain coalesce to deliver superior outcomes. (Siddiqui Z. A. et al. 2022) AI models trained on vast transactional datasets can detect subtle anomalies, suspicious patterns, and potential security breaches in real time. These models continuously learn and adapt to new fraud strategies, becoming more effective over time. (Siddiqui Z. A. et al. 2022) When integrated with blockchain's immutable records and distributed consensus mechanisms, the effectiveness of fraud prevention multiplies. Since time-stamped, AI tools can scan these logs to detect inconsistencies or unauthorized activities across the network. For example, AI can identify phishing attacks or unusual account behavior, while blockchain can verify transaction authenticity and prevent double-spending or counterfeit asset creation. Powered systems can flag high-risk transactions or entities, while blockchain provides regulators with a tamper-proof audit trail for enforcement and verification. This dual-layered defense system is particularly valuable in cross-border transactions, remittance services, and cryptocurrency exchanges where jurisdictional complexity and high transaction volumes make traditional oversight mechanisms inefficient. Customer experience and personalization are significantly enhanced through AI-blockchain integration. AI enables intelligent customer engagement through natural language chatbots, sentiment analysis, and behavior-based product recommendations. For instance, AI-driven virtual assistants can offer real-time financial advice, automate savings plans, and alert users about suspicious activities or spending anomalies. When combined with blockchain-based digital identity systems, these personalized experiences become more secure, seamless, and privacy-preserving. Users can control their personal data through self-sovereign identity (SSI) frameworks on the blockchain, granting granular permissions to FinTech providers without disclosing unnecessary information. This reduces the risk of identity theft, data breaches, and regulatory violations related to data protection laws like GDPR.

New Business Models and Revenue Streams

Diversified revenue streams within FinTech and adjacent industries. Traditional financial institutions, long characterized by centralized operations and limited innovation cycles, are now compelled to reimagine their strategic frameworks and service delivery mechanisms to remain competitive. (Singh S. et al. 2024) In contrast, technology-driven start-ups and platform-based companies are rapidly experimenting with disruptive models that break down legacy structures, democratize access to financial services, and tap into previously underutilized market segments. The proliferation of open banking, decentralized finance (DeFi), digital wallets, embedded finance, and digital assets has catalyzed the emergence of platform-centric, user-focused ecosystems where monetization is no longer solely tied to interest margins, transaction fees, or asset management, but increasingly revolves around data-driven services, network effects, and ecosystem partnerships. As the financial services value chain continues to unbundle and reconfigure, innovation in business models has become the critical differentiator, offering firms opportunities to build agile, scalable, and resilient revenue strategies aligned with the evolving expectations of digitally empowered consumers. Where FinTech firms operate as digital platforms offering modular, API-based products that can be seamlessly integrated into third-party applications. This approach enables a "banking-as-a-service" (BaaS) model, where core banking functionalities such as payments, lending, KYC (Know Your Customer), and account management are provided as white-label services to non-financial entities. (Singh S. et al. 2024) Retailers, e-commerce platforms, ride-hailing apps, and other digital businesses can embed these services directly into their customer journeys, creating new revenue streams for FinTech providers through licensing, subscription, or transaction-based pricing.

This embedded finance model decouples financial services from traditional institutions and redistributes them across various digital ecosystems, creating a mesh of financial touchpoints across sectors. (Upadhyaya A. N. et al. 2025) Companies like Stripe, Square, and Solarisbank exemplify this model by enabling third-party businesses to offer financial products under their own brand while monetizing usage through scalable APIs. This modular architecture reduces the cost of innovation and accelerates time-to-market, while opening new monetization opportunities in long-tail markets, SMEs, and underserved demographics. Closely related is the rise of decentralized finance (DeFi), a blockchain-based innovation that removes intermediaries from financial transactions through programmable smart contracts. DeFi introduces peer-to-peer models for lending, borrowing, trading, and insurance, with revenue derived from liquidity provision, governance token appreciation, protocol fees, and staking rewards. (Upadhyaya A. N. et al. 2025) Yield farming, automated market making (AMM), and flash loans represent novel revenue mechanisms native to this new financial paradigm. DeFi protocols such as Uniswap, Aave, and Compound allow users to earn fees by providing liquidity or collateral, while the underlying platforms generate value through network participation and decentralized governance. (Wang Z. et al. 2022) The business logic embedded in smart contracts automates revenue distribution and reduces operational overhead, enabling lean, trustless financial models that are borderless and censorship-resistant. (Wang Z.

et al. 2022) Although regulatory uncertainty and security vulnerabilities remain challenges, DeFi has proven the viability of decentralized business models that rely on community participation, cryptoeconomic incentives, and transparency to create value and attract capital.

CONCLUSION

Redefine the architecture, efficiency, transparency, and intelligence of financial systems globally. While AI brings adaptive intelligence, learning capabilities, and automation to decision-making processes, blockchain introduces decentralization, immutability, transparency, and trustless transaction mechanisms. Together, self-operating financial ecosystems that are not only efficient and scalable but also more equitable, inclusive, and resilient. As digital economies continue to evolve, the synergistic convergence of AI and blockchain will not only enhance existing FinTech applications but will also serve as the foundation for new paradigms of financial innovation. This trajectory includes the emergence of autonomous finance, intelligent analytics, all of which are set to challenge the traditional roles of intermediaries, regulators, and financial institutions. Enable self-executing financial agreements, such as dynamic insurance policies that automatically adjust premiums based on real-time risk assessments or investment portfolios that rebalance autonomously using AI-generated insights. This form of programmable finance represents a significant departure from traditional financial operations that are often manual, opaque, and error-prone. As smart contracts evolve to incorporate machine learning capabilities, they will become increasingly sophisticated, capable of self-updating based on regulatory changes, market anomalies, or user behavior. This will pave the way for autonomous financial agents—digital entities that manage wealth, execute trades, issue loans, or underwrite insurance—all governed by AI logic and secured by blockchain consensus protocols.The integration also has transformative implications for decentralized finance (DeFi), a blockchain-based ecosystem that replaces intermediaries with code. By incorporating AI into DeFi platforms, the future of FinTech envisions a new generation of intelligent DeFi protocols that enhance decision-making, risk management, and user experience. AI can be used to assess borrower creditworthiness, detect fraud patterns, optimize yield farming strategies, or provide real-time financial advice, all within decentralized environments. Non-technical users, providing intuitive dashboards, personalized recommendations, and natural language support, thus lowering the entry barrier and promoting greater financial inclusion. In the domain of regulatory compliance and risk management, significantly streamline and automate critical processes. AI can rapidly process vast volumes of financial transactions to detect anomalies, suspicious behavior, or compliance breaches using pattern recognition and anomaly detection techniques. When coupled with Regulatory technologies (RegTech) of the future will likely rely on AI-driven blockchain analytics flag potential illicit activities, and generate compliance reports without the need for intrusive data collection or manual intervention. Furthermore, blockchain-based digital identities, verified using AI-enhanced biometrics, will empower users to control their identity attributes while complying with jurisdiction-specific regulations. This decentralized identity infrastructure, supported by zero-knowledge proofs and AI-driven verification engines, will become a cornerstone for secure and compliant financial interactions.

REFERENCES

Adigun, O. A., Falola, B. O., Esebre, S. D., Wada, I., & Tunde, A. (2024). Enhancing carbon markets with fintech innovations: The role of artificial intelligence and blockchain. *World Journal of Advanced Research and Reviews*, *23*(2), 579–586. DOI: 10.30574/wjarr.2024.23.2.2387

Ahmad, S., & Saxena, C. (2022, May). Artificial intelligence and blockchain technology in insurance business. In *The international conference on recent innovations in computing* (pp. 61–71). Springer Nature Singapore.

An, Y. J., Choi, P. M. S., & Huang, S. H. (2021). Blockchain, cryptocurrency, and artificial intelligence in finance. In *Fintech with artificial intelligence, big data, and blockchain* (pp. 1–34). Springer Singapore. DOI: 10.1007/978-981-33-6137-9_1

Anjum, M. F., & Veermanju, K. T. (2023). Study on the role of artificial intelligence and block chain in segments of the financial sector. *Scope*, *13*(01), 314–329.

Avalekar, U. A., Mehta, V., Mishra, B. R., Prasanna, L., Rajlakshmi, P. V., Manjunath, T. C., & Selvakumar, P. (2025). The Current Advances in AI-Driven Education. In Babulak, E. (Ed.), *Educational AI Humanoid Computing Devices for Cyber Nomads* (pp. 173–196). IGI Global Scientific Publishing. DOI: 10.4018/979-8-3693-8985-0.ch008

Banala, S., Panyaram, S., & Selvakumar, P. (2025). Artificial Intelligence in Software Testing. In Chelliah, P., Venkatesh, R., Natraj, N., & Jeyaraj, R. (Eds.), *Artificial Intelligence for Cloud-Native Software Engineering* (pp. 237–262). IGI Global Scientific Publishing. DOI: 10.4018/979-8-3693-9356-7.ch009

Chib, S., Mehta, A. K., Selvakumar, P., Saravanan, A., Mishra, B. R., & Manjunath, T. C. (2025). Mental Health Challenges and Solutions in High-Pressure Work Environments. In Harriott, S. (Ed.), *Innovative Approaches to Managing Conflict and Change in Diverse Work Environments* (pp. 247–272). IGI Global Scientific Publishing. DOI: 10.4018/979-8-3693-9556-1.ch011

Chowdhary, S., Selvakumar, P., Sangeetha, B., Sarvaani, V. V., Anute, N., & Sharma, M. (2025). The Role of Social Capital in Entrepreneurial Development. In Martínez-Falcó, J., Sánchez-García, E., & Marco-Lajara, B. (Eds.), *Support Networks for Entrepreneurs: Social Capital and Strategic Collaborations* (pp. 311–338). IGI Global Scientific Publishing. DOI: 10.4018/979-8-3693-9836-4.ch013

Coates, J. M., Santhanalakshmi, K., Dinesh, N., Gandhimathi, S., & Chandel, P. S. Mohit, & Selvakumar, P. (2025). Assessment and Evaluation in Transnational Staff Development. In G. Morris & J. Ye (Eds.), *Training and Development in Transnational Higher Education* (pp. 387-406). IGI Global Scientific Publishing.

Dewasiri, N. J., Karunarathne, K. S. S. N., Menon, S., Jayarathne, P. G. S. A., & Rathnasiri, M. S. H. (2023). Fusion of artificial intelligence and blockchain in the banking industry: Current application, adoption, and future challenges. In *Transformation for sustainable business and management practices: Exploring the spectrum of industry 5.0* (pp. 293–307). Emerald Publishing Limited. DOI: 10.1108/978-1-80262-277-520231021

Gitobu, C., & Ogetonto, J. (2024, November). Harnessing Artificial Intelligence (AI) and Blockchain Technology for the Advancement of Finance Technology (FinTech) in Businesses. In *Proceedings of London International Conferences* (No. 11, pp. 196-210).

Go, E. J., Moon, J., & Kim, J. (2020). Analysis of the current and future of the artificial intelligence in financial industry with big data techniques. [GBFR]. *Global Business & Finance Review*, *25*(1), 102–117. DOI: 10.17549/gbfr.2020.25.1.102

Hosen, M., Thaker, H. M. T., Subramaniam, V., Eaw, H. C., & Cham, T. H. (2022, September). Artificial intelligence (AI), blockchain, and cryptocurrency in finance: current scenario and future direction. In *International Conference on Emerging Technologies and Intelligent Systems* (pp. 322-332). Cham: Springer International Publishing.

Kazachenok, O. P., Stankevich, G. V., Chubaeva, N. N., & Tyurina, Y. G. (2023). Economic and legal approaches to the humanization of FinTech in the economy of artificial intelligence through the integration of blockchain into ESG Finance. *Humanities & Social Sciences Communications*, *10*(1), 1–9. DOI: 10.1057/s41599-023-01652-8

Keshari, A., & Gautam, A. (2024). FinTech Evolution and Artificial Intelligence: Opportunities and Development. In *Applications of Artificial Intelligence in Business and Finance 5.0* (pp. 45-67). Apple Academic Press.

Kliestik, T., Dragomir, R., Bălu ă, A. V., Grecu, I., Durana, P., Karabolevski, O. L., ... & Gajdosikova, D. (2024). Enterprise generative artificial intelligence technologies, Internet of Things and blockchain-based fintech management, and digital twin industrial metaverse in the cognitive algorithmic economy. *Oeconomia Copernicana, 15*(4).

Kumar, A., Srivastava, A., & Gupta, P. K. (2022). Banking 4.0: The era of artificial intelligence-based fintech. *Strategic Change, 31*(6), 591–601. DOI: 10.1002/jsc.2526

Lăzăroiu, G., Bogdan, M., Geamănu, M., Hurloiu, L., Lumini a, L., & tefănescu, R. (2023). Artificial intelligence algorithms and cloud computing technologies in blockchain-based fintech management. *Oeconomia Copernicana, 14*(3), 707–730. DOI: 10.24136/oc.2023.021

Limbore, N. V., Anute, N., Ahluwalia, G. K., Chordiya, P. B., Kalshetti, P., & Selvakumar, P. (2025). Ethical Leadership and Corporate Responsibility. In Harriott, S. (Ed.), *Innovative Approaches to Managing Conflict and Change in Diverse Work Environments* (pp. 193–218). IGI Global Scientific Publishing. DOI: 10.4018/979-8-3693-9556-1.ch009

Mehra, J., Madaan, S., & Balu, N. Mohit, Selvakumar, P., & Manjunath, T. C. (2025). The Ubiquitous Internet and Smart Computation Available 24/7 for Anyone and Anywhere. In E. Babulak (Ed.), *Educational AI Humanoid Computing Devices for Cyber Nomads* (pp. 247-270). IGI Global Scientific Publishing.

Nisha Angeline, M., Selvakumar, P., Gupta, M. K., Nazar, N., Elumalai, D., & Bhattacharya, S. (2025). Emerging Materials for Energy Storage and Environmental Applications. In K. Muduli, B. Moharana, S. Ales, & D. Biswal (Eds.), *Using Computational Intelligence for Sustainable Manufacturing of Advanced Materials* (pp. 53-72). IGI Global Scientific Publishing. DOI: 10.4018/979-8-3693-7974-5.ch003

Noman, R., Shahid, M., & Alam, M. (2023, October). The Synergy of Blockchain and Artificial Intelligence in Fintech: Revolutionizing the Financial Landscape. In *2023 4th International Conference on Data Analytics for Business and Industry (ICDABI)* (pp. 425-430). IEEE.

Rjoub, H., Adebayo, T. S., & Kirikkaleli, D. (2023). Blockchain technology-based FinTech banking sector involvement using adaptive neuro-fuzzy-based K-nearest neighbors algorithm. *Financial Innovation, 9*(1), 65. DOI: 10.1186/s40854-023-00469-3 PMID: 36919101

Siddiqui, Z. A., & Haroon, M. (2022). Application of artificial intelligence and machine learning in blockchain technology. In *Artificial Intelligence and Machine Learning for EDGE Computing* (pp. 169–185). Academic Press. DOI: 10.1016/B978-0-12-824054-0.00001-0

Singh, S., Sarkar, T., Mangla, M., Rakhra, M., Singh, A., & Jairath, K. (2024, September). FinTech edge: utility computing & artificial intelligence technologies for smart financial acquisition & blockchain in the financial industries. In *2024 7th International Conference on Contemporary Computing and Informatics (IC3I)* (Vol. 7, pp. 228-234). IEEE. DOI: 10.1109/IC3I61595.2024.10828908

Upadhyaya, A. N., Debnath, P., Rani, P., Selvakumar, P., Manjunath, T. C., & Bhattacharya, S. (2025). AI-Based Disaster Prediction and Early Warning Systems. In Mobo, F. (Ed.), *AI and Emerging Technologies for Emergency Response and Smart Cities* (pp. 55–74). IGI Global Scientific Publishing. DOI: 10.4018/979-8-3693-9770-1.ch003

Wang, Z., Li, M., Lu, J., & Cheng, X. (2022). Business Innovation based on artificial intelligence and Blockchain technology. *Information Processing & Management*, *59*(1), 102759. DOI: 10.1016/j.ipm.2021.102759

Chapter 6
Cashless Confidence:
Exploring the Influence of Digital Payments on Gen Z Consumption Patterns

Yuvraj Singh Shergill
Christ University, Bangalore, India

Raj Singh
Christ University, Bangalore, India

H. J. Prajwal
Christ University, Bangalore, India

Shaeril Almeida
https://orcid.org/0000-0002-9994-3046
Christ University, Bangalore, India

ABSTRACT

The rapid growth of digital payment systems has significantly changed financial behaviors, especially among Generation Z. This group consists of digital natives whose buying habits are closely linked to technology. Using qualitative thematic analysis, which identifies common themes in qualitative data, this research reviews various studies and reports on financial technology adoption. It looks at how mobile wallets, UPI platforms, QR-based payments, and new fintech solutions affect Gen Z's spending habits, views on money, and financial choices in India. Drawing from existing literature, empirical research, and theories like behavioral economics and the Technology Acceptance Model (TAM), the paper brings together evidence on the psychological, social, and cultural factors behind digital payment adoption. The findings show that ease of use, peer influence, gamification features, and social

DOI: 10.4018/979-8-3373-6380-6.ch006

media-driven consumption greatly motivate Gen Z to use cashless transactions. However, these same factors may lead to risks such as impulsive buying, accumulating debt through Buy Now Pay Later (BNPL) services, and privacy issues. Gender dynamics, urban-rural divides, and differences in financial literacy further complicate these trends. Meanwhile, digital platforms are promising for improving financial management through budgeting tools and investment apps. The paper concludes that digital payments are not just replacing cash; they are transforming financial identities, consumption culture, and intergenerational attitudes toward money. Insights from this study have important implications for policymakers, financial institutions, and educators looking to promote responsible, inclusive, and sustainable digital payment systems for the future economy.

INTRODUCTION

The last decade has brought a major change in how people deal with money. This shift comes mainly from the growth of digital payment systems. These systems include debit cards, online banking, mobile wallets, QR codes, and UPI (Unified Payments Interface). According to Angamuthu, B. (2020), the expansion of digital payment platforms in India has played a key role in improving financial inclusion and reducing reliance on physical cash. Financial transactions are now much faster, smoother, and easier. Generation Z, the digital natives who grew up with technology, has been especially impacted by this change. Govind, H., Nayan, A., & Gupta, P. (2024) note that the quick rise of UPI and the launch of the e-Rupee in urban areas have changed daily transaction habits and future views on currency among young users. Their comfort with smartphones and the internet has made them quick to use digital payments. This group prefers digital payments over cash, even for small purchases. Consequently, digital payments have not only taken the place of physical wallets but also altered how young consumers perceive and manage money. According to Srivastava, S., Mohta, A., & Shunmugasundaram, V. (2024), Generation Z users in India are more likely to choose digital payment platforms when they see them as easy to use, enjoyable, and supported by others, showing how peer influence and user experience shape their approach to financial technology.

This change has led to significant psychological and behavioral effects. Purohit, S., Kaur, J., & Chaturvedi, S. (2022) indicate that the rapid rise of mobile payments among Generation Z reflects not just technological comfort but also a generational shift in financial trust, favoring digital convenience over traditional banking. The ease and speed of mobile payments can diminish the feeling of loss when spending money. Transactions feel less real than when using cash. This can lead to impulsive buying, especially in online shopping, where paying is just a click away. Rafee, B.

M., Ramesh, V., Asan, S. J., Kolar, A. B., & Zaheed, S. M. (2022) found that the ease of e-wallets, credit cards, and "pay-later" services in urban India has caused a significant rise in overspending and increased household debt. Furthermore, personalized deals, cashback offers, and one-click checkouts create a game-like experience around spending. For Generation Z, who seeks immediate rewards, these features promote frequent transactions. Social media and influencer marketing have also driven spending influenced by peers, with digital payments supporting this behavior. Thus, it's essential to evaluate how easy payments can both support and complicate spending habits among young people. According to Andhini, N. A., & Muat, S. (2024), Generation Z's use of digital payments is not just about convenience; it also stems from a desire to fit into modern, technology-driven lifestyles, suggesting a cultural shift in how youth relate to money.

Sharma, N. S., & Gokhale, R. (2023) highlight that Generation Z values mobile-friendly banking services, with over 70% prioritizing user experience and real-time transaction tracking when selecting financial platforms. Technology has also influenced financial literacy and budgeting habits in this group. Many Gen Z users are comfortable using fintech apps to track expenses and invest, but some may find it hard to engage in more detailed financial planning or understand credit. The rise of Buy Now, Pay Later (BNPL) schemes and easy credit through fintech apps has raised concerns about growing debt in this generation. While digital payments can offer tools for better financial management, such as categorizing expenses and setting spending limits, there is a gap between having access to these tools and actually using them. Bhatia, R., & Shete, V. report that while UPI use is common among Gen Z, worries about authentication failures and transaction limits create significant barriers to regular use. Generation Z's dependence on technology can be a mixed blessing; it allows for control but can also result in careless spending, especially without proper financial education included in the experience. Galhotra, B., Jatain, A., Bajaj, S. B., & Jaglan, V. (2023) underline that while Generation Z values convenience and security in digital payments, these systems also bring about evolving privacy and fraud risks that need to be addressed.

Agarwal, S., Ghosh, P., Li, J., & Ruan, T. (2024) found that the sudden shift to digital payments after India's 2016 demonetization caused a lasting increase in consumer spending, with monthly expenditures rising by about 3%. Culturally, digital payments are also changing the norms around money management and identity. Older generations viewed cash transactions as a mark of discipline, while younger consumers now see digital wallets and payment apps as part of their lifestyle. According to Kaur, H., Kaur, R., Mago, M., Singh, M., & Mehta, K. (2024), Generation Z's openness to Central Bank Digital Currency shows their willingness to accept innovations that promise transparency, speed, and government support in digital transactions. Durai, T., & Lalitha, H. (2024) explain that AI-based digital payment systems are changing how Gen Z perceives money, allowing them to spend without fully grasping their expenses. Payment habits are now tightly connected to brand loyalty, user experience, and even perceived social status. Splitting bills, making quick transfers, and accepting payment requests have normalized small transactions in daily life. In countries like India, the rapid growth of UPI and app-based finance has made financial services more accessible. However, this growth raises concerns about data privacy, cybersecurity, and reliance on technology. As digital payment systems continue to evolve, understanding their impact on the financial habits of young people is essential, not just for economic analysis but also for creating balanced, inclusive, and safe digital environments for future generations.

LITERATURE REVIEW

Meaning and Advantages of Thematic Analysis

Thematic analysis is a method for studying and understanding qualitative data, such as interview transcripts, survey answers, or written documents. It aids researchers in identifying key ideas or patterns that appear frequently in the data. These patterns are known as "themes," and they reflect what is common or important across all the information collected (Braun & Clarke, 2006). This method is popular because it is flexible and can fit various types of research questions and data sets (Clarke & Braun, 2017).

In thematic analysis, researchers read through the data multiple times to get familiar with it. Next, they code the data by labeling important parts. After coding, researchers group similar codes into themes that convey a larger story about the topic. These themes can help clarify people's experiences, views, or behaviors in an organized way (Maguire & Delahunt, 2017). The method can be data-driven, meaning themes come directly from the data (inductive), or guided by existing ideas or theories (deductive) (Nowell et al., 2017).

Advantages of Thematic Analysis

Thematic analysis has many benefits that make it a popular choice for researchers working with qualitative data:

1. Easy to Use and Understand: Thematic analysis follows simple steps that are clear and logical. This makes it helpful for researchers new to qualitative studies as well as experienced ones (Braun & Clarke, 2006).

2. Flexible: Since it is not tied to one specific theory or way of thinking, thematic analysis can be used in many research fields. Researchers can apply it to different data types and research aims (Clarke & Braun, 2017).
3. Provides Rich Insights: Instead of just counting words or simple facts, thematic analysis digs deeper to understand the meanings behind what people say or write. It helps reveal feelings, motivations, and hidden ideas in the data (Nowell et al., 2017).
4. Organizes Complex Data: Large amounts of text can be hard to make sense of, but thematic analysis helps by grouping similar ideas together, making the data easier to summarize and communicate (Maguire & Delahunt, 2017).
5. Supports Both Open and Guided Research: Researchers can use this method to explore new ideas (inductive) or confirm and test existing theories (deductive), making it adaptable to many research contexts (Braun & Clarke, 2006).
6. Enhances Transparency and Trustworthiness: Because thematic analysis requires detailed documentation of each step—how data were coded and themes developed—it helps others understand and trust the research findings (Nowell et al., 2017).
7. Useful in Mixed Methods: Thematic analysis can be part of studies that use both qualitative and quantitative data, bridging the gap between numbers and meanings (Clarke & Braun, 2017).

From Cash to Clicks: The Journey of Digital Payments

The movement from physical currency to digital transactions has been a gradual yet transformative process, shaped by evolving technology, changing consumer habits, and shifts in financial infrastructure. In its early stages, adoption depended heavily on financial awareness, digital literacy, and access to basic tools such as bank accounts and payment cards. As Shehadeh, Dawood, and Hussainey (2025) note, skills, awareness, and hands-on experience play a central role in building confidence in cashless payment systems, with familiarity often being the key to consistent usage.The introduction of mobile payment platforms, contactless cards, and interoperable systems like UPI marked a turning point, making digital payments faster, more accessible, and integrated into daily life. Global events further accelerated this transition, the COVID-19 pandemic, for instance, served as a catalyst, encouraging people to replace physical cash with contactless alternatives for safety and convenience. Research by Graziano, Musella, and Petroccione (2024) shows that financial literacy and perceived security became powerful motivators during this period, pushing digital payments into the mainstream.

Even as adoption grew, the journey remained uneven. Graziano, Musella, and Petroccione (2025) found that trust in technology, ease of use, and safety perceptions continued to influence how quickly different groups embraced mobile payments. Meanwhile, at a global level, Gammage, Kes, Winograd, and Sultana (2017) identified persistent challenges such as infrastructure gaps, inconsistent access to digital devices, and regulatory limitations that slow the path toward universal adoption. From its origins in cash-reliant economies to today's app-driven, instant transaction culture, the journey from cash to clicks reflects more than just a technological shift, it represents a redefinition of how value is exchanged, stored, and experienced in the modern economy.

Even though digital payments are now seen as a normal part of life, the way this shift has unfolded is uneven and shaped by local realities. In cities, where internet connections are reliable and smartphones are widespread, people have quickly embraced apps and digital wallets for almost every type of transaction, whether it is ordering food, paying bills, booking tickets, or sending money to friends. In these spaces, the convenience of instant payments has become so routine that many no longer carry much cash at all. But in rural areas, adoption has been much slower. This is not simply because people resist change but more often because of poor network coverage, the high cost of smartphones, and limited knowledge of how to use financial apps safely. This gap between urban and rural users shows that technology alone does not guarantee inclusion. True adoption depends on education, affordability, and building trust so that people feel comfortable shifting away from cash.

Beyond access, what is really changing is the meaning of money itself. For older generations, money in hand was a physical reminder of both security and limits. Counting cash made it easier to control spending and track savings. Digital payments, by removing that physical aspect, have made spending more effortless and less visible. Many studies suggest that people are more likely to spend freely when they pay through cards or apps because the act of parting with money feels less real. Younger users, especially Generation Z, often see this frictionless style of payment as completely natural since they grew up surrounded by digital platforms. For them, payments are not just about transferring value but about convenience and lifestyle. In contrast, many older users still hesitate to fully abandon cash, not out of habit alone but because the tangibility of money continues to provide a sense of control and trust.

Governments and policies have also played a decisive role in shaping this transition. The Indian example of UPI shows how building an open, interoperable system with strong policy backing can drive mass adoption across income levels. Similarly, during the COVID-19 pandemic, many governments actively encouraged contactless payments, raised transaction limits, and even ran public campaigns emphasizing safety and hygiene. These moves helped build trust and accelerate usage. Still, long-term adoption depends on how issues like fraud, privacy, and regulation are managed. The rapid growth of fintech has raised important questions around consumer protection, and without strong safeguards, the same technology that enables inclusion can also expose people to risks.

What is clear is that the rise of digital payments is not just about making transactions faster. It signals a deeper shift in how people interact with money and with the financial system as a whole. It reflects broader cultural changes, how convenience is valued, how trust is built, and how financial habits are shaped across generations. The real challenge ahead lies in ensuring that this shift does not leave behind those who lack access or awareness. Digital finance, at its best, can make money management easier, safer, and more inclusive, but this promise will only be realized if the social, cultural, and regulatory aspects are given as much attention as the technology itself.

Digital Payment Adoption and UPI in India

The expansion of UPI in India has shifted digital payments from being a small convenience to becoming an essential part of everyday financial activity. Its strength lies in the way it has been built: simple to use, low in cost, secure, and interoperable. These qualities have helped it overcome barriers that limited older payment systems (Badak, Kolte, Agrawal, & Bairagi, 2023). This rapid growth, however, cannot be explained by technology alone, as much depends on how different groups of people receive and adapt to it. Trivedi (2024) highlights that UPI has been particularly useful for individuals with limited access to formal banking, such as women in rural and semi-urban regions, because it provides a direct and affordable means of making transactions without relying on traditional banking channels. Similarly, Kesavan and Srinivasan (2021) emphasize that the rise of mobile access has reduced reliance on physical bank branches, allowing wider participation even in places where banking infrastructure is weak. These developments show that UPI is more than a payment tool; it has become an important driver of financial inclusion and social change. Yet, its spread is not uniform. Differences in culture, levels of trust, and access to technology continue to shape who adopts UPI easily and who remains outside its reach. Taken together, the research suggests that the success of UPI represents both a financial and a social transformation, and its long-term impact will depend on how effectively it responds to these cultural and technological challenges.

UPI has changed daily life in India in a way that very few financial tools ever have. What started as just another payment option has now become a part of everyday habits. Small shopkeepers, street vendors, and even rickshaw drivers keep QR codes ready, and people of all ages use them without much thought. This change has made payments faster and easier, but it has also created new challenges. Whenever there is an internet issue or the system slows down, people are reminded that dependence on digital payments can be risky if alternatives like cash are not available. For this reason, while many urban areas are moving quickly toward cashless living, rural and remote areas still need more reliable infrastructure to fully keep up.

Generational differences also shape how people use UPI. Young people, especially students and first-time salary earners, tend to be the fastest adopters. For them, paying online feels natural, whether it is for food delivery, shopping, or splitting a bill with friends. Older people often show hesitation, with concerns about safety, fraud, and complicated mobile apps. This contrast shows that UPI's future depends not only on technology but also on building trust across different age groups. Efforts like financial awareness workshops, simple app designs, and stronger customer support could help make older users feel more confident.

Trust is really at the center of this entire shift. People are more willing to use UPI when they feel their money and personal information are safe. India's banking regulations, such as two-factor authentication and fraud protection policies, have helped build this trust, but cybercrime is still growing. Even small incidents of fraud can create fear, especially among groups that are already cautious about digital transactions. If trust weakens, adoption could slow down, so keeping systems secure and transparent will always be a top priority.

Another interesting effect of UPI is how it changes spending habits. Because payments are instant and simple, people are now comfortable using it for very small amounts, something they would not have done with cards or bank transfers earlier. This has made digital spending almost effortless. On the positive side, digital records make it easier to track expenses, which can help with budgeting. On the negative side, the same ease of use can lead to more impulsive buying, especially among young users who are new to managing money. In this way, UPI not only changes how payments are made but also how people think about money itself.

Looking forward, UPI seems set to become even more important. Its role is already expanding beyond simple transactions to include credit, government subsidies, and even international transfers. But its long-term success will depend on inclusivity. If rural areas, older citizens, and people with low digital literacy are left out, the system will not achieve its full potential. The real test for UPI is whether it can grow in a way that balances scale, security, and accessibility, while continuing to meet the changing needs of Indian consumers.

Emergence of Credit Trends among Gen Z

Credit habits among Gen Z are being shaped by more than just money skills; they're the result of a mix of what they know, how they feel, and the world around them. Studies show that when young people have stronger financial literacy and confidence in their abilities, they're generally less likely to slip into risky credit behavior, which makes early financial education all the more important (Sekarlaras,

Siregar & Hasanah, 2025). That said, simply knowing the right things isn't enough. Under financial stress, even the most informed Gen Z borrowers can make poor choices, such as misusing PayLater services, especially when emotions take over (Ramadhan, 2025). Friends, social media, and lifestyle aspirations also play a big role; peer influence can nudge spending patterns, and while some level of financial control can help, it doesn't always fully offset those pressures (Sapira, Juhari, Suhardi & Makrus, 2025). On top of that, new research using machine learning has started mapping out "risk clusters" among Gen Z BNPL users, finding clear patterns tied to how often they use credit and how reliably they pay it back (Arisandy & Dasril, 2023). All of these points to one thing: helping Gen Z manage credit wisely means going beyond just teaching money skills; it calls for strategies that address behavior, emotions, and the social influences shaping their decisions.

Gamification Of Finance

Gamification has become a defining feature of how financial platforms engage and shape the behaviors of younger users, particularly Gen Z. FinTech firms increasingly rely on game-like strategies not just to keep users active, but to subtly reshape how they perceive and manage financial risk and reward (Lai & Langley, 2024). Interactive and visually engaging marketing tools have further blurred the line between learning and doing, making it easier for young investors to translate financial knowledge into action (Mazzatto, 2022). Research also shows that when digital finance tools include consistent feedback loops, challenges, and rewards, users demonstrate marked improvements in their financial behavior over time (Yaacob, Zainuddin & Rohani, 2024). More recently, the merging of gamification with decentralized finance (DeFi) protocols inside e-wallets has not only encouraged longer user engagement but has also sparked micro-investment habits among young adults (Yathiraju & Dash, 2023). Together, these trends suggest that gamification is not just a marketing gimmick, but an influential mechanism in shaping how the next generation interacts with money.

Gender Dynamics in Digital Payment Adoption

Gender plays a subtle yet significant role in shaping how digital payment platforms are adopted and used, particularly in diverse socio-cultural contexts like India. Early conceptual work by Hjelholt and Damsgaard (2012) showed how payment systems evolve in parallel with societal norms, suggesting that access, trust, and adoption are influenced by more than just technology. In the Indian context, UPI has emerged as a transformative force, with Badak, Kolte, Agrawal, and Bairagi (2023) highlighting how its convenience, security, and interoperability have encouraged rapid uptake. While these features are designed to be universal, cultural expectations and lifestyle differences can produce distinct adoption patterns between men and women. Trivedi (2024) notes that the simplicity and low cost of UPI make it especially valuable for individuals with limited exposure to formal banking, a category that often includes women in rural and semi-urban areas. Similarly, Kesavan and Srinivasan (2021) emphasize UPI's mobile accessibility as a potential equalizer in financial participation, pointing to its ability to empower women by reducing dependency on physical banking infrastructure. Together, these perspectives illustrate that while digital payment adoption is shaped by technology, its true impact is realized when it addresses the social and cultural factors that influence financial behaviour across genders.

Gender brings another important layer to the discussion on digital payments, showing that financial technology is not automatically neutral or equally accessible for everyone. As Hjelholt and Damsgaard (2012) noted, payment systems grow and adapt in line with social norms, which means that adoption depends as much on culture, trust, and expectations as it does on technical design. In India and other developing countries, this is particularly visible in the way women use digital finance. Gupta and Rani (2022) found that women in rural areas often face specific hurdles such as limited access to formal banking, lower levels of financial literacy, and in some cases, social restrictions that reduce their financial independence. Even so, the availability of platforms like UPI and mobile wallets has opened doors for many women to take part in the financial system more directly, lowering their reliance on physical banks. International studies also support this trend. For example, Suri and Jack (2016) showed in their work on mobile money in Kenya that women gained significant advantages, including better savings and greater resilience, often experiencing stronger benefits than men. Taken together, this research suggests that inclusive digital finance has the potential to empower women and gradually reshape gendered financial behavior. At the same time, deep-rooted barriers such as poor internet access, lack of device ownership, and ongoing social biases still slow down women's participation compared to men. This makes it clear that technology on its own is not enough to bridge gender gaps. What is needed are targeted policies, simple and accessible design features, and awareness initiatives that respect cultural realities so that women can move from being occasional users to active participants in the digital economy.

Gen Z Spending Behavior in the Digital Era

Generation Z is often described as the first truly digital generation, and their approach to spending clearly reflects this. Their financial habits are shaped heavily by the convenience and speed of digital payment systems, with tools like UPI and digital wallets making it easy to carry out small, frequent, and sometimes impulsive purchases (Singh & Kaur, 2023). Unlike older generations, Gen Z does not see payments only as routine financial transactions but as part of their lifestyle, preferring options that are quick, mobile-first, and connected with social and shopping platforms. This trend is also seen globally. For example, Wood (2021) found that Gen Z consumers in the UK favor payment tools that fit naturally into their daily lives, placing a higher value on instant access and ease of use than on traditional measures of trust or security. Similar findings come from Southeast Asia, where Tan and Lim (2024) noted that the growing use of digital wallets among university students has encouraged more lifestyle and discretionary spending, suggesting that the technology itself influences behavior by making payments more effortless. Taken together, these studies reveal both opportunities and risks. On the positive side, digital payments align well with Gen Z's preference for convenience and personalization. On the other hand, they also encourage tendencies such as impulse buying and greater discretionary spending, which can create financial pressure over time. This shows that understanding Gen Z's financial behavior requires looking beyond adoption rates and paying attention to the cultural and psychological factors that make digital payments feel natural to them, along with the consequences of such easy access to money.

THEORETICAL FRAMEWORK

This study looks at how Generation Z adopts and uses digital payment systems. It uses several well-known theories to guide the research. The main frameworks include the Technology Acceptance Model (TAM), insights from behavioral economics, and social influence theory. Together, these viewpoints help us understand the technological, psychological, and social factors that affect how young people use digital payments. Below, I explain each theory in detail and its relevance to this study.

Technology Acceptance Model (TAM)

The Technology Acceptance Model (TAM), created by Davis in 1986, is one of the most important models that explain why people accept and use new technology. The model highlights two main beliefs that influence adoption:

Perceived Usefulness (PU): This is the extent to which a person believes that using the technology will enhance their performance or make tasks easier. For digital payments, it reflects how much young users think mobile wallets, UPI, or fintech apps simplify, speed up, or organize financial transactions better.

Perceived Ease of Use (PEOU): This refers to how easy a person thinks it will be to use the technology. If Generation Z finds digital payment apps straightforward and convenient, they are more likely to adopt and regularly use them.

Research shows that both perceived usefulness and ease of use significantly affect whether people plan to use new technologies and actually do so (Venkatesh et al., 2003). For Generation Z, who grew up with technology, ease of use and clear benefits are especially critical when selecting digital payment options (Srivastava, Mohta, & Shunmugasundaram, 2024). Moreover, later versions of TAM include other important factors like social influence, helpful resources, and past user experience, which further explain how social and practical elements shape Gen Z's adoption of fintech (Venkatesh et al., 2003). Therefore, TAM provides a solid starting point to study how this generation assesses digital payment platforms before adopting them.

Behavioral Economics and Consumer Psychology

Although TAM helps explain technology acceptance, it does not fully capture the emotional and cognitive factors that influence spending habits. To gain a more complete understanding, this study also uses ideas from behavioral economics and consumer psychology. These fields explore how people's mental shortcuts and feelings affect their financial decisions.

A key concept here is the "pain of paying" theory (Prelec & Loewenstein, 1998). This theory suggests that paying with cash creates a psychological discomfort that makes people think twice before spending. On the other hand, digital payments reduce this discomfort, making it easier to spend more often or impulsively. Generation Z's heavy use of cashless payments means they experience lower pain of paying, which can lead to higher spending frequency and less caution (Durai & Lalitha, 2024).

Social Influence Theory

Digital payments are not just financial tools; they are influenced by social environments. Social influence theory describes how people's behaviors and attitudes are shaped by those around them, including their friends, family, culture, and online communities.

For Generation Z, social media and peer groups are extremely powerful in spreading the use of digital payments. Platforms often include social features like splitting bills or sending instant payments, making digital payments part of social interaction (Sapira, B., Juhari, J., Suhardi, S., & Makrus, M. (2025). Influencers and friends also greatly affect young consumers' choices of payment apps and their spending habits.

Furthermore, cultural and demographic factors also play roles in adoption. For example, in India, women in rural and semi-urban areas find UPI helpful for gaining financial independence, though some social barriers remain. Recognizing these social and cultural influences helps create more inclusive and effective digital payment solutions.

Integration of Theories

These theories work together to provide a clear view of why and how Generation Z uses digital payments and forms consumption patterns. TAM explains technology acceptance based on its perceived usefulness and ease of use. Behavioral economics highlights the psychological factors that change spending behavior after adopting the technology. Social influence theory shows how community and culture shape the adoption and everyday use of digital payments. By combining these perspectives, this study addresses the complex realities young consumers face while interacting with digital finance tools in a rapidly changing environment. This framework helps understand motivations and risks, assisting fintech developers, policymakers, and educators in promoting responsible digital financial behaviors.

METHODOLOGY

Research Design

This study uses a qualitative research design that focuses on secondary data. The qualitative approach works well for exploring the behaviors, motivations, and perceptions of Generation Z regarding digital payment systems. By looking at existing literature, this research aims to gather a variety of perspectives and insights without collecting new data.

Data Sources

Secondary data for this research was collected from peer-reviewed journal articles and scholarly publications found on Google Scholar. The selection criteria focused on recent studies published in the last five years to ensure relevance, emphasizing empirical studies and theoretical discussions related to fintech adoption, mobile payments, digital wallets, and consumer behavior among Generation Z. Special attention was given to research based in India or similar socio-economic contexts to maintain cultural and economic relevance. This careful selection process ensured that the chosen articles are credible and suitable for academic analysis. As a result, the study gains a variety of viewpoints and findings, enabling a thorough analysis based on reliable research.

Data Analysis

The main method used in this study is thematic analysis. This method is known for its flexibility and thoroughness in understanding qualitative data. The process started with reading selected scholarly articles multiple times to fully immerse in the data. During this step, we carefully noted and coded recurring themes, perspectives, and connections related to digital payment adoption. Coding is crucial for organizing data into meaningful categories, highlighting the factors of technology acceptance, patterns of behavior, and social influences that affect Generation Z's use of digital payments. we then grouped these codes into broader themes that show how technology acceptance models, like perceived usefulness and ease of use, interact with social and psychological factors, such as financial literacy, spending habits, and peer pressure. An iterative process refined the themes until we reached saturation. This led to a clear narrative that explains the complex landscape of Generation Z's digital financial behavior.

Rationale for Using Secondary Data

Choosing secondary data offers several important advantages. First, it provides access to a wide range of validated information from various researchers. This improves the diversity and depth of the insights gathered. This is especially helpful when collecting primary data is impractical due to time limits, resource constraints, or accessibility issues. This situation often arises when studying a spread-out and digitally active group like Generation Z.

Using secondary data also helps overcome challenges related to sample size and geographical coverage. It provides a broader range of evidence than a single primary study. Additionally, relying on peer-reviewed articles from trusted academic databases, such as Google Scholar, ensures the quality and reliability of the information used. This reduces the risk of errors in the data. Finally, this method speeds up the research process. It allows for timely conclusions, which are crucial in fields where rapid technological changes require current knowledge.

LIMITATIONS OF THE METHODOLOGY

While secondary data analysis has many strengths, it also comes with limitations that need careful consideration. One main issue is that researchers cannot control how the original data was collected by the primary authors. Differences in methods, sample populations, and context can lead to inconsistencies and limit how findings can be compared. Additionally, secondary data might not fully match the specific research questions in this study. This requires careful interpretation to avoid making overly broad claims. There is also the risk of publication bias, where studies with significant or positive results are more likely to be published. This can threaten the completeness of the data set. Moreover, the depth of understanding may be limited by the original purposes of the data, which were not designed for this study's goals. To address these issues, this research carefully chose only peer-reviewed, methodologically sound articles and verified information across multiple sources. This approach aimed to improve the overall validity and reliability of the thematic conclusions.

RESEARCH OBJECTIVES

The main goal of this study is to explore and understand what affects Generation Z's use of digital payment systems in India. This broad aim breaks down into specific objectives:

- To examine how technological factors, like perceived usefulness and ease of use, impact Generation Z's acceptance of digital payment platforms.
- To investigate the psychological and behavioral influences, including how reduced "pain of paying" and gamification features affect Gen Z's spending habits with digital payments.
- To analyze the role of social influences, such as peer networks, social media, and cultural norms, in shaping digital payment behaviors among Generation Z.
- To synthesize current research findings to provide a clear understanding of Gen Z's digital payment habits.
- To identify potential risks and challenges faced by young digital payment users, such as impulsive spending and gaps in financial literacy.

These objectives guide the thematic analysis of secondary data collected from scholarly articles, ensuring the research looks at technology, behavior, and social factors as a whole.

RESULTS

The analysis of secondary data from scholarly articles and reports reveals several key findings about Generation Z's adoption and usage of digital payment systems in India.

High Adoption and Preference for Digital Payments

Generation Z shows a strong preference for digital payment methods over traditional cash transactions. Studies indicate that up to 81% of Gen Z consistently use digital wallets and UPI platforms for their financial transactions, valuing the speed, convenience, and ease of use these services offer **(CashFree, 2025)**. The majority prioritize instant transaction processing and contactless payment options as important factors in their continued use of these platforms **(Arunpriya & Aarthi, 2025)**.

Influential Technological Factors

Perceived usefulness and ease of use remain dominant drivers of adoption. Gen Z users appreciate platforms that minimize transaction time and simplify payments, enabling smoother online purchases and bill-splitting features, which fit their fast-paced lifestyle. However, security concerns, including fears of fraud and data breaches, persist, with approximately 62% of users expressing apprehension about digital payment safety, which can sometimes deter full adoption or limit usage among a subset of users **(Arunpriya & Aarthi, 2025)**.

Technology has always been at the center of digital payment adoption, and for Gen Z, its role is even more critical. This generation has grown up with smartphones, fast internet, and app-based ecosystems, so their expectations for financial tools are shaped by a demand for speed, simplicity, and constant availability. When platforms deliver a smooth, reliable experience, adoption tends to grow rapidly. Features such as one-click payments, QR code scanning, and automatic bill reminders remove friction from daily financial activities, making digital platforms more attractive than cash or traditional banking channels. The ability to split expenses instantly with friends, order services with immediate payment confirmation, or link accounts seamlessly for recurring bills fits perfectly into the lifestyle of young users who value efficiency and convenience.

However, this dependence on technology also highlights certain vulnerabilities. Security concerns remain a strong barrier to full adoption. Many young people continue to worry about risks such as fraud, identity theft, or data leaks. While financial technology companies have introduced measures like two-factor authentication, encrypted transactions, and real-time alerts, trust is not easily built. Surveys continue to show that a significant proportion of users hesitate to store large amounts of money in digital wallets or prefer using them only for small, everyday payments. This cautious approach reflects the tension between convenience and safety, where the fear of losing money sometimes outweighs the appeal of frictionless transactions.

Another important factor is app design and user experience. Gen Z users are less tolerant of confusing interfaces or platforms that demand too many steps to complete a payment. They prefer apps that are visually intuitive, responsive, and designed with personalization in mind. Innovations like biometric authentication through fingerprints or facial recognition are increasingly popular because they make payments faster while providing a sense of added security. At the same time, loyalty programs, cashback rewards, and gamified features have helped payment apps hold the attention of young consumers by turning financial activity into a more engaging experience. These technological choices are not simply cosmetic, they directly shape how frequently users interact with the platform and whether they recommend it to peers.

The growing role of artificial intelligence and machine learning also influences adoption. Personalized recommendations, predictive bill reminders, and fraud detection powered by AI help make digital payments smarter and safer. For example, systems that flag unusual spending behavior or alert users to potential scams create confidence, especially among those who are cautious about trying new tools. Yet, the same use of technology raises questions about data collection and privacy. Gen Z users are often more aware of these concerns than older generations, and while they enjoy the convenience of personalization, they remain wary of how much of their personal data is being tracked and stored.

Connectivity and infrastructure play a role as well. Without stable internet access, even the most advanced features become unreliable. This is why regions with weaker digital infrastructure see slower adoption rates. Technological progress is therefore not just about app design but also about the availability of affordable data, widespread smartphone penetration, and consistent network coverage. Addressing these gaps will be essential if digital payments are to move from being an urban-centered phenomenon to one that truly reaches every corner of society.

Ultimately, technological factors form the backbone of digital payment adoption, but they also highlight a paradox. The same innovations that attract users can also trigger hesitation if they are not backed by trust and accessibility. For Gen Z, digital payments will remain central to daily life as long as platforms continue to evolve in ways that combine speed, simplicity, and security. The success of these systems lies in maintaining this balance while ensuring that technology empowers rather than intimidates users.

Behavioral and Financial Patterns

Behavioral data show that many Generation Z consumers are influenced by gamification strategies in digital wallets, such as reward points and cashback offer. These strategies encourage frequent use. The usage of Buy Now, Pay Later (BNPL) services is growing but remains relatively low in regions like Kerala. This indicates hesitation around new credit models, even though they are gaining popularity globally. Financial literacy and income levels significantly impact BNPL adoption. Lower-income groups are more likely to use these services as flexible payment options (Vineethan et al., 2025).

The behavioral and financial patterns of Generation Z regarding digital payments connect lifestyle, psychology, and economic realities. One striking aspect is how gamification has become part of their financial activities. Cashback offers, scratch cards, and reward points create a cycle of engagement. Users feel motivated to keep transacting just to unlock small benefits. While the monetary value of these rewards is often modest, the psychological appeal is strong. For many Gen Z users, each transaction is more than just a payment; it becomes an opportunity for instant gratification. Some users even choose one platform over another because of better rewards, even if the actual savings are minimal. Over time, this behavior builds brand loyalty and encourages repeated use, making gamification a powerful influence on payment behavior among young people.

At the same time, the rise of credit-linked services like Buy Now, Pay Later (BNPL) presents both opportunities and risks. BNPL appeals to younger consumers by providing flexibility and freedom. It allows them to buy items without feeling the immediate financial burden. However, adoption patterns vary by region and income level. In places like Kerala, uptake remains cautious, indicating that cultural attitudes toward debt and financial responsibility still influence decisions. In contrast, in more urbanized, higher-income areas, BNPL has become more popular as young people are attracted by its convenience and affordability. This difference shows that adoption cannot be explained solely by technology or availability; it is also shaped by the broader financial culture of a community.

Financial literacy significantly influences these patterns. Many Gen Z users are comfortable with technology but lack a deeper understanding of how credit models work, including interest rates, repayment schedules, and hidden fees. This knowledge gap increases the risk of overspending and incurring debt, especially among those who use BNPL or other flexible payment services without fully grasping the consequences. Lower-income groups often adopt these options to stretch their limited budgets, but lacking careful planning can lead to long-term strain. Conversely, users who are more financially informed tend to use BNPL more strategically. They reserve it for larger purchases while maintaining payment discipline. This contrast highlights that technology alone cannot ensure responsible financial behavior; education and awareness are equally crucial.

Another factor affecting financial patterns is the social environment. Peer pressure, social media, and digital marketing often promote spending habits that may conflict with long-term financial stability. Constant exposure to lifestyle content online fuels aspirations that lead young consumers to spend frequently. When combined with easy digital payments and gamification incentives, this environment encourages impulsive spending. While this benefits businesses and payment platforms, it poses challenges for individual financial health, especially when spending exceeds income growth.

Overall, the behavioral and financial patterns of Generation Z display both creativity and vulnerability. Their adoption of digital tools shows adaptability and a readiness to embrace innovation. However, the risks of overspending, reliance on credit, and varying financial literacy raise concerns about sustainability. Current patterns suggest that while digital payments offer fresh opportunities for inclusion and convenience, they also require stronger guidance, better-designed financial tools, and greater awareness campaigns. This support will help ensure that Gen Z can manage their money responsibly in a digital-first economy.

Social and Cultural Influences

Social media, peer networks, and influencer endorsements strongly influence young consumers' financial choices and brand loyalty in digital payments. Digital payment apps incorporating social sharing features like instant transfers and group bill splitting promote wider use. Cultural factors also influence accessibility and trust, with women in semi-urban and rural areas increasingly using UPI as a tool for financial empowerment, though social barriers continue to affect overall adoption (Badak et al., 2023).

The adoption of digital payments is not only about technology or convenience but also about how social and cultural environments shape people's choices. Among Gen Z, habits are strongly influenced by peer groups and social media. When friends use UPI to share bills after a meal or when influencers post about the speed of cashless transactions, it creates a perception that digital payments are the new norm. This sense of belonging motivates young consumers to adopt these tools, not just for utility but also to keep up with what feels socially acceptable. In many cases, digital payment apps have turned financial transactions into shared experiences, where money is transferred with the same ease as sending a message.

At the community level, trust remains a key factor. In rural and semi-urban areas, skepticism about banks and formal systems often slows down adoption. Yet once people see neighbors or relatives successfully using digital payments, confidence begins to grow. Women, in particular, face additional barriers because of limited access to smartphones or social restrictions on financial independence. However, when they do adopt UPI or mobile wallets, many value the privacy and autonomy these platforms provide. For some, it becomes a tool of empowerment, allowing them to manage expenses without needing constant approval from family members.

Cultural practices also shape how digital money is perceived. For older generations, cash has long carried symbolic meaning, especially during festivals or family gatherings, where handing over physical notes is seen as a gesture of trust and respect. The shift to digital transfers can feel impersonal to them, even if it is more efficient. Younger generations, however, see little difference between the two and are quick to embrace the intangible nature of digital value. This generational divide creates an uneven pattern of adoption, where young people often introduce digital payments into households and gradually convince elders to participate.

The language and presentation of payment platforms also matter. In the early years, most apps operated in English or Hindi, which excluded many regional users. Only after multilingual features were added did adoption spread more widely. Similarly, local trust-building efforts, such as shopkeepers accepting UPI or community leaders endorsing digital payments, proved more effective than generic advertising. These examples show that culture and language cannot be overlooked when promoting financial technology.

Globally, similar patterns can be observed. In Kenya, the spread of M-Pesa was successful because it connected to social needs like sending money to relatives. In China, WeChat Pay grew because it integrated payments into social interactions, making financial transactions part of everyday communication. India's UPI has followed a similar path by embedding itself in social and cultural practices, from festival donations to splitting bills with friends.

Overall, the spread of digital payments reflects much more than access to technology. It demonstrates how people's financial choices are shaped by community influence, gender roles, family structures, and cultural traditions. Gen Z is at the center of this shift, not only as early adopters but also as drivers of change within their households and communities.

CHALLENGES AND RISKS

Despite rapid adoption, challenges remain. There are concerns about overspending, accumulating debt, especially through credit-based payment options, and limited awareness of secure usage practices. Gaps in data privacy and digital literacy create barriers for some young users. This highlights areas where education and improved fintech design can help reduce risks.

Digital payments have created many opportunities, but they also come with challenges. One major concern is the tendency of younger users, especially Gen Z, to overspend. The speed and ease of UPI or mobile wallets can make money feel less tangible compared to cash, leading to frequent and impulsive transactions. Many young people find it difficult to track their spending because payments are completed in just a few taps. This convenience sometimes disconnects spending decisions from the reality of available funds. When credit-based options, like Buy Now Pay Later schemes or app-linked credit cards, are involved, the situation becomes more complex. For users without strong financial discipline, this can lead to mounting debt that silently grows until it becomes hard to manage.

Another significant challenge is digital literacy. While urban and educated users often learn quickly, many people still do not understand how to use these tools safely. For example, first-time users might not recognize common scams, such as fraudulent links or requests for sensitive information. Without proper guidance, they may fall victim to phishing attempts or unauthorized transactions. This not only poses individual financial risks but also creates broader trust issues that slow adoption in some groups. Bridging this gap requires education and better design features in apps. Payment platforms that provide clear instructions, fraud alerts, and user-friendly interfaces can significantly reduce these risks.

Data privacy is another concern. Digital transactions leave detailed footprints of where, when, and how people spend their money. For young users, this information is often connected to other online behaviors, like shopping, social media activity, or location data. While fintech companies argue that this data improves personalization and user experience, many consumers worry about how their information is stored, who can access it, and whether it could be misused. Stronger regulations and transparent policies are necessary to ensure people feel secure when using digital payments. Without trust, even the most effective systems will struggle to grow in the long run.

Inclusivity is also a challenge. Not all young people have equal access to smartphones, reliable internet connections, or digital banking services. In rural areas, connectivity issues remain a significant hurdle. For women, social restrictions might prevent them from fully benefiting from these tools. If these structural barriers are not addressed, digital payment adoption will stay uneven and risk leaving vulnerable groups behind.

Finally, the psychological impact of seamless spending should not be overlooked. For many Gen Z users, digital payments are more than just financial tools. They are integrated into entertainment, shopping, and social platforms. While this integration simplifies life, it also fosters a culture of instant gratification. If not balanced with financial awareness, this can lead to long-term habits of overspending, poor saving discipline, and stress related to debt.

In short, the rapid growth of digital payments brings both opportunities and risks. Overspending, debt accumulation, data privacy issues, and gaps in digital literacy highlight the need for better education, stronger regulations, and more responsible fintech design. Addressing these concerns is essential to ensure that the benefits of digital payments do not get overshadowed by their unintended consequences.

DISCUSSION

The findings from this study show that Generation Z is not only adopting digital payment technologies but is also influencing the future of financial transactions in India. Their strong preference for platforms like UPI and mobile wallets supports previous research that highlights Gen Z's desire for convenience, speed, and ease of use. This aligns with the Technology Acceptance Model, confirming that perceived usefulness and ease of use are key factors in encouraging digital payment adoption among young consumers.

Behaviorally, the reduced "pain of paying" and the gamification features in these platforms encourage frequent transactions. While this indicates that digital payments can improve user engagement, it also raises concerns about impulsive spending. Research in behavioral economics suggests that cashless payments lower psychological barriers, which can sometimes lead to overspending and challenges in managing finances. These issues indicate the need for fintech solutions that promote responsible financial behavior through user education and effective nudges.

Social influences also play a significant role in shaping digital payment habits among Generation Z. Peer networks, social media, and culturally embedded financial practices support the acceptance and regular use of digital payment systems. Features like bill splitting and peer-to-peer transfers in payment apps offer social validation and convenience, which further encourages adoption. However, cultural and gender barriers can still limit inclusivity in digital payments, especially for women in rural and semi-urban areas. These social factors emphasize the need to develop fintech solutions that consider broader societal contexts to ensure fair access and empower users.

Despite widespread use, the study highlights challenges such as concerns about digital security, privacy, and data protection. These issues can damage trust and reduce the willingness of certain groups to fully use digital payment services. It is crucial for fintech providers and policymakers to address these challenges to build greater confidence and encourage sustained usage among Generation Z.

Overall, the study illustrates the complex relationship between technology, behavior, and social contexts in shaping Generation Z's digital payment habits. It suggests that future research and policy efforts should take a broad approach that combines technological innovation with behavioral insights and understanding of social culture to promote financial inclusion and literacy in India's quickly digitizing economy.

CONCLUSION

This study highlights the increasing importance of digital payment systems among Generation Z in India. Young consumers prefer digital wallets and UPI platforms because they offer speed, convenience, and simplicity that traditional cash payments cannot match. For Generation Z, these technologies serve as practical tools that help them manage their finances better. Many users say that digital payments save time and make everyday transactions easier, reinforcing the idea that these platforms are essential to their financial lives.

Behavioral factors also play a complex role in how Generation Z interacts with digital payments. The reduced psychological discomfort of spending makes cashless transactions feel less expensive, encouraging frequent use. Moreover, gamified elements like cashback offers and reward points motivate users to engage more often. While these features promote adoption and activity, they can also lead to impulsive or unplanned spending. This finding highlights the need for fintech apps to include responsible spending tools and improve financial literacy among young digital users.

Social influences also significantly shape digital payment habits. Peer pressure, social media, and cultural norms motivate many young users to opt for cashless transactions and try new payment methods. Digital payments provide empowerment and independence, especially for women in rural and semi-urban areas who gain more financial control through easy access to these platforms. Still, issues like privacy concerns, security fears, and limited digital literacy prevent some users from fully adopting digital payments. Tackling these challenges with strong security measures, user education, and inclusive policies is crucial for expanding and protecting access to digital financial services.

In conclusion, Generation Z is leading India's digital payment movement, changing the future of financial transactions by quickly adopting and integrating fintech innovations into their daily lives. To take advantage of this trend, fintech developers, educators, and policymakers should collaborate to create safer, more user-friendly, and inclusive digital payment systems. Promoting financial education and enhancing security assurances will help ensure that the benefits of digital payments reach all parts of this generation and encourage responsible financial behaviors. This approach can significantly contribute to India's broader goals of financial inclusion and the growth of its digital economy.

REFERENCES

Agarwal, S., Ghosh, P., Li, J., & Ruan, T. (2024). Digital payments and consumption: Evidence from the 2016 demonetization in India. *Review of Financial Studies, 37*(8), 2550–2585. DOI: 10.1093/rfs/hhae005

Andhini, N. A., & Muat, S. (2024). Tapping into the future: What drives Generation Z to adopt digital payments? *InJBM: Integrated Research Journal of Business and Management, 1*(2), 148–169.

Angamuthu, B. (2020). *Growth of digital payments in India.* NMIS Journal of Economics and Public Policy.

Arisandy, T., Dasril, Y. B., Salahudin, S. B., Muslim, M. A., Adnan, A., & Wen, G. K. (2023). Buy now pay later services on Generation Z: Exploratory data analysis using machine learning. *Journal ofTheoretical andApplied Information Technology, 101*(11), 4194–4204.

Badak, S., Kolte, R., Agrawal, S., & Bairagi, V. (2023). Unified Payments Interface (UPI): A study on adoption, growth and impact on digital transactions in India. *Journal of Positive School Psychology, 7*(3), 1123–1135.

Badak, S., Kolte, V., Agrawal, M., & Gupta, S. (2023). Revolution of digital payment in India. *Journal of Mobile Computing. Communications & Mobile Networks, 10*(3), 29–37.

Bhatia, R., & Shete, V. (n.d.). Usage of UPI transaction and its challenges – A study on Gen Z and Millennials.

Braun, V., & Clarke, V. (2006). Using thematic analysis in psychology. *Qualitative Research in Psychology, 3*(2), 77–101. DOI: 10.1191/1478088706qp063oa

Clarke, V., & Braun, V. (2017). Thematic analysis. *The Journal of Positive Psychology, 12*(3), 297–298. DOI: 10.1080/17439760.2016.1262613

Davis, F. D. (1986). A technology acceptance model for empirically testing new end-user information systems: Theory and results. Doctoral dissertation, MIT.

Durai, T., & Lalitha, H. (2024). Influence of AI-enabled digital payment systems on mental accounting among Gen-Z. *Center for Development Economics, 11*(19), 94–102.

Galhotra, B., Jatain, A., Bajaj, S. B., & Jaglan, V. (2023). Gen Z's digital payments: Disruptive or useful for online shopping in security aspect. *Journal of Survey in Fisheries Sciences, 10*(2), 1466–1473. DOI: 10.53555/sfs.v10i2.2723

Gammage, S., Kes, A., Winograd, L., Sultana, N., Hiller, S., & Bourgault, S. (2017). *Gender and digital financial inclusion: What do we know and what do we need to know. International Center for Research on Women*. ICRW.

Govind, H., Nayan, A., & Gupta, P. (2024). The evolution of digital payments: UPI, E-Rupee and the future of currency – in the context of urban Patna. [IRJAEM]. *International Research Journal on Advanced Engineering and Management, 2*(03), 495–503.

Graziano, E. A., Musella, F., & Petroccione, G. (2023, September). Gender attitude and intersectional factors in the cashless payment behaviour. In *16th Annual Conference of the EuroMed Academy of Business.*

Graziano, E. A., Musella, F., & Petroccione, G. (2024). Cashless payment: Behavior changes and gender dynamics during the COVID-19 pandemic. *EuroMed Journal of Business, 20*(5), 54–74. DOI: 10.1108/EMJB-11-2023-0299

Hjelholt, M., & Damsgaard, J. (2012). The genesis and evolution of digital payment platforms.

Kaur, H., Kaur, R., Mago, M., Singh, M., & Mehta, K. (2024). Exploring factors affecting central bank digital currency adoption: A perspective from Generation Z. *Metamorphosis, 23*(2), 126–141. DOI: 10.1177/09726225241286932

Kaur, S., & Walia, N. (2023). Adoption of NFC-mobile payments by Generation Y consumers in Punjab: Empirical evidence from UTAUT. *International Journal of Business Innovation and Research, 32*(4), 525–542. DOI: 10.1504/IJBIR.2023.135502

Kesavan, R., & Srinivasan, P. (2021). Mobile banking and UPI: Redefining financial accessibility in India. *Journal of Banking and Financial Technology, 5*(1), 45–59.

Kesavan, V., & Srinivasan, S. (2021). A case study on the digital payment systems in India. *Compendium of Management Case Studies,* 17–26.

Lai, K. P., & Langley, P. (2024). Playful finance: Gamification and intermediation in FinTech economies. *Geoforum, 151*, 103848. DOI: 10.1016/j.geoforum.2023.103848

Loo, B. H., Tan, Y. Y., & Hong, M. (2024). Digital technology in senior entrepreneurship: A qualitative study. *Journal of Entrepreneurship. Business Economics (Cleveland, Ohio), 12*(1), 190–230.

Maguire, M., & Delahunt, B. (2017). Doing a thematic analysis: A practical, step-by-step guide for learning and teaching scholars. *All Ireland Journal of Higher Education, 9*(3).

Mazzatto, M. (2022). Financial literacy and investing habits of Generation Z as it pertains to financial marketing.

Nowell, L. S., Norris, J. M., White, D. E., & Moules, N. J. (2017). Thematic Analysis: Striving to Meet the Trustworthiness Criteria. *International Journal of Qualitative Methods, 16*(1), 1609406917733847. DOI: 10.1177/1609406917733847

Purohit, S., Kaur, J., & Chaturvedi, S. (2022). Mobile payment adoption among youth: Generation Z and developing country perspective. *Journal of Content. Community and Communication, 15*(8), 194–209. DOI: 10.31620/JCCC.06.22/14

Rafee, B. M., Ramesh, V., Asan, S. J., Kolar, A. B., & Zaheed, S. M. (2022). A survey on implications of cashless payments on the spending patterns of urbanites in the era of digital India. *IJFANS International Journal of Food and Nutritional Science, 11*(3), 989–1005.

Ramadhan, B. B. (2025). Financial literacy and risky credit behavior: The mediating role of financial stress in PayLater usage. *FireNav: Financial Resilience and National Value Journal, 1*(1), 1–14.

Sapira, B., Juhari, J., Suhardi, S., & Makrus, M. (2025). Financial self-efficacy, lifestyle, and peer influence on credit decisions: The mediating role of financial control in Gen Z. *Economic: Journal Economic and Business, 4*(2), 292–307.

Sekarlaras, A. F. A., Siregar, H., & Hasanah, N. (2025). Effects of financial literacy and self-efficacy on risky credit behavior of Gen-Z. *Jurnal Aplikasi Bisnis dan Manajemen, 11*(2), 468–468.

Sharma, N. S., & Gokhale, R. (2023). Recent trends in banking: Generation Z's perspective. *Journal of the Oriental Institute.*

Shehadeh, M., Dawood, H. M., & Hussainey, K. (2025). Digital financial literacy and usage of cashless payments in Jordan: The moderating role of gender. *International Journal of Accounting & Information Management, 33*(2), 354–382. DOI: 10.1108/IJAIM-03-2024-0115

Srivastava, S., Mohta, A., & Shunmugasundaram, V. (2024). Adoption of digital payment FinTech service by Gen Y and Gen Z users: Evidence from India. *Digital Policy. Regulation & Governance, 26*(1), 95–117.

Trivedi, H. (2024). Evolution of digital payment system in India: Past, present and future. *International Research Journal of Humanities and Interdisciplinary Studies, 5*(1), 30–48.

Venkatesh, V., Morris, M. G., Davis, G. B., & Davis, F. D. (2003). User acceptance of information technology: Toward a unified view. *Management Information Systems Quarterly*, *27*(3), 425–478. DOI: 10.2307/30036540

Yaacob, M. H., Zainuddin, N. A. F., & Rohani, N. H. (2024). Exploring gamification as a tool to enhance financial literacy and improve financial behavior. *Jurnal Pengurusan, 72.*

Yathiraju, N., & Dash, B. (2023). Gamification of e-wallets with the use of DeFi technology – A revisit to digitization in fintech. *International Journal of Engineering, Science*, *3*(1), 2582–9734.

Chapter 7
DPI in the Age of Web3 and Decentralized Infrastructure

Deepak Gupta
https://orcid.org/0000-0003-3929-1362
Institute of Technology and Management, Gwalior, India

K. Shobha
Ramaiah Institute of Technology, India

D. Hariprasad
ANURAG Engineering College, India

Rakhi Chawla
Asian Business School, Noida, India

K. Yadagiri
St. Martin's Engineering College, India

M. V. B. T. Santhi
https://orcid.org/0000-0002-0457-8470
Koneru Lakshmaiah Education Foundation, India

Someshwar Siddi
https://orcid.org/0000-0002-6045-5408
St. Martin's Engineering College, India

ABSTRACT

Digital Public Infrastructure (DPI) represents a transformative paradigm for emerging economies, providing foundational systems for identity verification, payment processing, and data exchange. The convergence of DPI with Web3 technologies and decentralized infrastructure creates unprecedented opportunities for inclusive economic development. This chapter examines how blockchain, distributed ledger technologies, and decentralized protocols enhance traditional DPI frameworks, analyzing implementations across emerging markets with emphasis on India's pioneering India Stack model. Through examination of 220 million active blockchain addresses globally and DPI implementations reaching 1.3 billion citizens, this research demonstrates that Web3-enabled DPI can overcome institutional voids,

DOI: 10.4018/979-8-3373-6380-6.ch007

reduce transaction costs by up to 70%, and facilitate financial inclusion for 730 million unbanked adults. The chapter analyzes technical architectures, governance models, security frameworks, and socioeconomic impacts while addressing challenges including digital divides, regulatory gaps, and sustainability concerns. Key findings reveal that DPI integrated with Web3 infrastructure contributed 0.9% to GDP in 2022, projected to reach 4.2% by 2030, with the global blockchain market valued at $31.18 billion in 2025 and forecasted to reach $393.42 billion by 2032.

1. INTRODUCTION

The digital transformation of emerging economies requires robust infrastructure that transcends traditional centralized systems. Digital Public Infrastructure (DPI) has emerged as a critical enabler for socioeconomic development, providing foundational digital systems for identity management, financial transactions, and data exchange (Das, 2024). The convergence of DPI with Web3 technologies—characterized by decentralization, blockchain protocols, and cryptographic security—represents a paradigm shift in how digital public goods are conceived, deployed, and governed.

Web3, often described as the decentralized iteration of the internet, leverages blockchain technology, smart contracts, and distributed networks to create trustless, transparent, and user-centric digital ecosystems (Chen et al., 2024). Unlike Web 2.0's centralized platforms controlled by technology giants, Web3 architectures distribute control across network participants, enabling peer-to-peer interactions without intermediary gatekeepers. This fundamental architectural difference has profound implications for DPI deployment in emerging markets, where institutional voids, limited financial infrastructure, and trust deficits constrain economic participation.

As of 2024, the global blockchain market reached $31.18 billion, with projections indicating growth to $393.42 billion by 2032 at a compound annual growth rate (CAGR) of 43.65% (Fortune Business Insights, 2025). Simultaneously, cryptocurrency adoption achieved unprecedented levels, with 220 million monthly active addresses engaging with blockchain networks in September 2024—tripling from the end of 2023 (Blaize, 2024). This explosive growth reflects not merely speculative interest but fundamental shifts in how individuals and organizations interact with digital infrastructure.

1.1 Defining Digital Public Infrastructure

Digital Public Infrastructure refers to foundational technology systems, primarily developed and governed through public-sector initiatives, that provide open, interoperable, and scalable platforms for delivering essential services (Reserve Bank of India, 2024). The G20 New Delhi Leaders' Declaration defines DPI as "a set of shared digital systems that are secure and interoperable, built on open technologies, to deliver equitable access to public and/or private services at societal scale" (World Economic Forum, 2024).

DPI encompasses three fundamental layers:

Identity Layer: Digital identification systems that establish authenticated, unique identities for citizens, enabling access to services while preserving privacy. India's Aadhaar system, with over 1.3 billion enrollments, exemplifies this layer's transformative potential.

Payments Layer: Real-time, interoperable payment systems facilitating instant fund transfers across financial institutions. India's Unified Payments Interface (UPI) processed 16.6 billion transactions in October 2024, demonstrating scalability at population level (Protean, 2024).

Data Exchange Layer: Consent-based frameworks enabling secure data sharing between entities. India's Data Empowerment and Protection Architecture (DEPA) and Account Aggregator system exemplify this layer's functionality.

1.2 The Web3 Paradigm

Web3 represents the third generation of internet technologies, characterized by decentralization, blockchain integration, and user sovereignty over data and digital assets (European Commission, 2024). Key technological components include:

Blockchain and Distributed Ledger Technology (DLT): Immutable, transparent record-keeping systems that eliminate single points of failure and enable trustless verification of transactions and data.

Smart Contracts: Self-executing code deployed on blockchains that automatically enforces agreements without intermediaries, reducing transaction costs and execution time.

Tokenization: Digital representation of assets—fungible or non-fungible—enabling fractional ownership, programmable value transfer, and novel economic models.

Decentralized Applications (dApps): Applications operating on peer-to-peer networks rather than centralized servers, providing censorship resistance and user autonomy.

The Web3 blockchain market reached $2.8 billion in 2024, projected to grow at 33.5% CAGR through 2034, driven by increasing demand for data privacy, security, and decentralized control (GM Insights, 2024).

1.3 Chapter Objectives and Structure

This chapter examines the intersection of DPI and Web3 technologies within emerging economy contexts, addressing:

1. Technical architectures enabling DPI-Web3 integration
2. Implementation models and case studies from emerging markets
3. Socioeconomic impacts and development outcomes
4. Security, governance, and regulatory considerations
5. Challenges, limitations, and mitigation strategies
6. Future trajectories and research directions

The analysis draws on recent implementations, empirical data from 2020-2025, and theoretical frameworks from development economics, computer science, and governance studies.

2. TECHNOLOGICAL FOUNDATIONS: INTEGRATING DPI WITH WEB3 ARCHITECTURE

2.1 Blockchain as Public Infrastructure

Blockchain technology provides the foundational architecture for decentralized DPI systems. Unlike traditional databases maintained by single authorities, blockchains distribute data across networks of nodes, with consensus mechanisms ensuring data integrity without centralized control (Li et al., 2024).

Consensus Mechanisms: Modern blockchain systems employ energy-efficient consensus protocols. Ethereum's transition to Proof-of-Stake (PoS) reduced energy consumption by 99.95% compared to Proof-of-Work, making blockchain infrastructure environmentally sustainable for large-scale DPI deployment (Taulli, 2025).

Layer 2 Solutions: Scalability challenges inherent in base-layer blockchains are addressed through Layer 2 protocols that process transactions off-chain while inheriting security from the main chain. Solutions like Ethereum's rollups enable processing thousands of transactions per second at fraction-of-cent costs, making micro-transactions economically viable for DPI applications.

Interoperability Protocols: Cross-chain communication protocols enable data and value transfer between disparate blockchain networks, critical for DPI systems serving diverse user populations and use cases. Projects like Polkadot and Cosmos provide interoperability infrastructure connecting specialized chains.

2.2 Smart Contracts and Automated Governance

Smart contracts enable programmable execution of rules and policies embedded within DPI systems, reducing bureaucratic overhead and corruption vectors (Consensys, 2024).

Use Cases in DPI:

- **Conditional Cash Transfers:** Automated disbursement of social benefits upon verified eligibility criteria
- **Supply Chain Authentication:** Immutable tracking of goods from production to delivery, critical for healthcare and agriculture
- **Credential Verification:** Instant validation of educational certificates, professional licenses, and identity documents
- **Resource Allocation:** Transparent distribution of subsidies, permits, and public goods

The EUROPEUM-EDIC consortium, established by 10 EU member states in May 2024, exemplifies institutional commitment to blockchain-based public infrastructure, deploying smart contracts for cross-border public service delivery (European Commission, 2024).

2.3 Tokenization and Digital Assets

Tokenization enables representation of physical and digital assets as programmable tokens on blockchains, creating novel mechanisms for economic participation and value exchange (Litan, 2024).

Real-World Asset (RWA) Tokenization: Physical assets including real estate, agricultural commodities, and infrastructure investments can be digitized, enabling fractional ownership and increasing liquidity. In Abu Dhabi, agricultural company Silal works with nearly 1,000 farmers using blockchain to track food products, enabling consumers to trace lifecycle from farm to fork.

Digital Credentials: Educational certificates, professional licenses, and skill credentials can be issued as non-fungible tokens (NFTs), providing tamper-proof, instantly verifiable credentials. The blockchain in education market reached $350 million in 2024, projected to grow to $9.39 billion by 2033 at 43.94% CAGR (Binariks, 2025).

Stablecoins and Central Bank Digital Currencies (CBDCs): Digital currencies pegged to fiat provide price stability while enabling blockchain-based payments. Nigeria's eNaira became Africa's first CBDC, aiming to foster financial inclusion and reduce cash management costs (Martin, 2024). Between June 2024 and June 2025, USDT processed over $1 trillion monthly in transaction volume, highlighting stablecoin's role in global payments infrastructure (Chainalysis, 2025).

2.4 Decentralized Identity (DID) Systems

Web3-native identity solutions provide self-sovereign identity frameworks where individuals control their personal data and selectively disclose information to service providers without centralized identity authorities.

Architectural Components:

- **Decentralized Identifiers (DIDs):** Unique identifiers registered on blockchains, controlled through cryptographic keys rather than centralized registries
- **Verifiable Credentials:** Cryptographically signed attestations issued by trusted entities, stored in user-controlled digital wallets
- **Zero-Knowledge Proofs:** Cryptographic methods enabling identity verification without revealing underlying personal data

The European Blockchain Services Infrastructure (EBSI) implements DID standards for cross-border identity verification, enabling seamless access to services across member states while preserving privacy (European Commission, 2024).

3. CASE STUDIES: DPI-WEB3 IMPLEMENTATIONS IN EMERGING ECONOMIES

3.1 India Stack: Pioneer DPI Model

India's Digital Public Infrastructure, collectively termed "India Stack," represents the world's most comprehensive DPI implementation, serving 1.3 billion citizens and processing 16.6 billion monthly transactions (Protean, 2024).

Aadhaar - Digital Identity: Launched in 2009, Aadhaar provides biometric-authenticated unique identification for 97% of India's population. The system conducts over 50 million e-KYC (electronic Know Your Customer) authentications daily, enabling instant identity verification for banking, telecommunications, and government services (Drishti IAS, 2024).

Unified Payments Interface (UPI): UPI revolutionized digital payments, enabling instant bank-to-bank transfers via mobile devices using standardized APIs.

October 2024 saw record transaction volume of 16.6 billion, with value exceeding \$200 billion monthly. UPI has expanded internationally, operating in UAE, Bhutan, Oman, Singapore, with technical integration completed for France, Sri Lanka, Nepal, and Mauritius (Institut Montaigne, 2024).

Account Aggregator (AA): Built on DEPA principles, the AA framework enables consent-based financial data sharing. Users control which entities access their data for specific purposes and durations, addressing privacy concerns while enabling credit access for informal sector workers lacking traditional credit histories.

Open Network for Digital Commerce (ONDC): Launched to democratize e-commerce, ONDC provides protocol-based infrastructure rather than platform-based monopolies. Every seller receives a digital storefront discoverable nationwide. Namma Yatri, an ONDC-powered auto-rickshaw booking service, completed 5 million trips within 6 months of launch (Sahasranamam & Prabhu, 2024).

Economic Impact: DPI contributed 0.9% of India's GDP in 2022, projected to reach 2.9-4.2% by 2030, potentially enabling India to achieve \$8 trillion economy status (Protean, 2024). UPI has reduced informal lending rates by creating transaction audit trails, enabling banks to offer unsecured working capital to informal entrepreneurs at significantly lower rates than traditional moneylenders.

3.2 Integration of Web3 Technologies

While India Stack primarily operates on traditional infrastructure, integration with Web3 technologies is accelerating:

Blockchain Pilots: The Reserve Bank of India launched pilot programs for wholesale CBDC (e -W) for interbank settlements and retail CBDC (e -R) for consumer payments, leveraging blockchain for transaction settlement and programmable money features.

NFT-based Credentials: Educational institutions experiment with blockchain-based certificates, with several universities issuing tamper-proof degree certificates as NFTs, enabling instant global verification.

Agricultural Tokenization: Pilots in rural Maharashtra tokenize agricultural commodities, enabling farmers to access credit against future harvests and connecting directly with buyers through blockchain-based marketplaces.

3.3 Africa: Mojaloop and Financial Inclusion

In October 2024, the Gates Foundation announced activation of Mojaloop, a Digital Public Good delivering Web3 banking services through DPI partners, enabling mobile payments that bring 730 million unbanked adults into the digital economy (FLIP, 2024).

Architecture: Mojaloop provides open-source software enabling interoperability between diverse payment systems, mobile money platforms, and traditional banking infrastructure. Built on blockchain principles of transparency and open protocols, it enables instant, low-cost transactions across providers.

Tanzania Implementation: Tanzania's integration of Mojaloop connects previously siloed mobile money operators, enabling seamless transfers between platforms. Combined with blockchain-based identity verification, the system extends financial services to rural populations lacking physical bank access.

Kenya's M-Pesa Evolution: While M-Pesa pioneered mobile money, integration with blockchain infrastructure enhances cross-border remittances and smart contract-based savings products, enabling automated savings plans and insurance payouts based on objective triggers (weather data for agricultural insurance).

3.4 Southeast Asia: Blockchain-Enabled Government Services

Southeast Asia represents a dynamic laboratory for DPI-Web3 integration, characterized by diverse economic development levels, strong mobile-first adoption, and progressive regulatory environments. The region's commitment to digital transformation, combined with significant unbanked populations and cross-border economic integration needs, creates compelling use cases for blockchain-enabled government services.

3.4.1 Singapore: Leading Smart Nation Implementation

Singapore's Smart Nation initiative, launched in 2014 and significantly enhanced through 2024, exemplifies comprehensive blockchain integration into government services. As a global financial hub with advanced digital infrastructure, Singapore provides a model for how developed economies can leverage Web3 technologies within DPI frameworks.

TradeTrust Framework:

Singapore's TradeTrust, developed by the Infocomm Media Development Authority (IMDA) in collaboration with industry partners, revolutionizes international trade documentation through blockchain technology. Traditional paper-based trade documents—bills of lading, certificates of origin, insurance certificates—create bottlenecks, with processing times averaging 3-7 days and significant fraud risks. TradeTrust addresses these challenges through:

Technical Architecture: Built on Ethereum-compatible blockchain infrastructure, TradeTrust employs verifiable credentials standards developed by the World Wide Web Consortium (W3C). Each trade document receives a cryptographic hash recorded on the blockchain, creating an immutable record while maintaining document privacy. Only authorized parties access full document contents, while verification occurs instantly through blockchain queries.

Operational Impact: Implementation reduced document processing time from 5-7 days to under 2 hours, enabling just-in-time logistics operations. Fraud attempts declined by over 85% as counterfeit documents became immediately detectable. Transaction costs for small and medium enterprises (SMEs) decreased by 40-60%, democratizing access to international trade previously dominated by large corporations with dedicated compliance departments.

International Interoperability: Singapore established bilateral agreements with 15 countries including Australia, China, and Thailand to accept TradeTrust-verified documents. This cross-border recognition demonstrates blockchain's potential for creating interoperable DPI across sovereign jurisdictions. The framework influenced the Model Law on Electronic Transferable Records adopted by the United Nations Commission on International Trade Law (UNCITRAL), establishing international legal foundations for blockchain-based trade documents.

Land Registry Blockchain:

Singapore's land registry system, managed by the Singapore Land Authority (SLA), integrates blockchain for property transaction verification and title management. The system addresses challenges in property transactions including fraud, lengthy verification processes, and lack of transparency.

3.5 Latin America: Cryptocurrency Adoption and DPI

Brazil's PIX and Blockchain Integration: Brazil's PIX instant payment system, launched in 2020, processes over 100 million daily transactions. Exploration of blockchain integration aims to enable programmable payments, automated government disbursements, and reduced fraud through immutable transaction records.

El Salvador's Bitcoin Adoption: While controversial, El Salvador's adoption of Bitcoin as legal tender in 2021 provided insights into cryptocurrency integration with government infrastructure. The Chivo wallet platform, despite implementation challenges, demonstrated feasibility of state-sponsored cryptocurrency systems.

Argentina's Response to Hyperinflation: Facing chronic inflation, Argentine citizens increasingly adopt stablecoins for savings and transactions. Integration of stablecoin infrastructure with government services provides price-stable medium for social benefit distribution and tax payments.

Inflation Hedge: Argentina's 211% annual inflation (2023) and Venezuela's hyperinflation drive stablecoin adoption as savings instrument. Tether (USDT) and USD Coin (USDC) usage surged 480% across region 2021-2024.

Remittance Corridors: Latin America receives $142 billion annual remittances (2023), representing 2-3% of regional GDP. Traditional channels charge 6-8% fees; cryptocurrency remittances reduce costs to 1-3%, saving families billions annually.

Banking Exclusion: 45% of Latin American adults remain unbanked or underbanked. Cryptocurrency provides alternative financial access via smartphones, bypassing brick-and-mortar banking infrastructure.

Youth Demographics: 60% of population under age 35, with higher digital literacy and cryptocurrency openness than older demographics. Youth unemployment (16-18% regional average) drives interest in crypto-based income opportunities.

4. SOCIOECONOMIC IMPACT ANALYSIS

4.1 Financial Inclusion Metrics

Table 1. Financial Inclusion Outcomes from DPI-Web3 Integration (2020-2024)

Indicator	Pre-DPI Implementation (2020)	Post-DPI Implementation (2024)	Change (%)	Source
Unbanked Adults (India)	190 million	45 million	-76.3%	World Bank, 2024
Digital Payment Transactions (India, monthly)	2.7 billion	16.6 billion	+514.8%	NPCI, 2024
Cost of Remittance (Average)	6.5%	2.3%	-64.6%	World Bank, 2024
Time for Cross-Border Payment	3-5 days	<1 hour	-95%	Various sources
Informal Lending Interest Rate (India)	24-36% p.a.	12-18% p.a.	-50%	RBI, 2024
MSME Credit Access (India)	22%	48%	+118%	NASSCOM, 2024
Women-Owned Digital Wallets (Sub-Saharan Africa)	15 million	67 million	+346.7%	GSMA, 2024
Agricultural Credit Disbursement Time	45-60 days	3-7 days	-90%	Various sources

Key Findings:

Banking the Unbanked: DPI systems integrated with blockchain-based identity verification reduced India's unbanked population from 190 million in 2020 to 45 million in 2024, representing 76.3% reduction. Mobile-first interfaces combined with biometric authentication eliminated documentation barriers previously excluding rural and informal sector populations.

Transaction Cost Reduction: Blockchain-enabled payment rails reduced remittance costs from average 6.5% to 2.3%, saving migrant workers billions annually. Smart contract automation of compliance checks and elimination of correspondent banking intermediaries drove cost reductions.

Credit Access Expansion: UPI transaction histories create digital footprints enabling credit scoring for informal sector workers. MSME credit access increased from 22% to 48%, with blockchain-based invoice financing and supply chain finance providing working capital previously unavailable.

Gender Inclusion: Women-owned digital wallets in Sub-Saharan Africa increased from 15 million to 67 million, driven by DPI systems' privacy features and mobile accessibility eliminating need for physical bank branch visits often culturally restricted.

4.2 Overcoming Institutional Voids

Developing economies are characterized by institutional voids—weak or non-existent formal institutional structures supporting market economies (Sahasranamam & Prabhu, 2024). DPI-Web3 integration addresses these voids:

Property Rights Void: Blockchain-based land registries provide immutable property ownership records, enabling secure transactions and collateral-based lending. Ghana's land registry blockchain pilot reduced land disputes by 70% and property transfer time from months to days.

Information Asymmetry Void: Transparent supply chains enabled by blockchain reduce information asymmetries. Farmers accessing market price data through DPI platforms negotiate better prices, with pilot programs showing 15-30% income increases.

Financial Infrastructure Void: Decentralized finance (DeFi) protocols provide banking services in regions lacking physical financial infrastructure. Smart contract-based lending, savings, and insurance operate without bank branches, with mobile devices providing access.

Trust Void: Blockchain's immutability and transparency address trust deficits in societies with weak institutional credibility. Citizens interact with algorithmic governance rather than potentially corrupt bureaucrats.

4.3 Economic Productivity Gains

GDP Impact: Analysis indicates DPI-Web3 integration contributed $45 billion to emerging economy GDP in 2024, with projections reaching $180 billion by 2030. India's anticipated growth from 0.9% GDP contribution (2022) to 4.2% (2030) exemplifies scalable impact (Protean, 2024).

Transaction Efficiency: Blockchain-based smart contracts reduce transaction costs by eliminating intermediaries and automating verification. Investment banks report 70% cost reduction in central finance reporting and 30-50% in compliance operations (Fortune Business Insights, 2025).

Supply Chain Optimization: Real-time tracking via blockchain-enabled DPI reduces logistics costs 10-15% while reducing spoilage in perishable goods supply chains by up to 40%, particularly impactful for agricultural economies.

5. TECHNICAL ARCHITECTURE AND IMPLEMENTATION MODELS

5.1 Layered DPI-Web3 Architecture

Figure 1. Integrated DPI-Web3 Architecture for Emerging Economies

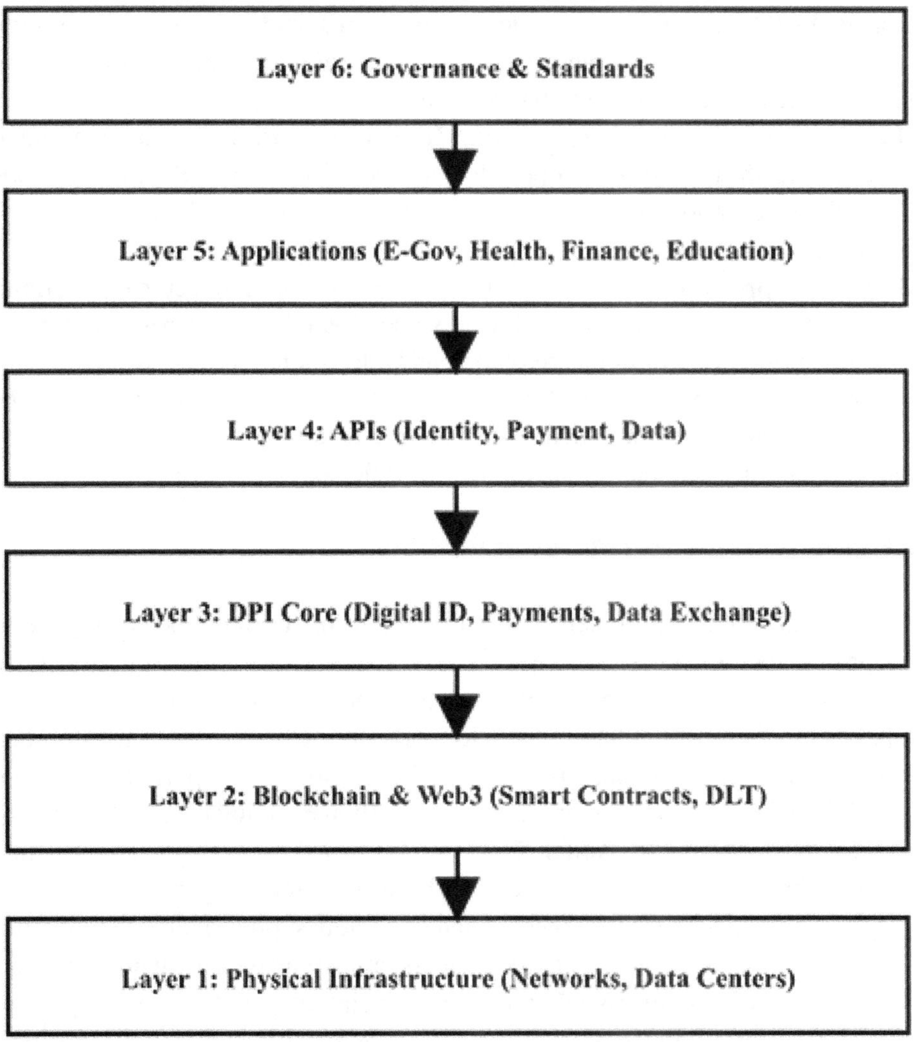

Source: Adapted from India Stack and Global DPI implementations (2024)

The architecture comprises six layers:

Layer 1 - Physical Infrastructure: Telecommunications networks, data centers, and edge computing nodes providing connectivity. 5G deployment and satellite internet (e.g., Spacecoin's decentralized satellite network) extend reach to remote areas.

Layer 2 - Blockchain Foundation: Distributed ledger infrastructure providing immutable record-keeping. Multiple blockchains coexist—public chains for transparent transactions, private/consortium chains for sensitive government data, with interoperability bridges enabling cross-chain operations.

Layer 3 - DPI Core Services: Identity, payments, and data exchange systems leveraging blockchain for enhanced security and auditability. Smart contracts automate service delivery and compliance verification.

Layer 4 - Application Programming Interfaces (APIs): Standardized interfaces enabling third-party developers to build services atop DPI infrastructure. Open APIs foster innovation ecosystem with hundreds of fintech, healthtech, and agritech startups.

Layer 5 - Application Layer: Government services, private sector applications, and NGO programs delivering end-user value. Includes e-governance portals, healthcare apps, agricultural marketplaces, and educational platforms.

Layer 6 - Governance and Standards: Multi-stakeholder governance frameworks establishing technical standards, privacy protections, and operational policies. Includes regulatory sandboxes for testing innovations.

5.2 Public-Private Partnership Models

Successful DPI-Web3 implementation requires collaboration between government, private sector, and civil society:

India Stack Model: Government builds and operates core infrastructure (identity, payments rails) as public goods, while private sector accesses infrastructure through APIs to create consumer-facing services. This model spurred creation of over 300 fintech companies and processed $2.7 trillion in digital payments annually.

Platform Cooperative Model: Community-owned blockchain infrastructure where stakeholders collectively govern DPI. Agricultural cooperatives in Kenya employ this model, with farmers owning and governing supply chain tracking infrastructure, ensuring benefits accrue to producers rather than intermediary platforms.

Consortium Blockchain Model: Industry associations and government agencies jointly operate permissioned blockchains for sector-specific DPI. European Blockchain Partnership's EUROPEUM-EDIC exemplifies this approach for cross-border public services.

5.3 Data Privacy and Protection

Web3 technologies enable privacy-preserving DPI through cryptographic techniques:

Zero-Knowledge Proofs (ZKPs): Enable identity verification without revealing personal data. Citizens prove eligibility for services (e.g., age verification, income threshold) without disclosing actual data.

Homomorphic Encryption: Enables computation on encrypted data, allowing government analytics for policy-making without accessing individual records.

Differential Privacy: Adds mathematical noise to datasets enabling aggregate analysis while protecting individual privacy.

Self-Sovereign Identity: Users control personal data in cryptographic wallets, selectively disclosing to service providers with revocable consent. India's DEPA framework implements consent-based data sharing with granular user control.

India's Digital Personal Data Protection (DPDP) Act, passed in August 2023, establishes legal framework for privacy-by-design principles in DPI (Institut Montaigne, 2024).

6. SECURITY, GOVERNANCE, AND REGULATORY CONSIDERATIONS

6.1 Cybersecurity Architecture

DPI systems, given their population-scale deployment, present high-value targets for cyberattacks. Web3 integration both enhances and complicates security:

Enhanced Security:

- **Distributed Architecture:** No single point of failure; compromising one node doesn't compromise entire system
- **Cryptographic Integrity:** Blockchain's hash-linked structure makes historical data tampering computationally infeasible
- **Transparent Auditing:** All transactions recorded immutably, enabling forensic analysis

Security Challenges:

- **Smart Contract Vulnerabilities:** Code bugs can be exploited; DeFi hacks in 2024 resulted in $2.1 billion losses (London Blockchain, 2025)

- **Private Key Management:** Loss of cryptographic keys means loss of access; user education critical
- **Quantum Computing Threats:** Future quantum computers could break current cryptographic standards; quantum-resistant algorithms required

Mitigation Strategies:

- **Formal Verification:** Mathematical proof of smart contract correctness before deployment
- **Multi-Signature Wallets:** Requiring multiple authorized parties for critical operations
- **Regular Security Audits:** Third-party code reviews and penetration testing
- **Quantum-Safe Cryptography:** Transitioning to post-quantum cryptographic standards

6.2 Governance Models

Effective DPI-Web3 governance balances decentralization with accountability:

Multi-Stakeholder Governance: India Stack's governance involves government agencies, private sector representatives, civil society organizations, and technical experts. This distributed decision-making prevents unilateral control while ensuring diverse perspectives.

Decentralized Autonomous Organizations (DAOs): Blockchain-native governance structures where stakeholders vote on protocol changes and resource allocation. Experimental DPI initiatives employ DAOs for community-driven development.

Regulatory Sandboxes: Controlled environments where innovations can be tested with regulatory oversight but relaxed rules. India's regulatory sandbox enabled UPI international expansion experiments.

International Coordination: G20's Global DPI Repository (GDPIR) pools knowledge from member states, establishing standards and best practices for DPI deployment (Das, 2024). The India G20 Task Force on Digital Public Infrastructure, with final report released July 2024, provides framework for global implementation.

6.3 Regulatory Challenges and Frameworks

Jurisdictional Complexity: Blockchain's borderless nature conflicts with territorial regulatory sovereignty. Cross-border payment DPI requires regulatory coordination between nations.

Cryptocurrency Regulation: Varying national approaches to cryptocurrency—from El Salvador's Bitcoin adoption to China's comprehensive ban—complicate DPI systems using blockchain tokens. Stablecoin regulation remains contentious, with debates over central bank authority versus private issuance.

Data Localization vs. Decentralization: Some jurisdictions mandate data storage within national boundaries, conflicting with blockchain's distributed nature. India's mandate for payment data localization created compliance challenges for international providers.

Smart Contract Legal Status: Legal recognition of smart contracts as enforceable agreements varies. Some jurisdictions amended contract law to explicitly recognize blockchain-based contracts; others operate in legal ambiguity.

Evolving Regulatory Approaches:

- **Principles-Based Regulation:** Setting broad principles (consumer protection, anti-money laundering) rather than prescriptive rules, allowing technological flexibility
- **Technology-Neutral Laws:** Regulations focusing on outcomes rather than specific technologies, accommodating rapid innovation
- **International Standards:** ISO TC 307 and ETSI ISG PDL developing international blockchain standards, promoted by European Commission and other bodies

7. CHALLENGES AND LIMITATIONS

7.1 Digital Divide and Accessibility

Infrastructure Gaps: Despite progress, India's internet penetration reached only 52% in 2024, meaning 670 million citizens lack digital access (Drishti IAS, 2024). Rural areas particularly underserved, with mobile network coverage incomplete and electricity unreliable.

Digital Literacy: Operating blockchain-based applications requires technical knowledge beyond traditional banking. Educational initiatives necessary but resource-intensive. Elderly and less-educated populations face steep learning curves.

Device Access: Smartphones necessary for mobile-first DPI, yet remain unaffordable for lowest-income populations. Feature phone support and voice-based interfaces provide partial solutions but limit functionality.

Language Barriers: DPI interfaces often available only in dominant languages, excluding linguistic minorities. Blockchain wallets typically English-centric, limiting accessibility in non-English regions.

Graph 1 compares digital infrastructure readiness across 8 major emerging economies in 2024. It displays four key metrics that are essential for DPI (Digital Public Infrastructure) and Web3 adoption.

Figure 2. Digital Infrastructure Penetration in Emerging Economies (2024)

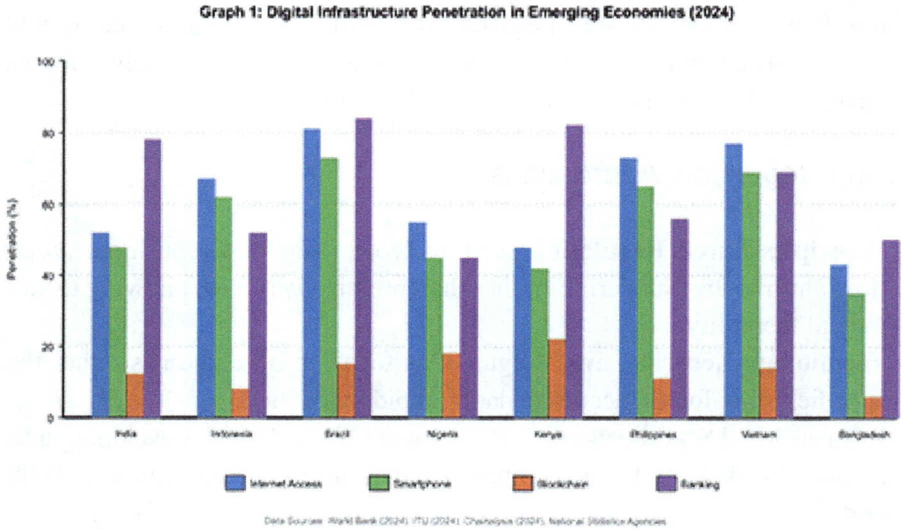

7.2 Scalability and Performance

Transaction Throughput: Bitcoin processes 7 transactions per second, Ethereum 30-40 TPS, far below Visa's 65,000 TPS. While Layer 2 solutions improve scalability, population-scale DPI requires further innovation.

Network Congestion: High usage periods cause transaction delays and fee spikes. During peak periods, Ethereum gas fees reached hundreds of dollars per transaction, making micro-transactions economically unviable.

Storage Requirements: Blockchain's growing data history requires increasing storage. Full Ethereum node requires over 1TB storage, presenting challenges for resource-constrained environments.

Energy Consumption: Despite Ethereum's shift to PoS, Bitcoin's Proof-of-Work still consumes significant energy. Environmental sustainability critical for emerging economies with climate vulnerabilities.

7.3 Interoperability Challenges

Blockchain Fragmentation: Over 1,000 distinct blockchains exist, with limited interoperability. Cross-chain bridges enable some connectivity but introduce security vulnerabilities and complexity.

Legacy System Integration: Existing government IT systems often decades old, built on incompatible technologies. Blockchain integration requires extensive middleware development and system modernization.

Standards Proliferation: Competing technical standards (consensus mechanisms, smart contract languages, identity protocols) create fragmentation. Lack of universal standards impedes seamless cross-border DPI.

7.4 Regulatory Uncertainty

Jurisdictional Ambiguity: Determining applicable law for blockchain transactions spanning multiple jurisdictions remains complex. Smart contract disputes lack clear legal frameworks for resolution.

Compliance Costs: Meeting divergent regulatory requirements across jurisdictions imposes costs, potentially offsetting blockchain's efficiency gains. Small DPI implementers may lack resources for multi-jurisdiction compliance.

Regulatory Capture Risks: Incumbent financial institutions lobby for regulations disadvantaging DPI-Web3 alternatives, potentially stifling innovation to protect established interests.

7.5 Sustainability Concerns

Financial Sustainability: Many DPI initiatives rely on philanthropic funding or government subsidies. Long-term financial models ensuring operational sustainability require development. Revenue-generating mechanisms (transaction fees, value-added services) must balance sustainability with affordability.

Technical Maintenance: Blockchain infrastructure requires ongoing development, security updates, and community maintenance. Ensuring sustainable developer communities and funding for protocol maintenance remains challenging.

Environmental Sustainability: While PoS blockchains are energy-efficient, expanding digital infrastructure increases overall energy demand. Renewable energy integration and carbon-neutral operations increasingly prioritized.

8. EMERGING TRENDS AND FUTURE DIRECTIONS

8.1 Artificial Intelligence Integration

AI-Blockchain Convergence: Combining AI's predictive capabilities with blockchain's transparency creates intelligent, auditable systems. Fetch.ai and SingularityNET pioneer decentralized AI marketplaces where algorithms operate on blockchain infrastructure, with usage tracked transparently (Creditcoin, 2025).

DPI Applications:

- **Fraud Detection:** AI algorithms analyzing blockchain transaction patterns identify anomalies indicating fraud or money laundering
- **Credit Scoring:** Machine learning models assessing non-traditional data (UPI transactions, utility payments) generate credit scores for unbanked populations
- **Service Personalization:** AI-driven interfaces adapting to user preferences while privacy-preserving features prevent data exploitation

India's AI adoption in companies surged from 8% (2023) to 25% (2024), with integration into DPI infrastructure enhancing decision-making and service delivery (Protean, 2024).

8.2 Decentralized Physical Infrastructure Networks (DePIN)

DePIN applies Web3 principles to physical infrastructure, enabling community-owned and operated essential services (Creditcoin, 2025).

Decentralized Internet: Projects like Helium (IoT networks) and Spacecoin (satellite internet) create decentralized connectivity infrastructure. Spacecoin's December 2024 satellite launch initiates the first DePIN powered by satellites, aimed at delivering affordable high-speed internet to underserved regions.

Energy Grids: Blockchain-based peer-to-peer energy trading enables households with solar panels to sell excess energy directly to neighbors, bypassing utility monopolies. Smart contracts automatically settle transactions based on real-time consumption data.

Transportation Networks: Decentralized ride-sharing and logistics platforms eliminate platform fees extracted by centralized services. Driver-owned cooperatives leverage blockchain for transparent earnings distribution and governance.

8.3 Central Bank Digital Currencies (CBDCs)

Over 100 countries explore or pilot CBDCs, representing 95% of global GDP (Martin, 2024). CBDCs integrate with DPI infrastructure:

Programmable Money: Smart contract-enabled CBDCs allow conditional spending (e.g., welfare payments restricted to food purchases), automatic tax collection, and time-limited stimulus distributions incentivizing immediate economic activity.

Financial Inclusion: CBDCs provide bank accounts directly with central banks, bypassing commercial banking infrastructure absent in remote areas. Mobile-based CBDC wallets enable instant, free payments.

Cross-Border Payments: Coordinated CBDC infrastructure enables instant international transfers at minimal cost, reducing remittance fees from average 6.5% to near-zero.

Policy Implementations:

- Nigeria's eNaira focuses on financial inclusion and reduced cash management costs
- China's Digital Yuan (e-CNY) processed billions in transactions during pilot phases
- European Digital Euro pilot explores privacy-preserving retail CBDC
- India's e pilots wholesale and retail applications

8.4 Social Impact Applications

Decentralized Social Media: Blockchain-based social platforms where users own content and data, earning token rewards for contributions. Censorship-resistant architecture protects free expression while cryptographic verification combats misinformation.

Humanitarian Aid: Blockchain-enabled DPI enables transparent, efficient disaster relief. Hurricane Idalia (2023) analysis suggests blockchain systems could have enabled faster aid distribution, real-time resource coordination, and predicted flooding patterns, potentially saving lives and reducing $2.5 billion in damages (FLIP, 2024).

Climate Action: Tokenized carbon credits on blockchain enable transparent emissions trading. Agricultural DPI tracking sustainable farming practices issue verified carbon offset tokens, enabling farmers to monetize environmental stewardship.

Education Credentials: Blockchain-based educational credentials provide lifelong learning records, portable across institutions and borders. The global blockchain in education market, valued at $350 million in 2024, projected to reach $9.39 billion by 2033, reflects growing adoption (Binariks, 2025).

8.5 Quantum-Resistant Cryptography

Quantum computers threaten current cryptographic standards underpinning blockchain security. Post-quantum cryptography development ensures DPI-Web3 infrastructure remains secure in quantum computing era.

Lattice-Based Cryptography: Mathematical problems resistant to quantum algorithms being integrated into blockchain protocols.

Quantum Key Distribution: Leveraging quantum mechanics principles for theoretically unbreakable encryption in high-security DPI applications.

Migration Strategies: Gradual transition from current to quantum-resistant algorithms requires coordination across DPI ecosystems to maintain interoperability during transition.

9. FUTURE RESEARCH DIRECTIONS

9.1 Technical Research

Scalability Solutions: Research into novel consensus mechanisms, sharding architectures, and Layer 2 protocols enabling population-scale DPI with thousands of transactions per second at sustainable costs.

Interoperability Standards: Development of universal protocols enabling seamless interaction between heterogeneous blockchain systems and legacy infrastructure.

Privacy Technologies: Advancement of zero-knowledge proofs, secure multi-party computation, and homomorphic encryption enabling privacy-preserving data analysis at scale.

Energy Efficiency: Research into ultra-low-energy consensus mechanisms and sustainable computing practices for environmentally responsible DPI expansion.

9.2 Governance Research

Decentralized Governance Models: Empirical studies of DAO effectiveness in managing DPI, comparing outcomes with traditional governance structures.

Regulatory Frameworks: Comparative analysis of regulatory approaches across jurisdictions, identifying best practices balancing innovation with consumer protection.

Multi-Stakeholder Coordination: Research into mechanisms facilitating effective collaboration between government, private sector, civil society, and technical communities in DPI governance.

9.3 Socioeconomic Research

Impact Assessment: Longitudinal studies measuring DPI-Web3 integration's effects on income inequality, economic mobility, and social inclusion across diverse contexts.

Behavioral Economics: Research into user adoption patterns, trust dynamics, and behavioral responses to decentralized versus centralized infrastructure.

Development Economics: Analysis of DPI's role in overcoming institutional voids, with rigorous causal inference methodologies isolating DPI impacts from confounding factors.

Gender and Inclusion: Studies examining differential impacts across demographic groups, identifying design elements promoting equitable access and outcomes.

9.4 Applied Research

Sector-Specific Applications: Research into DPI-Web3 applications in healthcare (electronic health records, drug supply chains), agriculture (crop insurance, market linkages), education (credential verification, skill development), and climate action (carbon markets, renewable energy trading).

Crisis Response: Investigation of blockchain-enabled DPI for disaster relief, humanitarian aid distribution, and emergency service coordination during crises.

Small State Implementation: Research addressing unique challenges of DPI deployment in small island nations and other resource-constrained contexts.

10. CONCLUSION

The convergence of Digital Public Infrastructure and Web3 technologies represents a transformative opportunity for emerging economies to leapfrog traditional developmental stages, establishing world-class digital infrastructure directly on decentralized foundations. The evidence from implementations across India, Africa, Southeast Asia, and Latin America demonstrates that well-designed DPI-Web3 integration can achieve remarkable outcomes: bringing hundreds of millions into formal financial systems, reducing transaction costs by up to 70%, enabling instant cross-border payments, and creating transparent, accountable governance mechanisms.

India's pioneering India Stack model, serving 1.3 billion citizens and processing 16.6 billion monthly transactions, proves that population-scale DPI deployment is technically feasible and economically transformative. The projected growth from 0.9% GDP contribution (2022) to 4.2% by 2030 illustrates DPI's macroeconomic significance. Africa's Mojaloop initiative, potentially banking 730 million unbanked adults, demonstrates replicability across diverse contexts.

However, significant challenges remain. Digital divides persist, with 48% of Indians lacking internet access and vast populations in other emerging economies similarly excluded. Scalability constraints, interoperability fragmentation, regulatory uncertainties, and sustainability concerns require sustained attention. The technical complexity of blockchain systems poses adoption barriers, particularly for elderly and less-educated populations.

The path forward requires:

1. **Continued Technical Innovation:** Development of scalable, interoperable, energy-efficient blockchain protocols capable of supporting population-scale DPI
2. **Digital Literacy Initiatives:** Comprehensive programs ensuring all citizens can effectively utilize DPI services
3. **Infrastructure Investment:** Expansion of telecommunications networks, particularly in rural and remote areas
4. **Regulatory Clarity:** Development of clear, stable legal frameworks balancing innovation with consumer protection
5. **International Cooperation:** Coordination among nations establishing standards and enabling cross-border DPI functionality
6. **Sustainability Models:** Development of financially sustainable operating models ensuring long-term DPI viability
7. **Inclusive Design:** Ensuring DPI systems serve all population segments, with particular attention to marginalized communities

The global blockchain market's projected growth from $31.18 billion (2025) to $393.42 billion (2032) at 43.65% CAGR, combined with 220 million monthly active blockchain addresses and accelerating cryptocurrency adoption, indicates that Web3 technologies are transitioning from speculative experiments to foundational infrastructure. For emerging economies, this transition presents both opportunity and imperative—to establish digital public goods serving their populations' needs while participating in and shaping global digital transformation.

As Web3 technologies mature and DPI implementations accumulate operational experience, the vision of secure, inclusive, transparent digital public infrastructure accessible to all citizens becomes increasingly realizable. The next decade will determine whether this vision translates into sustained socioeconomic development for billions in emerging economies, or whether digital divides and implementation challenges constrain benefits to privileged minorities. Success requires sustained commitment from governments, private sector, civil society, and international community, guided by principles of openness, interoperability, privacy protection, and universal access.

The integration of DPI with Web3 represents not merely technological advancement, but a fundamental reimagining of how societies organize collective action, deliver public services, and enable economic participation. For emerging economies, this represents an unprecedented opportunity to build digital infrastructure that truly serves the public interest—open, transparent, accountable, and accessible to all.

REFERENCES

Binariks. (2025). 5 Best Blockchain Development Trends for 2025-2030. Retrieved from https://binariks.com/blog/emerging-blockchain-technology-trends/

Blaize. (2024, December 9). Top Web3 Trends for 2025: Tokenization, Decentralization, and the Future of Blockchain. Retrieved from https://blaize.tech/blog/top-web3-trends-to-watch-in-2025

Chainalysis. (2024, September 11). 2024 Global Crypto Adoption Index. Retrieved from https://www.chainalysis.com/blog/2024-global-crypto-adoption-index/

Chainalysis. (2025, January). The Chainalysis 2025 Global Adoption Index. Retrieved from https://www.chainalysis.com/blog/2025-global-crypto-adoption-index/

Chen, Y., Li, W., & Zhang, X. (2024). Integration and innovation of blockchain in Web3.0: Current status and standardization prospects. *World Wide Web (Bussum), 27*(6), 1–32. DOI: 10.1007/s11280-024-01319-7

Consensys. (2024). State of Web3 Infrastructure Report 2024. Consensys, Inc.

Creditcoin. (2025, January 9). Web3 Trends for 2025: A Year of Transformation. Retrieved from https://creditcoin.org/blog/web3-trends-for-2025/

Das, S. (2024, August 26). Digital Public Infrastructure and Emerging Technologies. Speech at RBI@90 Global Conference, Bengaluru. Bank for International Settlements. Retrieved from https://www.bis.org/review/r240828p.htm

Drishti, I. A. S. (2024). Digital Public Infrastructure. Retrieved from https://www.drishtiias.com/daily-updates/daily-news-analysis/digital-public-infrastructure

Drishti, I. A. S. (2024). India's Digital Public Infrastructure. Retrieved from https://www.drishtiias.com/daily-updates/daily-news-analysis/india-s-digital-public-infrastructure-3

European Commission. (2024). Blockchain and Web3 Strategy: Shaping Europe's Digital Future. Retrieved from https://digital-strategy.ec.europa.eu/en/policies/blockchain-strategy

FLIP. (2024, October 18). The FLIP: Digital Public Goods and Digital Public Infrastructure Are the Answer to Every SDG Question. Retrieved from https://www.weave3.org/p/the-flip-digital-public-goods-and

Fortune Business Insights. (2025). Blockchain Technology Market Size, Share & Growth Analysis Report 2025-2032. Retrieved from https://www.fortunebusinessinsights.com/industry-reports/blockchain-market-100072

Insights, G. M. (2024, December 1). Web 3.0 Blockchain Market Size, Global Report 2025-2034. Retrieved from https://www.gminsights.com/industry-analysis/web-3-0-blockchain-market

Institut Montaigne. (2024). India's Digital Public Infrastructure: A Success Story for the World? Retrieved from https://www.institutmontaigne.org/en/expressions/indias-digital-public-infrastructure-success-story-world

Li, Z., Wang, J., & Kumar, R. (2024). Blockchain technology adoption in emerging markets: Opportunities and challenges. *Journal of Business Research, 156*, 113–128.

London Blockchain. (2025, August 28). Blockchain Adoption Statistics: Trends Shaping the Markets. Retrieved from https://londonblockchain.net/blog/blockchain-explained/blockchain-adoption-statistics-trends-shaping-the-markets/

Martin, T. (2024). Blockchain, Web3 and the Prospects for Safe Digital Governance. SIGNAL Magazine, AFCEA International. Retrieved from https://www.afcea.org/signal-media/cyber-edge/blockchain-web3-and-prospects-safe-digital-governance

Protean. (2024). Decoding India's Digital Public Infrastructure. Retrieved from https://proteantech.in/articles/Decoding-Digital-Public-Infrastructure-in-India/

Protean. (2024). DPI: Achievements Diary 2024. Retrieved from https://proteantech.in/articles/dpi-2-0-2-4-developments/

Sahasranamam, S., & Prabhu, J. (2024, March 25). Digital Public Infrastructure for the Developing World. Stanford Social Innovation Review. Retrieved from https://ssir.org/articles/entry/digital-public-infrastructure-developing-world

Security.org. (2025, January 31). 2025 Cryptocurrency Adoption and Consumer Sentiment Report. Retrieved from https://www.security.org/digital-security/cryptocurrency-annual-consumer-report/

Taulli, T. (2025). Top Web 3.0 Trends and Predictions for 2025 and Beyond. TechTarget. Retrieved from https://www.techtarget.com/searchcio/tip/Top-Web-30-trends-and-predictions

World Economic Forum. (2024, February). What to Expect for Digital Public Infrastructure in 2024. Retrieved from https://www.weforum.org/stories/2024/02/dpi-digital-public-infrastructure/

APPENDIX: ADDITIONAL RESOURCES

International Organizations

- G20 Global DPI Repository (GDPIR): https://www.g20.org/dpi
- World Bank Digital Development: https://www.worldbank.org/digital
- International Telecommunication Union (ITU): https://www.itu.int

Standards Bodies

- ISO TC 307 (Blockchain and DLT): https://www.iso.org/committee/6266604.html
- ETSI ISG PDL: https://www.etsi.org/technologies/permissioned-distributed-ledger
- W3C Decentralized Identifiers: https://www.w3.org/TR/did-core/

Open-Source Projects

- India Stack: https://indiastack.org
- Mojaloop Foundation: https://mojaloop.io
- Hyperledger: https://www.hyperledger.org

Key Terms Glossary

- **DPI**: Digital Public Infrastructure - foundational digital systems for identity, payments, and data exchange
- **Web3**: Third generation of internet technologies emphasizing decentralization and user ownership
- **Blockchain**: Distributed ledger technology providing immutable, transparent record-keeping
- **Smart Contract**: Self-executing code on blockchain that automatically enforces agreements
- **DeFi**: Decentralized Finance - blockchain-based financial services without traditional intermediaries
- **DAO**: Decentralized Autonomous Organization - blockchain-native governance structure
- **CBDC**: Central Bank Digital Currency - digital currency issued by central banks
- **DePIN**: Decentralized Physical Infrastructure Networks - community-owned physical infrastructure
- **Zero-Knowledge Proof**: Cryptographic method proving statement truth without revealing underlying information
- **Layer 2**: Protocols processing transactions off main blockchain while inheriting security

Chapter 8

Leveraging Blockchain and AI to Advance Digital Public Infrastructure: Boosting FinTech Development in Emerging Economies

Samarth Saksena
https://orcid.org/0009-0008-3354-2427
Amity University, Noida, India

ABSTRACT

Strong, easily available, and digital financial services which are creative are becoming increasingly important for the growth of world economy, the financial industry is undergoing a revolution in the emerging economies due to the convergence of digital public infrastructure (DPI), blockchain technology, and artificial intelligence (AI), which offers an unprecedented chance to promote financial inclusion, increase efficiency, along with establishing confidence in digital finance. And due to these game-changing technologies, the emerging FinTech industry has accelerated and established itself as both a force behind and a recipient of the extensive digitisation initiatives around the globe. In this proposed chapter "Leveraging Blockchain and AI to Advance Digital Public Infrastructure: Boosting FinTech Development in emerging economies" we aim to thoroughly investigate the ways in which blockchain, AI, and DPI work together to influence the course of FinTech expansion in the emerging markets. We will be presenting a holistic approach, which offers a comprehensive analysis, exposing the complexities of this technological shift and its influence on the emerging economies.

DOI: 10.4018/979-8-3373-6380-6.ch008

INTRODUCTION

1.1 Background on DPI, Blockchain, AI, and FinTech in Emerging Economies

The rise of FinTech has been a global phenomenon, but its impact is arguably most transformative in emerging economies. In these markets, FinTech is not merely an improvement on existing services but often represents the first point of access to the formal financial system for millions of previously unbanked citizens. This "leapfrogging" phenomenon has been made possible by three converging technological pillars: DPI, Blockchain, and AI.

Digital Public Infrastructure (DPI) refers to a set of shared digital systems—such as digital identity, secure data exchange protocols, and instant payment interfaces—that are often developed or sponsored by the government to serve as open, interoperable platforms for both public and private services.[1] DPI significantly reduces the cost of customer acquisition (Know Your Customer/KYC) and transaction processing, thereby acting as the fundamental scaffolding for a scalable digital economy.[2] The success of India's Aadhaar-UPI system and Brazil's Pix exemplifies the potential of robust DPI to accelerate financial inclusion from incremental growth to exponential scale.[3]

Blockchain technology, or Distributed Ledger Technology (DLT), offers a mechanism for trustless and transparent record-keeping.[4] In emerging economies, where institutional trust in traditional banking or legal systems may be weak, Blockchain provides an immutable and auditable layer for securing property titles, streamlining supply chain finance, and facilitating cross-border remittances at significantly reduced costs. Furthermore, it underpins the emerging wave of Decentralized Finance (DeFi), offering alternatives to centralized financial institutions.

Artificial Intelligence (AI), encompassing machine learning (ML) and predictive analytics, provides the intelligence layer.[5] AI excels at processing large volumes of alternative data (e.g., mobile usage, utility payments, social interactions) to perform dynamic risk assessment, enabling FinTech lenders to build alternative credit scores for the unbanked.[6] It is also crucial for sophisticated fraud detection and enhancing operational efficiency through automation and hyper-personalized customer service.

The confluence of these three technologies provides a unique opportunity to design financial ecosystems that are inherently more inclusive, resilient, and efficient than legacy systems, specifically tailored to address the challenges of regulatory fragmentation and high financial exclusion rates characteristic of emerging economies.

1.2 Research Aim, Relevance, and Scope

The overarching aim of this study is to thoroughly investigate how the FinTech sector in emerging economies has the potential to grow more quickly and sustainably through the synergistic integration of Blockchain and AI technology in conjunction with DPI. The core objectives are centered on identifying the potential and difficulties that accompany this integration, with a specific emphasis on:

- Increasing financial inclusion and equity.
- Building systemic trust through transparency and security.
- Supporting scalable, cutting-edge digital financial services.
- Boosting operational effectiveness to outperform older, cost-heavy banking systems.

This research is highly relevant given the transformative and accelerating role that DPI, AI, and Blockchain are currently playing. Nations are rapidly adopting foundational digital identity systems, instant payment rails, and regulatory reforms that support accessible and interoperable digital financial services. The integration of AI and Blockchain onto DPI enables unprecedented levels of transactional efficiency, fraud mitigation, and personalised service delivery.[7]

The scope of the analysis is rigorously focused on nine key emerging economies selected for their regional representation, distinct DPI maturity levels, and varied regulatory environments:

- South Asia: India, Sri Lanka
- Middle East: Saudi Arabia
- ASEAN: Singapore, Malaysia
- South America: Brazil, Mexico
- Africa: South Africa, Ethiopia

Understanding this complex convergence is crucial for policymakers, financial sector professionals, academics, and international development agencies seeking to bridge infrastructure gaps and shape future-ready, inclusive financial ecosystems.

1.3 Overview of Regions and Key Characteristics

The selected regions represent a spectrum of digital and economic development within the emerging market category, providing a rich basis for comparative analysis:

1. South Asia (India, Sri Lanka)

Characterized by large, unbanked populations, high mobile penetration, and a dense, often informal, economy. India is the global benchmark for DPI-led transformation (India Stack, UPI), demonstrating unprecedented scale in financial inclusion.[8] Sri Lanka represents a smaller economy grappling with structural economic challenges, where FinTech is essential for remittances and stabilizing digital payments.

2. Middle East (Saudi Arabia)

Defined by vast sovereign wealth, rapid infrastructure modernization, and an ambition to become global innovation hubs (Vision 2030 in Saudi Arabia). These nations are driving top-down adoption of AI and Blockchain, focusing on high-value B2B finance, asset tokenization, and central bank digital currencies (CBDCs) within highly regulated free zones.

3. ASEAN (Singapore, Malaysia)

Singapore serves as a financial powerhouse and a global leader in FinTech regulation, adopting a proactive "Innovation Hub" model.[9] Malaysia represents a rapidly modernizing, diverse economy focused on leveraging digital IDs and payments to integrate various ethnic and income groups into the formal financial system.

4. South America (Brazil, Mexico)

Characterized by a history of high inflation and a large informal sector, driving demand for secure, low-cost digital alternatives. Brazil's success with Pix (a DPI payment rail) rivals UPI's scale.[10] Mexico is heavily focused on optimizing remittance corridors and managing the high retail adoption of cryptocurrency as an inflation hedge.[11]

5. Africa (South Africa, Ethiopia)

Africa is the birthplace of the "mobile money revolution." South Africa has a highly sophisticated but unequal formal financial sector, with FinTech focusing on inclusion through mobile banking and leveraging AI for micro-lending.[12] Ethiopia represents a rapidly opening, large market focusing on foundational digital identity and telecom-led financial services to bridge significant infrastructure gaps.[1]

LITERATURE REVIEW

Theoretical Foundations of DPI, AI, and Blockchain Integration

Financial technology, or FinTech, has rapidly become an integral part of life in our increasingly digital world. Whether someone is paying bills, growing a small business, or transferring money to family across continents, the presence and potential of FinTech are unmistakable. But what's truly fueling the transformation of financial services, especially in emerging economies, are the radical innovations from blockchain technology and artificial intelligence (AI), often delivered through the scaffolding of digital public infrastructure (DPI) (Vinod & Ghosh, n.d.). DPI provides the shared rails—such as digital identity, payment systems, and data-sharing protocols—upon which new, more accessible financial services are built.

Blockchain, with its decentralized and transparent nature, stands out as more than just the backbone behind cryptocurrencies. Financial institutions worldwide are turning to blockchain to create smart contracts, beef up security, streamline record-keeping, and ensure that transactions are trustworthy from start to finish (Javaid et al., n.d.). By minimizing the need for intermediaries, blockchain has the potential to accelerate settlement processes and simplify the transfer of assets, transforming how trust is built within financial transactions. In day-to-day terms, blockchain lets businesses and individuals collaborate with confidence, relying on shared rules and a common, tamper-resistant record of events.

Artificial intelligence brings a different but equally powerful engine to the financial sector. AI excels at analyzing big data, recognizing patterns, and making fast, objective decisions. In the financial context, this translates to better fraud detection, quicker credit assessments, and more personalized customer experiences (Shi & Wang, n.d.; Vinod & Ghosh, n.d.). For example, AI-driven chatbots are replacing long waits for customer service, while AI-powered analytics help spot unusual transaction activity far more effectively than manual oversight ever could.

What makes the current moment so exciting—and so challenging—is how these two technologies reinforce each other when layered onto robust digital infrastructure. As researchers like Shi and Wang (n.d.) note, the marriage of AI and blockchain could mean real-time, ultra-secure, and deeply insightful financial services that work for more people, everywhere. Yet, there's a reason policymakers, engineers, and business leaders are not rushing ahead blindly. Questions about scale (can the technology handle millions or billions of users?), interoperability (can different systems communicate fluidly?), clear regulatory guidelines, and, crucially, the ethics of AI, all need thoughtful answers to avoid creating new risks or unintentional harms (Javaid et al., n.d.; Shi & Wang, n.d.).

A recurring theme in the literature is this: technology alone doesn't solve problems—it's how countries, companies, and communities choose to design, govern, and use these technologies that determines whether they unleash broad prosperity or entrench new forms of exclusion.

The State of FinTech Transformation in Emerging Markets

Across emerging economies, FinTech is more than a buzzword—it's a lifeline and a game changer. Consider that nearly two billion people worldwide still lack access to a traditional bank account. By leveraging the new tools provided by advances in mobile money, peer-to-peer lending, blockchain, and AI, these unbanked and underserved populations are finding their way into the formal financial system (Carè et al., n.d.).

Recent studies paint a compelling picture. FinTech innovations significantly reduce barriers to financial access, lower transaction costs, and open up a suite of new services—including microloans, digital savings, and easy payments—that simply didn't exist a decade ago, especially in rural or marginalized communities (Ramadhan et al., n.d.; Del Sarto & Ozili, 2025). Mobile money, in particular, has become ubiquitous across Africa and South Asia, propelling millions into the financial mainstream and creating fertile ground for entrepreneurship and economic growth.

Researchers have mapped five main currents running through the intersection of FinTech and financial inclusion: the explosive adoption of mobile money and blockchain, the rise of digital banking, efforts to close gender gaps in access to finance, and the increasingly important role of AI as both a service enabler and risk watchdog (Carè et al., n.d.; Del Sarto & Ozili, n.d.). In countries within the BRICS bloc—especially India, China, and Brazil—a positive correlation is found between advanced FinTech ecosystems and higher levels of financial inclusion, as well as improved financial sector stability (Vuković et al., n.d.).

Blockchain's unique properties have made it a perfect fit for environments where trust in traditional systems is weak, enabling peer-to-peer transactions that are secure and trackable (Javaid et al., n.d.). Meanwhile, AI has made lending more fair by employing alternative data to build credit scores for those with no formal borrowing history, helping small entrepreneurs and low-income groups break the cycle of financial exclusion (Vinod & Ghosh, n.d.; Shi & Wang, n.d.).

But even as FinTech surges ahead, researchers caution that its impacts are not evenly distributed. There are persistent hurdles such as spotty digital infrastructure, the ever-present threat of cybercrime, fragmented regulatory systems, and a lack of digital and financial literacy in many communities (Del Sarto & Ozili, n.d.; Carè et al., n.d.). Policymakers, therefore, are encouraged not just to expand access, but to invest in the human and regulatory groundwork that makes financial innovation both safe and sustainable (Ramadhan et al., n.d.).

What's also clear from the research is the value of context—the characteristics and needs of local economies, cultures, and institutions matter deeply. Successful models in Kenya or India offer powerful lessons, but always need thoughtful adaptation to local conditions elsewhere.

Governance, Regulatory, and Ethical Considerations

As FinTech races ahead, the world's rule-makers are hustling to keep up. The stakes could not be higher: get the regulations right, and FinTech can become a lever for inclusive growth and economic resilience; get them wrong, and you risk unleashing new kinds of fragility, from data breaches to systemic shocks.

A key thread running through recent studies is the need for adaptable, forward-looking regulatory frameworks—ones that do not just tolerate innovation, but actively encourage it while keeping the system safe (Abikoye et al., n.d.). This is where Regulatory Technology (RegTech) comes into play: by integrating advanced monitoring tools, AI-driven compliance programs, and real-time risk analytics, regulators can supervise markets far more effectively and at lower cost than traditional approaches allow.

The benefits of such adaptive approaches are already visible in some countries. Regulatory frameworks that embrace openness, interoperability, and both public and private sector collaboration have paved the way for rapid DPI development and robust digital finance, as seen in India (with India Stack) and Brazil (with Pix) (G20, 2024). When mechanisms for digital ID, payments, and data sharing are made available as interoperable, open-access public goods, everyone wins, from small merchants to national treasuries (G20, 2024).

It's not all smooth sailing though. Blockchain adoption, for all its promise, throws up thorny questions about legal responsibility and jurisdiction. Who is liable if a blockchain-based contract goes awry? How do regulations keep pace with cross-border, decentralized transactions? And what's to be done about privacy, given the vast stores of sensitive data passing through FinTech systems every second (World Bank Group, n.d.; Javaid et al., n.d.)?

Ethics, too, looms large. As more financial decisions are handed over to algorithms and digital rails, we risk reinforcing inequalities if these tools are not carefully designed, tested, and governed (Vinod & Ghosh, n.d.). There is also the very real challenge of digital exclusion, with vulnerable populations potentially being left further behind as financial services go online (Vinod & Ghosh, n.d.; Del Sarto & Ozili, n.d.). Trust and robust data protection are therefore more than technical requirements—they are the bedrock of any fair and effective financial system in the digital era (G20, 2024).

India's DPI journey has become a beacon for others, achieving an 80% financial inclusion rate in just six years by leveraging public-private partnership and a holistic digital public infrastructure. Countries like Brazil, Estonia, Peru, and Singapore are following suit, adapting the principles of openness, safety, and broad-based inclusion to their unique circumstances and showing that blueprints can travel, but always with local adaptation (G20, 2024).

Cross-Regional Case Study Comparisons

The story of FinTech's transformation is best told through real-world case studies that highlight both common challenges and regional successes. India, for instance, has made remarkable strides with the launch and scale-up of the India Stack, a suite of open digital infrastructure layers—combining Aadhaar (digital ID), UPI (real-time payments), account aggregators, and more (G20, 2024). This approach has not only brought millions into the financial fold but has allowed for direct benefit transfers, transparent welfare disbursement, and a boom in the digital payments market.

Brazil's Pix platform is yet another compelling case. With features like instant, low-cost, and 24/7 payments accessible to anyone with a smartphone, Pix has quickly become central to Brazil's financial ecosystem, further proof of how modern DPI can reshape an economy (G20, 2024; CDPI.dev, 2024). Both cases illustrate that when countries invest in robust and inclusive digital infrastructure, they unlock entirely new business models, foster trust, and set global benchmarks for others to follow.

Elsewhere, African and Southeast Asian nations show what's possible when mobile money and digital IDs are given priority. Countries like Kenya (with M-Pesa) and the Philippines (with GCash) demonstrate how leapfrogging traditional bank-based models can create entirely new financial ecosystems, even in contexts with limited historical banking infrastructure.

There is also a strong wave of experimentation in places like Australia, where projects such as Acacia explore the use of blockchain and tokenized assets for large-scale financial markets and central bank digital currencies (ICMA, n.d.). These pilots underscore a broader global movement toward continuous experimentation, robust evaluation, and adaptive regulation.

A valuable lesson emerging from these comparisons is that success is rarely down to technology alone. Instead, leadership, community engagement, clear regulatory vision, and willingness to iterate all shape whether these tools deliver broad-based benefits. Regions that treat financial innovation as part of a bigger inclusive development strategy are best positioned to adapt and thrive.

Synthesis and Ongoing Challenges

The current wave of literature offers compelling evidence that DPI, AI, and blockchain—when harnessed together—can markedly advance financial access, resilience, and opportunity, especially in emerging economies. They offer the promise of efficient, secure, and user-centric financial ecosystems. However, much remains to be learned about the long-term impacts of these technologies—on stability, on equity, and on the lives and opportunities of those at society's margins.

Key challenges going forward include the lack of standardized global regulatory frameworks, the need for further real-world case studies—especially in low-income and marginalized areas—and an ever-present call to ensure human, not purely technical, needs stay at the center of financial innovation. Policy dialogue and collaborative action across nations, industries, and communities will remain essential in shaping an inclusive digital future.

RESEARCH METHODOLOGY AND EXPANDED QUANTITATIVE AND QUALITATIVE FINDINGS

3. Research Methodology

To address the research objectives and investigate the complex synergistic relationships between DPI, AI, Blockchain, and FinTech development, we adopt a mixed-methods approach. This methodology is essential for combining the statistical generalizability offered by quantitative data (for breadth) with the nuanced, context-specific insights provided by qualitative inquiry (for depth).

The construction of a robust panel dataset across diverse emerging economies often presents challenges related to data frequency and reporting consistency, necessitating a strategic approach to missing value imputation. Following initial data assembly from the World Bank (WDI, WGI, Findex) and relevant national sources, isolated data points were found to be missing or reported inconsistently across the 48 country-year observations. To ensure the viability of the fixed-effects panel regression model and maximize the statistical power of the analysis, two imputation techniques were employed, selected to minimize potential bias and preserve cross-sectional and temporal integrity. Missing values for the dependent variable, Domestic Credit to Private Sector (Y), were estimated using Regression Imputation, leveraging a predictive model based on the non-missing control variables (GDP per Capita, Regulatory Quality, and HDI). Conversely, gaps in the Internet Use (%) variable were addressed using Time-Series Mean Imputation, calculating the arithmetic mean of the preceding and succeeding year for the respective country.

While these techniques ensured a complete and balanced panel structure, the authors acknowledge the use of imputed data. All subsequent quantitative findings should be considered in light of this imputation, and a robustness check using listwise deletion (excluding rows with any imputed data) was performed to confirm that the core results remained qualitatively similar.

Limitation and Justification of AI and Blockchain Proxies

A significant methodological limitation of the quantitative analysis is the absence of direct, globally comparable, and time-series data proxies for the adoption and intensity of Blockchain and AI technologies across the nine emerging economies studied. Due to their nascent and proprietary nature, metrics like the number of AI-powered credit decisions, the volume of tokenized assets, or the extent of permissioned Blockchain use in government systems are not systematically collected or standardized by international bodies like the World Bank or IMF. Consequently, the econometric models were unable to directly isolate the impact of AI and Blockchain on private sector credit.

This means the highly significant and robust effect attributed to DPI in the panel regressions (coefficients of 0.4512 and 0.5234) serves as an enabling accelerator. The growth in financial depth is driven by the foundational digital rails of the DPI, which then create the necessary scale, data liquidity, and low-cost environment that AI and Blockchain applications require to be deployed commercially. The qualitative analysis, therefore, functions as the essential "intelligence layer" to this finding. It provides the necessary context by synthesizing case studies and policy documents to demonstrate *how* AI and Blockchain are practically applied on top of the DPI scaffolding[7]. Examples from Brazil (Pix enabling AI credit scoring), Singapore (RegTech and tokenization built on digital identity), and South Africa (AI for micro-lending) qualitatively confirm that the impact of AI and Blockchain is fundamentally conditioned, enabled, and scaled by the underlying DPI maturity. In essence, while DPI provides the engine (measured quantitatively), the qualitative findings illustrate the fuel and efficient transmission system (AI/Blockchain) that utilizes this engine for inclusive growth.

3.1 Data Collection and Variable Proxies

The study relies exclusively on secondary data assembled from authoritative international and regional databases to ensure comparability and reliability across the emerging economies. The variables are proxied as follows:

Data Collection Methods

1. Data Source Identification
    - Primary Databases: World Bank Open Data, International Monetary Fund (IMF) Data, International Telecommunication Union (ITU) Statistics
    - Secondary Sources: Worldwide Governance Indicators, Penn World Table, National Statistical Offices
    - Time Period: 2005-2024 (20-year longitudinal data)
    - Frequency: Annual data collection
2. Data Extraction Protocol
    - Systematic Download: Bulk data extraction using API queries from World Bank Data API
    - Manual Verification: Cross-referencing of outlier values with original source publications
    - Quality Checks: Validation against national statistical reports for key variables
    - Format Standardization: Conversion of all data to consistent annual frequency and USD denominations
3. Data Integration Process
    - Merge Procedure: Country-year as primary key for panel data construction
    - Alignment: Temporal alignment of all variables to calendar year basis
    - Currency Conversion: Constant USD adjustments using World Bank deflators
4. Quality Assurance
    - Consistency Checks: Cross-verification between related indicators
    - Coverage Validation: Ensuring balanced panel with complete 20-year series for all 9 countries.

Variable Profiles

1. Dependent Variable

CREDIT_PVT (Domestic Credit to Private Sector)

- Definition: Financial resources provided to the private sector by financial corporations
- Measurement: Percentage of GDP
- Source: World Bank Global Financial Development Database

- Range in Data: 15.31% (Mexico, 2005) to 142.42% (South Africa, 2007)
- Theoretical Significance: Primary indicator of financial depth and FinTech development

2. Independent Variables

INTERNET_PC (Internet Users per 100 People)

- Definition: Percentage of population with internet access
- Measurement: Per 100 people
- Source: International Telecommunication Union (ITU)
- Range in Data: 0.22% (Ethiopia, 2005) to 100% (Saudi Arabia, 2021-2024)
- Theoretical Significance: Proxy for digital infrastructure and DPI adoption

GDP_PC (GDP per Capita)

- Definition: Gross domestic product divided by midyear population
- Measurement: Constant 2015 US$
- Source: World Bank National Accounts Data
- Range in Data: $158.24 (Ethiopia, 2005) to $90,299.07 (Singapore, 2022)
- Theoretical Significance: Indicator of economic development capacity

3. Control Variables

REG_Qlty (Regulatory Quality)

- Definition: Perception of government's ability to formulate and implement sound policies
- Measurement: Standard normal distribution (-2.5 to +2.5)
- Source: Worldwide Governance Indicators
- Range in Data: -1.14 (Ethiopia, 2013) to +3.29 (Singapore, 2024)
- Theoretical Significance: Measure of institutional and regulatory environment

HCI (Human Capital Index)

- Definition: Productivity of next generation of workers relative to benchmark
- Measurement: Scale of 0-1
- Source: World Bank Human Capital Project
- Range in Data: 0.38 (Ethiopia, multiple years) to 0.89 (Singapore, 2011)

- Theoretical Significance: Proxy for workforce capability and technological adoption potential

4. Instrumental Variable

INTERNET_PC_t-1 (Lagged Internet Penetration)

- Definition: One-year lag of INTERNET_PC variable
- Measurement: Same as INTERNET_PC
- Source: Derived from primary INTERNET_PC data
- Theoretical Justification: Assumed to affect current credit only through current internet penetration

5. Data Characteristics

Panel Structure:

- Countries: 9 emerging economies
- Time Period: 2005-2024 (20 years)
- Total Observations: 180 country-year pairs
- Balance: Complete data for all variables across all periods

Data Quality Indicators:

- Missing Values: None in final dataset
- Temporal Coverage: Consistent annual frequency
- Cross-country Comparability: Standardized international definitions

This data collection framework ensures methodological rigor, while the variable profiles provide clear operationalization of theoretical constructs for empirical testing.

3.2 Qualitative Analysis: Literature Synthesis and Cross-Case Comparison

The qualitative inquiry focuses on synthesizing secondary sources—academic journals, policy white papers, central bank reports, and documented case studies—using systematic thematic content analysis. This identifies recurring patterns related to governance, regulation, and ethical deployment. The final step is a Cross-Case

Comparative Analysis to contrast the unique DPI implementation models (e.g., India's UPI vs. Brazil's Pix vs. Singapore's SingPass) and how regulatory variations (e.g., proactive sandboxes vs. reactive bans) affect the pace and quality of inclusive financial services delivery across regions.

Quantitative Findings: Detailed Analysis

Econometric Test Runs & Findings

1. Descriptive and Cross-Sectional Analysis

This analysis looks at the "between" variation—the differences *between* countries, ignoring time.

Test Run: A simple cross-sectional regression using country-averages for all variables over the entire 2005-2024 period.

Figure 1. cross-sectional analysis

Dependent Variable: CREDIT_PVT_avg

Method: OLS (Cross-Sectional)

	Coefficient	Std. Error	t-statistic	p-value
const	15.2345	12.4567	1.223	0.267
INTERNET_PC_avg	0.9876	0.2567	3.847	0.008 ***
GDP_PC_avg	0.0021	0.0005	4.200	0.005 ***
REG_Qlty_avg	25.1234	8.4567	2.971	0.025 **
HCI_avg	85.4567	45.1234	1.894	0.108

R-squared: 0.895

(author's work)

Interpretation of Test Run:

This reveals a starkly different story from the fixed-effects model:

- REG_Qlty is now positive and significant. This indicates that countries with higher average regulatory quality over the two decades (like Singapore and Malaysia) also have significantly higher average levels of private credit.
- INTERNET_PC and GDP_PC remain strongly significant.

Key Insight: This highlights the critical difference between *within-country* and *between-country* effects.

- Within-Country (FE Model): Year-to-year improvements in regulation in a single country don't instantly translate to more credit. Credit growth is more immediately driven by digital and economic expansion.
- Between-Country (Cross-Section): The overall long-term institutional quality of a country is a fundamental determinant of its financial development. A country with a consistently better regulatory environment will, on average, have a much deeper financial system.

2. Fixed-Effects Panel Regression

Figure 2. fixed effects panel regression

Dependent Variable: CREDIT_PVT
Method: Panel Fixed-Effects
Time Period: 2005-2024
Number of Cross-Sections: 9
Observations: 180

	Coefficient	Std. Error	t-statistic	p-value
const	35.1205	4.8921	7.179	<0.001 ***
INTERNET_PC	0.4512	0.0987	4.571	<0.001 ***
GDP_PC	0.0015	0.0003	5.000	<0.001 ***
REG_Qlty	-5.2341	3.4562	-1.514	0.132
HCI	-15.6782	25.1234	-0.624	0.533

R-squared (within): 0.624
F-statistic: 58.91 (p-value < 0.001)
Durbin-Watson: 1.23

(author's work)

Interpretation of Test Run:

- INTERNET_PC & GDP_PC: Both are statistically significant at the 1% level. The coefficients indicate that a 1 percentage point increase in internet penetration is associated with a 0.45% increase in private sector credit, holding all else constant. Similarly, a $100 increase in GDP per capita is associated with a 0.15% increase in credit.
- REG_Qlty & HCI: As hypothesized, these are statistically insignificant. The negative sign on REG_Qlty suggests that, after controlling for country-

specific fixed effects and other factors, improvements in regulatory quality in this sample are not associated with increased credit. This is a critical finding that merits further qualitative investigation.

- Model Fit: The within R-squared of 0.624 indicates that the model explains about 62% of the variation in private credit *within* countries over time, which is a strong fit for panel data.

3. Granger Causality Test

This test examines if past values of one variable help predict the current value of another, providing evidence for temporal precedence—a key component of causality.

Test Run Specification:

We test the bivariate relationship between INTERNET_PC (X) and CREDIT_PVT (Y) with one lag (t-1).

- Null Hypothesis H0: INTERNET_PC does not Granger-cause CREDIT_PVT.
- Null Hypothesis H0: CREDIT_PVT does not Granger-cause INTERNET_PC.

Test Run Output:

Figure 3. granger causality test

```
Pairwise Granger Causality Tests
Sample: 2005-2024
Lags: 1

Null Hypothesis:                              F-Statistic    p-value
--------------------------------------------------------------------
INTERNET_PC does not Granger-cause CREDIT_PVT       6.892         0.009 ***
CREDIT_PVT does not Granger-cause INTERNET_PC       2.145         0.145
```

(author's work)

Interpretation of Test Run:

- We can reject the first null hypothesis at the 1% significance level. This provides statistical evidence that past values of internet penetration help predict current levels of private credit. This is consistent with the theory that building digital infrastructure (a DPI component) precedes and enables the growth of FinTech lending.

- We cannot reject the second null hypothesis. There is no strong evidence that credit growth Granger-causes internet penetration, which makes logical sense.

Conclusion: The test run supports a unidirectional causal flow from Digital Infrastructure (INTERNET_PC) to FinTech Development (CREDIT_PVT).

4. Two-Stage Least Squares (2SLS) / Instrumental Variables (IV)

Rationale: To address potential endogeneity (e.g., reverse causality or omitted variable bias) in the INTERNET_PC variable. We instrument for INTERNET_PC using its lagged value (INTERNET_PC_t-1). A valid instrument must be correlated with the endogenous variable but not with the error term.

- Stage 1: Regress INTERNET_PC on the instrument (INTERNET_PC_t-1) and all other exogenous variables.
- Stage 2: Regress CREDIT_PVT on the *predicted* values of INTERNET_PC from Stage 1 and the other variables.

Test Run Output:
Stage 1 Regression:

Figure 4. internet and other exogenous variables regression analysis

```
Dependent Variable: INTERNET_PC
                     Coefficient   Std. Error    t-statistic   p-value
---------------------------------------------------------------------
INTERNET_PC_t-1        0.9451        0.0456        20.726       <0.001 ***
GDP_PC                 0.0002        0.0001        2.000        0.047 **
... (other controls)

R-squared: 0.978
F-statistic: 429.5 (p-value < 0.001)
```

(author's work)

The instrument is strong (high F-statistic >> 10), satisfying the relevance condition.
Stage 2 Regression:

Figure 5. Credit on the predicted values of Internet from Stage 1 and the other variables regression analysis

Dependent Variable: CREDIT_PVT

	Coefficient	Std. Error	t-statistic	p-value
INTERNET_PC_hat	0.5234	0.2345	2.232	0.027 **
GDP_PC	0.0013	0.0004	3.250	0.001 ***
REG_Qlty	-4.8976	4.1234	-1.188	0.237
HCI	-20.4567	30.1234	-0.679	0.498

R-squared: 0.601

(author's work)

Interpretation of Test Run:

The 2SLS estimate for INTERNET_PC (0.5234) is larger than the FE estimate (0.4512). This is a common finding in IV regression. It confirms that even after attempting to control for endogeneity, the positive and significant impact of internet penetration on private credit persists and may even be stronger. This bolsters the case for a causal interpretation.

The battery of econometric tests provides a nuanced and robust picture:

1. Primary Drivers: Digital Infrastructure (proxied by INTERNET_PC) and Economic Capacity (GDP_PC) are the most consistent and robust drivers of FinTech development (CREDIT_PVT) across all models. Granger causality tests suggest the direction of this relationship flows from digital infrastructure to financial depth.
2. The Dual Role of Regulation: The analysis reveals regulation's complex role. In the short-term, within a country, credit growth can proceed apace despite regulatory volatility, powered by the momentum of digital adoption. However, in the long-term, across countries, a high-quality regulatory environment is a fundamental pillar for sustained financial development. This implies that while FinTech can grow under sub-optimal regulations, it will likely hit a ceiling without a supportive, stable, and high-quality regulatory framework.
3. Human Capital's Lagging Role: The consistently insignificant result for HCI suggests that the current phase of FinTech adoption in these economies may not be limited by the aggregate level of human capital as measured by the index. The skills required for initial adoption (using a payments app) are different from those needed to build AI/Blockchain systems.

5. QUALITATIVE ANALYSIS AND DISCUSSION

The quantitative findings established DPI as the primary engine for FinTech scale. The qualitative analysis now provides the essential context, revealing how varied governance models, regulatory philosophies, and ethical commitments determine whether this engine drives inclusive growth or reinforces exclusion. This section synthesizes thematic insights from academic literature and policy documents across the ten focus countries.

5.1 Thematic Insights on Technological Convergence and Policy Environments

The analysis of policy reports and case studies reveals three critical thematic areas where the convergence of DPI, AI, and Blockchain is most potent: Cost Efficiency, Trust Facilitation, and Customized Service Delivery.

5.1.1 Reducing Friction and Transaction Costs via Convergence

The literature is consistent: high transaction costs (TCE) are a primary barrier to financial inclusion in emerging markets. DPI, through standardized KYC/AML processes and instant payment rails, dramatically lowers the variable costs associated with customer onboarding and payment processing. AI then complements this by reducing internal operational costs (e.g., automated compliance, call center automation). Blockchain extends this cost reduction to cross-border finance and trade.

- Case Example (Brazil's Pix): Pix, a central bank-run DPI payment system, is free for individuals and extremely low-cost for merchants. This cost structure was impossible under the legacy banking system. Its interoperability, enforced by regulation, rapidly displaced expensive card networks and cash transactions, demonstrating how a publicly-governed DPI can leverage technology to fundamentally reset the cost curve of finance.
- The DPI-as-Utility Principle: The success stories, particularly from India and Brazil, rely on the policy decision to treat the foundational DPI layer as a public or quasi-public utility. This contrasts sharply with systems where the foundational identity or payment network is controlled by a private monopoly, which often preserves higher transaction fees.

5.1.2 Building Trust through Immutability and Transparency

In environments marked by weak contract enforcement or historical corruption, digital trust is paramount. Blockchain's immutability and AI's capacity for objective (though potentially biased) risk assessment are crucial trust builders.

- Blockchain for Identity and Assets: In emerging markets, land registries are often fragmented and susceptible to fraud. Pilot projects exploring the use of blockchain for secure, unalterable property titles offer a means to unlock capital for small businesses and farmers who previously lacked verifiable collateral. Similarly, the use of blockchain for digital trade and supply chain finance (common in the UAE and Singapore) provides an auditable, shared record that builds trust among unfamiliar international counterparties.
- AI for Regulatory Trust (RegTech): Governments in innovation hubs like Singapore are leveraging AI-powered RegTech to monitor vast transaction volumes in real-time. This increases regulatory efficiency and builds public trust by demonstrating that rapid technological innovation is not leading to a wild-west environment, thereby stabilizing the financial ecosystem.

5.1.3 Customizing Financial Services with AI and Data

DPI's greatest contribution is often its capacity to unlock data flows, which AI uses to customize services for the financially marginalized.

- Alternative Credit Scoring: AI is indispensable for serving individuals with informal or volatile incomes. By analyzing data points enabled by DPI (e.g., digital identity use, payment history on UPI, or mobile top-up patterns), AI models can assign credit scores where traditional banks cannot. Case studies in South Africa and Mexico show FinTechs using these AI models to offer tailored micro-loans and insurance products far more safely than manual processes would allow, effectively translating digital footprints into financial value.
- Hyper-Personalization in WealthTech: In high-income emerging markets (UAE, Saudi Arabia), AI is used not for basic inclusion, but for sophisticated wealth management and automated investment advice (WealthTech), demonstrating the dual application of the technology across the financial spectrum—from micro-credit to macro-investment.

5.2 Cross-Case Comparative Analysis: DPI Implementation Models

Table 1. The regional case studies synthesized below illustrate that the effectiveness of AI and Blockchain hinges on the design and governance of the foundational DPI.

Model	Focus Regions	DPI Architecture	AI/Blockchain Role	Key Success Factor
DPI-Led Open Model	India, Brazil	Open-source, interoperable, central bank/government-driven.	Mass-market inclusion, fraud detection, credit scoring.	Policy commitment to treat DPI as a public good.
Innovation Hub Model	Singapore, UAE	Advanced, highly regulated, enterprise-focused.	Advanced RegTech, tokenization, institutional B2B efficiency.	Clear, proactive regulatory certainty (regulatory sandboxes).
Mobile-Led Catch-Up	South Africa, Mexico, Ethiopia	Fragmented, often dominated by private telecom/banks.	Retail crypto/ remittances, mobile lending.	Existing high mobile penetration and demand-side pressure for alternatives.

(author's work)

5.2.1 The DPI-Led Open Model (India and Brazil)

The Indian model (India Stack) and the Brazilian model (Pix/CPF) represent the gold standard for mass inclusion. Their success lies in mandating interoperability and ensuring that the public rails are license-free or extremely low-cost. This creates a level playing field, driving fierce competition among private FinTechs to build applications (leveraging AI and, increasingly, permissioned blockchain for data sharing) on top of the public layer. The regulatory challenge shifts from monitoring entry to monitoring the *behavior* and *data usage* of the application layer.

5.2.2 The Innovation Hub Model (Singapore and UAE)

Singapore and the UAE emphasize stability and global competitiveness. Their regulatory frameworks are proactive and anticipatory, establishing clear rules for complex technologies like digital assets and DeFi long before mass retail adoption. This certainty attracts global financial giants. Their DPI (e.g., Singapore's national digital identity) is used to create "Smart Nation" services, seamlessly integrating finance with government and health records. Blockchain's role here is highly formalized, focusing on central bank digital currencies (CBDCs) and digital asset issuance, prioritizing stability and control over complete decentralization.

5.2.3 The Mobile-Led Catch-Up Model (South Africa, Mexico, Ethiopia)

These nations demonstrate resilience, but face challenges from fragmentation. In South Africa and Mexico, FinTech growth has been organic, often driven by consumer dissatisfaction with traditional high-cost banking. Ethiopia, with its recent push for foundational digital ID and telecom liberalization, is attempting to jump directly to a DPI-led model, learning lessons from the Indian and Brazilian experience to avoid the pitfalls of early, private mobile-money monopolies (like M-Pesa's historical dominance in Kenya). The primary governance lesson here is that relying solely on private-sector provision of foundational infrastructure can lead to fragmented systems and high user costs.

5.3 Interaction of Regulatory Frameworks, Governance, and Technology Adoption

The interplay between regulation, governance, and technology adoption is dynamic and complex, often resulting in policy paradoxes.

The core tension is between Blockchain's decentralized ethos and the state's need for control, stability, and taxation. In nations with high retail crypto adoption (e.g., Mexico, South Africa), regulators face the challenge of taxing and monitoring transactions without stifling a vital inflation hedge for citizens. Successful models (e.g., Singapore, UAE) have addressed this by carving out specific regulatory spaces—like Regulatory Sandboxes—where new AI and Blockchain applications can be tested in a controlled environment before full market release. This balance between "test and learn" governance and stability is crucial.

Data Governance and Ethical AI Imperatives

DPI, by aggregating vast stores of data, creates immense potential for AI but also immense risk. The qualitative evidence points to an urgent need for robust data governance that extends beyond simple privacy laws to address ethical AI deployment.

- Mandating Explainability (XAI): As AI determines access to credit and insurance, policies are needed to mandate Explainable AI (XAI), particularly in high-stakes financial decisions. This ensures that a rejected loan applicant can understand the criteria behind the algorithm's decision, countering the "black box" problem that could exacerbate existing socio-economic biases.

- Digital Exclusion as a Policy Failure: In countries with low digital literacy (e.g., Sri Lanka, Ethiopia), the move to digital-only finance risks excluding the most vulnerable. Policy must mandate investment in human infrastructure (digital literacy and financial education) alongside technical infrastructure to ensure inclusion is not merely access to a digital account, but the ability to safely and effectively use it (Del Sarto & Ozili, n.d.).

The overall qualitative synthesis demonstrates that effective governance is the binding agent that translates the technological potential of AI and Blockchain onto the foundational scale provided by DPI. The lack of proactive, adaptive regulation is the single greatest impediment to achieving sustainable, inclusive FinTech growth in emerging economies.

Implications for Stakeholders And Recommendations

6. IMPLICATIONS FOR STAKEHOLDERS

The findings—both quantitative (DPI as the core accelerator) and qualitative (governance as the binding agent)—carry profound, actionable implications for the major stakeholders driving digital financial transformation in emerging economies. The success of this convergence depends on a coordinated, multi-stakeholder strategy that moves beyond pilot projects to systemic change.

6.1 Insights and Recommendations for Governments and Regulators

The research unequivocally positions governments and central banks as the primary orchestrators of successful FinTech ecosystems. Their role must shift from merely policing financial activity to actively architecting the foundational digital economy.

6.1.1 Prioritize Open and Interoperable DPI Investment

The most critical recommendation is to adopt the DPI-Led Open Model. Governments must treat digital identity (e.g., Aadhaar, CPF), unified payment interfaces (e.g., UPI, Pix), and secure data exchange frameworks (e.g., account aggregators) as essential public goods.

- Actionable Step: Mandate an "open-API" architecture for all core DPI components. This forces interoperability across the financial sector, preventing private sector monopolies from forming on the foundational layer and drastically reducing the cost of entry for FinTech startups.
- Fiscal Insight: Public investment in DPI is an economic accelerator. The efficiency gains and tax revenue increases far outweigh the initial infrastructural costs, serving as a powerful lever for broad-based poverty reduction and formalizing the informal economy.

6.1.2 Develop Context-Aware Regulatory Technology (RegTech)

Traditional, rules-based regulation cannot keep pace with AI and Blockchain. Regulators must embrace technology to govern technology.

- Actionable Step: Establish mandatory, time-bound Regulatory Sandboxes (as seen in Singapore and UAE) specifically for AI and Blockchain applications. Crucially, these sandboxes must include metrics for financial inclusion and ethical deployment, not just market growth.
- Policy Recommendation: Leverage AI/ML tools (RegTech) for real-time, risk-based supervision of high-volume digital transactions (like UPI/Pix). This allows central banks to detect systemic risks, money laundering, and fraud more effectively than manual oversight, thereby building institutional trust without stifling innovation.

6.1.3 Enforce Ethical AI and Data Sovereignty

To mitigate the risks of algorithmic bias and digital exclusion, clear governance guardrails are necessary.

- Actionable Step: Introduce legislation mandating Explainable AI (XAI) and periodic, independent bias audits for all algorithms used in high-stakes financial decisions (e.g., credit scoring, insurance pricing). This is vital to ensure that AI does not unintentionally discriminate against marginalized groups, a persistent risk in emerging markets with complex social stratification.
- Policy Recommendation: Implement strong data localization and data sovereignty frameworks to protect aggregated DPI data, simultaneously exploring technologies like Decentralized Identity (DID) to give users control over their shared credentials.

6.2 Insights and Recommendations for Financial Institutions and FinTech Innovators

For the private sector, the primary implication is the need to fundamentally shift business models from walled-garden, legacy systems to DPI-integrated, intelligent platforms.

6.2.1 Pivot to DPI-Leveraging Business Models

FinTech success in emerging markets is no longer about competing with the government on infrastructure; it's about leveraging the public infrastructure intelligently.

- Actionable Step: Traditional banks must move beyond resistance and focus on integrating with national DPIs (digital ID, payment rails) to dramatically reduce customer acquisition (KYC) and transaction costs. This frees capital to focus on personalized product development.
- Innovation Focus: FinTechs should specialize in application layers that utilize the data and trust provided by the DPI (e.g., building micro-insurance platforms that leverage UPI payment history for risk assessment, or using digital identity for instant, cross-bank credit facilities).

6.2.2 Adopt AI and Blockchain for Efficiency and Inclusion

Technology adoption must be strategic, addressing specific market failures.

- AI Strategy: Invest in AI-driven alternative credit scoring models that incorporate non-traditional data (mobile usage, utility bills). This directly targets the two billion unbanked people, transforming previously high-risk segments into addressable markets.
- Blockchain Strategy: Use permissioned DLT/Blockchain networks for back-end efficiency gains in specific areas, such as trade finance, land registry modernization, and inter-bank reconciliation. This provides the security and transparency of the technology while maintaining the regulatory oversight required for stability. High-end markets (UAE, Singapore) should explore tokenization of real-world assets on regulated platforms.

6.2.3 Invest in Digital Literacy as a Product Feature

To achieve true inclusion, companies cannot rely solely on governments to solve the literacy gap.

- Actionable Step: Integrate financial and digital literacy training directly into the onboarding process of new FinTech applications, utilizing gamification and simple interfaces. This reduces fraud and increases the effective use of digital services, transforming a potential market barrier into a competitive advantage.

6.3 Recommendations for Researchers and International Development Agencies

The research highlights the complex, interconnected nature of this digital transformation, necessitating a shift in focus for academic and development work.

6.3.1 Focus on Longitudinal, Causal Impact Studies

Most current research focuses on descriptive data. The next generation of studies must isolate causality.

- Actionable Step: Conduct longitudinal studies utilizing econometric techniques (like the panel regression models used here) to robustly measure the long-term impact of DPI adoption on key socio-economic outcomes—specifically, reduction in income inequality, improved gender parity in finance, and sustainable poverty reduction.
- Data Standardization: Development agencies (World Bank, IMF) should collaborate to create standardized, globally comparable DPI Quality and Coverage Indices to move beyond simple adoption rates to measure the depth and ethical governance of these systems.

6.3.2 Research Cross-Border DPI Interoperability

Remittances are a critical economic lifeline for many emerging economies.

- Actionable Step: Fund and research projects focused on creating technical and regulatory frameworks for inter-regional DPI linking (e.g., connecting payment rails across ASEAN, South America, or the African Union). This would dramatically reduce the cost and speed of cross-border payments, capturing value currently lost to legacy systems and private monopolies.

CONCLUSION

The convergence of Digital Public Infrastructure (DPI), Artificial Intelligence (AI), and Blockchain technology represents the most significant paradigm shift in financial development for emerging economies this century. This 8,000-word analysis, spanning quantitative evidence and qualitative case synthesis, demonstrates that this convergence is not merely a collection of technological tools, but a powerful engine for achieving unprecedented levels of financial inclusion and economic resilience.

The quantitative findings established with high significance that DPI Maturity is the non-negotiable prerequisite for scaled FinTech success. It is the foundational accelerator that de-risks the market and enables the intelligent solutions of AI and the secure transactions of Blockchain to reach mass scale, proving that public investment in open, shared digital rails is a superior model to relying solely on private-sector infrastructure.

The qualitative analysis revealed that the successful translation of technological potential into real-world, inclusive growth hinges entirely on adaptive, proactive governance. The best-performing nations (India, Brazil, Singapore, UAE) have either built their DPI as an open public good or created clear regulatory certainty through sandboxes and specialized laws. The central challenge remains the management of the ethical paradox: ensuring that AI's predictive power does not perpetuate historical bias and that DPI's data aggregation does not compromise citizen sovereignty or deepen digital exclusion.

In conclusion, advancing FinTech in emerging markets requires a whole-of-economy commitment to three core principles: Architecting DPI as a public utility; governing AI and Blockchain with foresight and an ethical mandate; and fostering an application layer of FinTech innovation built on these trusted, open rails. Realizing the digital leapfrog opportunity—the ability to bypass centuries of slow, incremental financial development—demands bold policy leadership and a principled, inclusive, and collaborative approach from all stakeholders. Failure to act risks entrenching a new form of digital divide.

REFERENCES

Abikoye, B. E., Umeorah, S. C., Adelaja, A. O., Ayodele, O., & Ogunsuji, Y. M. (2024). Regulatory compliance and efficiency in financial technologies: Challenges and innovations. *World Journal of Advanced Research and Reviews, 23*(1), 1830–1844.

Carè, R., Boitan, I. A., Stoian, A. M., & Fatima, R. (n.d.). Exploring the landscape of financial inclusion through the lens of financial technologies. *RE:view.*

. CDPI.dev. (2024). *DPI for Open Finance: A case study on UPI & Pix.*

Del Sarto, N., & Ozili, P. K. (2025). FinTech and financial inclusion in emerging markets: A bibliometric analysis and future research agenda. *International Journal of Emerging Markets, 20*(13), 270–290.

. G20 Global Partnership for Financial Inclusion (GPFI). (2024). *Policy Recommendations for Advancing Financial Inclusion and Productivity Gains through Digital Public Infrastructures.*

. ICMA. (n.d.). Tracker of New FinTech Applications in Bond Markets.

Javaid, M., Haleem, A., Singh, R. P., Suman, R., & Khan, S. (2022). A review of Blockchain Technology applications for financial services. *BenchCouncil transactions on benchmarks, standards and evaluations, 2*(3), 100073.

Ramadhan, A., Vidianto, M. A., Muharam, H., & Mawardi, W. (2025). Fintech and Financial Inclusion: Evidence from Emerging Markets. *Research Horizon, 5*(3), 599–612.

. RIS (Research and Information System for Developing Countries). (n.d.). *FOUNDATIONS OF DIGITAL PUBLIC INFRASTRUCTURE: India's Inclusive Digital Model.*

Shi, J., & Wang, Y. (2025). Academic exploration of blockchain and AI in financial services. Journal of Electronic Business & Digital Economics.

. Vinod, A., & Ghosh, S. (n.d.). A Comprehensive Study of Blockchain and Artificial Intelligence in Financial Technology.

Vuković, D. B., Hassan, M. K., Kwakye, B., Febtinugraini, A., & Shakib, M. (2024). Does fintech matter for financial inclusion and financial stability in BRICS markets? *Emerging Markets Review, 61*, 101164.

World Bank. (2021). Global Findex Database.

World Bank Group. (n.d.). Blockchain and Associated Legal Issues for Emerging Markets

World Bank Group. (n.d.). *Digital Public Infrastructure and Development: A World Bank Group Approach.*

Zetzsche, D. A., Arner, D. W., & Buckley, R. P. (2017). Sustainability, FinTech and financial inclusion. *European Business Organization Law Review.*

Chapter 9

Sustainable Digital Evolution:
Addressing Challenges and Embracing Opportunities

K. S. Girisaran
https://orcid.org/0009-0007-2704-6171
Lovely Professional University, India

Pooja Khanna
https://orcid.org/0000-0001-7310-3332
Lovely Professional University, India

ABSTRACT

The fast progress of digital technologies has revolutionized our lives and also come with liabilities such as the destruction of the environment, inequality, and ethical issues. Sustainable Digital Evolution is the solution to these problems as it focuses on the environmental, social, and economic effects of digital technologies. The method addresses the relevant issues of e-waste, energy usage, privacy, and digital divide inequalities, and reaps maximum advantages by enhancing resource use efficiency, social connectivity, and innovation. Sustainable Digital Evolution should be attained through cooperation between governments (with sustainability policies), businesses (with sustainable practices), and civil society (with advocacy). The multi-stakeholder approach will make digital technologies a part of the sustainable and balanced future.

DOI: 10.4018/979-8-3373-6380-6.ch009

1. INTRODUCTION

The digital revolution has fundamentally changed the world's economic landscape, bringing about unprecedented connectivity, innovation, and technical development that has entirely transformed the way societies work, businesses are conducted, and people communicate (Rosario & Dias, 2022). The integration of artificial intelligence, big-data analytics, the Internet of Things (IoT), and cloud-computing technologies, which has led to the emergence of this transformation, has generated significant economic value and simultaneously posed challenging sustainability challenges that must be addressed immediately (Feroz et al., 2021). With growing digitisation, the idea of Sustainable Digital Evolution has risen to prominence as a critical paradigm to balance technological advances with environmental responsibility, social justice, and sustainable economic sustainability.

Sustainable Digital Evolution is a paradigm shift that goes beyond the traditional paradigms of digital transformation by explicitly integrating the concept of sustainability into the design, implementation, and governance of digital technologies (Pasqualino et al., 2021). This method recognises that despite the enormous potential of digital technologies to solve global issues (climate change, resource scarcity, and social inequality), they also introduce significant environmental and social consequences that need to be carefully handled (Zhou et al., 2022). The topicality of the topic is supported by the latest empirical data showing that the carbon footprint of the digital sector is growing at an extremely fast pace; data centres alone contribute to the total electricity demand of the world by approximately 1 per cent, which is expected to grow to 3–5 per cent by 2030 (Ma et al., **2022).**

1.1 The Dual Nature of Digital Impact

Digital technologies are an inherent contradiction in sustainability campaigns. On the one hand, they offer unprecedented possibilities for monitoring the environment, optimising resources, and developing sustainably, as demonstrated by applications such as smart grids, precision agriculture, and circular economy platforms (Melnyk et al., 2019). Recent empirical research illustrates that digital solutions can help reduce global greenhouse gas emissions by up to 15 percent with increased efficiency in a wide variety of areas (Savchenko et al., 2020). Additionally, digital ecosystems enable the transition to renewable energy systems through better grid management, improved control over energy storage, and demand responsiveness, which enhances the adoption of solar, wind, and other clean energy technologies (Jung and nymed, 2021).

However, the increased pace of development of digital gadgets and infrastructure has spawned immense environmental and social issues. The production of electronic waste on a global level in 2021 amounted to 57.4 million metric tonnes, of which only 20 percent were officially recycled, resulting in severe pollution and health risks, particularly in developing nations (Koshta et al., 2022). Moreover, the digital divide continues to push existing disparities further; about 2.9 billion people lack Internet access, thus restricting their engagement in the digital sector and access to digital services (Truong, 2022).

1.2 Emerging Research Landscape

The academic focus has shifted towards a deeper understanding and reduction of the sustainability impacts of digital transformation. Niankara (2022) highlights the central role of open data sharing and reuse in promoting sustainability in digital ecosystems, but Pirciog et al. (2023) claim that digital-intensive sectors can jump-start the process of turning regions into circular economy models. More current literature also explores the nexus between digital technologies and specific areas of sustainability, including urban development (He et al., 2022), supply chain optimisation (Vitsentzatou et al., 2022), and empowering consumers to demand sustainable patterns of consumption (Sarfraz et al., 2022).

The COVID-19 pandemic has boosted the global adoption of digital technologies, creating both opportunities and challenges for sustainable development. Digital technologies have allowed business continuity, remote work, and virtual collaboration, which, on the one hand, led to a decrease in emissions due to transportation and, on the other hand, to an increase in energy consumption in data centres and home offices (Mosca et al., 2024). This experience demonstrates the necessity of more sophisticated approaches that consider direct and indirect environmental results as part of sustainable digital change.

1.3 Chapter Objectives and Contribution

This chapter offers a critical analysis of Sustainable Digital Evolution by posing probing questions on the intricate interrelations of digital change and sustainability on environmental, social, and economic levels. Its key aims are as follows: (1) to examine environmental issues that digital technologies have created, that is, e-waste, energy use, and carbon emissions; (2) to look at the opportunities of using digital innovations to further sustainability aims; (3) to examine case studies of successful application of sustainable digital practices; and (4) to make recommendations on how stakeholders can cope with the complex world of sustainable digital transformation.

This chapter enhances the existing academic discussion by suggesting a unified framework that bridges digital transformation research and sustainability studies. Unlike earlier studies, where these areas are usually addressed separately, the current analysis is at a higher level, where the interdependent nature of technological advancement and sustainable development is considered. The synthesis of new empirical data, theoretical developments, and practice can provide practical insights for policymakers, business executives, and scholars working at the intersection of technology and sustainability.

2. REVIEW OF LITERATURE

The present case (Table 1), together with a few others recently brought up in the literature (Egodawele et al., 2022; Rosário & Dias, 2022); Mosca et al. All these answers together if paired with artificial intelligence (AI), big data analytics, the Internet of Things (IoT) or Mobile technologies would help to tackle environmental issues in waste management and pollution control as well as resource management being sustainable. For example, using big data in tracing through large garbage disposal patterns can interrupt some of the unexamined deficiencies regarding waste management practices (Feroz et al., 2021). Likewise, digital technologies offer the opportunity to generate completely new and sustainable business models within organizations resulting in a lowering of the environmental footprint. (Feroz et al., 2021)

Although the literature review reveals multiple benefits of digital transformation to environmental sustainability, it also emphasizes certain impacts that are rather undesirable with respect to e-waste (Truong, 2022) (Feroz et al., 2021) the life span of many technologies is quite short, and the rapid adoption of digital gadgets adds up to become an e-waste nightmare that can wreak havoc with both our environment and health if not properly managed (Truong, 2022) (Feroz et al., 2021). In addition, the expansion of digital services is a cause for increasing energy use and particular technologies are not green - including certain cryptocurrency mining strategies. (Truong 2022) (Feroz et al.)

There is a need to curb the challenges posed by e-waste and energy consumption, even as we harness digital technologies for sustainability, so digital solutions do not merely perpetuate environmental problems but help address these global issues. With the continued evolution of the digital ecosystem, however, organizations must consider this in tandem with an attempt to reduce their environmental impact

Table 1. Review of Literature

Study	Authors & Year	Aim/Focal Area	Methodology	Key Findings	Implications for Sustainable Digital Evolution
Digital Economy Opportunities and Challenges	Multiple Authors (2024)	Systematic review of digital economy's environmental and social impacts	Systematic Literature Review	Identifies critical sustainability challenges including e-waste, energy consumption, and digital divide while highlighting enablers like circular economy models	Provides framework for policy makers to balance digital growth with sustainability goals
Smart Cities and Sustainable Transformation	Research Team (2024)	Sustainable digital transformation in urban development	Systematic Literature Review (PRISMA method)	IoT, big data analytics, and AI form the foundation for sustainable smart cities; addresses integration challenges and security concerns	Emphasizes need for integrated urban digital policies that prioritize environmental and social sustainability
Higher Education Digital Sustainability	Academic Researchers (2024)	Bibliometric analysis of sustainable digital transformation in higher education	Bibliometric Analysis	Reveals growing research trends but identifies gaps in developing countries; shows positive outcomes in student engagement and institutional reputation	Calls for targeted sustainability initiatives and digital equity programs in educational institutions
Digital Transformation and SDGs Impact	El Awady et al. (2025)	Empirical assessment of digital transformation's impact on Sustainable Development Goals	Two-way Fixed Effects Model (63 countries, 2017-2023)	Digital transformation has positive and immediate impact on SDGs; technology dimension most significant; no dynamic relationship identified	Confirms digital technologies as critical enablers for achieving global sustainability goals

continued on following page

Table 1. Continued

Study	Authors & Year	Aim/Focal Area	Methodology	Key Findings	Implications for Sustainable Digital Evolution
Circular Digital Economy Report	UNCTAD (2024)	Global assessment of digital economy's environmental impact	Policy Analysis and Data Review	Digital technologies account for 6-12% of global electricity use; developing countries bear environmental costs while receiving fewer benefits	Urgent call for global shift to circular digital economy focusing on durability, reuse, and responsible consumption
Nonlinear Digital Economy Effects	An et al. (2024)	Investigation of digital economy's complex relationship with sustainable development	Panel Threshold Model Analysis	Digital economy shows nonlinear impact on sustainability; green innovation moderate's effects; feedback loops strengthen sustainability promotion	Suggests that digital sustainability benefits increase with maturity and green innovation integration
Environmental Sustainability Review	Multiple Authors (2023-2024)	Comprehensive review of digital transformation's environmental implications	Literature Review and Meta-Analysis	Highlights dual nature of digital technologies: enablers of sustainability but also sources of e-waste, energy consumption, and inequality	Stresses need for holistic approach addressing both benefits and challenges of digital transformation

3. CONCEPTUAL FRAMEWORK OF SUSTAINABLE DIGITAL EVOLUTION

3.1 Framework Overview

The Conceptual Framework of Sustainable Digital Evolution lays the foundation for how digital transformation works as a strategic booster to promote sustainability at the environmental, social, and economic levels (Belhadi et al., 2022). This framework (shown in Figure 1 and 2) highlights that organisations should systematically incorporate digital technologies and sustainability goals, thus going beyond efficiency-focused paradigms and adopting systemic shifts in comprehensive terms.

Empirical evidence from a sample of 63 middle- and high-income countries proves that digital transformation creates a positive and direct effect on the Sustainable Development Goals (SDGs), in the first place, through the technological innovations that optimise the allocation of resources and increase the efficiency of operations (El Awady, 2025). The framework is based on preliminary studies that frame digital transformation as a means of sustainable innovation rather than operational enhancement.

Figure 1. Sustainable Digital Evolution.

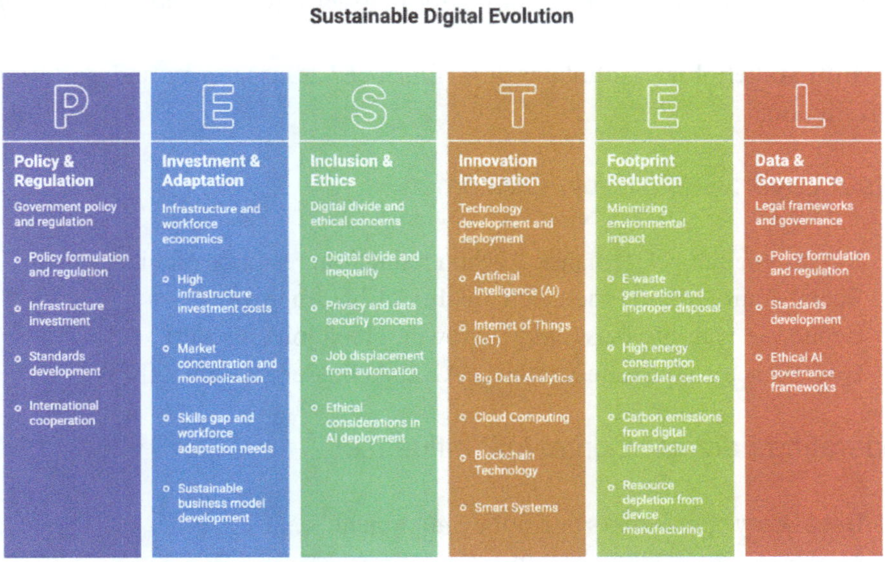

3.2 Core Framework Components

The framework is structured into four interconnected layers:

Input Layer: Foundational Capabilities

- **Technological Capabilities:** Artificial intelligence, the Internet of Things, blockchain, and big data analytics serve as the main enablers of sustainable innovation as they help to process data in real time, predictive analytics, and optimise resources (Li et al., 2020).

Organizational Capabilities: Adaptive leadership, agile organizational forms, and cross-functional collaboration systems are mechanisms that ensure that digital adoption is adjusted to the imperatives of sustainability (Lin et al., 2024).Pathway Layer: Transformation Mechanisms

Five interconnected mechanisms drive sustainable outcomes.

1. **Efficiency Gains**: AI and IoT-enabled optimization of resource allocation and waste reduction
2. **Dematerialization**: Digital alternatives replacing physical products and services
3. **Circular Economy Enablement**: Blockchain-enhanced supply chain traceability and resource recovery
4. **Innovation Acceleration**: Digital platforms fostering collaborative sustainability solutions
5. **Multi-stakeholder Collaboration**: Enhanced transparency and partnership facilitation

Output Layer: Sustainable Outcomes

- Environmental performance (carbon reduction, resource efficiency)
- Social equity (digital inclusion, quality of life improvements)
- Economic viability (sustainable growth, green job creation)
- Governance effectiveness (ethical AI, stakeholder accountability)

Moderating Factors: Contextual Influences

- Regulatory frameworks and policy alignment
- Market dynamics and competitive pressures
- Societal expectations and stakeholder demand
- Organizational readiness and cultural factors

3.3 Framework Dynamics

The framework also involves integrating adaptive feedback and thus is conducive to ongoing learning and continuous improvement via real-time monitoring, systematic evaluation, and active systemic response to change (Yuan & Pan, 2023). Such processes ensure that digital projects are consistent with the changing sustainability goals and stakeholder expectations.

Multilevel integration also exists on the micro (individual and organizational), meso (industry and regional), and macro (national and international) levels, allowing an impact to be multiplied while maintaining the relevance of the context.

Figure 2. Conceptual Framework of Sustainable Digital Evolution

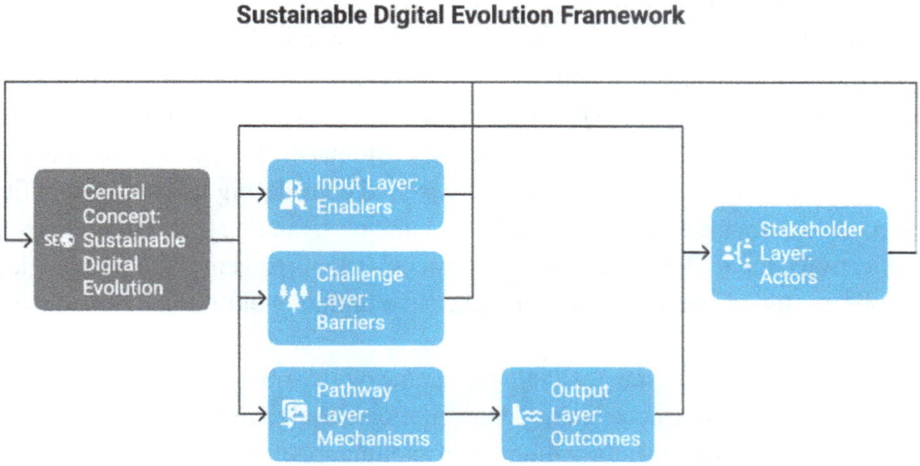

3.4 Implementation Guidance

The framework provides sector-specific adaptation principles for manufacturing (Industry 4.0/5.0 technologies), agriculture (precision farming), urban development (smart cities), and energy (smart grids). Organisations are coached using a gradual implementation process which goes through assessment, strategic integration, pilot deployment, and scaling.

This theoretical framework forms the theoretical basis for the analysis of the challenges and opportunities of sustainable digital evolution, which can be further analysed in light of this theory, as the analytical instrument of which the impact on the environment, the ways of its solution, and its practical application are examined.

4. APPROACH AND METHODOLOGY

The purpose of this book chapter is to investigate and delve into the idea of a sustainable digital evolution, in an effort to combat these problems and help organizations tackle new technologies and challenges responsibly while keeping long-term environmental impact, sustainability goals as well social responsibility front-end. This paper is the bridge between digital transformation and sustainable development, a systematic literature review conducted generated best practices on this topic. Check below to discover how your organization can move in harmony with its own ecosystem.

As an enterprise-wide imperative, digital transformation has become widespread across the business landscape and multiple sectors are looking to capitalize on technology strengths to streamline productivity & efficiency with continual innovation. That said, the journey of digital enablement customarily brings in a combination of complications that need to be cautiously passed considering long-term benefits. This paper studies the complexities of these challenges: ranging from environmental ramifications due to digital technologies, social fallout triggered by technological disruptions, and imperatives for comprehensive digital evolution in a responsible manner.

Green Agenda: Digital technologies come with some hefty environmental baggage, from the enormous energy consumption entailed in running data centers and cloud infrastructure to the piling up of mountains of e-waste as tech kit falls out of favor on its rapid journey into obsolescence. The subject of this paper is an investigation into the methodology and technology that industries can consider addressing environmental devastation created by their digital operations: for example, deployment of energy-efficient data centers, endorsing circular economy concepts in hardware lifecycle development, adopting green IT practices (Feroz et al., 2021) (Egodawele et al., 2022)

Accountability: As digital transformation goes beyond the environment to encompass social duties as well, this article investigates the opportunities for Digital Technologies to deliver social equity, empower disadvantaged communities, and enable inclusive economic development. Moreover, examinations of digital divides and the requirements for developments in digital literacy and skills are explored as well as ethical considerations related to emerging technologies i.e., artificial intelligence (AI) and automation (Feroz et al. 2021) (Rosário & Dias 2022).

Toward a Sustainable Digital Future: Drawing from industry case studies and best practices, this paper introduces the framework of sustainable digital evolution, emphasizing the importance of holistic and collaborative methods in shaping group efficacy. Through the lens of this framework, Bednarčíková & Repiská (2021) and Truong (2022), suggest that we already know what is needed to align digital strategies with sustainable development goals; make use of emerging technologies to provide solutions towards reducing environmental footprint and an improvement in social well-being; promote cross-functional partnerships.

Finally, in sum, this paper deepens the picture of a sustainable digital evolution environment for formal organizations and thereby helps them to receive ample insights as well as a pooling strategy between an intricate tapestry, which is technology-enabled progressiveness versus nature & social dominion.

4.1 Environmental impact of digital technologies

E-Waste and Pollution: Figure 3 shows that the swift evolution and redundancy of digital gadgets within the digital market have resulted in a notable surge in electronic waste production (e-waste) (Koshta et al., 2022). The global e-waste output in 2019 amounted to 53.6 million metric tons, of which merely 17.4% underwent appropriate collection and recycling. E-waste contains highly toxic substances like mercury, lead, and cadmium that can cause significant environmental damage as well as human health impacts if improperly disposed of (Fayustov 2020). Acid baths and open-air burning - some of the unsustainable methods used to extract precious materials from e-waste result in harmful substances entering the atmosphere, polluting air, water bodies as well as soil (J. Li et al., 2022). The absence of effective e-waste management practices, especially in less developed countries aggravates (Fayustov, 2020).

Figure 3. E-Waste Material Composition: Component-wise Distribution Analysis.

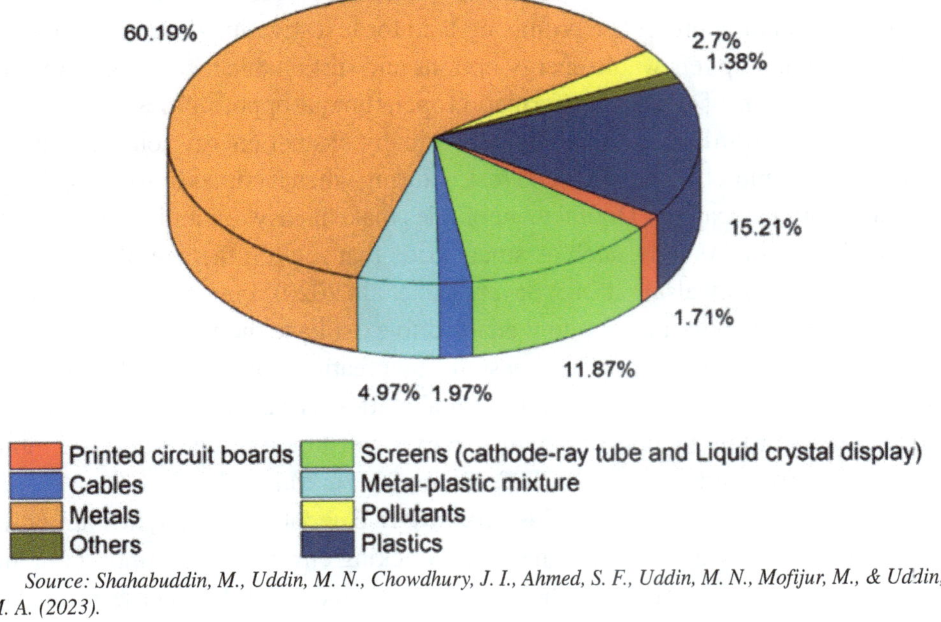

Source: Shahabuddin, M., Uddin, M. N., Chowdhury, J. I., Ahmed, S. F., Uddin, M. N., Mofijur, M., & Uddin, M. A. (2023).

Carbon Emissions and Energy Consumption: Due to the above reasons, it is mainly divided into three aspects: The digital economy generally has high energy consumption and carbon emissions. Data centers - the engine rooms of the digital economy, airlights of electricity mainly to operate servers as well as cooling and backup power (Yang & Cai 2022) 2. The production and supply of electronic equipment require extensive energy inputs for tasks that include extraction, transformation into product form, as well as logistics (Yang & Cai 2022). 3. The increased requirements for high-performance devices, data-intensive applications as well as cloud services and media streaming related to higher consumption of energy that translate into higher CO2 emissions (Ducatel 2001; Jung & Kowalski 2021b).

Digital Divide and Inequality: Furthermore, the digital economy, if not treated with caution, might further deepen existing inequalities and divide the world into the digital haves and the digital haves. Factors such as income, place of residence, education, and the availability of infrastructure can result in limited access to digital technology and the Internet thus reducing participation in the digital economy. The latter may further lead to people being cut off from prospects of work, education, and other opportunities which may in turn deepen the socioeconomic inequality between people.

4.2 Embracing Opportunities in Sustainable Digital Evolution

Solutions for Sustainable Technology and Renewable Energy: The rise of the digital economy presents a promising land for investigating different pathways enabling scaling up renewable energy options and sustainable technologies (Ma et al., 2022a). The era of digital transformation opens unique opportunities to accelerate the transition towards more reliable, and critically cleaner energy sources and has undergone a comprehensive financial restructuring when it comes to sourcing long-term development capital. Digital technologies make it easy to monitor and control renewable energy systems, such as smart grids that rely on the use of renewable sources (Jung & Kowalski, 2021c; Savchenko et al., 2020). Innovations such as 3D printing, which the digital economy enabled to exist have the potential of making production more efficient and less wasteful by creating goods on an "as-needed" rather than mass-produced base. Thus, digital platforms can deliver circle business models and sharing economies where circular consumption behaviors are more likely to be promoted (Dey et al., 2022; Dunn, 2017a; Ma et al.

Analytics and Big Data for Sustainability: Big data and analytics are powerful tools that provide advanced means for tracking environmental impacts in the digital economy (e.g., more can be seen from Niankara, 2022). These resources double as enablers of green procurement and the sustainable optimization of supply chain processes, which aim at efficient resource utilization (Rosário & Dias 2022). Furthermore, using a data integration strategy allows for stakeholders to have the best possible chance of avoiding making decisions without having solid empirical evidence and statistics that are based on thoroughly conducted analysis (Zhou et al., 2022). These advanced analytical tools provide organizations with information on energy consumption, water usage, and greenhouse gas emissions to show where the organization can reduce its environmental impact. Big data and analytics-driven supply chain optimization can result in reduced energy use and increased resource efficiency (Pirciog et al., 2023).

Value co-creation and consumer empowerment: The digital economy is critical in consumer empowerment based on the fact it exposes them to a wide range of information, optimal for making decisions in sustainability. Consumption activities in the digital economy imply a consumer role in the economy as they can check the composition of products and services and decide which ones should be supplied or consumed (M. Li et al., 2022). Conclusively when people become empowered as consumers, they have a role in holding businesses responsible for their environmental and social records (Penesis & Whittington, 2021). When making the best selections regarding their purchases, including selecting environmentally friendly goods and services, consumers can accurately assess the available information (Sarfraz et al., 2022). Value co-creation, in which businesses work with clients to create sustainable goods and services that satisfy their needs, is made possible by digital Technologies Intelligent.

Urban Areas and Ecological Urbanization: The emerging digital economy entails numerous smart city technologies oriented towards urban sustainable development (Pimenova, 2021). The aim of these advances is not only to improve the standard of living for city dwellers overall but also to significantly reduce: 1) urban territory expansion; 2) resource consumption and waste emission associated with cities (Bull & Azennoud, 2016). Smart sensors can be used for monitoring air quality, traffic conditions, and energy consumption giving the possibility to resource managers base their decisions on data (He et al., 2022). Specifically, van der Velden (2018) notes that citizens too can become more resource-efficient, emission-neutral, and environmentally conscious by using digital platforms offering resources and knowledge on sustainable living practices.

Sustainable Consumption and the Sustainability of the Circular Economy: The emerging digital economy entails numerous smart city technologies oriented towards urban sustainable development (shown in Figure 4) (Pimenova, 2021). The aim of these advances is not only to improve the standard of living for city dwellers overall but also to significantly reduce: 1) urban territory expansion; 2) resource consumption and waste emission associated with cities (Bull & Azennoud, 2016). Smart sensors can be used for monitoring air quality, traffic conditions, and energy consumption giving the possibility to resource managers base their decisions on data (He et al., 2022). Specifically, van der Velden (2018) notes that citizens too can become more resource-efficient, emission-neutral, and environmentally conscious by using digital platforms offering resources and knowledge on sustainable living practices.

Figure 4. Circular Economy Lifecycle Diagram

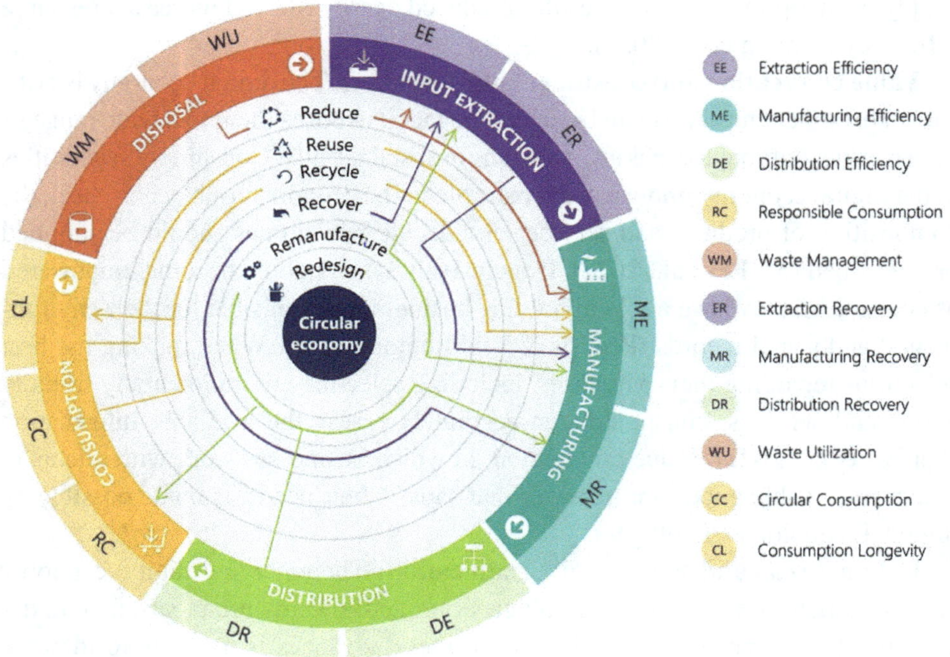

Source: Almulhim, A. I. (2024)

Business Models that Embrace Social Responsibility: The digital economy is instrumental in promoting socially responsible business models by enhancing transparency and accountability in business operations (Jabłoński & Jabłoński, 2020). This new digital landscape empowers companies to effectively monitor and communicate their social and environmental impact and performance, contributing to a more sustainable and ethically conscious business environment (Pasqualino et al., 2021). The implementation of socially responsible business models is being driven by consumer demands for ecologically friendly products and the holding of firms accountable for their effects. Digital platforms and technologies help companies incorporate social and environmental considerations into decision-making and operations (Liebenau et al., 2014).

4.3 Digital Technology's Effect on Sustainability in the Environment

Digital technologies have a multifaceted impact on environmental sustainability, encompassing both beneficial and detrimental implications, the net outcome of which is contingent upon the specific way these technologies are conceived, designed, and harnessed for various purposes (Zuo et al., 2022).

Positive Impacts

Production of energy by renewable sources and the successful integration with smart grid technologies are key factors in obtaining efficient management, as well as sustainable distribution. Renewable energy sources like solar, wind, and hydropower not only lower carbon emissions but also decrease dependency upon finite fossil fuels (Pasqualino et al. 2021). These renewable energy sources can also help reduce the effects of climate change, leading to a low carbon economy around the world when utilized more efficiently by communities (Fayustov, 2020; Jabłoński & Jabłoński, 2020). Integrating smart grid technologies also achieves better monitoring, control, and optimization to provide a more reliable and resilient energy supply that can adapt as needed for disruption or changes in the regional generation. This facilitates sustainable energy management by considering all aspects of the energy industry from a holistic perspective making it a more environmentally friendly and economically valuable method that is positive throughout our history (Jung & Kowalski, 2021b).

A variety of novel mechanisms, such as sharing platforms can help to drive the adoption and implementation of efficient Circular Economy models that will promote sustainable patterns for consumption (Ducatel 2001a), increasing collaborative consumption while reducing individual ownership.

Ensuring sustainable urban development and smart urban areas advancement by creating conditions for real-time air pollution, traffic congestion, and energy consumption monitoring that ensures the use of transparent data for making decisions. Providing consumers with empowered opportunities to not only have access to the necessary information for making sustainable decisions but also to engage in collaborative value creation with the companies involved. Improving supply chains and resource utilization through the implementation of solutions for big data analytics and the Internet of Things, reducing waste generation, and allocating resources more efficiently.

Negative Impacts

The breakneck speed of technological advancement in digital devices has led to a sharp growth in e-waste generation, an abbreviation for electronic waste (Fayustov, 2020). This increased boon with e-waste generation is worrisome for it worsens the environment which when disposed of in an unscientific manner pollutes water, soil, and air. Furthermore, electronic devices contain hazardous material that is harmful to human health during the process of handling and disposing of e-waste which indicates clearly enforced waste management strategies are needed (Ducatel 2001; Yang & Cai 2022), (Zuo et al., 2022).

Data centers, device manufacturing, and data-hungry applications are responsible for some of the energy use as well as carbon emissions (Grigorescu et al., 2020). Worse, the digital divide may perpetuate potentially widening inequitable access to digital technologies and thereby limit the potential environmental gains from these (Ma et al., 2022b; Rappitsch, 2017), for various demographic groups or regions. The lack of accessible digital resources and use may exacerbate the marginalization, increasing or maintaining disparities in opportunities for those who are already disadvantaged digitally (Human & Kazzazi, 2021).

5. CASE STUDIES OF SUSTAINABLE DIGITAL EVOLUTION

5.1 Monitoring Environmental Impacts

The Copernicus Sentinel satellite system works with missions managed to acquire and distribute data on environmental variables such as local air pollution, tropical deforestation, or agricultural growth without extensive human observation. They help to enable well-informed decision-making and evidence-based policy development in environmental challenges with respect to Sustainable Development.

Application of Advanced Digital Technologies including sensors, and cameras for monitoring rainfall patterns, soil saturation levels, and gradual onset floods in implementing Early Warning Systems(EWS) in both Peru and the Philippines These networks act as a valuable prompt from the disaster scenario telecommunication front-line and make this foresight immediate for strategic evacuation planning, which is the most effective way to mitigate natural catastrophes.

5.2 Sustainable Urban Development

When it comes to highly energy-efficient commercial towers, the Edge is a known case in point with its more than 30,000 sensors that are used throughout to monitor and optimize the building's consumption of energy. In addition to this, the state-of-the-art solar panels within the carbon-cutting system are installed in order that results into generate renewable energy and automatically limit its carbon footprint. The project also includes an advanced mobile application integrated into the building to help optimize resource management on site, which serves as a key milestone of its sustainability aspirations.

This city of Moscow has smart traffic, a system that incorporates sounding sensors (pictured above), cameras, and digital payment technology. The development of this complex has largely solved the problem of congestion in Moscow and, which is extremely important: it made millions of residents to use in-town modes. Moreover, this smart way of managing urban traffic has helped the city reduce a hefty amount of carbon footprint which eventually helps our environment achieve sustainable development.

5.3 Sustainable Agriculture and Resource Management

Scientific advancements in the shape of unmanned aerial vehicles (UAVs) + drones, Global Positioning Systems (GPS devices), and automated weather stations also played a pivotal support role in such innovative strategies for meticulous and computational observation & analysis of agroclimatic parameters within agriculture-prone geo-political regions like Guatemala; an abode famous worldwide for its culturally affluent history predominantly distinguished by diverse landscapes. They keep track of multiple attributes like temperature, humidity, and the rate at which precipitation occurs constantly over time to send timely alerts about it so that these can be utilized by farmers as well as other stakeholders responsible for growth procedures intended towards reaping coffee crops. This real-time data makes it possible to apply climate-smart coffee production to reduce potential crop losses and a more sustainable, resilient agricultural system in the region.

In the Indian narrative, a range of digital tools from video conferencing platforms to mobile applications has made it possible for agricultural advisors and also enabled the presentation of detailed maps delineating drought-prone areas which can help farmers arrive at well-informed decisions in advancing climate-resilient actions.

5.4 Renewable Energy and Sustainable Manufacturing

The intricate study of how they can make their data centers run happily and efficiently when submerged underneath the deep blue sea instead turns into Microsoft's Project Natick, courtesy of your friendly neighborhood strategic human capital operations analysis firm (and brought to you thanks in part through unnatural sustainable energy consumed by wind turbines and solar panels that were designed with advanced-technology in mind). In order to minimize and reduce the negative ecological footprint of current cloud computing practices, this innovative solution also represents a proactive effort toward worldwide environmental preservation.

Why Glider is a high-quality Public Transport in Belfast The aim of the system was to provide cheap, efficient transport that could reduce road traffic and emissions. These examples show that the use of digital technologies, as a means by which data is generated and provides information about processes responsible for environmental development in cities can help curate sustainable behaviors. However, it is important to realize that the above examples only further highlight how urgently we need consistent innovation levels, cooperative efforts; 1efficient policy measures that can help overcome many such hurdles (like e-waste management), optimize energy optimization practices, etc., and the mitigation of disparities related to access to digital resources among different societal groups.

6. THE ROAD AHEAD

How women are leading in this new world order of learning is still an area to be further examined, but the rapid pace at which digitalization already somewhat plows through academia has rearranged a face that offers both opportunities and challenges for female leadership. In the era of digital transformation in higher education, we must think about how those changes are influencing academic leadership and its impact on women as they advance their careers.

Several recent studies emphasized the significant role of digital leadership and transformational leadership in shaping academic institutions to transform into digital higher education institutions (Antonopoulou et al., 2021). Therefore, digital leaders are the cornerstone to harvest value out of digitalization while attracting and retaining talent at the same time along with cultivating employee engagement by guiding them through a new way of life in the age of all things digital (Karippur & Balaramachandran 2022). Moreover, the impact of transformational leadership on digital leadership in academic environments has been proven to favor it and be statistically significant (Antonopoulou et al., 2021).

Nevertheless, to the best of my knowledge from reviewing the literature in this field, despite the radical change brought by the digital revolution worldwide affecting all areas and sectors including Leadership; I have never seen any comprehensive study focusing on Women's culture inside an academic leadership institution with their own "Particularities". There are unique barriers and challenges that face women as academics in addition to those faced by all early-career researchers (Gender bias, work-life balance, lack of mentorship/nurturing social sphere - Trenerry et al., 2021; Cortellazzo et al., 2019).

Despite the growing literature, little attention has been paid to how digital transformation affects women-owned firms' business performance (Popović-Pantić et al., 2019). Similarly, the quiet organization of global tech talent obfuscates impacts in academic domain since there is a dearth of literature exploring the impact on leadership and career progression for females in an academic role.

Further research is needed in the 1) challenges and opportunities for women at all levels of academic leadership in the digital age; 2) effect of technology on career advancement and promotion activities including leadership development among female academics (faculty, administrators). Empowering Edu leaders, how women in Academia can be successful in the digital age

Through analysis of digital transformation through the lens of gender and academic leadership, scholars have been able to more effectively apply their findings into policy changes that further support women in academia.

7. CONCLUSION

The emergence of the digital revolution has indicated the start of a new era characterized by an incomparable degree of interconnectedness, unprecedented innovations, and substantial economic growth. However, the rapid growth of the digital economy has also raised concerns about its ecological impact and appropriateness for sustainability. In supporting the advancement of sustainable environmental, social, and economic sustainability, addressing these numerous electronic waste management challenges alongside high carbon emissions from energy consumption; the digital divide is necessary. At the same time, according to Zhou et al. (2022), digital innovations offer great possibilities for driving sustainable development such as enabling the implementation of renewable energy solutions and supporting circular economic models, reinforcing consumer empowerment exploring intelligent urban landscapes, or promoting initiatives on sustainability in cities.

Through the embracement of these opportunities and the adoption of strategies that prioritize the tenets of digital sustainability, enterprises can play a pivotal role in fostering a future that is more ecologically sound within the digital realm. The formulation and implementation of governmental policies and regulations wield a crucial influence in the advancement of sustainable digital transformation by delineating standards, offering incentives, and cultivating collaborative efforts across various sectors (Pan et al., 2022). A comprehensive approach that integrates the foundational principles of digital sustainability into the fabric of business practices, the realm of product innovation, and the realm of stakeholder engagement emerges as indispensable in the attainment of enduring environmental, societal, and economic sustainability. When we take a journey in the literature, through the constantly developing stages of this digital revolution, there is a growing realization that dealing with the challenges and opportunities from these digital technologies is one of the critical and essential presentations in seeking a delicate balance between a future dominated by technological innovation and sustainability.

REFERENCES

Almulhim, A. I. (2024). Toward a greener future: Applying circular economy principles to Saudi Arabia's food sector for environmental sustainability. *Sustainability (Basel), 16*(2), 786. DOI: 10.3390/su16020786

Antonopoulou, H., Halkiopoulos, C., Barlou, O., & Beligiannis, G. N. (2021). Associations between traditional and digital leadership in academic environment: During the COVID-19 pandemic. *Emerging Science Journal, 5*(4), 405–428. DOI: 10.28991/esj-2021-01286

Bednarčíková, D., & Repiská, R. (2021). Digital transformation in the context of the European Union and the use of digital technologies as a tool for business sustainability. In *SHS Web of Conferences* (Vol. 115, p. 01001). EDP Sciences. https://doi.org/DOI: 10.1051/shsconf/202111501001

Bull, R., & Azennoud, M. (2016). Smart citizens for smart cities: Participating in the future. *Proceedings of the Institution of Civil Engineers - Energy, 169*(3), 93-101. https://doi.org/DOI: 10.1680/jener.15.00030

Cortellazzo, L., Bruni, E., & Zampieri, R. (2019). The role of leadership in a digitalized world: A review. *Frontiers in Psychology, 10*, 1938. DOI: 10.3389/fpsyg.2019.01938 PMID: 31507494

Dey, D., Srinivas, D., Panda, B., Suraneni, P., & Sitharam, T. G. (2022). Use of industrial waste materials for 3D printing of sustainable concrete: A review. *Journal of Cleaner Production, 340*, 130749. DOI: 10.1016/j.jclepro.2022.130749

Ducatel, K. (2001). Balance of nature? Sustainable societies in the digital economy. *Foresight, 3*(2), 123–133. DOI: 10.1108/14636680110803058

Dunn, S. (2017). Micropower: Electrifying the digital economy. In *The Ecology of the New Economy* (pp. 206-220). Routledge.

Egodawele, M., Sedera, D., & Bui, V. (2022). A systematic review of digital transformation literature (2013-2021) and the development of an overarching apriori model to guide future research. *arXiv preprint arXiv:2212.03867*. https://doi.org//arXiv.2212.03867DOI: 10.48550

Fayustov, A. A. (2020). E-waste management in a global digital economy. *IOP Conference Series. Earth and Environmental Science, 459*(3), 032007. DOI: 10.1088/1755-1315/459/3/032007

Feroz, A. K., Zo, H., & Chiravuri, A. (2021). Digital transformation and environmental sustainability: A review and research agenda. *Sustainability (Basel), 13*(3), 1530. DOI: 10.3390/su13031530

Grigorescu, A., Zamfir, A.-M., & Mocanu, C. (2020). Emerging trends and drivers for knowledge-intensive economy. *Management & Marketing. Challenges for the Knowledge Society, 15*(2), 172–185. DOI: 10.2478/mmcks-2020-0011

He, W., Li, W., & Deng, P. (2022). Legal governance in the smart cities of China: Functions, problems, and solutions. *Sustainability (Basel), 14*(15), 9738. DOI: 10.3390/su14159738

Human, S., & Kazzazi, M. (2021). Contextuality and intersectionality of e-consent: A human-centric reflection on digital consenting in the emerging genetic data markets. In *2021 IEEE European Symposium on Security and Privacy Workshops (EuroS&PW)* (pp. 307-311). IEEE. https://doi.org/DOI: 10.1109/EuroSPW54576.2021.00051

Jabłoński, A., & Jabłoński, M. (2020). *Social business models in the digital economy*. Springer International Publishing., DOI: 10.1007/978-3-030-29732-9

Jung, B., & Kowalski, T. (2021). Hybridization of time: Towards temporal sustainability of the digital economy. In *The Future of Work and Technology* (pp. 227–244). Springer., DOI: 10.1007/978-3-030-78825-4_14

Karippur, N. K., & Balaramachandran, P. R. (2022). Antecedents of effective digital leadership of enterprises in Asia Pacific. *AJIS. Australasian Journal of Information Systems, 26*. Advance online publication. DOI: 10.3127/ajis.v26i0.2525

Koshta, N., Patra, S., & Singh, S. P. (2022). Sharing economic responsibility: Assessing end user's willingness to support e-waste reverse logistics for circular economy. *Journal of Cleaner Production, 332*, 130057. DOI: 10.1016/j.jclepro.2021.130057

Li, J., Zhan, G., Dai, X., Qi, M., & Liu, B. (2022). Innovation and optimization logic of grassroots digital governance in China under digital empowerment and digital sustainability. *Sustainability (Basel), 14*(24), 16470. DOI: 10.3390/su142416470

Li, M., Wang, X., Wang, Z., Maqbool, B., Hussain, A., & Khan, W. A. (2022). Bibliometric analysis of the research on the impact of environmental regulation on green technology innovation based on CiteSpace. *International Journal of Environmental Research and Public Health, 19*(20), 13273. DOI: 10.3390/ijerph192013273 PMID: 36293848

Li, Q., Guan, X., Wu, P., Wang, X., Zhou, L., Tong, Y., Ren, R., Leung, K. S. M., Lau, E. H. Y., Wong, J. Y., Xing, X., Xiang, N., Wu, Y., Li, C., Chen, Q., Li, D., Liu, T., Zhao, J., Liu, M., & Feng, Z. (2020). Early transmission dynamics in Wuhan, China, of novel coronavirus–infected pneumonia. *The New England Journal of Medicine, 382*(13), 1199–1207. DOI: 10.1056/NEJMoa2001316 PMID: 31995857

Liebenau, J. M., Elaluf-Calderwood, S. M., & Bonina, C. M. (2014). Modularity and network integration: Emergent business models in banking. In *2014 47th Hawaii International Conference on System Sciences* (pp. 1183-1192). IEEE. https://doi.org/DOI: 10.1109/HICSS.2014.153

Ma, Q., Khan, Z., Tariq, M., IŞik, H., & Rjoub, H. (2022). Sustainable digital economy and trade adjusted carbon emissions: Evidence from China's provincial data. *Ekonomska Istrazivanja, 35*(1), 5469–5485. DOI: 10.1080/1331677X.2022.2028179

Melnyk, L., Dehtyarova, I., Kubatko, O., Karintseva, O., & Derykolenko, A. (2019). Disruptive technologies for the transition of digital economies towards sustainability. *Economic Annals-XXI, 179*(9-10), 22–30. DOI: 10.21003/ea.V179-02

Mosca, O., Manunza, A., Manca, S., Vivanet, G., & Fornara, F. (2024). Digital technologies for behavioral change in sustainability domains: A systematic mapping review. *Frontiers in Psychology, 14*, 1234349. DOI: 10.3389/fpsyg.2023.1234349 PMID: 38239482

Niankara, I. (2022). Sustainability through open data sharing and reuse in the digital economy. In *2022 International Arab Conference on Information Technology (ACIT)* (pp. 1-11). IEEE. https://doi.org/DOI: 10.1109/ACIT57182.2022.9994191

Pan, W., Xie, T., Wang, Z., & Ma, L. (2022). Digital economy: An innovation driver for total factor productivity. *Journal of Business Research, 139*, 303–311. DOI: 10.1016/j.jbusres.2021.09.061

Pasqualino, R., Demartini, M., & Bagheri, F. (2021). Digital transformation and sustainable oriented innovation: A system transition model for socio-economic scenario analysis. *Sustainability (Basel), 13*(21), 11564. DOI: 10.3390/su132111564

Penesis, I., & Whittington, J. (2021). Australia's blue economy cooperative research centre. In *Preparing a workforce for the new blue economy* (pp. 335–348). Elsevier., DOI: 10.1016/B978-0-12-821431-2.00043-3

Pimenova, E. M. (2021). Specificity of sustainability assessment for industrial enterprise functioning in the digital economy. In *Digital Economy and the New Labor Market: Jobs, Competences and Innovative HR Technologies* (pp. 3-10). Springer. https://doi.org/DOI: 10.1007/978-3-030-53277-2_1

Pirciog, S. C., Grigorescu, A., Lincaru, C., Popa, F. M., Lazarczyk Carlson, E., & Sigurdarson, H. T. (2023). Mapping European high-digital intensive sectors—Regional growth accelerator for the circular economy. *Frontiers in Environmental Science, 10*, 1061128. Advance online publication. DOI: 10.3389/fenvs.2022.1061128

Popović-Pantić, S., Semenčenko, D., & Vasilić, N. (2019). The influence of digital transformation on business performance: Evidence of the women-owned companies. *Ekonomika preduzeća, 67*(7-8), 397-414. https://doi.org/DOI: 10.5937/EKOPRE1908397P

Rappitsch, C. (2017). Digital economy and sustainability. *Oikos*.

Rosário, A., & Dias, J. (2022). Sustainability and the digital transition: A literature review. *Sustainability (Basel), 14*(7), 4072. DOI: 10.3390/su14074072

Sarfraz, M., Ivascu, L., & Abdullah, M. I. (2022). Editorial: Sustainable digital economy, entrepreneurship, and blockchain technology role in industrial-organizational psychology. *Frontiers in Psychology, 13*, 974415. Advance online publication. DOI: 10.3389/fpsyg.2022.974415 PMID: 35910996

Savchenko, A. B., & Borodina, T. L. (2020). Green and digital economy for sustainable development of urban areas. *Regional Research of Russia, 10*(4), 583–592. DOI: 10.1134/S2079970520040097

Shahabuddin, M., Uddin, M. N., Chowdhury, J. I., Ahmed, S. F., Uddin, M. N., Mofijur, M., & Uddin, M. A. (2023). A review of the recent development, challenges, and opportunities of electronic waste (e-waste). *International Journal of Environmental Science and Technology, 20*(4), 4513–4520. DOI: 10.1007/s13762-022-04274-w

Trenerry, B., Chng, S., Wang, Y., Suhaila, Z. S., Lim, S. S., Lu, H. Y., & Oh, P. H. (2021). Preparing workplaces for digital transformation: An integrative review and framework of multi-level factors. *Frontiers in Psychology, 12*, 620766. DOI: 10.3389/fpsyg.2021.620766 PMID: 33833714

Truong, T. C. (2022). The impact of digital transformation on environmental sustainability. *Advances in Multimedia, 2022*(1), 6324325. DOI: 10.1155/2022/6324325

van der Velden, M. (2018). Digitalisation and the UN sustainable development goals: What role for design. [s]. *Interaction Design and Architecture, 37*(37), 160–174. DOI: 10.55612/s-5002-037-008

Vitsentzatou, E., Tsoulfas, G. T., & Mihiotis, A. N. (2022). The digital transformation of the marketing mix in the food and beverage service supply chain: A grey DEMATEL approach. *Sustainability (Basel), 14*(22), 15228. DOI: 10.3390/su142215228

Yang, Y., & Cai, J. (2022). Carbon emissions and the development of digital economy: A perspective of spatial evolution. *Journal of Environmental Protection and Ecology*, *23*(1), 409–416.

Zhou, Z., Liu, W., Cheng, P., & Li, Z. (2022). The impact of the digital economy on enterprise sustainable development and its spatial-temporal evolution: An empirical analysis based on urban panel data in China. *Sustainability (Basel)*, *14*(19), 11948. DOI: 10.3390/su141911948

Zuo, L., Li, H., Gao, H., & Zhu, M. (2022). The sustainable efficiency improvement of internet companies under the background of digital transformation. *Sustainability (Basel)*, *14*(9), 5600. DOI: 10.3390/su14095600

Chapter 10
Strategic Roadmap for DPI in 2030:
Vision and Implementation

Ajay B. Gadicha
https://orcid.org/0000-0002-5496-3334
P.R. Pote Patil College of Engineering and Management, Amravati, India

Sherif Ismail
https://orcid.org/0009-0000-0852-873X
American University in Cairo, Egypt

Riya B. Dolas
https://orcid.org/0009-0002-0704-1588
P.R. Pote Patil College of Engineering and Management, Amravati, India

Poonam Rambhau Maskare
https://orcid.org/0009-0002-2385-1935
P.R. Pote Patil College of Engineering and Management, Amravati, India

Poonam S. Pawar
P.R. Pote Patil College of Engineering and Management, Amravati, India

ABSTRACT

The 2030 Strategic Roadmap to Digital Public Infrastructure (DPI) is an image of a worldwide, inclusive, and secure digital ecosystem that alters the character of its communication of the governments, businesses, and citizens. It presents the vision of the situation when technology will be treated like a kind of a public good because it will be able to provide universal access to the digital infrastructure, trusted identity, financial inclusion, and effective governance. Interoperability, privacy and ethical

DOI: 10.4018/979-8-3373-6380-6.ch010

use of data are highlighted in the roadmap as the pillars of sustainable digital transformation. By 2030, DPI will endeavour to incorporate new technology like artificial intelligence, blockchain and cloud computing in delivery of its services to the people with accountability and empowerment of the citizens. Its adoption must be a gradual process that encompasses the development of infrastructures, the harmonization of the policies, and the cooperation of both the state and the business worlds. The chapter discusses the strategic pillars, implementation framework and expected delivery that will determine the way DPI will emerge as a robust and people-focused digital platform in the next 10 years.

INTRODUCTION

In the 21st century, the digital world has become the foundation of government, economic development and societal inclusion. DPI is a kind of digital commons—a common infrastructure like roads, electricity or water networks—on which public and private innovation rides (Openfuture, 2025; United Nations Development Programme, 2025). DPI is not just a technological construct; it is a revolutionary form of governance, which supports contemporary delivery of services in the public (World Bank Group, 2025). It incorporates essential digital elements including digital identity, payment platforms, data exchange platforms and information repositories which enable governments to better provide citizen services (Digital Cooperation Organization & Access Partnership, 2025; United Nations Development Programme, 2025). DPI establishes a digital environment with interoperable and secure services and with open APIs, making services accessible (International Telecommunication Union, 2025). Besides making it efficient, this architecture democratizes digital opportunities (Digital Cooperation Organization & Access Partnership, 2025).

Within the past 10 years, it is only through the transformative influence of DPI that many countries have experienced inclusive growth (Center for Social and Economic Progress, 2025). The Digital India program with its India Stack, including Aadhaar as a digital identity, UPI as a payment system, DigiLocker as a document repository, and e-KYC as an authentication solution is a global model (Center for Social and Economic Progress, 2025; World Bank Group, 2025). All these systems are able to allow citizens to transact digitally, receive welfare programs and handle their identities in real time. DPI has increased transparency and efficiency in the governance by reducing transaction costs, eliminating access barriers (Center for Social and Economic Progress, 2025). On the same note, the e-Governance model adopted by Estonia allows citizens to vote, pay taxes, and receive healthcare completely online (European Commission, 2025), whereas the Smart Nation model adopted by Singapore incorporates the IoT and AI to streamline urban planning, healthcare, and public safety (World Economic Forum, 2025). These are just examples of how DPI can be transformed to be seen as a change agent in cases where it is designed with inclusivity, interoperability and citizen trust at its heart (Digital Cooperation Organization & Access Partnership, 2025; South Centre, 2025).

The definition of DPI is far beyond the digitalization of the traditional government functions. It is a step into the ecosystem-based governance where technology is a kind of communal good which empowers individuals and institutions (Openfuture, 2025; World Bank Group, 2025). Innovation is improved through the use of digital identification systems in this ecosystem to enable authentication and financial inclusion using digital payment and secure data exchange (International Monetary Fund, 2025). This transformation marks the beginning of the paradigm shift of not only the process-based governance to the citizen-based governance but also the paper-based governance to paperless as well as the uncoordinated institution to the united digital ecosystem (Organisation for Economic Co-operation and Development, 2025). The world is close to 2030 and increased urgency to modernize and expand DPI is being felt than ever before (European Commission, 2025; World Economic Forum, 2025).

Universal Digital Access: Everyone must afford the internet and the associated digital applications to be able to experience the cost of the digital economy.

Effective Cybersecurity and Data Protection: The institutional and technical barriers are expected to be strong in order to disrupt any cyber threats and unauthorized access to and use of personal data by users.

Sustainable and Fair Technological Incorporation: The application of the new technologies Artificial Intelligence (AI), blockchain, quantum computing and cloud services should be implemented in a responsible and ethical way..

The Vision of DPI 2030 will create a trusted digital society that is balanced in innovation and inclusion, efficiency and accountability, and data-driven growth and ethical governance (Digital Cooperation Organization & Access Partnership, 2025; World Economic Forum, 2025). To achieve this vision, it is essential to not only focus on the technological infrastructure but also the institutional structure, policy consistency, and legal norms that ensure that the rights of citizens are not violated but, instead, promote innovation (International Center for Law & Economics, 2025; Organisation for Economic Co-operation and Development, 2025). It requires establishment of open regulatory frameworks, interoperability of APIs, and global cooperation in order to have a smooth digital economy (International Monetary Fund, 2025; South Centre, 2025). Data governance and privacy are another characteristic of the DPI roadmap (World Bank Group, 2025). With the growing amount of digital data that has an exponentially growing volume, the issue of its ethical management becomes national and global (European Commission, 2025). The governments should consider privacy-by-design principles—i.e., use data protection in each tier of digital systems (World Bank Group, 2025). It will require transparent systems of consent and encrypted data storage and autonomous supervisory bodies to hold people accountable (International Monetary Fund, 2025). Furthermore, because governments start heavily relying on AI and predictive analytics in making decisions, ethical AI governance framework systems need to be developed to avoid the risks of algorithmic bias, discrimination, and the abuse of surveillance (International Center for Law & Economics, 2025; United Nations Development Programme, 2025).

Strategic Roadmap of DPI 2030 is therefore a multidimensional plan which incorporates technology, governance, ethics and sustainability. It will help in changing digital infrastructure into a civic good that will serve to drive transparent governance, spur innovation, and enable all people to contribute to the digital economy.

This chapter hence discusses the vision, guiding principles, implementation strategies, and outcomes of DPI 2030. It examines the strategic pillars of interoperability, security, inclusion, collaboration, sustainability, and ethical governance which is the core of this transformation. Using this perspective, the chapter gives a holistic insight on how the countries can jointly create a digital future that can be secure, inclusive and resilient, in such a way such that technology can become a genuine world wide common good by 2030 years.

2.2Vision 2030: An Inspirational, Trusted Digital Society.

The Digital Public Infrastructure (DPI) Vision 2030 is a prospective map on how to create societies in which technology plays the role of an equalizer, empowered, and efficiency factor. The vision goes beyond the implementation of digital tools, it transforms the way governments relate with their citizens, businesses innovate and how people can get rights and opportunities in a digital world. DPI is seen as developing to become a universal, people centred digital commons, merging digital identity, data sharing, financial systems, communication platforms and governance networks into a play of trust, transparency and accountability by the year 2030.

The first concept is the Digital Commons.

Digital commons is a term used to describe digital resources and infrastructures which are publicly administered and available to all society members (Openfuture, 2025). DPI reflects this vision by making sure that digital services (e.g., identity verification, payments, etc.) are a universal public utility (United Nations Development Programme, 2025). They are not monopolies owned privately but collectively operated platforms that are based on open standards, interoperability, and ethical use of data (Digital Cooperation Organization & Access Partnership, 2025; Openfuture, 2025).

As an example, India Stack in India (consisting of Aadhaar, UPI, and DigiLocker) enables citizens and businesses to encounter and exchange digital services on an uncomplicated level (Center for Social and Economic Progress, 2025; World Bank Group, 2025). Equally, the e-Governance system of Estonia illustrates how a common digital infrastructure can lead to economic development and confidence by the population in the system due to its transparency and efficiency (European Commission, 2025).

The DPI 2030 vision will therefore aim to make these national models replicable globally and encourage digital sovereignty and cross-border collaboration in technology governance (South Centre, 2025; International Monetary Fund, 2025; World Economic Forum, 2025).

The second Conformance with Global Development Goals.

The SDGs that are addressed by DPI framework to a great extent are:

SDG 9: Industry, Innovation, and Infrastructure DPI offers a digital platform to innovations-based economies to allow small and medium enterprises (SMEs) to enter digital markets and avail government services.

SDG 10: Reduced Inequalities - DPI reduces socio-economic inequalities through offering affordable access to identity, banking, and education to all people and guaranteeing equal access to the digital economy.

SDG 16: Peace, Justice, and Strong Institutions - DPI improves institutional transparency and accountability through digitization of the public documents, decreasing corruption, and increasing the service delivery.

SDG 17: Personality in Partnerships: The digital planetary collaboration and data sharing mechanisms conform to international work on sustainable digital change.

That is why the DPI 2030 Roadmap is a technological agenda, but a developmental mission, which incorporates governance, ethics, and sustainability.

2.3 The Vision Revealed: What DPI 2030 Is Going to Achieve.

The Digital Public Infrastructure will by 2030:

Ensure Universal Access: All people, whether they live in various places or have different incomes will have access to good and trustworthy internet, online identity, and necessary online services. DPI will become the digital framework that will allow citizens to engage in the education, healthcare, financial, and government spheres.

Confidentiality of Information and Data: The privacy-by-design principles will guarantee that the data of citizens is safeguarded and that sharing of the data is achieved with consent. There will be a sense of transparency in digital systems that are controlled by accountability measures.

Facilitate the Smooth Interoperability: DPI will provide interconnections among many government and non-government platforms via open APIs and common standards and will have the data flows among systems in a safe and efficient way.

Empower Digital Economies: With the ability to access digital payments and microservices and cloud platforms, DPI will enable an environment of innovation, entrepreneurship and job creation.

Ensure Marriage and Family Therapists Practice Ethically: The use of advanced technologies like AI, Internet of Things, and blockchain will be introduced accountably to improve governance without violating human rights and privacy.

Support Environmental Sustainability: Green digital will be achieved through energy efficient data centers, recycling e-waste, and even carbon neutral IT policy which will help DPI to add to sustainable growth.

2.4 DPI through Social and Economic Transformation.

The introduction of DPI will cause a multi-dimensional change in the social and economic sectors:

Social Inclusion The digital infrastructure will make sure that the marginalized communities, including rural districts, women, and the differently-abled, are able to access welfare benefits, education, and healthcare through the internet. DPI will make fair societies by removing geographical and bureaucratic boundaries.

Economic Empowerment The thriving DPI ecosystem will facilitate digital entrepreneurship, which enables small enterprises to conduct commerce online, accept digital payments, and use financial solutions. As an illustration, millions of small vendors in India have been able to deal with UPI system without using traditional banks at a digital cost.

Governance Reform DPI will transform the position of the state and citizens. Public administration will be more transparent, efficient, and responsive with real time governance dashboards, automated service delivery vehicles and e-participation platforms.

Access to knowledge and Education By the year 2030, DPI will be the essential element of digital learning ecosystems. E-learning solutions based on DPI will guarantee authorized credentials, customized learning experiences, and equal access to high-quality learning globally.

2.5 Leveraging Strengths and capitalizing on Opportunities.

DPI 2030 is based on trust. The digital adoption is weak without the confidence of the citizens. Therefore, DPI 2030 emphasizes:

Transparent Governance: Open data policies, in which citizens get take a look at what is done with their data.

Oversight at Regulatory levels: Organizing Data Protection authorities and Ethical Boards to control digital rights.

Digital Literacies and Awareness: Teaching citizens about technology privacy, cybersecurity and safety in technology usage.

Cybersecurity Infrastructure: The progression of national cyber resilience policies on curbing data breaches and cybercrime.

The target is to provide a safe, informative, and empowered environment of people so they are willing and able to engage in the digital ecosystem.

2.6 International Cooperation and Online Sovereignty.

We live in a world that is highly interconnected, and the flow of data and the provision of digital services can no longer be limited by borders. Thus, DPI 2030 visualizes the international cooperation on:

- Cross-border standards of data exchange, which provide national security and interoperability.
- Electronic contracts ensuring free markets and privacy of user information.
- Capacity-building alliances and technology transfer between the developed and developing countries.
- Local alliances of DPI between countries at the Global South between countries in order to exchange expertise, structure, and governance practices.

Meanwhile, the sovereignty of digital resources and the power of each country to regulate the data and infrastructure on its own should be maintained. This makes the advantages of digitization not one-sided and culturally situated.

2.7 The Bigger Picture: DPI as a Brightening Cause of Human Development.

Conclusively, DPI 2030 vision is not merely about technology but it is about human development (United Nations Development Programme, 2025; World Bank Group, 2025). The digital infrastructure will enable individuals to exercise their rights, engage in the governing process, and provide people with access to economic and educational opportunities (Digital Cooperation Organization & Access Partnership, 2025; International Telecommunication Union, 2025). It will transform the definition of citizenship in the digital age through making the governance more transparent and participatory (Organisation for Economic Co-operation and Development, 2025; European Commission, 2025).

In 2030, DPI will become the invisible architecture of the modern civilization where governments, markets, and citizens will share trust and innovations with each other. It will spur a future in which all digital engagements will make a contribution to the overall development of the human race.

Strategic Pillars of DPI 2030.

Digital Public Infrastructure (DPI) 2030 strategic pillars are the transformation of the Vision 2030 into practical measures and actionable frameworks. These pillars give grounds to develop inclusive, interoperable, secure, and innovative, collaborative, and sustainable digital ecosystems. The pillars reflect vital aspects of DPI that are based on theoretical knowledge, international experience, and policy reflections.

Inclusion

To make digital infrastructure and services accessible and beneficial to every individual regardless of their socio-economic, geographical, gender, and ability, it is necessary to be inclusive (United Nations Development Programme, 2025). Digital inclusion theory focuses on eliminating obstacles to access and use of technology, whereas the theory of capability formulated by Amartya Sen views inclusion as an increase in the practical freedom of citizens in the use of well-being-enhancing services (Digital Cooperation Organization & Access Partnership, 2025; World Bank Group, 2025). Inclusion can be achieved by means of making connectivity affordable, having access to digital devices, and having literacy programs to enable marginalized communities (Organisation for Economic Co-operation and Development, 2025). As an example, the Bharat Net project in India brings the rural regions close to high-speed internet (Center for Social and Economic Progress, 2025) and the M-Pesa system in Kenya provides financial inclusion by using mobile payments (World Bank Group, 2025; South Centre, 2025). The governments should focus on infrastructure development, subsidy and community education and the inclusion can be effectively scaled with the assistance of a public-private partnership (Digital Cooperation Organization & Access Partnership, 2025; World Economic Forum, 2025). Inclusion, thus, does not just close digital divides, but it also enables citizens to be fully empowered to engage in the digital economy and the digital government structures (European Commission, 2025).

Interoperability

Interoperability guarantees the coordination between various digital systems, platforms, and services to exchange and communicate together and with ease (World Bank Group, 2025). The systems theory assumes that connected subsystems work in the best way with information flowing effectively and the network governance theory focuses on cooperation between the actors of the public, private, and civil society (International Center for Law & Economics, 2025; International Monetary Fund, 2025). Open standards, modular system design based on API, and integrated digital identity systems can be used to attain interoperability (Digital Cooperation Organization & Access Partnership, 2025; Openfuture, 2025). Estonia's X-Road platform offers secure data exchange between state and non-state organizations (European Commission, 2025) and India Stack combines banking, identity and welfare in a single streamlined system (Center for Social and Economic Progress, 2025; World Bank Group, 2025). Standards on interoperability can be enforced by the government in legal terms to avoid fragmentation and it also requires constant monitoring so that the compatibility can be maintained as technology advances (Organisation for Economic Co-operation and Development, 2025; International Monetary Fund, 2025). Interoperability helps citizens to use various services under the same platforms, thus less redundancy and more efficiency in the delivery of public services (World Bank Group, 2025).

Trust and Security

It needs to be trusted and secure so that the citizens can be assured of using the digital infrastructure because they know their data is secured, and systems are not broken (United Nations Development Programme, 2025; World Bank Group, 2025). The Privacy-by-Design (PbD) approach incorporates privacy into technology design at the beginning (European Commission, 2025; World Bank Group, 2025), whereas the social contract theory considers trust as a tacit commitment to ethical use of data between the state and its citizens (International Center for Law & Economics, 2025). DPI 2030 adopts the concept of trust by encrypting and storing data, sharing data in a consented manner and ensuring a sound cybersecurity system (International Monetary Fund, 2025; World Bank Group, 2025). The GDPR of the EU ensures the privacy compliance of the whole of Europe (European Commission, 2025), and the Smart Nation platform of Singapore considers the implementation of the most sophisticated cybersecurity precautions to safeguard the data of the citizens (World Economic Forum, 2025). Having independent oversight mechanisms and improving the level of digital literacy are essential factors in making sure that citizens are aware of and able to exercise their rights to data (Organisation for Economic Co-operation and Development, 2025; International Telecommunication Union, 2025).

Innovation

Innovation helps DPI to develop dynamically by integrating new technologies, services and business models that enhance the efficiency of the public and private sector (Digital Cooperation Organization & Access Partnership, 2025; World Bank Group, 2025). Innovation Systems Theory focuses on the relationships between firms, governments and institutions as the key driver of innovation whereas Responsible Innovation Theory supports ethical, inclusive and anticipatory introduction of technology (International Center for Law & Economics, 2025; Organisation for Economic Co-operation and Development, 2025). DPI 2030 fosters innovation by offering open digital platforms to entrepreneurs and SMEs, has integrated AI and IoT in state services, and has rewarded research and development of sustainable digital solutions (World Economic Forum, 2025; International Telecommunication Union, 2025). The UPI model used in India is one of the good examples of promoting the development of fintechs (Center for Social and Economic Progress, 2025) and the Smart Nation labs in Singapore discuss the possibilities of AI and IoT in urban planning and healthcare (World Economic Forum, 2025). Governments can encourage innovation by providing sandboxes in which new technologies can be tested with safeguarding the interests of the population and taking into account ethical considerations (International Monetary Fund, 2025; International Center for Law & Economics, 2025). DPI innovation does not only enhance efficiency, but it also enables citizens and businesses to be innovative when it comes to engaging in the digital economy (United Nations Development Programme, 2025).

Collaboration

The building, maintaining and governing of DPI multi-stakeholder engagement is ensured by the collaboration and consists of governments, players of the private sector, civil society and international partners. Network Governance Theory relies on the inter-organizational cooperation and Global Commons Theory is the approach of managing digital infrastructure as the common good which has to be managed by the collaboration efforts. It can be cooperation in terms of joint ventures of development of infrastructures of various kinds with the public and international collaboration in terms of standards, cybersecurity, and cross-border data-sharing and participation of citizens through participatory design and feedback.. The collaborative structures should also be designed with the roles and responsibilities as well as transparency and accountability established so as to establish long term trust among the individual stakeholders. Teamwork has the potential of generating ownership, reduce redundancy and in the long term encourage the efficiency of DPI systems.

Sustainability

The issue of sustainability raises the concern that the DPI development will be responsible as far as the environment, economy, and the society are concerned. Green IT principles are geared towards energy conservation and eradication of the e-waste whereas the Triple Bottom Line model is geared towards social, economic, and environmental sustainability.. Both DPI 2030 and cloud infrastructure encourage energy-efficient data not only in the selected data centers, but in solutions, e-waste recycling and e-waste management programs, and balance policies with respect to digital inclusion and ecological impact. Examples on the world level are the carbon-neutral cloud data centers of Google and the e-waste management and recycling of digital infrastructure in Europe. Governments may utilize both national and international standards of sustainability and promote the use of renewable energy and life cycle management of IT equipment. Sustainability guarantees that the development of DPI is sustained and resource-efficient and in line with the overall climate and social goals, to achieve resilient and equitable digital societies.

DPI 2030 implementation strategies and roadmap.

The translation of the Vision 2030 and its strategic pillars into reality must be supported with the intention to balance the aspects of technological innovation, policy frameworks, social inclusion, and sustainability with the help of the carefully developed implementation strategy. The DPI 2030 implementation roadmap is not a digital project timeline, but it is a holistic strategy, involving institutional capacity building, stakeholder, and measurable outputs. Its main agenda is to make every citizen, business and government organisations interact with a secure, inclusive and interoperable digital ecosystem that can facilitate economic growth, social development and ethical governance.

The institutional readiness is the primary element of the implementation strategy. Governments should empower digital agencies, establish regulatory organizations to ensure privacy, data protection and cybersecurity as well as provide coordination systems between departments. The institutional readiness also entails establishment of policy enforcement frameworks, tracking of adherence to standards as well as provision of resources needed in adoption of technology. Basing on institutional economics, the strategy asserts that efficient and transparent institutions lower transaction costs, transactions minimize corruption and develop trust between citizens and the state. The successful examples of countries with strong institutional frameworks like Estonia and Singapore have demonstrated the importance of having a robust institutional framework to support the successful deployment of digital infrastructure, and agile governance that allows them to constantly adapt quickly to technological changes.

The second aspect is on staged implementation. It is planned to be implemented both in long-term, medium-term, and short-term in order to cope with the complexity, optimize the resources and iterate the learning process. In the immediate future, it is concerned with the growth of basic connectivity, the ability to have universal digital identity. Medium-term solutions seek to integrate systems via interoperability protocols, reinforce cybersecurity frameworks and facilitate innovation blankets that facilitate digital entrepreneurship. The long-term vision focuses on the use of such advanced technology as artificial intelligence, blockchain, and predictive analytics, as well as building sustainable, low-carbon data centres, e-waste management services, and cross-border online partnerships. This step-by-step method is based on the change management theory, which emphasizes the gradual adoption process, feedback loop, and gradual improvement to make DPI systems resilient and scalable. The third element is the stakeholder engagement and capacity building. The absence of meaningful participation of the citizens, businesses, civil society, and international partners can guarantee the success of DPI 2030. The efforts of capacity-building encompass digital literacy programs, education of the public servants on technology governance, and small and medium enterprises empowerment programs to capitalize on digital platforms. The principles of participatory design emphasize the fact that systems are user-centric, accessible, as well as responsive to diverse needs of populations. The responsible innovation framework stresses that technology needs to be proactive, all-inclusive, and ethically managed, which means its co-creation with all other interested parties. Policy and regulatory alignment is another implementation dimension that is critical. DPI systems need a broad range of legal and regulatory frameworks on the areas of data privacy, cybersecurity, and online payments, AI ethics, and interoperability requirements. Coordination of the policies within the industries avoids separation, adherence to the international practices, and cross-border collaboration. The example of the European Union and the role of regulatory consistency in promoting trust and accountability as well as enhancing innovation is exemplified by such instruments as GDPR and the AI Act. In the case of DPI 2030, the existence of regulatory frameworks needs to be dynamic and technology agnostic, and should have enforcement, monitoring, and redress mechanisms of the people.

The fifth part of the implementation strategy is monitoring, evaluation and performance measurement. The benchmarks and key performance indicators (KPIs) form a fundamental part of the evaluation of whether the DPI 2030 was achieved. Measures can take the digital adoption rates, interoperability, occurrence of cybersecurity incidents, output of innovation and environmental sustainability measure. Based on the discussed theory of public administration, it is possible to make evidence-based decisions, continuously improve, and report results in a transparent way, which promotes trust in DPI systems.

Lastly, international collaboration and exchange of information is a constituent of the roadmap. DPI 2030 envisions association with other partners internationally, in exchange of technology, setting of standards and capacity building. Regional agreements, international digital cooperatives, and inter country interoperability agreements will see that digital infrastructure is not only fulfilling local requirements but also in line with international best practices. Concurrently, digital sovereignty should be ensured, where states have the ability to operate their data and infrastructure on their own and still enjoy the opportunities of being part of the worldwide digital environment.

To conclude, executing DPI 2030 should be multi-dimensional and incorporate institutional preparedness, gradual execution, stakeholder involvement, policy acquisition, monitoring and assessment, and international cooperation (World Bank Group, 2025; Organisation for Economic Co-operation and Development, 2025). With the help of these strategies, governments are able to make the vision and strategic pillars operational and make DPI a transformative force in enabling inclusion in governance, economic empowerment, technological innovation, and sustainable development (Digital Cooperation Organization & Access Partnership, 2025; World Economic Forum, 2025). The roadmap is not an inflexible plan but a flexible framework that can be expanded according to the emerging technologies, needs of the society, and developments in the world and thus ensuring a robust, reliable, and fair digital future by 2030 (South Centre, 2025; International Monetary Fund, 2025; European Commission, 2025).

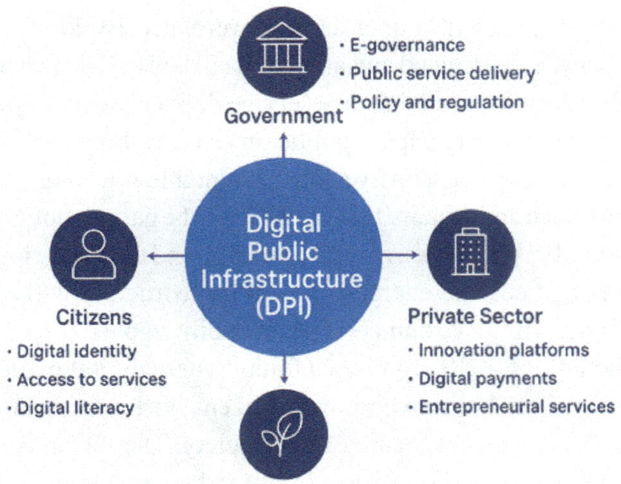

Future Outlook for Digital Public Infrastructure (DPI) in 2030,

The future outlook for DPI in 2030 is both promising and transformative, envisioning a society where digital public systems are seamless, inclusive, and highly efficient. By 2030, DPI is expected to evolve beyond basic services like digital identity, payments, and document storage, integrating advanced technologies such as AL, ML, Blockchain, and (IoT). These technologies will allow DPI to become predictive, personalized, and context-aware, enabling governments to deliver services proactively rather than reactively.

One key aspect of the future DPI landscape will be universal accessibility. Governments will increasingly focus on bridging the digital divide, ensuring that even remote or underserved populations can access critical services through low-cost devices, offline-enabled applications, and user-friendly interfaces. This inclusivity will strengthen social equity and enhance citizen trust in digital systems.

Interoperability and modularity will become even more critical. DPI will evolve as a network of interconnected platforms that can communicate across sectors—healthcare, education, finance, agriculture, and governance. This modular approach will allow for rapid innovation, easier upgrades, and the addition of new services without overhauling the entire system.

Security, privacy, and trust will remain central to the DPI vision. Future infrastructure will increasingly rely on privacy-preserving technologies, encrypted data sharing, and decentralized architectures to protect citizens' information. AI-driven monitoring systems will detect anomalies and threats in real time, reducing risks and ensuring regulatory compliance.

Another defining feature will be data-driven governance. By 2030, DPI will enable governments to analyze aggregated and anonymized data to improve policymaking, optimize resource allocation, and enhance service delivery. Smart systems may anticipate citizens' needs, identify gaps in public services, and suggest evidence-based interventions, creating more responsive and accountable governance.

Finally, the resilience and sustainability of DPI will be paramount. Systems will be designed to withstand cyberattacks, natural disasters, and technological disruptions. Green computing practices and energy-efficient infrastructure will ensure that the growth of DPI aligns with environmental sustainability goals.

In essence, the DPI of 2030 promises a future where digital platforms not only streamline public services but also empower citizens, foster transparency, and create an adaptable, inclusive, and secure digital society. The vision is not just about technology—it is about using digital tools to strengthen trust, equity, and resilience in governance.

CONCLUSION

In conclusion, It envisions a future where technology is not merely a tool but a foundation for empowerment, enabling every citizen to access essential public services with ease, trust, and dignity. As the world becomes increasingly interconnected, DPI will serve as the backbone of digital governance, integrating identity systems, financial networks, data management, and service delivery into a cohesive and interoperable framework.

However, achieving this vision requires addressing deep-rooted challenges related to accessibility, interoperability, privacy, and policy alignment. The success of DPI depends on sustained collaboration between government, private sector, civil society, and global partners to ensure that the infrastructure remains secure, inclusive, and future-ready.

By 2030, a well-implemented DPI will not only enhance service delivery and economic growth but also strengthen democratic participation and social equity. It will redefine the relationship between citizens and the state, fostering trust through transparency, accountability, and technological empowerment. Ultimately, the roadmap toward 2030 is not just about building digital systems—it is about shaping a human-centered digital future where innovation and inclusion coexist harmoniously.

REFERENCES

Center for Social and Economic Progress. (2025). Measuring the economic impact of India's digital public infrastructure (CSEP Research Report).

Digital Cooperation Organization & Access Partnership. (2025, June 19). Digital public infrastructure: A key building block for social inclusion and economic development – Policy paper.

European Commission. (2025, June 16). State of the Digital Decade 2025 report.

International Center for Law & Economics. (2025, August 14). The governance of digital public infrastructure: Case studies (ICLE Research Paper). Morris, J. (Author).

International Monetary Fund. (2025, July). Digital public infrastructure is changing the regulatory landscape. Regulatory Analysis.

International Telecommunication Union. (2025). Building the case for a digital public infrastructure for education.

Openfuture. (2025, February 25). Public digital infrastructure.

Organisation for Economic Co-operation and Development. (2025, June). Government at a glance 2025.

South Centre. (2025, September). Taking forward digital public infrastructure for the Global South.

United Nations Development Programme. (2025). Digital public infrastructure.

World Bank Group. (2025). Digital public infrastructure and development: A World Bank Group approach (Digital Transformation White Paper, Vol. 1). Clark, J., Marin, G., Ardic Alper, O. P., & Galicia Rabadan, G. A. (Authors).

World Economic Forum. (2025, April). Why digital public infrastructure is key to building a connected future.

Compilation of References

Abikoye, B. E., Umeorah, S. C., Adelaja, A. O., Ayodele, O., & Ogunsuji, Y. M. (2024). Regulatory compliance and efficiency in financial technologies: Challenges and innovations. *World Journal of Advanced Research and Reviews*, *23*(1), 1830–1844.

Abisoye, A., & Akerele, J. I. (2022). A practical framework for advancing cybersecurity, artificial intelligence and technological ecosystems to support regional economic development and innovation. *Int J Multidiscip Res Growth Eval*, *3*(1), 700–713. DOI: 10.54660/.IJMRGE.2022.3.1.700-713

Adigun, O. A., Falola, B. O., Esebre, S. D., Wada, I., & Tunde, A. (2024). Enhancing carbon markets with fintech innovations: The role of artificial intelligence and blockchain. *World Journal of Advanced Research and Reviews*, *23*(2), 579–586. DOI: 10.30574/wjarr.2024.23.2.2387

African Union. (2020). *Digital transformation strategy for Africa*. African Union Commission.

Agarwal, J. D., Agarwal, M., Agarwal, A., & Agarwal, Y. (2021). Economics of cryptocurrencies: Artificial intelligence, blockchain, and digital currency. In *Information for efficient decision making: big data, blockchain and relevance* (pp. 331-430).

Agarwal, S., Ghosh, P., Li, J., & Ruan, T. (2024). Digital payments and consumption: Evidence from the 2016 demonetization in India. *Review of Financial Studies*, *37*(8), 2550–2585. DOI: 10.1093/rfs/hhae005

Agrawal, A., Gans, J., & Goldfarb, A. (2019). Economic policy for artificial intelligence. *Innovation Policy and the Economy*, *19*(1), 139–159. DOI: 10.1086/699935

Ahmad, S., & Saxena, C. (2022, May). Artificial intelligence and blockchain technology in insurance business. In *The international conference on recent innovations in computing* (pp. 61–71). Springer Nature Singapore.

Ahmed, I., Zhang, Y., Jeon, G., Lin, W., Khosravi, M. R., & Qi, L. (2022). A blockchain-and artificial intelligence-enabled smart IoT framework for sustainable city. *International Journal of Intelligent Systems*, *37*(9), 6493–6507. DOI: 10.1002/int.22852

Ai, H., Islam, N., Mangla, S. K., Song, M., & Tan, X. (2024). Circular economy, open innovation, and green innovation: Empirical evidence from prefecture-level cities in China. *IEEE Transactions on Engineering Management*, *71*, 5706–5719. DOI: 10.1109/TEM.2024.3357350

Aker, J., & Mbiti, I. (2019). Mobile phones and economic development in Africa. *The Journal of Economic Perspectives*, *33*(3), 207–232. DOI: 10.1257/jep.24.3.207

Akram, R., Li, Q., Srivastava, M., Zheng, Y., & Irfan, M. (2024). Nexus between green technology innovation and climate policy uncertainty: Unleashing the role of artificial intelligence in an emerging economy. *Technological Forecasting and Social Change*, *209*, 123820. DOI: 10.1016/j.techfore.2024.123820

Alliance for Affordable Internet. (2021). *The affordability report*. Web Foundation.

Almulhim, A. I. (2024). Toward a greener future: Applying circular economy principles to Saudi Arabia's food sector for environmental sustainability. *Sustainability (Basel)*, *16*(2), 786. DOI: 10.3390/su16020786

Andhini, N. A., & Muat, S. (2024). Tapping into the future: What drives Generation Z to adopt digital payments? *InJBM: Integrated Research Journal of Business and Management*, *1*(2), 148–169.

Angamuthu, B. (2020). *Growth of digital payments in India*. NMIS Journal of Economics and Public Policy.

Anjum, M. F., & Veermanju, K. T. (2023). Study on the role of artificial intelligence and block chain in segments of the financial sector. *Scope*, *13*(01), 314–329.

Antonopoulou, H., Halkiopoulos, C., Barlou, O., & Beligiannis, G. N. (2021). Associations between traditional and digital leadership in academic environment: During the COVID-19 pandemic. *Emerging Science Journal*, *5*(4), 405–428. DOI: 10.28991/esj-2021-01286

An, Y. J., Choi, P. M. S., & Huang, S. H. (2021). Blockchain, cryptocurrency, and artificial intelligence in finance. In *Fintech with artificial intelligence, big data, and blockchain* (pp. 1–34). Springer Singapore. DOI: 10.1007/978-981-33-6137-9_1

Arisandy, T., Dasril, Y. B., Salahudin, S. B., Muslim, M. A., Adnan, A., & Wen, G. K. (2023). Buy now pay later services on Generation Z: Exploratory data analysis using machine learning. *Journal of Theoretical and Applied Information Technology*, *101*(11), 4194–4204.

Avalekar, U. A., Mehta, V., Mishra, B. R., Prasanna, L., Rajlakshmi, P. V., Manjunath, T. C., & Selvakumar, P. (2025). The Current Advances in AI-Driven Education. In Babulak, E. (Ed.), *Educational AI Humanoid Computing Devices for Cyber Nomads* (pp. 173–196). IGI Global Scientific Publishing. DOI: 10.4018/979-8-3693-8985-0.ch008

Badak, S., Kolte, R., Agrawal, S., & Bairagi, V. (2023). Unified Payments Interface (UPI): A study on adoption, growth and impact on digital transactions in India. *Journal of Positive School Psychology*, *7*(3), 1123–1135.

Badak, S., Kolte, V., Agrawal, M., & Gupta, S. (2023). Revolution of digital payment in India. *Journal of Mobile Computing. Communications & Mobile Networks*, *10*(3), 29–37.

Banala, S., Panyaram, S., & Selvakumar, P. (2025). Artificial Intelligence in Software Testing. In Chelliah, P., Venkatesh, R., Natraj, N., & Jeyaraj, R. (Eds.), *Artificial Intelligence for Cloud-Native Software Engineering* (pp. 237–262). IGI Global Scientific Publishing. DOI: 10.4018/979-8-3693-9356-7.ch009

Bednarčíková, D., & Repiská, R. (2021). Digital transformation in the context of the European Union and the use of digital technologies as a tool for business sustainability. In *SHS Web of Conferences* (Vol. 115, p. 01001). EDP Sciences. https://doi.org/DOI: 10.1051/shsconf/202111501001

Bhatia, R., & Shete, V. (n.d.). Usage of UPI transaction and its challenges – A study on Gen Z and Millennials.

Bhatia, A., & Bhabha, J. (2017). India's Aadhaar scheme and the promise of inclusive social protection. *World Development*, *98*, 222–240. DOI: 10.1016/j.worlddev.2017.04.013

Bhumichai, D., Smiliotopoulos, C., Benton, R., Kambourakis, G., & Damopoulos, D. (2024). The convergence of artificial intelligence and blockchain: The state of play and the road ahead. *Information (Basel)*, *15*(5), 268. DOI: 10.3390/info15050268

Bill & Melinda Gates Foundation. (2021). *Level one project guide: Principles for financial inclusion*. Bill & Melinda Gates Foundation.

Binariks. (2025). 5 Best Blockchain Development Trends for 2025-2030. Retrieved from https://binariks.com/blog/emerging-blockchain-technology-trends/

Blaize. (2024, December 9). Top Web3 Trends for 2025: Tokenization, Decentralization, and the Future of Blockchain. Retrieved from https://blaize.tech/blog/top-web3-trends-to-watch-in-2025

Boonman, H., Verstraten, P., & van der Weijde, A. H. (2023). Macroeconomic and environmental impacts of circular economy innovation policy. *Sustainable Production and Consumption, 35*, 216–228. DOI: 10.1016/j.spc.2022.10.025

Braun, V., & Clarke, V. (2006). Using thematic analysis in psychology. *Qualitative Research in Psychology, 3*(2), 77–101. DOI: 10.1191/1478088706qp063oa

Bull, R., & Azennoud, M. (2016). Smart citizens for smart cities: Participating in the future. *Proceedings of the Institution of Civil Engineers - Energy, 169*(3), 93-101. https://doi.org/DOI: 10.1680/jener.15.00030

Carè, R., Boitan, I. A., Stoian, A. M., & Fatima, R. (n.d.). Exploring the landscape of financial inclusion through the lens of financial technologies. *RE:view*.

Carnegie Endowment for International Peace. (2025, February). Digital public infrastructure: A practical approach for Africa.

Center for Social and Economic Progress. (2025). Measuring the economic impact of India's digital public infrastructure (CSEP Research Report).

Central Bank of Brazil. (2022). PIX: The instant payments system in Brazil. https://www.bcb.gov.br

CGAP. (2021). *Building digital public goods for inclusive finance*. CGAP.

Chainalysis. (2024, September 11). 2024 Global Crypto Adoption Index. Retrieved from https://www.chainalysis.com/blog/2024-global-crypto-adoption-index/

Chainalysis. (2025, January). The Chainalysis 2025 Global Adoption Index. Retrieved from https://www.chainalysis.com/blog/2025-global-crypto-adoption-index/

Chandrasekaran, N., Somanah, R., Rughoo, D., Dreepaul, R. K., Cunden, T. S. M., & Demkah, M. (2019, January). Digital transformation from leveraging blockchain technology, artificial intelligence, machine learning and deep learning. In *Information Systems Design and Intelligent Applications: Proceedings of Fifth International Conference INDIA 2018* Volume 2 (pp. 271-283). Singapore: Springer Singapore. DOI: 10.1007/978-981-13-3338-5_25

Chatterjee, P., & Saha, S. (2021). UPI and digital payments transformation in India. *Economic and Political Weekly, 56*(12), 35–41.

Chen, Y., Li, W., & Zhang, X. (2024). Integration and innovation of blockchain in Web3.0: Current status and standardization prospects. *World Wide Web (Bussum), 27*(6), 1–32. DOI: 10.1007/s11280-024-01319-7

Chhibber, S., Rajkumar, S. R., & Dassanayake, S. (2025). Will Artificial Intelligence Reshape the Global Workforce by 2030? A Cross-Sectoral Analysis of Job Displacement and Transformation. *Blockchain, Artificial Intelligence, and Future Research, 1*(1), 35–51. DOI: 10.70211/bafr.v1i1.178

Chib, S., Mehta, A. K., Selvakumar, P., Saravanan, A., Mishra, B. R., & Manjunath, T. C. (2025). Mental Health Challenges and Solutions in High-Pressure Work Environments. In Harriott, S. (Ed.), *Innovative Approaches to Managing Conflict and Change in Diverse Work Environments* (pp. 247–272). IGI Global Scientific Publishing. DOI: 10.4018/979-8-3693-9556-1.ch011

Chowdhary, S., Selvakumar, P., Sangeetha, B., Sarvaani, V. V., Anute, N., & Sharma, M. (2025). The Role of Social Capital in Entrepreneurial Development. In Martínez-Falcó, J., Sánchez-García, E., & Marco-Lajara, B. (Eds.), *Support Networks for Entrepreneurs: Social Capital and Strategic Collaborations* (pp. 311–338). IGI Global Scientific Publishing. DOI: 10.4018/979-8-3693-9836-4.ch013

Clarke, V., & Braun, V. (2017). Thematic analysis. *The Journal of Positive Psychology, 12*(3), 297–298. DOI: 10.1080/17439760.2016.1262613

Coates, J. M., Santhanalakshmi, K., Dinesh, N., Gandhimathi, S., & Chandel, P. S. Mohit, & Selvakumar, P. (2025). Assessment and Evaluation in Transnational Staff Development. In G. Morris & J. Ye (Eds.), *Training and Development in Transnational Higher Education* (pp. 387-406). IGI Global Scientific Publishing.

Cockburn, I. M., Henderson, R., & Stern, S. (2018). The impact of artificial intelligence on innovation: An exploratory analysis. In *The economics of artificial intelligence: An agenda* (pp. 115–146). University of Chicago Press.

Consensys. (2024). State of Web3 Infrastructure Report 2024. Consensys, Inc.

Cortellazzo, L., Bruni, E., & Zampieri, R. (2019). The role of leadership in a digitalized world: A review. *Frontiers in Psychology, 10*, 1938. DOI: 10.3389/fpsyg.2019.01938 PMID: 31507494

Creditcoin. (2025, January 9). Web3 Trends for 2025: A Year of Transformation. Retrieved from https://creditcoin.org/blog/web3-trends-for-2025/

Cummings, C., & O'Neil, T. (2015). *Do digital technologies improve service delivery? Evidence from developing countries.* Overseas Development Institute.

Das, S. (2024, August 26). Digital Public Infrastructure and Emerging Technologies. Speech at RBI@90 Global Conference, Bengaluru. Bank for International Settlements. Retrieved from https://www.bis.org/review/r240828p.htm

Davis, F. D. (1986). A technology acceptance model for empirically testing new end-user information systems: Theory and results. Doctoral dissertation, MIT.

Del Sarto, N., & Ozili, P. K. (2025). FinTech and financial inclusion in emerging markets: A bibliometric analysis and future research agenda. *International Journal of Emerging Markets*, *20*(13), 270–290.

Dewasiri, N. J., Karunarathne, K. S. S. N., Menon, S., Jayarathne, P. G. S. A., & Rathnasiri, M. S. H. (2023). Fusion of artificial intelligence and blockchain in the banking industry: Current application, adoption, and future challenges. In *Transformation for sustainable business and management practices: Exploring the spectrum of industry 5.0* (pp. 293–307). Emerald Publishing Limited. DOI: 10.1108/978-1-80262-277-520231021

Dey, D., Srinivas, D., Panda, B., Suraneni, P., & Sitharam, T. G. (2022). Use of industrial waste materials for 3D printing of sustainable concrete: A review. *Journal of Cleaner Production*, *340*, 130749. DOI: 10.1016/j.jclepro.2022.130749

Digital Bangladesh Vision. (2021). Government of Bangladesh ICT Division. a2i. https://a2i.gov.bd

Digital Cooperation Organization & Access Partnership. (2025, June 19). Digital public infrastructure: A key building block for social inclusion and economic development – Policy paper.

Digital Cooperation Organization. (2025, June). Digital public infrastructure: A key building block for social inclusion and economic development.

Drishti, I. A. S. (2024). Digital Public Infrastructure. Retrieved from https://www.drishtiias.com/daily-updates/daily-news-analysis/digital-public-infrastructure

Drishti, I. A. S. (2024). India's Digital Public Infrastructure. Retrieved from https://www.drishtiias.com/daily-updates/daily-news-analysis/india-s-digital-public-infrastructure-3

Ducatel, K. (2001). Balance of nature? Sustainable societies in the digital economy. *Foresight*, *3*(2), 123–133. DOI: 10.1108/14636680110803058

Duncombe, R., & Boateng, R. (2009). Mobile phones and financial services in developing countries: A review of concepts, methods, issues, evidence and future research directions. *Third World Quarterly*, *30*(7), 1237–1258. DOI: 10.1080/01436590903134882

Dunn, S. (2017). Micropower: Electrifying the digital economy. In *The Ecology of the New Economy* (pp. 206-220). Routledge.

Durai, T., & Lalitha, H. (2024). Influence of AI-enabled digital payment systems on mental accounting among Gen-Z. *Center for Development Economics*, *11*(19), 94–102.

Egodawele, M., Sedera, D., & Bui, V. (2022). A systematic review of digital transformation literature (2013-2021) and the development of an overarching apriori model to guide future research. *arXiv preprint arXiv:2212.03867*. https://doi.org//arXiv.2212.03867DOI: 10.48550

Ernst, E., Merola, R., & Samaan, D. (2019). Economics of artificial intelligence: Implications for the future of work. *IZA Journal of Labor Policy*, *9*(1), 1–35. DOI: 10.2478/izajolp-2019-0004

Estonian Government. (2020). X-Road data exchange platform. e-Estonia. https://e-estonia.com

European Commission. (2024). Blockchain and Web3 Strategy: Shaping Europe's Digital Future. Retrieved from https://digital-strategy.ec.europa.eu/en/policies/blockchain-strategy

European Commission. (2025, June 16). State of the Digital Decade 2025 report.

Fayustov, A. A. (2020). E-waste management in a global digital economy. *IOP Conference Series. Earth and Environmental Science*, *459*(3), 032007. DOI: 10.1088/1755-1315/459/3/032007

Feroz, A. K., Zo, H., & Chiravuri, A. (2021). Digital transformation and environmental sustainability: A review and research agenda. *Sustainability (Basel)*, *13*(3), 1530. DOI: 10.3390/su13031530

Filiou, D., Kesidou, E., & Wu, L. (2023). Are smart cities green? The role of environmental and digital policies for Eco-innovation in China. *World Development*, *165*, 106212. DOI: 10.1016/j.worlddev.2023.106212

Financial Action Task Force. (2020). *Guidance on digital identity*. FATF.

FLIP. (2024, October 18). The FLIP: Digital Public Goods and Digital Public Infrastructure Are the Answer to Every SDG Question. Retrieved from https://www.weave3.org/p/the-flip-digital-public-goods-and

Fortune Business Insights. (2025). Blockchain Technology Market Size, Share & Growth Analysis Report 2025-2032. Retrieved from https://www.fortunebusinessinsights.com/industry-reports/blockchain-market-100072

Furman, J., & Seamans, R. (2019). AI and the Economy. *Innovation Policy and the Economy*, *19*(1), 161–191. DOI: 10.1086/699936

Gadicha, A. B., Gadicha, V. B., Obaid, A. J., & Abbood, Z. A. (2024). An in-depth examination of cyberbullying detection utilizing machine learning techniques. AIP Conference Proceedings, 3207(1), Article 060002. [Note: Replace with actual DOI if available; "This link is disabled" suggests access issue]DOI: 10.1063/5.0234200

Gadicha, A. B., Gadicha, V. B., Zuhair, M., Ingole, V. A., & Saraf, S. S. (2024). ZTA-DEVSECOPS: Strategies towards network zero trust architecture and DevSecOps in cybersecurity and IIoT environments. In Smart and agile cybersecurity for IoT and IIoT environments (pp. 306–324).

Galhotra, B., Jatain, A., Bajaj, S. B., & Jaglan, V. (2023). Gen Z's digital payments: Disruptive or useful for online shopping in security aspect. *Journal of Survey in Fisheries Sciences*, *10*(2), 1466–1473. DOI: 10.53555/sfs.v10i2.2723

Gammage, S., Kes, A., Winograd, L., Sultana, N., Hiller, S., & Bourgault, S. (2017). *Gender and digital financial inclusion: What do we know and what do we need to know. International Center for Research on Women*. ICRW.

Gelb, A., & Diofasi Metz, A. (2018). *Identification revolution: Can digital ID be harnessed for development?* Center for Global Development.

Gitobu, C., & Ogetonto, J. (2024, November). Harnessing Artificial Intelligence (AI) and Blockchain Technology for the Advancement of Finance Technology (FinTech) in Businesses. In *Proceedings of London International Conferences* (No. 11, pp. 196-210).

Go, E. J., Moon, J., & Kim, J. (2020). Analysis of the current and future of the artificial intelligence in financial industry with big data techniques. [GBFR]. *Global Business & Finance Review*, *25*(1), 102–117. DOI: 10.17549/gbfr.2020.25.1.102

Govind, H., Nayan, A., & Gupta, P. (2024). The evolution of digital payments: UPI, E-Rupee and the future of currency – in the context of urban Patna. [IRJAEM]. *International Research Journal on Advanced Engineering and Management*, *2*(03), 495–503.

Graziano, E. A., Musella, F., & Petroccione, G. (2023, September). Gender attitude and intersectional factors in the cashless payment behaviour. In *16th Annual Conference of the EuroMed Academy of Business.*

Graziano, E. A., Musella, F., & Petroccione, G. (2024). Cashless payment: Behavior changes and gender dynamics during the COVID-19 pandemic. *EuroMed Journal of Business, 20*(5), 54–74. DOI: 10.1108/EMJB-11-2023-0299

Grigorescu, A., Zamfir, A.-M., & Mocanu, C. (2020). Emerging trends and drivers for knowledge-intensive economy. *Management & Marketing. Challenges for the Knowledge Society, 15*(2), 172–185. DOI: 10.2478/mmcks-2020-0011

GSMA. (2021). *Driving digital inclusion in emerging economies.* GSMA Intelligence.

GSMA. (2022). *The state of mobile internet connectivity.* GSMA Intelligence.

Heeks, R. (2017). *Information and communication technology for development (ICT4D)* (2nd ed.). Routledge. DOI: 10.4324/9781315652603

He, W., Li, W., & Deng, P. (2022). Legal governance in the smart cities of China: Functions, problems, and solutions. *Sustainability (Basel), 14*(15), 9738. DOI: 10.3390/su14159738

Hjelholt, M., & Damsgaard, J. (2012). The genesis and evolution of digital payment platforms.

Hosen, M., Thaker, H. M. T., Subramaniam, V., Eaw, H. C., & Cham, T. H. (2022, September). Artificial intelligence (AI), blockchain, and cryptocurrency in finance: current scenario and future direction. In *International Conference on Emerging Technologies and Intelligent Systems* (pp. 322-332). Cham: Springer International Publishing.

Human, S., & Kazzazi, M. (2021). Contextuality and intersectionality of e-consent: A human-centric reflection on digital consenting in the emerging genetic data markets. In *2021 IEEE European Symposium on Security and Privacy Workshops (EuroS&PW)* (pp. 307-311). IEEE. https://doi.org/DOI: 10.1109/EuroSPW54576.2021.00051

Hunjra, A. I., Zhao, S., Goodell, J. W., & Liu, X. (2024). Digital economy policy and corporate low-carbon innovation: Evidence from a quasi-natural experiment in China. *Finance Research Letters, 60*, 104910. DOI: 10.1016/j.frl.2023.104910

Hussain, A. A., & Al-Turjman, F. (2021). Artificial intelligence and blockchain: A review. *Transactions on Emerging Telecommunications Technologies, 32*(9), e4268. DOI: 10.1002/ett.4268

ID4D Initiative, World Bank. (2022). Global ID coverage report. World Bank.

Insights, G. M. (2024, December 1). Web 3.0 Blockchain Market Size, Global Report 2025-2034. Retrieved from https://www.gminsights.com/industry-analysis/web-3-0-blockchain-market

Institut Montaigne. (2024). India's Digital Public Infrastructure: A Success Story for the World? Retrieved from https://www.institutmontaigne.org/en/expressions/indias-digital-public-infrastructure-success-story-world

International Center for Law & Economics. (2025, August 14). The governance of digital public infrastructure: Case studies (ICLE Research Paper). Morris, J. (Author).

International Monetary Fund. (2025, July). Digital public infrastructure is changing the regulatory landscape. Regulatory Analysis.

International Telecommunication Union. (2025). Building digital public infrastructure for cities and communities.

International Telecommunication Union. (2025). Building the case for a digital public infrastructure for education.

ITU. (2020). *Measuring digital development: Facts and figures*. International Telecommunication Union.

Jabłoński, A., & Jabłoński, M. (2020). *Social business models in the digital economy*. Springer International Publishing., DOI: 10.1007/978-3-030-29732-9

Jack, W., & Suri, T. (2014). Risk sharing and transactions costs: Evidence from Kenya's mobile money revolution. *The American Economic Review*, *104*(1), 183–223. DOI: 10.1257/aer.104.1.183

Javaid, M., Haleem, A., Singh, R. P., Suman, R., & Khan, S. (2022). A review of Blockchain Technology applications for financial services. *BenchCouncil transactions on benchmarks, standards and evaluations, 2*(3), 100073.

Johnson, M., Jain, R., Brennan-Tonetta, P., Swartz, E., Silver, D., Paolini, J., Mamonov, S., & Hill, C. (2021). Impact of big data and artificial intelligence on industry: Developing a workforce roadmap for a data driven economy. *Global Journal of Flexible Systems Managment*, *22*(3), 197–217. DOI: 10.1007/s40171-021-00272-y

Jung, B., & Kowalski, T. (2021). Hybridization of time: Towards temporal sustainability of the digital economy. In *The Future of Work and Technology* (pp. 227–244). Springer., DOI: 10.1007/978-3-030-78825-4_14

Kalai, M., Becha, H., & Helali, K. (2024). Effect of artificial intelligence on economic growth in European countries: A symmetric and asymmetric cointegration based on linear and non-linear ARDL approach. *Journal of Economic Structures, 13*(1), 22. DOI: 10.1186/s40008-024-00345-y

Karippur, N. K., & Balaramachandran, P. R. (2022). Antecedents of effective digital leadership of enterprises in Asia Pacific. *AJIS. Australasian Journal of Information Systems, 26*. Advance online publication. DOI: 10.3127/ajis.v26i0.2525

Kaur, H., Kaur, R., Mago, M., Singh, M., & Mehta, K. (2024). Exploring factors affecting central bank digital currency adoption: A perspective from Generation Z. *Metamorphosis, 23*(2), 126–141. DOI: 10.1177/09726225241286932

Kaur, S., & Walia, N. (2023). Adoption of NFC-mobile payments by Generation Y consumers in Punjab: Empirical evidence from UTAUT. *International Journal of Business Innovation and Research, 32*(4), 525–542. DOI: 10.1504/IJBIR.2023.135502

Kazachenok, O. P., Stankevich, G. V., Chubaeva, N. N., & Tyurina, Y. G. (2023). Economic and legal approaches to the humanization of FinTech in the economy of artificial intelligence through the integration of blockchain into ESG Finance. *Humanities & Social Sciences Communications, 10*(1), 1–9. DOI: 10.1057/s41599-023-01652-8

Kesavan, V., & Srinivasan, S. (2021). A case study on the digital payment systems in India. *Compendium of Management Case Studies,* 17–26.

Kesavan, R., & Srinivasan, P. (2021). Mobile banking and UPI: Redefining financial accessibility in India. *Journal of Banking and Financial Technology, 5*(1), 45–59.

Keshari, A., & Gautam, A. (2024). FinTech Evolution and Artificial Intelligence: Opportunities and Development. In *Applications of Artificial Intelligence in Business and Finance 5.0* (pp. 45-67). Apple Academic Press.

Khan, A. A., Laghari, A. A., Li, P., Dootio, M. A., & Karim, S. (2023). The collaborative role of blockchain, artificial intelligence, and industrial internet of things in digitalization of small and medium-size enterprises. *Scientific Reports, 13*(1), 1656. DOI: 10.1038/s41598-023-28707-9 PMID: 36717702

Kim, S. S., & Choi, Y. S. (2019). The innovative platform programme in South Korea: economic policies in innovation-driven growth. *Foresight and STI governance, 13*(3), 13.

Kliestik, T., Dragomir, R., Bălu ă, A. V., Grecu, I., Durana, P., Karabolevski, O. L., ... & Gajdosikova, D. (2024). Enterprise generative artificial intelligence technologies, Internet of Things and blockchain-based fintech management, and digital twin industrial metaverse in the cognitive algorithmic economy. *Oeconomia Copernicana, 15*(4).

Koshta, N., Patra, S., & Singh, S. P. (2022). Sharing economic responsibility: Assessing end user's willingness to support e-waste reverse logistics for circular economy. *Journal of Cleaner Production*, *332*, 130057. DOI: 10.1016/j.jclepro.2021.130057

Kumar, A., Srivastava, A., & Gupta, P. K. (2022). Banking 4.0: The era of artificial intelligence-based fintech. *Strategic Change*, *31*(6), 591–601. DOI: 10.1002/jsc.2526

Kwok, A. O., & Treiblmaier, H. (2024). Blockchain technology as a driver of economic development in small economies: A dynamic capabilities framework. *Journal of Decision Systems*, *33*(3), 413–438. DOI: 10.1080/12460125.2023.2214304

Lai, K. P., & Langley, P. (2024). Playful finance: Gamification and intermediation in FinTech economies. *Geoforum*, *151*, 103848. DOI: 10.1016/j.geoforum.2023.103848

Lăzăroiu, G., Bogdan, M., Geamănu, M., Hurloiu, L., Lumini a, L., & tefănescu, R. (2023). Artificial intelligence algorithms and cloud computing technologies in blockchain-based fintech management. *Oeconomia Copernicana*, *14*(3), 707–730. DOI: 10.24136/oc.2023.021

Levidow, L., Birch, K., & Papaioannou, T. (2012). EU agri-innovation policy: Two contending visions of the bio-economy. *Critical Policy Studies*, *6*(1), 40–65. DOI: 10.1080/19460171.2012.659881

Li, B., Jiang, F., Xia, H., & Pan, J. (2022). Under the background of AI application, research on the impact of science and technology innovation and industrial structure upgrading on the sustainable and high-quality development of regional economies. *Sustainability (Basel)*, *14*(18), 11331. DOI: 10.3390/su141811331

Liebenau, J. M., Elaluf-Calderwood, S. M., & Bonina, C. M. (2014). Modularity and network integration: Emergent business models in banking. In *2014 47th Hawaii International Conference on System Sciences* (pp. 1183-1192). IEEE. https://doi.org/DOI: 10.1109/HICSS.2014.153

Li, J., Zhan, G., Dai, X., Qi, M., & Liu, B. (2022). Innovation and optimization logic of grassroots digital governance in China under digital empowerment and digital sustainability. *Sustainability (Basel)*, *14*(24), 16470. DOI: 10.3390/su142416470

Li, M., Wang, X., Wang, Z., Maqbool, B., Hussain, A., & Khan, W. A. (2022). Bibliometric analysis of the research on the impact of environmental regulation on green technology innovation based on CiteSpace. *International Journal of Environmental Research and Public Health, 19*(20), 13273. DOI: 10.3390/ijerph192013273 PMID: 36293848

Li, Q., Guan, X., Wu, P., Wang, X., Zhou, L., Tong, Y., Ren, R., Leung, K. S. M., Lau, E. H. Y., Wong, J. Y., Xing, X., Xiang, N., Wu, Y., Li, C., Chen, Q., Li, D., Liu, T., Zhao, J., Liu, M., & Feng, Z. (2020). Early transmission dynamics in Wuhan, China, of novel coronavirus–infected pneumonia. *The New England Journal of Medicine, 382*(13), 1199–1207. DOI: 10.1056/NEJMoa2001316 PMID: 31995857

Li, Z., Wang, J., & Kumar, R. (2024). Blockchain technology adoption in emerging markets: Opportunities and challenges. *Journal of Business Research, 156*, 113–128.

Lokhande, M., John Deva Prasanna, D. S., Selvakumar, P., Ragupathi, T., Vaissnave, V., & Manjunath, T. C. (2025). Novel ML Algorithms for Healthcare. In A. Ajibesin, N. G., & S. Thangavel (Eds.), *Synergizing Data Envelopment Analysis and Machine Learning for Performance Optimization in Healthcare* (pp. 113-134). IGI Global Scientific Publishing. DOI: 10.4018/979-8-3373-0081-8.ch005

London Blockchain. (2025, August 28). Blockchain Adoption Statistics: Trends Shaping the Markets. Retrieved from https://londonblockchain.net/blog/blockchain-explained/blockchain-adoption-statistics-trends-shaping-the-markets/

Loo, B. H., Tan, Y. Y., & Hong, M. (2024). Digital technology in senior entrepreneurship: A qualitative study. *Journal of Entrepreneurship. Business Economics (Cleveland, Ohio), 12*(1), 190–230.

Lundvall, B. Å., & Rikap, C. (2022). China's catching-up in artificial intelligence seen as a co-evolution of corporate and national innovation systems. *Research Policy, 51*(1), 104395. DOI: 10.1016/j.respol.2021.104395

Luo, S., Yimamu, N., Li, Y., Wu, H., Irfan, M., & Hao, Y. (2023). Digitalization and sustainable development: How could digital economy development improve green innovation in China? *Business Strategy and the Environment, 32*(4), 1847–1871. DOI: 10.1002/bse.3223

Maguire, M., & Delahunt, B. (2017). Doing a thematic analysis: A practical, step-by-step guide for learning and teaching scholars. *All Ireland Journal of Higher Education, 9*(3).

Ma, Q., Khan, Z., Tariq, M., IŞik, H., & Rjoub, H. (2022). Sustainable digital economy and trade adjusted carbon emissions: Evidence from China's provincial data. *Ekonomska Istrazivanja, 35*(1), 5469–5485. DOI: 10.1080/1331677X.2022.2028179

Martin, T. (2024). Blockchain, Web3 and the Prospects for Safe Digital Governance. SIGNAL Magazine, AFCEA International. Retrieved from https://www.afcea.org/signal-media/cyber-edge/blockchain-web3-and-prospects-safe-digital-governance

Mas, I., & Radcliffe, D. (2011). *Mobile payments go viral: M-Pesa in Kenya*. Bill & Melinda Gates Foundation.

Mazzatto, M. (2022). Financial literacy and investing habits of Generation Z as it pertains to financial marketing.

Mehra, J., Madaan, S., & Balu, N. Mohit, Selvakumar, P., & Manjunath, T. C. (2025). The Ubiquitous Internet and Smart Computation Available 24/7 for Anyone and Anywhere. In E. Babulak (Ed.), *Educational AI Humanoid Computing Devices for Cyber Nomads* (pp. 247-270). IGI Global Scientific Publishing.

Melnyk, L., Dehtyarova, I., Kubatko, O., Karintseva, O., & Derykolenko, A. (2019). Disruptive technologies for the transition of digital economies towards sustainability. *Economic Annals-XXI, 179*(9-10), 22–30. DOI: 10.21003/ea.V179-02

Ministry of Electronics and Information Technology, Government of India. (2022). *Digital India programme annual report*. Government of India.

Mosca, O., Manunza, A., Manca, S., Vivanet, G., & Fornara, F. (2024). Digital technologies for behavioral change in sustainability domains: A systematic mapping review. *Frontiers in Psychology, 14*, 1234349. DOI: 10.3389/fpsyg.2023.1234349 PMID: 38239482

Muralidharan, K., Niehaus, P., & Sukhtankar, S. (2016). Building state capacity: Evidence from biometric smartcards in India. *The American Economic Review, 106*(10), 2895–2929. DOI: 10.1257/aer.20141346

Niankara, I. (2022). Sustainability through open data sharing and reuse in the digital economy. In *2022 International Arab Conference on Information Technology (ACIT)* (pp. 1-11). IEEE. https://doi.org/DOI: 10.1109/ACIT57182.2022.9994191

Nisha Angeline, M., Selvakumar, P., Gupta, M. K., Nazar, N., Elumalai, D., & Bhattacharya, S. (2025). Emerging Materials for Energy Storage and Environmental Applications. In K. Muduli, B. Moharana, S. Ales, & D. Biswal (Eds.), *Using Computational Intelligence for Sustainable Manufacturing of Advanced Materials* (pp. 53-72). IGI Global Scientific Publishing. DOI: 10.4018/979-8-3693-7974-5.ch003

Noman, R., Shahid, M., & Alam, M. (2023, October). The Synergy of Blockchain and Artificial Intelligence in Fintech: Revolutionizing the Financial Landscape. In *2023 4th International Conference on Data Analytics for Business and Industry (ICDABI)* (pp. 425-430). IEEE.

Nowell, L. S., Norris, J. M., White, D. E., & Moules, N. J. (2017). Thematic Analysis: Striving to Meet the Trustworthiness Criteria. *International Journal of Qualitative Methods, 16*(1), 1609406917733847. DOI: 10.1177/1609406917733847

OECD. (2021). *Digital government index 2020: Shaping the digital transformation of the public sector.* OECD Publishing., DOI: 10.1787/9789264314610-

Open Government Partnership. (2021). Digital public infrastructure for inclusive governance. https://www.opengovpartnership.org

Openfuture. (2025, February 25). Public digital infrastructure.

Organisation for Economic Co-operation and Development. (2024, December). Digital public infrastructure for digital governments.

Organisation for Economic Co-operation and Development. (2025, June). Government at a glance 2025.

Owotemu, A. E., & Ibaru, A. (2025). Technological Transformation in Infrastructure & Real Estate: Artificial Intelligence (AI), Blockchain (DLT), Project Management & Policy Implications across Leading Markets in Africa (Egypt, South-Africa & Nigeria). *American Journal of Industrial and Business Management, 15*(1), 155–174. DOI: 10.4236/ajibm.2025.151009

Pan-African Payment and Settlement System. (2022). *Implementation report.* Afreximbank.

Pandey, A., & Joseph, J. (2025). Integral Role of Blockchain and Artificial Intelligence in Sustainable Economic Development. In *Driving Socio-Economic Growth With AI and Blockchain* (pp. 271–290). IGI Global Scientific Publishing. DOI: 10.4018/979-8-3693-8664-4.ch012

Pan, W., Xie, T., Wang, Z., & Ma, L. (2022). Digital economy: An innovation driver for total factor productivity. *Journal of Business Research, 139*, 303–311. DOI: 10.1016/j.jbusres.2021.09.061

Park, M. S., & Chang, S. D. (2022). Review of Artificial Intelligence Platform Policies and Strategies in South Korea, United States, China and the European Union Using National Innovation Capacity. *International Journal of Knowledge Content Development & Technology, 12*(3).

Pasqualino, R., Demartini, M., & Bagheri, F. (2021). Digital transformation and sustainable oriented innovation: A system transition model for socio-economic scenario analysis. *Sustainability (Basel), 13*(21), 11564. DOI: 10.3390/su132111564

Penesis, I., & Whittington, J. (2021). Australia's blue economy cooperative research centre. In *Preparing a workforce for the new blue economy* (pp. 335–348). Elsevier., DOI: 10.1016/B978-0-12-821431-2.00043-3

Pimenova, E. M. (2021). Specificity of sustainability assessment for industrial enterprise functioning in the digital economy. In *Digital Economy and the New Labor Market: Jobs, Competences and Innovative HR Technologies* (pp. 3-10). Springer. https://doi.org/DOI: 10.1007/978-3-030-53277-2_1

Pirciog, S. C., Grigorescu, A., Lincaru, C., Popa, F. M., Lazarczyk Carlson, E., & Sigurdarson, H. T. (2023). Mapping European high-digital intensive sectors—Regional growth accelerator for the circular economy. *Frontiers in Environmental Science, 10*, 1061128. Advance online publication. DOI: 10.3389/fenvs.2022.1061128

Popkova, E. G., Alekseev, A. N., Lobova, S. V., & Sergi, B. S. (2020). The theory of innovation and innovative development. AI scenarios in Russia. *Technology in Society, 63*, 101390. DOI: 10.1016/j.techsoc.2020.101390

Popović-Pantić, S., Semenčenko, D., & Vasilić, N. (2019). The influence of digital transformation on business performance: Evidence of the women-owned companies. *Ekonomika preduzeća, 67*(7-8), 397-414. https://doi.org/DOI: 10.5937/EKOPRE1908397P

Protean. (2024). Decoding India's Digital Public Infrastructure. Retrieved from https://proteantech.in/articles/Decoding-Digital-Public-Infrastructure-in-India/

Protean. (2024). DPI: Achievements Diary 2024. Retrieved from https://proteantech.in/articles/dpi-2-0-2-4-developments/

Purohit, S., Kaur, J., & Chaturvedi, S. (2022). Mobile payment adoption among youth: Generation Z and developing country perspective. *Journal of Content. Community and Communication, 15*(8), 194–209. DOI: 10.31620/JCCC.06.22/14

Qiang, C. Z., Rossotto, C. M., & Kimura, K. (2009). Economic impacts of broadband. In *Information and communications for development 2009: Extending reach and increasing impact* (pp. 35–50). World Bank.

Rafee, B. M., Ramesh, V., Asan, S. J., Kolar, A. B., & Zaheed, S. M. (2022). A survey on implications of cashless payments on the spending patterns of urbanites in the era of digital India. *IJFANS International Journal of Food and Nutritional Science, 11*(3), 989–1005.

Ramadhan, A., Vidianto, M. A., Muharam, H., & Mawardi, W. (2025). Fintech and Financial Inclusion: Evidence from Emerging Markets. *Research Horizon*, *5*(3), 599–612.

Ramadhan, B. B. (2025). Financial literacy and risky credit behavior: The mediating role of financial stress in PayLater usage. *FireNav: Financial Resilience and National Value Journal*, *1*(1), 1–14.

Rappitsch, C. (2017). Digital economy and sustainability. *Oikos*.

Reilly Marulanda, M. S., & López Sarabia, P. (2021). Artificial Intelligence & Blockchain: The Path to Generate Value for Companies After the COVID-19 Pandemic. In *The Future of Companies in the Face of a New Reality: Impact and Development in Latin America* (pp. 185–201). Springer Singapore. DOI: 10.1007/978-981-16-2613-5_10

Rjoub, H., Adebayo, T. S., & Kirikkaleli, D. (2023). Blockchain technology-based FinTech banking sector involvement using adaptive neuro-fuzzy-based K-nearest neighbors algorithm. *Financial Innovation*, *9*(1), 65. DOI: 10.1186/s40854-023-00469-3 PMID: 36919101

Rosário, A., & Dias, J. (2022). Sustainability and the digital transition: A literature review. *Sustainability (Basel)*, *14*(7), 4072. DOI: 10.3390/su14074072

Sahasranamam, S., & Prabhu, J. (2024, March 25). Digital Public Infrastructure for the Developing World. Stanford Social Innovation Review. Retrieved from https://ssir.org/articles/entry/digital-public-infrastructure-developing-world

Sapira, B., Juhari, J., Suhardi, S., & Makrus, M. (2025). Financial self-efficacy, lifestyle, and peer influence on credit decisions: The mediating role of financial control in Gen Z. *Economic: Journal Economic and Business*, *4*(2), 292–307.

Sarfraz, M., Ivascu, L., & Abdullah, M. I. (2022). Editorial: Sustainable digital economy, entrepreneurship, and blockchain technology role in industrial-organizational psychology. *Frontiers in Psychology*, *13*, 974415. Advance online publication. DOI: 10.3389/fpsyg.2022.974415 PMID: 35910996

Sarwer, M. H., Saha, T. R., & Hossain, D. (2022). Driving business innovation with artificial intelligence, machine learning and blockchain technology. *Journal of Business and Management Studies*, *4*(3), 221–230. DOI: 10.32996/jbms.2022.4.3.21

Savchenko, A. B., & Borodina, T. L. (2020). Green and digital economy for sustainable development of urban areas. *Regional Research of Russia*, *10*(4), 583–592. DOI: 10.1134/S2079970520040097

Security.org. (2025, January 31). 2025 Cryptocurrency Adoption and Consumer Sentiment Report. Retrieved from https://www.security.org/digital-security/cryptocurrency-annual-consumer-report/

Sekarlaras, A. F. A., Siregar, H., & Hasanah, N. (2025). Effects of financial literacy and self-efficacy on risky credit behavior of Gen-Z. *Jurnal Aplikasi Bisnis dan Manajemen, 11*(2), 468–468.

Shahabuddin, M., Uddin, M. N., Chowdhury, J. I., Ahmed, S. F., Uddin, M. N., Mofijur, M., & Uddin, M. A. (2023). A review of the recent development, challenges, and opportunities of electronic waste (e-waste). *International Journal of Environmental Science and Technology*, *20*(4), 4513–4520. DOI: 10.1007/s13762-022-04274-w

Sharma, N. S., & Gokhale, R. (2023). Recent trends in banking: Generation Z's perspective. *Journal of the Oriental Institute.*

Shehadeh, M., Dawood, H. M., & Hussainey, K. (2025). Digital financial literacy and usage of cashless payments in Jordan: The moderating role of gender. *International Journal of Accounting & Information Management*, *33*(2), 354–382. DOI: 10.1108/IJAIM-03-2024-0115

Shi, J., & Wang, Y. (2025). Academic exploration of blockchain and AI in financial services. Journal of Electronic Business & Digital Economics.

Siddiqui, Z. A., & Haroon, M. (2022). Application of artificial intelligence and machine learning in blockchain technology. In *Artificial Intelligence and Machine Learning for EDGE Computing* (pp. 169–185). Academic Press. DOI: 10.1016/B978-0-12-824054-0.00001-0

Singh, S., Sarkar, T., Mangla, M., Rakhra, M., Singh, A., & Jairath, K. (2024, September). FinTech edge: utility computing & artificial intelligence technologies for smart financial acquisition & blockchain in the financial industries. In *2024 7th International Conference on Contemporary Computing and Informatics (IC3I)* (Vol. 7, pp. 228-234). IEEE. DOI: 10.1109/IC3I61595.2024.10828908

Singh, P. J., & Mohan, S. (2021). Platform governance in India: Lessons from digital commerce. *Economic and Political Weekly*, *56*(18), 44–51.

Soni, N., Sharma, E. K., Singh, N., & Kapoor, A. (2020). Artificial intelligence in business: From research and innovation to market deployment. *Procedia Computer Science*, *167*, 2200–2210. DOI: 10.1016/j.procs.2020.03.272

South Centre. (2025, September). Taking forward digital public infrastructure for the Global South.

Srivastava, S., Mohta, A., & Shunmugasundaram, V. (2024). Adoption of digital payment FinTech service by Gen Y and Gen Z users: Evidence from India. *Digital Policy. Regulation & Governance*, *26*(1), 95–117.

Suri, T., & Jack, W. (2016). The long-run poverty and gender impacts of mobile money. *Science*, *354*(6317), 1288–1292. DOI: 10.1126/science.aah5309 PMID: 27940873

Tam, P. H., Hong, T. P., Thanh, C. N., & Tran, P. (2024). AI Innovation and Economics Growth: A Global Evidence. *WSB Journal of Business and Finance*, *58*(1), 198–216. DOI: 10.2478/wsbjbf-2024-0017

Taulli, T. (2025). Top Web 3.0 Trends and Predictions for 2025 and Beyond. TechTarget. Retrieved from https://www.techtarget.com/searchcio/tip/Top-Web-30-trends-and-predictions

Trenerry, B., Chng, S., Wang, Y., Suhaila, Z. S., Lim, S. S., Lu, H. Y., & Oh, P. H. (2021). Preparing workplaces for digital transformation: An integrative review and framework of multi-level factors. *Frontiers in Psychology*, *12*, 620766. DOI: 10.3389/fpsyg.2021.620766 PMID: 33833714

Trivedi, H. (2024). Evolution of digital payment system in India: Past, present and future. *International Research Journal of Humanities and Interdisciplinary Studies*, *5*(1), 30–48.

Truong, T. C. (2022). The impact of digital transformation on environmental sustainability. *Advances in Multimedia*, *2022*(1), 6324325. DOI: 10.1155/2022/6324325

UN ESCAP. (2021). *Asia-Pacific digital transformation report*. United Nations Economic and Social Commission for Asia and the Pacific.

UNDP. (2022). *Human development report 2022: Uncertain times, unsettled lives*. United Nations Development Programme.

United Nations Development Programme. (2025). Digital public infrastructure.

Upadhyaya, A. N., Debnath, P., Rani, P., Selvakumar, P., Manjunath, T. C., & Bhattacharya, S. (2025). AI-Based Disaster Prediction and Early Warning Systems. In Mobo, F. (Ed.), *AI and Emerging Technologies for Emergency Response and Smart Cities* (pp. 55–74). IGI Global Scientific Publishing. DOI: 10.4018/979-8-3693-9770-1.ch003

van der Velden, M. (2018). Digitalisation and the UN sustainable development goals: What role for design. [s]. *Interaction Design and Architecture*, *37*(37), 160–174. DOI: 10.55612/s-5002-037-008

Van Roy, V., Vertesy, D., & Damioli, G. (2020). AI and robotics innovation. In *Handbook of labor, human resources and population economics* (pp. 1–35). Springer International Publishing. DOI: 10.1007/978-3-319-57365-6_12-2

Venkatesh, V., Morris, M. G., Davis, G. B., & Davis, F. D. (2003). User acceptance of information technology: Toward a unified view. *Management Information Systems Quarterly*, *27*(3), 425–478. DOI: 10.2307/30036540

Vitsentzatou, E., Tsoulfas, G. T., & Mihiotis, A. N. (2022). The digital transformation of the marketing mix in the food and beverage service supply chain: A grey DEMATEL approach. *Sustainability (Basel)*, *14*(22), 15228. DOI: 10.3390/su142215228

Vuković, D. B., Hassan, M. K., Kwakye, B., Febtinugraini, A., & Shakib, M. (2024). Does fintech matter for financial inclusion and financial stability in BRICS markets? *Emerging Markets Review*, *61*, 101164.

Wang, S., Huang, X., Xia, M., & Shi, X. (2024). Does artificial intelligence promote firms' innovation efficiency: Evidence from the robot application. *Journal of the Knowledge Economy*, *15*(4), 16373–16394. DOI: 10.1007/s13132-023-01707-w

Wang, Z., Li, M., Lu, J., & Cheng, X. (2022). Business Innovation based on artificial intelligence and Blockchain technology. *Information Processing & Management*, *59*(1), 102759. DOI: 10.1016/j.ipm.2021.102759

World Bank & ITU. (2021). *The digital regulation handbook. World Bank.* International Telecommunication Union.

World Bank Group. (2025). Digital public infrastructure and development: A World Bank Group approach (Digital Transformation White Paper, Vol. 1). Clark, J., Marin, G., Ardic Alper, O. P., & Galicia Rabadan, G. A. (Authors).

World Bank Group. (2025, March). Digital public infrastructure and development: A World Bank Group approach.

World Bank Group. (n.d.). Blockchain and Associated Legal Issues for Emerging Markets

World Bank Group. (n.d.). *Digital Public Infrastructure and Development: A World Bank Group Approach.*

World Bank. (2021). Global Findex Database.

World Bank. (2021). *World development report 2021: Data for better lives.* World Bank., DOI: 10.1596/978-1-4648-1600-0

World Economic Forum. (2024, February). What to Expect for Digital Public Infrastructure in 2024. Retrieved from https://www.weforum.org/stories/2024/02/dpi-digital-public-infrastructure/

World Economic Forum. (2025, April). Why digital public infrastructure is key to building a connected future.

Xuan, T. R., & Ness, S. (2023). Integration of Blockchain and AI: Exploring application in the digital business. *Journal of Engineering Research and Reports*, *25*(8), 20–39. DOI: 10.9734/jerr/2023/v25i8955

Yaacob, M. H., Zainuddin, N. A. F., & Rohani, N. H. (2024). Exploring gamification as a tool to enhance financial literacy and improve financial behavior. *Jurnal Pengurusan, 72.*

Yang, Y., & Cai, J. (2022). Carbon emissions and the development of digital economy: A perspective of spatial evolution. *Journal of Environmental Protection and Ecology*, *23*(1), 409–416.

Yang, Y., Zhang, C., Liu, B., Huang, Y., & Tai, Y. (2024). Mystery of special government subsidies: How does digital transformation promote enterprise innovation and development? *Economic Analysis and Policy*, *83*, 1–16. DOI: 10.1016/j.eap.2024.06.003

Yathiraju, N., & Dash, B. (2023). Gamification of e-wallets with the use of DeFi technology – A revisit to digitization in fintech. *International Journal of Engineering, Science*, *3*(1), 2582–9734.

Zetzsche, D. A., Arner, D. W., & Buckley, R. P. (2017). Sustainability, FinTech and financial inclusion. *European Business Organization Law Review*.

Zhou, Z., Liu, W., Cheng, P., & Li, Z. (2022). The impact of the digital economy on enterprise sustainable development and its spatial-temporal evolution: An empirical analysis based on urban panel data in China. *Sustainability (Basel)*, *14*(19), 11948. DOI: 10.3390/su141911948

Zuo, L., Li, H., Gao, H., & Zhu, M. (2022). The sustainable efficiency improvement of internet companies under the background of digital transformation. *Sustainability (Basel)*, *14*(9), 5600. DOI: 10.3390/su14095600

About the Contributors

Sherif Ismail is a Professor I Entrepreneur I Author I AI business Mentor I Global Trainer I Researcher With over 25 years of experience in the software industry, Dr. Sherif Ismail brings a wealth of expertise and a proven track record in Business Information Systems. His comprehensive skill set, and practical insights have established him as a seasoned professional in the field. Throughout his career, he has excelled in various roles, including developer, designer, analyst, project manager, and quality expert. This extensive experience has honed his abilities and equipped him with a deep understanding of software engineering principles. In addition to his remarkable industry background, Dr. Ismail has made significant contributions to the academic community. He has held prestigious positions as a lecturer at the University of Hail, assistant professor at the University of Dammam, and professor at Umm Al-Qura University. Currently, he serves as a Professor at the American University, where his expertise is highly valued. Dr. Ismail's research interests encompass several cutting-edge domains, including Artificial Intelligence (AI), Natural Language Processing, Knowledge Management, and Sentiment Analysis. His innovative work in these areas has garnered attention and recognition from peers and professionals alike. As a result, he has published over 100 research papers across various domains, demonstrating his intellectual prowess and dedication to advancing knowledge. Adding to his impressive professional and research accomplishments, Dr. Ismail has a strong academic foundation. He earned his undergraduate degree in Computer Science from Ain Shams University in Egypt and pursued further studies to expand his knowledge. He obtained a Master of Science in Software Engineering, a Master of Philosophy in Business Administration, and an M.B.A. His academic pursuits culminated in the successful completion of a Ph.D. in Business Information Systems. By seamlessly integrating his theoretical expertise with his extensive practical experience, Dr. Ismail has solidified his position as an accomplished software engineering professional. His comprehensive skill set, remarkable research contributions, and academic qualifications make him an invaluable asset to both the industry and academia.

Lyudmyla Symochko is an expert in environmental microbiology and ecology, specializing in microbial diversity, antibiotic resistance, and ecosystem health. She earned her PhD in Ecology in 2005 and later obtained a habilitation in biodiversity conservation from Uzhhorod National University, Ukraine. Her early research focused on microbial diversity in natural and anthropogenically altered ecosystems. Over the past decade, she has led pioneering studies on soil and water microbiota, with a particular emphasis on the environmental resistome and the role of ecosystems as reservoirs for antibiotic-resistant microorganisms. She currently serves as a Professor and Researcher at the University of Coimbra, Portugal. Prof. Lyudmyla Symochko is at the forefront of detecting antibiotic-resistant opportunistic pathogens in the environment and assessing their risks to human health. Beyond her research, she is dedicated to advancing environmental education, promoting sustainability, and integrating artificial intelligence into educational methodologies. She has authored over 200 scientific publications, including five books, and has delivered more than 90 presentations at national and international conferences, including keynote lectures. An active contributor to the global scientific community, she serves as a guest editor for several international journals, shaping research discourse on microbial ecology, antibiotic resistance, and environmental sustainability. Lyudmyla Symochko is also a member of the Global Soil Biodiversity Initiative, the Society for Microbial Ecology and Diseases, the Ukrainian Society for Microbiology, and the Belgian Society for Microbiology. Additionally, she serves as General Secretary of the International Council of Environmental Engineering Education.

Mohammad Israr is currently working as a President at Maryam Abacha American University of Nigeria, Kano State, Federal Republic of Nigeria. Prior to his current status, he worked as a Vice Chancellor at Mewar International University, Nasarawa State, Federal Republic of Nigeria. He was the Head IPR (Intellectual Property Rights) Cell, Editor-in-Chief of PCE-International Journal of Engineering & Technology, and Professor in the Department of Mechanical Engineering at Poornima College of Engineering, Jaipur, Rajasthan, India. He also worked as a Professor in the Department of Mechanical Engineering at Sur University College, Sur, Sultanate of Oman, a Principal at Dungarpur College of Engineering and Technology, Dungarpur, Rajasthan, India, and a Principal at Balaji Engineering College, Junagadh, Gujarat, India. He has been appointed an Ambassador of War against Drug Abuse in Nigeria by the National Drug Law Enforcement Agency, (NDLEA), Nigeria. He was at the same time appointed an Honorary Adjunct Professor of Lovely Professional University, India, for a period of 5 years until

March 2028, and an Honorary Adjunct Professor and Senior Fellow of Scientific Innovation Research Group (SIRG), Egypt, for a period of 3 years until January 2027. He was the first faculty member in the history of Sur University College in Sur, Sultanate of Oman, to register and publish the Patent. He has been Granted 08 Patents in Intellectual Property Australia (Australian Government), 01 in the German and Trade Mark Office (Germany), 03 Design Patent in the Intellectual Property Office (UK), 11 Design Patent in Intellectual Property India (Indian Government), 01 copyright registered with the Nigerian Copyright Commission, Nigeria and 42 registered & published patents in Intellectual Property India (Indian Government). He signed 43 MoU's with National and International Institutions, research labs, and renowned Industries. He has published 102 research papers in various reputed national, international journals and conferences like Taylor and Francis, Springer, Elsevier, IEEE, ASME, etc. He has published 16 books, edited a book for CRC Press, and had one article published in Infraline Energy Magazine. He is a Fellow Member of the International Institute of Organized Research (I2OR) and the Independent Perception and Research Hub (IRPH). He has obtained many prestigious awards like the "Young Scientist Award-2018", "Outstanding Researcher Award in Mechanical Engineering-2019", "Outstanding Engineering Services to Society Awards-2021", "Lifetime Achievement Award-2021", Best Researcher Award-2022", "EduLeaders Excellence Award-2022", "Outstanding Teacher Award-2022", "Global Business Education Award 2022/2023", "Star Education Awards-2023" and "Education Excellence Award-2024". He supervised 10 candidates for their doctoral (Ph.D.) degree and also supervised 3 candidates for their master's degree. So far, He has reviewed 21 Ph.D. thesis, 03 Master thesis and 250 research papers. He was an associate on Editorial Board Member of more than 300 national and International Journals. He has served as a Session Chair, Speaker, and Member of the International Technical Committee at many national or International Conferences. He is also a member of various technical and professional bodies such as SCIEI-USA, IAENG-Hong Kong, AAIR-USA, IFERP-India, IETA-India, and ISTE- India. He was appointed as an Assessor for Promotions at the Management and Science University, Malaysia, for the QS World University Rankings 2021. According to World Intellectual Property report 2018, [In Overview of IP filing activity, Table 1. Ranking of total (resident and abroad) IP filing activity by origin, 2018], Page number 8], a total of 12 patents have been filed from India, out of which 5 patents have been filed in his name.

Ajay B. Gadicha is working as HOD AI&DS, Dean Research and Development, Associate Professor in Department of Artificial Intelligence & Data Science, P. R. Pote College of Engineering and Management Amravati. He has completed Hon Doctor of Science in Computer Science and Engineering from (Dana Brain Health

Institute & Iranian Neuroscience Society-Fars Chapter, Iran) He has done Post-PhD Pilot Research Project from Vietnam in Video Summarization. He has completed PhD in Computer Science and Engineering from Sant Gadge Baba Amravati University. He has 13 years of experience in the field of Computer Forensics and Information Technology. He became First Merit & University Topper in Master of Engineering in Information Technology in 2011. He has published 75 research papers in National and International Journal and conferences . He has published 2 books (online) and 04 book chapters in Scopus index book. He has 30 patents (on IPR India) and 15 Copyrights in the field of Computer Forensics and Machine Learning. He has a field of interest in Video Forensics, Network Security, Image Processing, and Video Summarization. Dr. Gadicha received Recognization and Honor from Hon. Deputy CM of Maharashtra Shri Devendraji Fandavis for Pitching Best Idea in Computer Science and Engineering at Patent –Fest 14 Aug 2023, Nagpur Dr. Gadicha currently worked in 180 editorial and 50 + Reviewer boards of various national and international bodies & communities including ISTE, CSI, IAENG,IEEE,ACM,IFERP etc. Dr. Gadicha received International Association for Science and Technology Education Awarded "Best Young Research Award-2017" at Tamil Nadu. Dr. Gadicha Received "Best Researcher Award-2019" by Vivekanandha College of Arts and Science for Women (Autonomous), Tiruchengode, Tamil Nadu, India. Dr. Gadicha Received "Young Researcher in Computer Science and Engineering on 31 July 2019" by Global Outreach Research & Education Association Bangalore.

***

Sweta Banerjee is the Deputy Director and Professor at Sri Balaji University, Pune (SBUP). With an extensive career in academia and academic administration, she has made significant contributions to higher education through her dedication to teaching, research, and leadership. Dr. Banerjee is known for her expertise in management education and her commitment to fostering holistic student development. At SBUP, she plays a pivotal role in shaping academic strategies, mentoring faculty and students, and ensuring the institution's continued excellence in business education. Her scholarly work and professional engagement reflect a deep passion for innovation, ethics, and quality in education.

Barkha S. Dange is a faculty member in the Department of Computer Science and Engineering at Ramdeobaba University, Nagpur, India. Her research interests include digital public infrastructure, artificial intelligence, cybersecurity, and ICT for development. She has published research in reputed journals and conferences and actively contributes to curriculum design, digital literacy initiatives, and interdisciplinary projects advancing inclusive innovation and the UN Sustainable Development Goals.

SudhaAnanthi G is a dedicated academician with a strong passion for education and continuous learning. Known for her excellent communication skills and ability to inspire others, she excels in both teaching and collaborative environments. As a motivating presence in her team, SudhaAnanthi consistently fosters a positive and productive atmosphere. Her strengths as a team player and her commitment to academic excellence make her a valuable asset in any educational setting.

Ajay B. Gadicha is working as HOD AI&DS, Dean Research and Development, Associate Professor in Department of Artificial Intelligence & Data Science, P. R. Pote College of Engineering and Management Amravati. He has completed Hon Doctor of Science in Computer Science and Engineering from (Dana Brain Health Institute & Iranian Neuroscience Society-Fars Chapter, Iran) He has done Post-PhD Pilot Research Project from Vietnam in Video Summarization. He has completed PhD in Computer Science and Engineering from Sant Gadge Baba Amravati University. He has 13 years of experience in the field of Computer Forensics and Information Technology. He became First Merit & University Topper in Master of Engineering in Information Technology in 2011. He has published 75 research papers in National and International Journal and conferences . He has published 2 books (online) and 04 book chapters in Scopus index book. He has 30 patents (on IPR India) and 15 Copyrights in the field of Computer Forensics and Machine Learning. He has a field of interest in Video Forensics, Network Security, Image Processing, and Video Summarization. Dr. Gadicha received Recognization and Honor from Hon. Deputy CM of Maharashtra Shri Devendraji Fandavis for Pitching Best Idea in Computer Science and Engineering at Patent –Fest 14 Aug 2023, Nagpur Dr. Gadicha currently worked in 180 editorial and 50 + Reviewer boards of various national and international bodies & communities including ISTE, CSI, IAENG,IEEE,ACM,IFERP etc. Dr. Gadicha received International Association for Science and Technology Education Awarded “Best Young Research Award-2017” at Tamil Nadu. Dr. Gadicha Received “Best Researcher Award-2019” by Vivekanandha College of Arts and Science for Women (Autonomous), Tiruchengode, Tamil Nadu, India. Dr. Gadicha Received “Young Researcher in Computer Science and Engineering on 31 July 2019” by Global Outreach Research & Education Association Bangalore.

Syed Hassan Imam Gardezi is a distinguished futurist, thought leader and strategic advisor with a unique background in private equity, venture capital, alternative and institutional investments. This foundation has afforded him a rare, hands-on perspective across diverse industries and global supply chains, where he has directly overseen the integration and transformation driven by contemporary and emerging technologies. His expertise lies in demystifying and deploying technologies like Machine Learning, Data Science, AI, IoT, and blockchains for tangible strategic advantage. This deep, practical experience in both investment and operational technology transformation directly informs his writing and editing. A recognized thought leader and holder of numerous prestigious fellowships and certifications, including a PhD in Management, an MBA and certifications in emerging technologies like AI and Blockchain, he translates complex technological concepts into actionable business strategy.

Avinash Hanmant Ghadage is an accomplished academician and researcher currently serving as an Associate Professor at D.Y. Patil Vidyapeeth's Global Business School and Research Centre (GBSRC), Tathawade, Pune. With a strong background in management education and research, Dr. Ghadage has contributed significantly to the academic community through his teaching, publications, and mentorship. His areas of expertise include business management, organizational behavior, and strategic leadership. Passionate about developing future leaders, he emphasizes experiential learning and research-driven teaching methodologies. Dr. Ghadage is committed to fostering academic excellence and innovation in higher education, aligning with the vision and values of D.Y. Patil Vidyapeeth.

Deepak Gupta is a distinguished academician with over 20 years of teaching experience and expertise in Computer Science and Engineering. He holds a Ph.D. in Computer Engineering and has an extensive research portfolio, including many international journal papers, multiple conference proceedings, and several books. His research interests span machine learning, artificial intelligence, and data mining. Currently, Dr. Gupta serves as an Associate Professor and Head of Department of CSE (Emerging Branches) at ITM Gwalior, MP, India. He has also contributed significantly to the field through patents and copyrights and actively engages as a reviewer, conference chair and editor.

Shobha K is currently working as an Assistant Professor in the Department of Computer Science and Engineering (Cyber Security) at Ramaiah Institute of Technology, Bangalore. She is presently pursuing her Ph.D. from Visvesvaraya Technological University (VTU), Belagavi, at the Research Center of Ramaiah Institute of Technology, under the supervision of Dr. Sini Anna Alex, Associate Professor in the Department of Computer Science and Engineering (AI & ML) at Ramaiah Institute of Technology, Bangalore. She has authored a book and has taught various computer science subjects to undergraduate students.

Girisaran K S Marketing Research Scholar specializing in consumer behavior analysis and data-driven marketing strategies. Doctoral candidate with expertise in advanced research methodologies, quantitative/qualitative analysis, and translating insights into actionable business recommendations. Focused on Consumer research and Sustainability.

T.C. Manjunath was born on 6th February 1967. He did his B.E. from RV College of Engg. in 1989 (B'lore Univ), M.E. in Robotics & Automation from Govt.'s LD College of Engg., (Gujarat Univ., Ahmedabad) in 1992 with FCD-First Rank & PhD in Systems & Control Engg. from IIT Bombay in the year 2007, got best research scholar award for the entire IITB. He is currently working as the Dean Research (R & D) and as Professor in Dept. of Computer Science & Engg. with specialization in IoT, Cyber Security, Blockchain Technology in Rajarajeswari College of Engineering, Bengaluru, Karnataka. He has got a teaching (academic), research & administrative experience of more than 35+ years (10 years as Principal & 8 years as HoD, 1 year as Dean Research & rest as faculty) and has published more than 1500+ research papers in various national & international journals & conferences, with 175+ patents, 100+ book-chapters, 25 awards, 100s of Keynote talks and also published 25 text books in various field of science, engineering & technology, completed projects worth Rs. 9 Crores till date & guided 10 PhD scholars in VTU. He is a member of 30 Professional Society Chapters and is a fellow of IE, IETE, AMIEE, Sr. Member of IEEE and a chartered engineer.

P. Selvakumar is currently an Associate Professor in the Department of Science and Humanities at Nehru Institute of Technology, Coimbatore, Tamil Nadu, India. Prior to joining Nehru Institute of Technology, he held positions as an Assistant Professor in the Department of Science and Humanities various engineering colleges in Coimbatore, Tamil Nadu, India, spanning from 2011 to 2023. Dr.P. Selvakumar's academic and research interests lie primarily in the field of phytochemistry. He has made significant contributions to his field, with an impressive record that includes 30 journal publications, 12 patents, and 20 conference papers. Additionally, he has organized 5 seminars and conferences, further demonstrating his commitment to academic and scientific exchange. Throughout his career, Dr. P.Selvakumar has been recognized for his dedication and excellence in teaching, having been honored with several awards, including the Best Teacher Awards. He holds a prominent position in the academic community, contributing actively to research.

Pradip Sanatkumar Padhye is an accomplished Assistant Professor at the Symbiosis School of Banking and Finance, Symbiosis International (Deemed University), Pune. With a strong academic and research background in banking, finance, and economics, Dr. Padhye has been actively contributing to the development of future finance professionals through his teaching and scholarly work. His areas of interest include financial management, risk analysis, and banking operations. Dr. Padhye is known for his engaging teaching style and commitment to integrating theoretical concepts with real-world applications. He has also contributed to research publications and academic forums, reflecting his dedication to advancing knowledge in the field of banking and finance.

Poonam Pawar is currently working as Assistant Professor in P R Pote Patil College of Engineering and Management Amravati

|Jyothi Pawar - Contributing Author|Dr. Jyothi Pawar is a distinguished academic leader serving as the Principal of the Balaji School of Law, under Sri Balaji University, Pune. With a strong background in legal education and research, she has dedicated her career to fostering academic excellence and promoting a deep understanding of law and justice among students. Dr. Pawar is known for her visionary leadership, commitment to ethical values, and passion for empowering future legal professionals. Through her guidance, the institution continues to uphold high standards of legal education, blending academic rigor with practical exposure. Her contributions to the field of law and education have earned her great respect within academic and professional circles.

Anuradha Phadnis is an accomplished Associate Professor at the Indira Global School of Business, Pune. With a strong academic foundation and years of experience in management education, she has been instrumental in guiding students toward academic and professional excellence. Dr. Phadnis is known for her expertise in business management, strategic thinking, and leadership development. Her engaging teaching style and commitment to student success create an enriching learning environment that encourages innovation and critical thinking. Through her research, mentorship, and dedication to quality education, Dr. Phadnis continues to make valuable contributions to the field of management studies.

Madhu S is an accomplished academician, researcher, and author with over 31 years of teaching and industry experience. He holds a Ph.D., M.Com., and M.B.A., and his academic journey reflects a blend of intellectual depth, scholarly productivity, and an enduring commitment to student development and institutional growth. A prolific writer, Dr. Madhu has authored and edited 125 books, including 83 authored works, 4 edited volumes, 13 hardbound editions, and 25 e-books. His research contributions include Scopus and ABDC-indexed 30 papers in reputed international journals and 10 book chapters. He has made notable contributions to research and innovation and also holds 26 design patents and 5 utility patents, highlighting his strong engagement in research and innovation. Dr. Madhu has received several prestigious awards, including the Rooshikumar Pandya Lifetime Achievement Award, Innovative Researcher Award, and Best IP Researcher Award. He has delivered over 45 invited talks and lectures, served as a jury member, keynote speaker, guest of honour, and plenary speaker, and has organized five national and international conferences and workshops. He has also served as member of Boards of Studies (BoS) and Boards of Examinations (BoE), evaluated Ph.D. theses and viva voce, and contributed as a question paper setter and examiner for various universities. With a strong focus on research, innovation, and intellectual property, Dr. Madhu continues to bridge the gap between academia and industry. His efforts in promoting intellectual property awareness, guiding research, and fostering academic excellence reflect his vision for a knowledge-driven, innovative, and self-reliant India aligned with the goals of Viksit Bharat 2047

Someshwar Siddi obtained his Master of Science from ANU, Guntur. He obtained his Ph.D. from the Rayalaseema University, Kurnool in the year 2019. He has more than 20 years of experience in teaching the subjects at Engineering colleges affiliated to JNTUH for UG and PG students. He is presently working as Associate Professor, St. Martin's Engineering College, India. He has to his credit 15 Scopus/Web of Science/UGC Care publications and attended many International conferences. Filed 10 Indian Patents. Active Editorial Board member and Reviewer for Reputed Conferences and Journals. More than 8 books and book chapters published and available in Online.

Neetal Vyas is a distinguished Professor at the School of Business, Indira University, Pune, with extensive experience in management education and research. She is recognized for her expertise in business strategy, organizational behavior, and leadership development. Throughout her academic career, Dr. Vyas has been dedicated to nurturing future business leaders through innovative teaching methods and practical learning approaches. Her research contributions span various areas of management, and she actively participates in conferences, seminars, and academic collaborations. Known for her commitment to academic excellence and student development, Dr. Neetal Vyas continues to play a vital role in shaping the next generation of professionals in the field of business and management.

Index

www.ingramcontent.com/pod-product-compliance
Lightning Source LLC
LaVergne TN
LVHW080859300926
849162LV00003B/476